AN INNOCENT GOES
TO WAR

AN INNOCENT GOES TO WAR

Denys Montgomery

The Book Guild Ltd
Sussex, England

A copy of this manuscript is held in
The Imperial War Museum Archive.

The Book Guild Ltd
25 High Street,
Lewes, Sussex

First published 1999
© Denys Montgomery, 1999
Set in Times
Typesetting by Keyboard Services, Luton

Printed in Great Britain by
Antony Rowe Ltd,
Chippenham, Wiltshire

A catalogue record for this book is
available from the British Library

ISBN 1 85776 319 X

This story is a tribute to all my stalwart, unsung companions in arms, who laboured so devotedly like galley slaves behind the 'front line', often in danger, frequently in appalling conditions – whose work tended to be unseen and unrecognised – to keep the sinews of war in the proper trim, required by their combatant brothers in the Army, thus assuring victory.

CONTENTS

AUTHOR'S NOTE

In case the reader feels doubtful as to the accuracy of the content of the book I should emphasise that the events were recorded in letters home, as soon as this was permitted by the Censor, usually after the elapse of a year (when such information was of no use to the enemy). After the War these rough notes were embodied in typescript by me. I can assure the reader these events really took place, and no attempt has been made, with hindsight, to glamorise them.

PART ONE

THE HAPPY WARRIORS

*I must have the gentleman to haul and draw with the
mariner and the mariner with the gentleman*

Sir Francis Drake

1

"My" war might properly be said to have started in March 1939, when the Germans marched into Czechoslovakia. I had been observing the news for about a year, and had come to the decision that a major war was imminent that would involve Britain. That day the newspapers carried an official advertisement for men with an engineering background to register with the Army Officers' Emergency Reserve. I reckoned I had the necessary qualifications and put my name forward. I received an acknowledgement, indicating that I was to hold myself in readiness and would be called up in due course.

At that time, I was a recently qualified engineer, a new addition to the staff of the English Electric Company at Stafford, working in the sales engineering sub-section of the Rectifier Substation Section (RSS) and, whilst I liked the work, I saw little chance of advancement since the two other members of the sales section were only slightly senior to me and likely to remain so. The military option appealed to me as an adventure, a means of "seeing the world" and at the same time gaining valuable new experience.

By the end of August, things began to hot up. Gas masks had been issued in the spring of that year – horrid little things in cardboard boxes, which one was now supposed to carry everywhere, "just in case" of an unexpected gas attack. But by now children were being evacuated to the West Country and those in the English Electric Company who were in the TA or equivalent in other arms of the Services were summoned to the colours. Several of my friends disappeared and I was left wondering when it would be my turn. I was worried that, if hostilities started, engineering would be declared a "reserved occupation", like mining and agriculture, thereby frustrating my hopes.

On September 3, in the digs where I was living at the time, we listened to Neville Chamberlain announcing that we were now in a state of war with Germany and, since there seemed to be little we could do about that, we hired a couple of rowing boats from near the old mill on the Sow and rowed up the river as far as we could get, to near Chebsey, and back again.

In late November, I received a summons to attend a Medical Board in Birmingham. Here, in a vast room in some school, a series of desks were arranged round the walls, at each of which sat a specialist in one of the particular aspects of health that had to be certified as acceptable. With some two hundred other young men, I was passed round the desks and subjected to examinations: eyes, ears, throat, heart, chest, and so on, before reaching the reception desk, where I was informed that I was fit enough for general service and told to await further orders. I was getting somewhere.

Several months then passed and I was getting restive, because English Electric was exerting increasing pressure on me to call it off. Then, in February, I received a missive informing me that I had been gazetted Lieutenant, OME (Ordnance Mechanical Engineer) Fourth Class, in the RAOC and instructing me to report to the RAOC Command Workshops at Aldershot by a certain date. I was to learn that, in the RAOC, engineering officers were graded in classes, First Class being lieutenant colonels; Second were majors; Third were captains; and Fourth were lieutenants. At that time there was no Fifth Class, although it was instituted later in the war for second lieutenants. The OMEs were differentiated from the stores side where the corresponding ranks were OEOs (Ordnance Executive Officers).

Unfortunately, by this time I was in quarantine for some infectious disease, chicken pox, measles or something, so I phoned the reference on the call-up letter and was told not to report until I was "clean". It appeared that the "phoney war" in France was not producing any significant vacancies and the Army could afford to wait.

I duly reported in February and was attached to the Command Workshops, Aldershot Command, along with six other newly commissioned lieutenants, where we were subjected to short courses in arms drill, "square-bashing", Army law and military finance. As a result of my recent service in the school OTC, the arms and square drill were no problem to me, but two of the seven newcomers were veterans from the 1914–18 war and found things a bit hard. During this time, I was billeted with a civilian family in Aldershot, but ate in the Command Officers' Mess and did duties there such as Orderly Officer.

The Workshops were staffed entirely by civilians and it was the practice for the new officers to be allocated to one of the shops as if in nominal command. The reason for this apparently daft arrangement seemed to be that all requisitions and returns had to be signed ("approved") by an officer, which he did on the say-so of the civilian foreman. As a result of this, the workforce viewed the officers concerned with a sort of genial contempt and were always seeking to "take the mickey" out of them. I remember that once, when I was put in the position of Officer i/c Tank Workshops, I was expected to sign the testing pass-out for one of the little Mark VIc light tanks and I rather foolishly said that perhaps first I ought to see the test run performed, before signing anything. This was accepted with alacrity by the civilian tester and he suggested that I would get the best view if I stood up in the turret and shut its rear lid behind me, so as not to fall out. This I did and the rejoicing test driver took the little tank over a fearsome obstacle course, in the hope of making me either sick or unable to stay the course. He didn't actually make the vehicle sit up and beg, or turn "base over apex" at the bottom of a steep slope, but it was the most exciting ride I had ever experienced. At the end of the test, which I suspect was much more virulent than required, he presented his pass-out form and I signed it, with a steady hand. I think my reputation improved after this and they were much more cordial thereafter.

While I was in Aldershot the Germans invaded Denmark and Norway and I received an "immediate" posting to the LAD (Light Aid Detachment) of a medium regiment RA. The LAD was being hastily formed at Aldershot, but I never saw it, which was a good thing for all concerned, because I was still as green as grass and had no idea how an LAD worked. I learned later that it consisted of a single officer with about eight skilled men to carry out "first-line" repairs on the regiment's guns, which were 5.5"s, about which I knew precisely nothing. The regiment was already on a ship bound for Norway and they disembarked at Andalsnes, to find the Germans had beaten them to it. I was told afterwards that they just had time to throw their guns into the fjord, before hurriedly re-embarking on an impatiently waiting destroyer and being brought back to the UK.

Soon after came the invasion of the Low Countries and the evacuation from Dunkirk, bringing the Aldershot workshops virtually into the front line, and the tank shop was filled with ancient armoured fighting vehicles from World War I onwards, which we were supposed to put into working order as stop-gap replacements for the modern stuff that had been lost in the BEF debâcle. Some of these dinosaurs were the original heavy tanks of the type that made the first breakthrough in 1917, for example. I really think that some of these must have been chipped out of the plinths of war memorials! There were also several 1926-vintage Medium tanks and one extraordinary Ford V8-engined prototype Infantry Tank Mk 1, which had never been put into production, since it had a top speed on the flat of some five miles per hour and enormous exposed wide tracks. It had been replaced by the Mk 2 "Matildas", (which had gone to France in numbers and had been lost by the BEF earlier that year). It must have been found in some military museum. We made them all work, after a fashion, but it was a good thing that the Germans didn't follow up Dunkirk with a full-scale invasion. They'd have died laughing!

There were lots of unemployed, but experienced, RAOC tank fitters going spare at this time and I was taken off the tank repairs, given an Austin 8 pickup truck and a map, and sent out to make a log of all the major garages in the Aldershot Command with adequate lifting gear and high doors which might be used for dispersal workshops. The map was an essential, because all the signposts had been removed and anyone you asked about the whereabouts of places assumed you were a German spy and refused to give any information. It was about this time that I saw my first bomb damage in the Aldershot area. The sole bomb, aimed I suppose at the barracks, had demolished a timber-framed cottage at Crookham, a nearby village.

In August, I was directed to the work that was to be my speciality for the next couple of years. I was sent on the 2nd AA OMEs Course on anti-aircraft weaponry. The course venue had been hastily moved from Lydd in Kent, where the previous, 1st course had found itself a bit too near the invasion and the students on it had spent most of their time manning trenches for Defence of the Realm.

The personnel and equipment had been shipped to Stoke on Trent (for guns) and to Bury (for fire control). I spent six weeks at Stoke and two of us were billeted with a very pleasant lady, an ex-dance-instructress, next to the Michelin factory, from which we commuted daily to the Stoke Drill Hall for the course.

Here we were introduced to the 3.7" standard mobile Heavy AA gun, the larger static 4.5", and the almost obsolescent mobile 3". There was also the mobile Light AA Bofors 40mm Mk 1, which was now coming into general service. We were also shown the prototype semi-mobile Mk 2, in which the sprung chassis had been replaced by an unsprung platform for manufacturing economy, and in which large soft pneumatic tyres replaced the big springs of the Mk 1 platform.

While at Stoke, I took a bus to Stafford and looked up my former workmates in the English Electric Rectifer Section. They were all pleased to see me and envied me my freedom.

The Battle of Britain was now well under way, but made no impression on me. The newspapers seemed to regard it as a sort of match – UK versus Germany – and published the numbers of aircraft shot down in the manner of a football score (for example, RAF 15 aircraft lost, but 10 pilots rescued. Germany 44 aircraft lost, 15 claimed hit).

After six weeks at Stoke, the course moved to Bury and I was billeted with a pleasant ex-amateur motor racing driver in

Prestwich, a suburb of Manchester, from where I commuted to Bury on the electric Manchester–Bury line. Here, at some school, we were indoctrinated in the theory, construction and use of range-finders, sound-locators and predictors. The usual predictor was the one in use for the 3.7" HAA guns, but a new lightweight instrument was now being introduced which operated with the 40mm LAA guns and was supposed to make them "even more effective" by eliminating much of the human element.

While I was at Prestwich, the night bombing campaign began in earnest and was in full swing all the time I was there. The target was Manchester and we heard the waves of aircraft come over most nights. My landlord retired to the cellar every time the siren went, but I reckoned I was just as safe in my bedroom, since the cellar was far from bomb-proof.

At the end of the course, we were all returned to our originating bases and I was given a week's leave. My parents were then living with my grandmother in Criccieth in north Wales and I intended to join them there. The rail journey was quite exciting; there was an air raid on as I left Aldershot and, by the time I arrived in Waterloo, it was just over. I managed to secure a lone taxi to take me by a devious route through the rubble to Euston and by the time I reached there, the raid was renewed. While waiting for something to happen, (there were no trains) we took cover from the falling bits of AA shells under the main overbridge and watched the searchlights wandering around in the sky. Eventually, the train came and we all piled in, hoping not to have to disembark and take cover again. When we got going at last, the train proceeded slowly north-westwards, through Rugby and Crewe, where we stopped for a long time. When we restarted for Chester, we saw the reason: beside the line were two large bomb craters. It was getting dark by the time we reached Bangor and I had to change trains on to the branch line for Pwllheli and Criccieth. My parents had agreed to meet me at the little halt at Afon Wen, rather than going on to Pwllheli, and I was so late that they were wondering whether I was coming at all.

My father was in the Criccieth Home Guard and during my

8

stay, there was a "flap" one night which put all the defences on alert. Apparently, it was an invasion scare and I wondered what I was supposed to do, so far from Aldershot. However, it proved to be a false alarm and I was able to finish my leave and return at the proper time.

Once back in Aldershot, I received another posting. I was to report to a Mobilisation Centre at Arnold, near Nottingham, to join a new unit, the 2nd LAA Regiment Workshops Section, which was being formed there. On my arrival, I learned that a LAA Workshops was a unit of 40 men, commanded by a lieutenant. It was quite a large unit for a lieutenant's command – eventually it was upgraded to a captain – but I had to do everything myself, with the aid of a sergeant clerk, an Irishman, Sgt Hughes, to handle the paperwork. I was billeted with a family in Hucknall a few miles away and I drew a 15cwt truck to provide the necessary mobility, with which I went back and forth between Hucknall and Arnold, trying to get the right men to make up my unit's strength.

Apart from myself, I was supposed to have one Warrant Officer class two, designated an Armament Quartermaster Sergeant (AQMS), a Staff Sergeant (fitter), two Sergeants (including the clerk), three Corporals and thirty-one other ranks – fitters, drivers, instrument mechanics and general duties. I was eventually posted an AQMS (Holgate), a S/Sgt (MT) (Dean), a corporal fitter (White), and a corporal storeman (Benoit), and the rest were much about the same age and inexperience as myself. The average age was about 26 and only S/Sgt Dean and Corporals White and Benoit had seen any active service in the BEF.

My AQMS was, I think, a bit out of his depth. He should, by rights, have been my second i/c and run the workshop side, but he was only a reasonable artisan and had been promoted above his capacity. The backbone of the workshop was S/Sgt Dean, who came from Chester-le-Street in Co. Durham and the star artisan was Lance Corporal Siddle, my blacksmith, although I didn't realise his true worth until we were in the desert. Sgt Hughes got the pay situation sorted out and I was able to open

9

an Imprest Account with the advice of the adjutant at Arnold. He also scrounged a very second-hand typewriter from somewhere, I think from the Arnold HQ, and settled down to organise his filing and correspondence system.

As soon as we were nearly up to strength, the unit was moved, lock, stock and barrel, to the requisitioned Blue Ball roadhouse at Risley, on the road to Derby, where we shared the accommodation with two Mobile Bath Units, each about ten strong. In spite of the fact that their combined strength was less than mine, each was commanded by a Captain; Husbands and Smith. I didn't let this affect our personal relations and we settled down easily to await the future intentions of the War Office.

Once again, nothing seemed to happen and we were apparently forgotten for five months. During that time the two Mobile Bath Units moved on and I saw them no more. Keeping the men happy and interested on my own was a problem. I organised route marches round the countryside, to keep us reasonably fit, and once I was persuaded to join in a "field day" against the local Home Guard. A retired major was raked in to adjudicate. I never heard what his verdict was, but a good time was had by all. On another occasion, some ladies in the next village committed me to providing the male actors for a little play, which we put on in the Blue Ball. I was adjudged by the ladies to be the most suitable man to play the principal role opposite a very personable damsel, Peggy Mitchell, and Dean told me afterwards that he kept order during the more passionate scenes by threatening to put anyone making rude noises on a charge. To my surprise, the play revealed the acting ability of Cpl Benoit, a Channel Islander, who had to impersonate a Frenchman.

Then, in March 1941, we received orders to go overseas, were issued with khaki drill tropical kit (I had to purchase mine, being an officer) and were given seven days' embarkation leave. We were allocated a number to be stencilled on all our baggage and kit: Serial 29893. G15 L. I went off to stay with my parents at Criccieth, and had been there only three days when I was recalled to Risley to organise the move out of the place. Everyone else returned on time, I was relieved to find, and the whole unit was given a magnificent send-off in the bar of the Blue Ball by our local friends and their ladies. As a result, we were all more than a little merry by the time a fleet of trucks turned up to carry us away to Derby railway station, bound, rather the worse for wear, for an unknown destination.

This proved, initially, to be Glasgow, where we were dumped on the arrival platform at about 7.00 a.m., after an all-night virtually sleepless journey. I am not sure whether I should have received a first-class seat, but it seemed proper to stay in the thirds with the lads, most of them young and somewhat disorientated at the thought of leaving Britain and their families for somewhere thousands of miles away in a war zone.

Leaving the Section on the platform with AQMS Holgate, I reported to the Railway Transport Officer (RTO) at the station for further orders. I found they knew about us. We were booked to join Convoy G.15, which was assembling down the Clyde and we must get a move on, since the ship we were to sail in, the requisitioned Orient liner *Otranto*, would be pulling out into the river later that morning and then we would have to use a lighter to get on board. Packed into a three-ton lorry, we were driven down to Greenock and put down on the quayside. Here, another Movement Control Officer cursed me for being so late and we were shepherded smartly up a steep gangway on to the ship.

The *Otranto*, I was to learn, was a converted passenger liner of some 25,000 tons and was carrying over 3000 troops to somewhere requiring tropical kit. As the only war still going on in the "tropics" was that in the north African desert – the Italians having been driven out of Ethiopia – it was generally reckoned that we were bound for Egypt, but it might, of course, have been India, or even West Africa.

As a small unit, we were allocated a space several decks down, reached by a steep stairway from the deck above. Someone showed the lads where and how to sling the hammocks that the lesser ranks would be using and the senior NCOs were allotted bunks on another deck. I was told to see the purser about my own accommodation and found that, since I was the senior – in fact the only – RAOC officer on board, I rated a single cabin on the main deck with a porthole window looking

11

on to the promenade deck. I was also told where I could find the Adjutant of 2 LAA Regt HQ, who were also on board and to whom I should report.

With some difficulty, for the ship was a seething mass of uninterested soldiery, I located the adjutant, Captain the Hon. Claud Phillimore RA, a tall, fair man with a cultured drawl, who welcomed me in a friendly manner and asked if my men were all on the ship. I said they were, and foolishly expressed my opinion of the accommodation they had been allocated, to be told smartly that I shouldn't complain, because "even" the RA rank and file of his HQ were equally poorly housed and we would just have to put up with it. He said his RSM, a WO I called Bliss, would locate my senior NCOs and find if they had any comments, but this was a troopship in wartime, I must remember. I reflected somewhat guiltily that I was getting First Class accommodation and messing for myself.

Phillimore then located and introduced me to the CO, Lt Colonel Helby, the quartermaster, Lt(QM) Mckeown, the MO, Lt Messent, and RSM Bliss.

Shortly after our arrival, the ship was warped out into the middle of the river and loading proceeded by lighter. There was a massive noticeboard by the purser's office on which I found my name and table for the meals, which were being served in two sessions, because the ship was carrying, as I have said, over 3000 "bodies", of whom at least 600 were officers. Some of these latter were female, including the nursing sisters of No 3 General Hospital, also the Hadfield-Spears Field Ambulance Unit, the drivers of which were FANYs. These damsels, although their uniforms were like those of ATS officers, were distinguished from such lesser mortals by the wearing of red cloth-covered buttons as rank badges, instead of stars. The orderlies were mostly Quakers, quiet, self-effacing young men who had volunteered for this work, although refusing to take part in any warlike operations. I don't know who the Hadfield part of the sponsors was, but the driving force was Lady Spears, wife of Sir Edward Spears, a senior diplomat in the Middle East. In private life, she was Mary Borden the author, a stern, horse-faced woman sitting at the captain's table. The FANYs were generally called "The Tiller Girls", among the lesser or more ribald officers, or, simply, "Mary Borden's Chorus".

The *Otranto* was stuck in the Clyde for two days, during which I struck up an acquaintanceship with another lone officer, a Captain Jack Smith, the OC of yet another Mobile Bath Unit. I think he had his eye on one of the Sisters of the General Hospital and asked me to come along to support him. It appeared that the Sister who took his eye, a dark-haired Welsh girl called Megan Lloyd Hughes, was part of a foursome who had evidently decided to form a defensive square against the assaults of their predominantly male shipmates. My function was apparently to lure away one or more of the others, Breda Walton, Marie Howlett and Phyllis Ball. Jack's little ruse was unsuccessful, for Megan declined to be separated from her friends and Jack and I found ourselves apparently "squiring" this whole gaggle of girls, meeting several of their friends and taking part in the exercise they had determined beforehand, which was to walk round the deck daily the number of times that made up a mile, until the ship sailed. That was how I first met Phyllis Ball and, since my contemporaries all called me "Monty", that was the name by which I was introduced. She told me, in return, that her name was usually shortened to "Phyl". She came from Kent and we seemed to have similar interests.

One of the first things the ship got round to organising was the daily morning assembly at "Boat Stations", and I found I had to line up my Section, wearing our life-jackets, which we had to carry everywhere we went, in a double rank facing the sea, right in front of the Nursing Sisters, whom we could hear whispering behind us, but were not allowed to turn and look at. I wondered whether the whispering was about my unit and later Phyl told me that it was about me, as I looked so young (I was actually twenty-six) to be in charge of so many men older than myself! This boat drill took place every morning and we had to stand, rain or shine, for about two hours until dismissed by the OC Troops, after which our time was our own.

The convoy gathered for some four days in the Clyde and then, one night, the ships set off in the dark down to the Firth of Clyde in single file. During this operation, the untried convoy drill broke down and the *Stirling Castle* crashed into the stern of the *Reina del Pacifico*. The latter had to put back to Greenock with damaged steering, but the *Stirling Castle* continued to limp with us as far as Durban, although, with its damaged bow, it had difficulty in maintaining the requisite speed. We were told that the convoy commodore RN, becoming fed up with the laggard's wayward behaviour, felt moved to send a signal, visible to the entire convoy: 'Pardon me, Madam, but your ship is slowing!' This was apparently in the best Navy tradition and caused amusement all round.

Needless to say, as soon as we were on the high seas, the weak-stomached members of my Workshops were seasick and their fellows were much put to it to keep the place sanitary. Being in a small space in the depths of the ship with doubtful ventilation, their quarters were most unpleasant and on my daily visits I had to bear continuous complaints, which cut no ice with the ship's staff. (To jump ahead a little, when we came into subtropical waters, I wangled permission for as many as wished to to sleep on deck, as long as they didn't interfere with the work of the crew. This idea caught on and it was made a concession for other units, but I got no credit for starting it.)

Our initial course lay far out into the Atlantic; once we saw an iceberg in the distance, raising speculation that we were going to Canada; several times we saw a whale and there were innumerable porpoises round the ship most days. One thing we were relieved not to see was any sign of enemy activity, although our escort of destroyers ranged dangerously round and through the convoy at will. There was also a battleship travelling with us until we were in the latitude of Gibraltar, when it departed east, taking a number of our destroyer screen with it.

As we turned south the weather improved and the last of my seasick lads finally appeared on deck and were able to join in the lectures and discussions on weaponry that I persuaded the more experienced NCOs to deliver, sitting in the warm sun on the boat deck after boat drill. In order to combat boredom during this latter chore, I instituted, whilst "standing easy" and awaiting inspection, the time-honoured children's game of "Simon says", in its Army guise of "O'Grady says", which kept them awake. As this involved me facing the troops, I was amused to see some of the Sisters standing at the back going through the motions, until stopped by some female in authority.

As the weather grew warmer, convoy orders decreed a change from winter kit to "whites", which for us meant khaki drill and shorts, exposing some very white and knobbly knees. After a short time everyone became acclimatised to this and vied with each other to get brown. The Sisters were transformed overnight from little grey mice to white angels with snowy hats, far outshining the FANYs, who didn't seem to have a tropical version of their uniform.

After a couple of weeks, the convoy turned left and fetched up at Freetown in Sierra Leone to refuel. We were anchored in the mouth of a river, shaded from the cooling sea breezes, so that it was horribly hot and sticky. The authorities decided that, since the troops had been forbidden to wear their Army boots on board and had replaced them with plimsolls, their feet must be getting soft, and we were warned to expect a route march on shore (in the tropical sun!) to harden them up. Then, the good news came that this refined torture was cancelled, not due to common charity, but because there was an outbreak of some tropical fever in the town. This was replaced by the bad news: The ships' boats were provided for a regatta, with a member of the crew as "minder", to be rowed by teams from each unit, competing for a small prize, again in the broiling sun. I asked Dean to pick a team of twelve rowers and agreed I would go with them as cox. Curiously enough, the list was greatly oversubscribed, although I have since realised that no one had any idea what they were letting themselves in for in pulling a ship's lifeboat with heavy seagoing oars under those conditions.

There were about six boats in each heat and we were started with a gun fired from one of the destroyers. It was only then that I and all my crew really found out what we had blithely let ourselves in for. The rowers stripped to their singlets and, halfway along the course, we were leading RHQ's boat, coxed by Col Helby and with Howe-Browne, Asst Adjutant, as stroke. There had been much rivalry and betting between the units, but we finished last in our heat and behind RHQ, all the same. By the time we crossed the line, I was feeling like a piece of roast meat and the lads looked finished. We returned to the *Otranto* and handed back our boat for another gang of mugs to go out in; thereafter being inspected by a squad of unit medical officers for overexposure to the sun and given a chit for a couple of bottles of beer later that evening as finishers. I learned that my Workshops' boat had been loudly cheered on by the whole Hospital, because we were the only crew they really knew and I was commiserated with by several of the Sisters.

After nearly a week we set off again and were glad to get away from the heat and humidity. As we crossed the Equator there was much argument as to whether the water going down the plugholes had changed direction, but there was no decision. I learned that the Sisters were stacked sixteen to a cabin and a single shower and felt embarrassed at my own individual cabin.

Deck chairs were produced by the ship's company and laid out in lines on the upper deck, to be scrambled for by the younger officers and the Sisters. Phyl Ball and I came to an agreement that whoever came out first from our lunch would commandeer two chairs side by side and we sat thus together for most of the rest of the voyage, usually with either Breda or Megan as "duenna", for I believe that the Matron looked rather askance at one of her girls sitting alone with a single officer. Phyl and I were becoming fast friends by this time; we used to walk round the deck after dinner to lean over the rail above the other ranks' piece of deck in the stern and listen to them singing in the soft tropical dusk.

It couldn't last, of course. The air grew colder and the sea rougher and then the convoy split into two, one part going in to Capetown and the other – ours – going on to Durban. On one clear day, we had a brief glimpse of Table Mountain wreathed in clouds and then the weather broke. It was winter in the southern hemisphere, and the sea grew rougher and rougher, as a gale blew up. The tables emptied in the dining saloon and sitting on deck was quite out. Phyl and I seemed immune, but many of our companions were laid low for a second time.

Eventually, we steered into Durban harbour at about midday and tied up against a long quay. An announcement on the ship's tannoy said that only officers were to be allowed on shore that afternoon, but the Other Ranks would be let out the following morning. Phyl and her three friends were accompanied by Jack Smith and myself and we went down the gangway, acutely conscious of the envious eyes of the troops lining the rails. Jack had decided to put on full Service dress with Sam Browne belt and – of all things! – riding breeches and boots, to be followed by derisive hoots from the soldiery that he had forgotten his horse.

We hadn't gone more than a hundred yards down the quay, when a car stopped and a lady and gentleman asked if we knew our way and, if not, could they give us a lift. Phyl and I were driven to their house in the suburbs and these kindly people looked after us for the remainder of our stay. Others were doing the same thing all down the quay. It would seem that the entire Durban population was determined to make our visit to this new country as enjoyable as possible. Their name was Sluiter and they had two small children, a girl and a boy, about six and eight respectively. They gave us tea and we were offered freshwater baths, which we accepted with alacrity. Sea water never really gets one clean and the seawater soap provided on the ship never produced any lather. Carefully avoiding any attempt to gather military information, they found that we were likely to be there for several days and invited us to join them on a motor trip into the countryside the following day. Brushing aside our protests, they drove us out to a noted beauty spot, the "Valley of a Thousand Hills", where they produced a picnic at a viewpoint. Feeling we were imposing on their kindness a bit too much, we decided to go by ourselves to the beach the following day. We brought our bathing things and they drove us to what they said was the best spot, where we lounged about and took a dip every now and then.

17

I think Phyl had decided by now that she was getting too involved with me, so the next day she announced she was going shop-gazing with Megan and Breda. I took a sightseeing trip round the city and went to the cinema, where in the interval they encouraged the soldiers to join in with a number of well known songs, such as *Wish me luck as you wave me goodbye* and *Roll out the barrel*, which everyone did with gusto. Then the Master of Ceremonies announced they had a new song of which they knew the tune but not the words. Could the visitors supply them? And the organ struck up *The Quartermaster's Stores*. A warrant officer sitting next to me turned and said, 'I hope they don't!' for there were several barrack-room versions current, not fit for mixed company. But most of the audience sang the orthodox words, so all was well.

The Sluiters had promised to pick us up after breakfast the following day, but the ship was "closed" and no one was allowed off. Clearly, we were due to sail. We could see our hosts on the quay and waved to them, but the guards on the gangway prevented any closer contact. We never properly said goodbye, but after the *Otranto* had pulled out into the harbour, the purser's office said a basket of fruit had been delivered with my name on it. It was from the Sluiters with a note saying they were sorry we were apparently departing and wishing us bon voyage. They were indeed kind and charming people. The enormous amount of fruit in the basket was quite beyond the ability of Phyl and me to deal with before it went off, so most of my unit and some of the Hospital had a share.

During the convoy's stay in Durban, parties of troops set about unloading the damaged *Stirling Castle*, and its cargo and its troops were distributed anyhow among the remaining ships, with little consideration as to how it was all going to be sorted out at the other end. The lame duck was left behind in Durban and we set out north-east towards the Mozambique Channel.

Still not completely sure of our destination, we felt we were now on the home run. It could only be India or the Middle East now, as the convoy crept slowly up the coast of East Africa. As we neared the Equator again, it was decided to hold a knock-out mixed doubles deck-tennis tournament. Phyl and I had played this game a lot during the earlier stages of the voyage and our friends pressed us to enter, which we did and reached the semi-final, in which we came up against the OC Ship, Lt Colonel Greer, partnered by one of the statuesque Amazons from Mary Borden's Chorus. Although we gave them a good game, we were comprehensively beaten.

About this time there was our first submarine warning and all officers had to join their other ranks, ready to take command, should the emergency demand. I went down with the lads to their lower deck space, with that horrid narrow and steep stair up to the open air, and the lid was shut on us. We were there for some half an hour, feeling the explosions of depth charges shake the ship and wondering how on earth we were going to escape, should the need arise, which fortunately it didn't. There was an audible sigh of relief from everyone when the "All Clear" sounded and the entrance lid to our prison was lifted.

On another occasion, there was an air-raid warning during morning boat drill and we were ordered to stand our ground. The only aircraft we saw were our own fighter cover, but one of them had some trouble and the pilot baled out. For a long time we could see the parachute dropping towards the sea and presumably one of our destroyer screen diverted to pick the man up, although we didn't see that. The convoy wasn't allowed to slow or deviate.

We rounded the Horn of Africa and turned towards the Straits of Bab el Mandeb and Aden. This settled our last main question; we were bound for Egypt and not India. When we entered the Red Sea the weather, which had hitherto been just hot, became really roasting. The leading ships of the convoy were distorted by the heat-shimmer in odd manners; at one time they looked like flat barges, and then suddenly they appeared to grow to the size of the *Queen Mary*. This heat went on for days and most of us just hung around in whatever shade we could find on deck, with our tongues virtually hanging out. This was the moment, of course, for some of the most macho officers to decide on an inspection tour of the engine and boiler rooms! I didn't.

Eventually, ranges of barren hills began to appear on either side through the mirk and we realised this was the entrance to

19

the Gulf of Suez. Soon, the convoy arrived in some sort of harbour with white buildings on either shore. We all crowded to the rails and took in our first view of the glamorous East. The voyage was over. We had arrived.

2

Now that we were at our destination, the tight security practised by the ship's crew seemed to be relaxed slightly. We were told that the port on our west side was that of Port Tewfik at the southern end of the Suez Canal and the small town opposite on the eastern side gloried in the name of El Shatt. However, there seemed to be no rush to get us off the ship and life went on as usual, except that it was hotter than ever now we were anchored. Any wind that might have cooled us was shielded from our anchorage by barren, rocky hills on either side, which brooded above us like blue-black pieces of crumpled paper, partly obscured by the heat haze.

Our convoy must have carried something like 50,000 troops and large amounts of vehicles and equipment, but the port was incapable of dealing with more than two or three ships a day. While we waited for our turn to come round, we lazed about, trying to keep out of the sun and avoiding the rails, because of the blinding reflection of the sun, now nearly vertically over-head, off the still water. In a couple of days the sewage from the twenty or so ships, discharged into the tideless bit of sea, began to stink to high heaven and made things even more unpleasant. We were some three hundred yards from our promised destination, but, for all the good that did, we might have been back in Durban. And much more comfortable, too.

Eventually, it was the turn of the *Otranto* and all ranks of 2 LAA Regt were alerted to be ready to move off with full kit at 10.30 a.m. the following morning. Although I was fed up with the waiting, it saddened me to think that we were now to be separated from our friends in No 3 General Hospital, and in

21

particular from Phyllis Ball. We agreed that we would try to keep in touch and exchanged our unit addresses, as we sat in the ship's lounge and drank our last ten shillings in orange juice, for the bar was closed while in port.

In the hottest part of the following day, we donned our now-unaccustomed boots, drew our arms from the ship's armoury, shouldered our kit and filed down into a lighter. We were taken to the quay, where we were marshalled into ranks with RHQ 2 LAA Regt and then marched off to the adjacent railway sidings. No trains were in sight, but a harassed Movement Control corporal said our special train would leave at 3.00 p.m. from *this* siding. We downed our webbing kit on the dusty, dirty quay and sought some shelter from the blistering noon sun, only to be told that we were in the wrong place and that the train would leave from *that* siding, two hundred yards away. Wearily, we humped our kit over to the new place in an unmilitary straggle and settled down again, only to be told by Movement Control that again we were in the wrong place and we would board some hundred yards further on. Again we moved and this time no one told us to move again, so I told the lads they could go and patronise the EFI (Expeditionary Forces Institute), the overseas NAAFI, several hundred yards away.

On the way, I espied the Sisters in one of the covered goods sheds, sitting round a large tea urn, sadly watching their snowy "whites" suffering from the surroundings, and I promptly joined them. Subsequently, Jack Smith and Colin Travis (the 2 LAA Signals Officer) rolled up and joined the party.

Eventually a long train turned up at 4.30 and we packed into the coaches reserved for us, after throwing out a number of Egyptians who were already illegally there and hoping to cadge a free lift. The coaches had been standing in the sun for some time and were incredibly hot. We threw down the windows, but that did little good while we were stationary and when we started to move – which we did at 5.30 – we were enveloped with dust and sand.

After clanking along several sidings, the train got going in better form and we crowded into the corridor or hung out of the windows, absorbing our first views of Egypt and also a lot of dust and fumes from the oil-fired locomotive. Our route lay alongside a tree-edged canal – misnamed the "Sweetwater Canal", solely because the water in it was not salt. Everyone was looking for his first camel, but all we could see were lots of small, overburdened donkeys pattering along and ridden by dark-skinned men wearing loose, striped nightshirts and turbans. They took not the slightest notice of the train as we passed, not so much faster than the donkeys.

There was a "First Class" compartment at one end of our coach and I was sharing it with Lt Travis, Doc Messent and Howe-Browne. The Doc and I got fed up with watching the desert crawl by and went off down the corridor to see where the Sisters were, to find that the Hospital was in the rear of the train and also that they were in a worse state than we were; the girls were almost fainting from lack of water. The men on the trains had all come ashore wearing their webbing harness, now discarded for comfort, but this meant that each had a water bottle. With some prescience, I had instructed my lads to fill them before we left the ship, whereas the Sisters were in their "whites" with only handbags, all their other kit being somewhere on the train, but not within reach. It had not been thought necessary to provide them with a drink.

Chivalry prevailed. Feeling very virtuous, we upped and bore our full water bottles down as far as the entrance to their coach and passed them to a senior Sister standing in the end of the corridor, because men weren't allowed to enter the "women's quarters". She said 'Bless you' and in due course brought back the bottles to us. Phyl told me later that our water ration just about saved their lives!

As it was beginning to get dark, the train ground to halt at a scruffy little station, the Hospital filed out onto the platform in the inadequate light of some low-powered and widely spaced electric lamps and we saw them no more. The light wasn't good enough for me to pick out Phyl, but they all waved as the train moved off and we all leaned out of the windows and waved back.

Eventually, about an hour later, we arrived in one of the Cairo railway stations, of which there are at least three, serving lines going north to Alexandria, east to the Suez Canal – the one on which we had come – and south to Helwan, up the Nile. The train was met by a number of open 10-ton lorries, into which we were packed, standing against wooden side railings and feeling like cattle going to market.

At this hour of the evening, the heat of the day had rapidly decreased and, as we waited for the lorries to start, it was so much cooler than it had been at Port Tewfik, that we were shivering. It was here that we had our first encounter with the local population, who milled around our vehicles, all seeking to sell us beads, bottles of lemonade, flat pastries, fruit and other foods, all of which we had orders not to take. All ages were doing this, but they were mostly teenagers and the noise was deafening.

What most impressed itself on my consciousness was that the blackout we had become so used to in the UK was non-existent here and lights were everywhere among the trees along the streets.

After a while, our lorry convoy started and we drove through the brightly lit centre of Cairo, over a long bridge – was it the Nile? – and out into the country along a wide road. Then our vehicle suddenly turned left and bumped on an unsurfaced track beside a water-filled ditch, eventually to arrive at a large tented camp. This proved to be the Beni Yussef Collecting Centre.

Here we dismounted and were marched to a row of large marquee-like EPIP (English Privates Indian Pattern) tents, with two tent poles and a large flysheet, to insulate against the sun, each accommodating eight ORs or four officers. My lot were allowed four tents and I shared one with Messent, Travis, the Signals Officer and Howe-Browne. We were all given some form of meal, got our beds out, and packed down for the first night in Egypt, to be awakened at the crack of dawn by groups of natives perambulating through the camp, shouting out what sounded like "Hah-teer!" Apparently these were sellers of mugs of hot tea, which the troops were permitted to buy from them. At present this wasn't possible, because no one had any Egyptian money. Later that morning, however, arrangements were made to pay the troops in local currency. This was the Egyptian pound, or piastre – quickly dubbed the "disaster" – which divided up into 100 millemes – horrid little coins with a hole in the middle that the natives kept threaded on a string as small change.

We were a month or more at Beni Yussef, during which time we acclimatised ourselves to the heat and flies, parading at 0700 for unit PT, an hour's break from 0900 to 1000 for breakfast. Work continued until 1300 (1 p.m.) and then re-started at 1600 (4 p.m.), knocking off at 1830.

Most of the operations were under the control of the RAs (McKeown and Howe-Browne) and, although I didn't care for this, it left me free to go into Cairo and try to locate the transport that had supposedly come out on the same convoy. I also sought the items of necessary tools and equipment required to complete our G.1098 (War Equipment Table) for a LAA workshop. All this necessitated numerous visits to the main Base Ordnance Depot at Abbassia on the far side of the city. We had been issued in Risley with a 15cwt open truck, a 30cwt recovery lorry with crane and winch, a small machinery lorry with lathe, battery-charging facilities and benches, and a motorcycle. We lacked two 30cwt general purpose lorries for stores and personnel, but these were withheld and not issued until we actually moved out towards the Forward Area.

Since I had good reason for my journeys and vehicle to bear me, I went into Cairo much more than Messent or Howe-Browne and my first stop was often at the English Club near the city centre, where I let my driver, Cpl Thorne, go to the local EFI and slipped into the Club (at which newly arrived officers had been made temporary members) to order a quart jug of ice-cold shandy, before continuing. This set me up for the day.

Gradually, my equipment began to add up and, after the common "Unit Exercises" at 0700, I withdrew my lot to familiarise themselves with our new kit, and to find out a bit more about their capabilities and gain ideas as to what else we needed, whether it was on our War Equipment Table or not. We also drew a number of smaller RD (ridge double) tents that the powers-that-be in the ME deemed necessary for mobile units. The EPIP tents were far too big and took half an army to erect and lower. The RD had two wooden tent poles, small side walls and a flysheet to keep off the heat of the sun. Each slept eight men or one or two officers. They were still very labour-intensive to erect.

As they were supposed to be our shelter in the desert, it seemed highly desirable to be able to erect and dismantle them by ourselves as quickly as possible and we began to devise any drills we would have to use. I set to with the lads in this and we were hampered by sudden hot winds, which, on one occasion, brought down our half-erected tent and buried me beneath. I was soon dug out and the lads thought this frightfully funny. It made their day.

On another occasion, I had turned in with a shocking headache and was snugly in my camp bed when another sudden howling gust uprooted the tent pegs of our EPIP tent and it collapsed across me, enveloping me in fold after fold of heavy canvas. My headache was much alleviated by the effort of clawing my way out of the suffocating mess.

As time went on, we were joined by the 2 LAA Regt RASC Section with two officers, a Captain and a Lieutenant. They had been out there for some months and had their scale of vehicle transport already.

Beni Yussef was near Gizeh, we soon found, but no one felt strong enough to visit the Pyramids, or the Sphinx, just up the road. Our main concern wasn't with antiquities, but with mosquitoes from the water-filled drainage ditches much nearer the camp. Before the authorities decided to issue mosquito nets, we were bitten mercilessly and came out in large lumps, mainly on our faces, which made shaving very difficult.

Messent, who, like me, had special activities that took him out of the camp, returned one day to tell us that No 3 General Hospital was temporarily billeted with the Base Hospital at Helmieh, a few miles to the north of Cairo. He had been to see them and reported on the Sisters' well-being. They were not opened up and operational and, being only "visitors" at Helmieh, were able to come in to the Big City from time to time. He added, with a grin, that Sister Phyllis Ball had been asking after me and he had given her my best wishes. Had he been right in that?

By the time June arrived, we were about as ready as we ever would be and received orders to depart for the Forward Area. A couple of days before we were due to move out, Messent organised a small farewell party at the famed St James restaurant in Cairo and invited me and Travis to come with him. He had been successful in getting three Sisters from No 3 General to come as well if they could get off. Imagine my delight when I saw who they were! I noted in my next letter home that they included Breda Walton, Maisie Mitchell and "the incomparable Phyllis Ball"! My parents must have begun to wonder on reading this. It was wearing my heart on my sleeve with a vengeance!

Throwing our inhibitions to the wind, Phyl and I consumed large quantities of melon and glorious strawberries and cream, washed or unwashed, and dared the consequences. As it happened neither of us succumbed to the effects of "gippy tummy" afterwards, which was just as well.

It was a case of eat strawberries and be merry, for tomorrow we were going to be parted and would probably not see each other for months, or ever again. It was our last fling.

It was in early July 1941 that we set out to move up into the "Forward Area". This "we" consisted of RHQ 2 LAA Regt RA; the 2 LAA Regt Signals Section, R Sigs and the 2 LAA Regt Workshops RAOC. RHQ with its "auxiliaries" had nominally come out to regain command of its three LAA batteries that had come out earlier and were already up in the desert, but now they had arrived, the batteries were engaged elsewhere and no one seemed to want us.

Our column mustered some 120-odd souls – officers and men – some of them were pretty odd, too. My workshop consisted of a subaltern (me) and thirty-eight good men and true of assorted ages, trades and outlook on life. I have mentioned earlier that most of them were young and inexperienced, although a few of the more senior ones had been in France with the BEF, and a very few had been in Egypt before as regular soldiers. The rest were, like me, raw to the game and a bit vague about the finer points of soldiering.

While we had been rounding the Cape on the way here, the victorious Middle East Force – Wavell's Army of the Nile – had, in a few days, rolled back the Italian forces from one end of Cyrenaica to the other, but the Germans had come to their assistance and had pushed our troops back inside the Egyptian frontier to between Sollum on the border and Sidi Barrani well back in Egypt. Whilst we had sweated in Beni Yussef, training, route-marching and laboriously collecting our stores and transport from the Cairo base depots, two minor "shows" had come and gone and we were not involved in either. There had been a short, sharp "flare-up" on the frontier, to become known as the "June Battle", in which both sides claimed victory, but the line somehow seemed not to have been altered; and an army had marched into Syria against the Vichy French.

We had almost given up hope and there were whispers of disbandment in the air, when the warning order came, placing us under the command of 12 AA Brigade at Qasassin, a camp in the Eastern Desert between Cairo and the Canal, who were on the point of moving off themselves into that mysterious place, the Western Desert, about which we had heard and speculated so much.

On the so-called "Desert Road" between Mena, by the Pyramids, and Mareopolis, just outside Alexandria, there was just one building, part petrol station, part restaurant, rejoicing in the name of "The Halfway House" at about the mid-point between Cairo and Alexandria. It was, I understood, a popular calling point for pre-war motorists making the journey. This was the only sign of life the whole way.

Our convoy could hardly be called a brilliant effort. We had been ordered to maintain a hundred-yard interval between vehicles as a precaution against air attack – we also had such AA machine guns as we possessed mounted at the ready and manned on our vehicles – but our raw drivers seemed to be incapable of keeping station and the column closed up and opened out like a spring. Howe-Browne, leading the column – the CO and Phillimore had gone on ahead – was probably sticking to his scheduled 25mph, or whatever it was, but we, at the end of the convoy, were alternating rapidly between 15 and 45mph. Every few miles, as well, vehicles would ditch themselves in the soft sand in the verges and be left: "Workshops can deal with them", a common misapprehension on the part of the RA! We had a busy time.

A little way beyond the Halfway House we passed the Wadi Natrun, a steep-sided rift in the desert floor, renowned for its ancient Coptic monastery and its modern alkali deposits, but we saw little or nothing of it, since we were too far from the lip of the depression.

We had set out from Beni Yussef at 0700 and, by early afternoon, we came out of the sand country into terrain where the ground was definitely earth and some attempt had been made to cultivate it in straggly furrows. The subtropical vegetation of the Delta was visible on our right as a faint blue line and a board on a post in the middle of nowhere said this was Mareopolis. I was to know this place well later on. We came across a few palm trees at a place called Amriya with a railway line leading from Alexandria to Mersa Matruh in the far west, and went through a giant empty tented camp with Australian names on the sign boards. I supposed it had been where the Australian Divisions had formed up for the fighting of the previous winter.

On the far side of this deserted camp was a steep hill, at the bottom of which we passed over a causeway across Lake Mariout, a vast, shallow lagoon cut off from the sea by a narrow rocky ridge and stretching for miles to the westward and eastward, where the dim outline of the buildings of Alexandria showed up on the ridge between Mariout and the sea. Here was our first glimpse of the Mediterranean, amid land sparsely covered with stunted fig bushes and an occasional clump of lofty date palms. Except for a distant wireless or radar station, there was little sign of war, or even of human life.

Then we came to the Road. I give it a capital 'R', because, for the next two years, there was to be only one road for us – this

29

coast road stretching from Alexandria to the Tunisian frontier. It was the main feature of this uncompromising desert, to which we became singularly attached; the route whereby we went "up" to the front, or "down" to the Delta and leave. Certainly it merited the title, the honourable title, of *The* Road. We joined it at a T-junction where stood a small Military Police post and a battered metal signboard erected by the Royal Automobile Club of Egypt pointing west to Mersa Matruh.

Our spirits rose as we turned left on to this Road, for we were now leaving the Base Area of BTE (British Troops in Egypt) and were entering the territory of the famous Western Desert Force. There was a certain amount of traffic on this road; strings of loaded RASC vehicles heading west and other vehicles coming the other way. The westbound ones were trim and clean-looking, while the returning ones were battered, covered in dust, with unditching channels in racks and blackened containers made from petrol cans dangling from the chassis. Their crews looked bronzed and unshaven.

There was little change in the scenery for many miles. The road lay on a low ridge; to our right lay the sea, gleaming intensely blue in the afternoon sun; then a range of white sandhills; next a stretch of *sabakha* or dried salt marsh, now hard underfoot in the high summer, but treacherously soft in winter; then our road, bordered with the same half-hearted attempts at cultivation; and finally, on the left lay the desert itself, a dreary waste of undulating sand, dust, stone and rock. The Desert Railway ran along this latter portion and occasionally could be seen in the distance; every now and then a small side road branched off towards it, bearing the destination name of some sand-silted halt: Burg el Arab, Hammam, El Alamein and Tel el Eissa.

Burg el Arab was our goal for the night and we turned off towards it. I don't know what we were expecting in the way of staging accommodation, but what we got was a captain who waved a hand towards a particularly bare bit of desert, said 'That's your staging area' and faded away. We realised this was the normal way of passing the night while on convoy. We were learning! We cooked ourselves a supper of bully-beef stew,

30

biscuits and baked beans out of the "hard rations" we had been issued for the journey and went to sleep in the open under the stars, feeling somewhat deflated.

And the evening and the morning were the first day, some Biblical scholar among us was heard to say.

The following morning we were on the road betimes after wringing ourselves out – the dew in the desert was particularly heavy – and consuming a much-needed breakfast of boiled tinned bacon, biscuits, jam and comforting hot tea. For the entire morning, the scenery was much the same as the previous day. We passed Daba, where there was a large wayside NAAFI/EFI roadhouse and Fuka, where the road climbed a low escarpment in a couple of zigzags. Finally, we came to the outskirts of Ma'aten Bagush and at last some signs of military occupation began to be visible. Bagush was at that time the Rear HQ of the Western Desert Force and was fortified in quite an elaborate manner that was known locally as a "box", consisting of several concentric rings of barbed wire, an anti-tank ditch and a lot of marked minefields. These defences began among the white sandhills on the coast and wound up on to the escarpment behind, which ran parallel to the shore a couple of miles inland. Inside this "box" was an airfield and a very large array of tents, most of which were well dug into the ground, so that only their ridges were visible.

Guides met us at the entrance to the box, to conduct us to our destinations. It appeared that RHQ and the Signals were to be within the box itself, whereas we, the Workshops, were to carry on beyond Bagush, to Km 37 (from Matruh), where the Bde OME, a Major Estlin, was located with 1 (SA) AA Regt Workshops.

The whole set-up of AA in the desert, at that time, was so confused a patchwork that it seems of interest to list how it was composed. 12 AA Bde was in command of all AA units in the WDF area deployed in defence of the RAF landing grounds. In point of fact, that included nearly all the AA in the desert. It consisted of:

1 (SA) AA Regt, with three batteries, plus:
2 LAA Regt commanding 37 and 38 LAA Batteries, 23

(Hong Kong and Singapore) HAA Bty and 25 (City of Londonderry TA) HAA Bty.

37 and 38 LAA Btys were the headless body of 13 LAA Regt, the RHQ of which, with the remaining battery, were trapped in Tobruk; they were armed respectively with captured Italian 20mm Bredas and British 40mm Bofors. The three batteries of 1 (SA) AA Regt had ancient 3" AA guns, captured Italian 13.2mm Bredas and twin AA Lewis guns. 23 (HKS) Bty had a mixture of 3" and 3.7" mobile guns, while 25 HAA Bty were fully equipped with 3.7" mobiles. They had been left by their parent 9 HAA Regt in Alexandria, during the abortive June battle, to defend Sollum when captured, and were still in the desert after the failure of that party. 12 AA Bde had hung on to them.

All this miscellany of artillery was what the Bde Workshops were supposed to keep in reasonable firing condition! Thus 12 AA Bde's "parish" was a very large one, extending from Sidi Barrani in the far west to Fuka in the far rear and the AA defences were spread out in what would in later months have been regarded as a dangerously thin layer, although at that time no one seemed to think so. These batteries were distributed as follows:

37 LAA Bty	Sidi Barrani LG.
38 LAA Bty	Bagush and Sidi Haneish LGs.
23 (HKS) HAA Bty	Sidi Haneish Railhead and Fuka LG.
25 HAA Bty	Matruh and Fuka Satellite LGs.
1 (SA) AA Regt	Matruh and Sidi Haneish LGs.

Also under the command of 12 AA Bde was 14 LAA Wksps at Alam Halfa between Sidi Barrani and the forward area at Buq Buq, which had somehow got separated from 14 LAA Regt during the excitements of the previous spring and was rather nobody's baby now that its parent unit was bottled up in Tobruk. In an even vaguer way 12 AA Bde was partly responsible for the welfare of 122 LAA Bty, an independent Bty who had got hooked on to 22 Guards Bde, and for 1 LAA Regt with 7 Armoured Division. Both of these units were somewhere up forward and it was rumoured that the batteries that 2 LAA Regt HQ had come out to command – 1, 5 and 6 LAA Btys – were on the loose with some formation in the desert to the south. It was all mast confusing.

The Bagush – Sidi Haneish area was the advanced base of the Western Desert Force, and Sidi Haneish, within the Bagush Box, was the railhead, although Matruh was the actual end of the railway line.

Major Estlin had established himself well away from the rest of Bde HQ and had decided to form a sort of combined Bde workshop for the whole area, to cope with the differing requirements of the units in his "parish". It was to comprise an amalgamation of 1 (SA) Regt Wksps and mine, whether we liked it or not. As a matter of fact, we did not, but it was no use arguing. Capt Stephen, the OC of the South Africans, objected so much to Estlin's ideas that he was "attached for special duties" to Bde HQ to get him out of the way and, as I was senior to his 2 i/c Lt Hallack, I was put in command of the composite show, with Hallack to assist me. The Sergeant Major was a South African and the rest of us worked together "fully integrated". I can't say this arrangement was ever a brilliant success, as might be expected, but that it operated at all was due to the loyal cooperation from all to prevent friction, and it did an immense amount of good and useful work in the two months that it lasted. However, we were all glad when the split-up came and we reverted to being our individual selves again.

The workshop was at Ras Hawala, a lovely strip of sandy beach backed by an expanse of flat ground. Our tents were sited on the seashore, well dug in to minimise being spotted from the air, for I was told that nothing stands out so clearly as the shadows of ridge tents. The workshop area was on the flat, inland from us. I lived and messed with the RHQ of the South African Regt, and a very pleasant and friendly lot they were. They had but lately arrived in the ME from East Africa, where they had been engaged in the defeat of the Italians in Somaliland and Southern Ethiopia.

We "took over", if one can use such a word for so casual an affair, from an Australian workshop that was just moving out.

33

They were a weird and wonderful crowd of hard-bitten toughs who had gone through the whole of the previous winter's campaign and now, battered and thoroughly "browned off", were returning to the Delta to refit. I noticed with interest how they had made themselves completely mobile – everything they had was on wheels and ready to move at very short notice. The Australian captain, who had seen our arrival, reckoned we were far too static and advised me to remedy this shortcoming at once. How right he was!

We were pretty busy at once with such a large area to service and we quickly found that the type of work we had to do was very different from what we had imagined. Somehow, we had been expecting that the major portion of our work would be with the guns and we were much surprised to find that these caused little bother – at that time – for the great volume of absolutely unending work came from the repair of motor vehicles. The appalling pot-holed roads, or where there were no roads at all, the rocky and uneven desert tracks, made broken springs an almost daily occurrence even with the most careful of drivers. With the dry and dusty atmosphere by day and heavy dew at night, engines lasted but a paltry 10,000 miles before replacement. Also, bodywork rattled to bits, electrical gear gave trouble and we found that our combined strengths of fitters (MT) were only just able to keep our heads above water.

It was fortunate that we were not yet in a mobile role, and that we had this period of static operation in which to find our feet and devise, with the help of old desert stagers, various preventative and curative measures to cope with the troubles. Our efforts did, I think, make some slight improvement, but for the next two years our main job remained that of trying to keep a maximum of regimental vehicles on the road at any time. It was a daunting job.

By contrast, we had little trouble with the guns and fire-control instruments. These went wrong as well, but, since they were not mobile, they caused far fewer headaches.

The HQ of the Brigade Workshops organisation, which figures so largely in my account from now on, consisted of two officers, the Major K. S. Estlin I have mentioned, and an instrument specialist, skilled in the repair of fire-control equipment, a Lieutenant, AOME 4th Class, whose name I forget. At the time we joined the Bde, he was an older man who didn't impress himself on me, and was later to be superseded by someone younger, Lt Wray, who was more of a live wire.

The small Bde staff included a Warrant Officer Class 1, ASM Bill Smith, whose job was to liaise with the Battery fitters on matters of maintenance and training, and a chief clerk, Staff Sergeant Lewis, who ran the office side and was the administrative backbone of the HQ. There were also Estlin's batman driver and a junior clerk, who assisted Lewis.

Estlin was aged about thirty-five and was ex-TA. He had been in his present position for quite a long time, so he knew exactly what his workshop officers were expected to do and how they should do it. He ruled us with a rod of iron, or rather spring steel, for he was always prepared to listen to sensible suggestions. His approval of one's performance was something to be striven for, no matter what it cost one in time and energy.

He was tall, of robust build, prematurely bald and with a round, ruddy face. His manner was informal, but he never minced words; he knew the "book" inside out and was merciless in his correction of faults. At least one knew exactly where one was because, if one found him a beast on occasion, he was a just beast. As a newcomer, my relations with him developed through a spectrum: apprehension; sheer terror; respect; admiration; to real friendship. In retrospect, I think he rather liked me, and those whom he liked he chastened; I got a lot of chastening. He would breeze into my workshop office, saluting rigorously according to the convention, no matter what the rank of the occupant was, and then dismiss my clerk, before starting to commend my progress, or "tear a strip" off me. He never criticised anyone in the hearing of someone of lower rank.

His one aim in life was to ensure that the equipment of 12 AA Bde was, as far as was practicable, in the best condition possible, and he would bend any rules to attain this. He turned a blind eye to the malfeasances of his workshop officers, if they broke rules to attain this desirable end. He had the ear of the Brigadier and shamelessly wangled what he wanted to provide the best service for his Brigade, RA or RAOC alike. In short, he was a great man; one of the best and it was a privilege to serve under him. We only realised how great when he was moved and promoted and another, lesser mortal replaced him.

His idea of locating my workshop in the same spot as his HQ was very trying, for he was always checking up for himself what we were doing.

We lived, as I have said, right on the shore at Ras Hawala, which was fine for keeping clean by an evening bathe, but man needs water to drink as well as for ablutions. Fresh water was scarce and rationed to two gallons per man per day for all purposes: cooking, drinking, washing, shaving, washing up and filling the radiators of our vehicles if they boiled away their contents. Water had to be fetched daily from an Army water point in Bagush. Immediately we came up against a snag; we had no means of fetching it except for the few two-gallon cans our scale of equipment allowed, whereas our South African neighbours had a number of 100-gallon water trailers.

However necessity is the mother of invention; we found a large derelict Italian water tank designed to hold 2000 gallons out in the desert and, when we had sawn the middle third out of it to make it a more handy size, mounted it on an old 15cwt truck chassis, bent the ends together to take a towing eye and added springs and wheels from somewhere in the desert. We then had a towable water trailer. Estlin watched with a blind eye the way we were breaking the rules in not returning the old chassis to Base for repair as we should have done and approvingly looked the other way when we towed the trailer to the water point. That tank lasted us through the whole of the ensuing winter campaign, giving invaluable service and endless trouble. By the following May, out of the original set-up only the tank itself remained unaltered.

This shortage of water didn't worry us unduly; there was enough for our needs. Nor were the rations bad or inadequate, even though our two cooks, RA general-duty men, had little or no previous experience of cooking and were pretty unskilled. We had our "Hydra" petrol cooker and we improvised an oven, so that our messing could have been a lot worse.

Our senior NCOs soon fixed themselves up with a good Mess, to which the South Africans of equivalent rank were invited and eager guests, and we started a large and flourishing unit canteen which did a roaring trade. Beer, cigarettes and eatables were available from the EFI/NAAFI depot at Qasaba, some three miles away, and a daily truck served to keep us well supplied. Decidedly, things could have been worse.

The two main health problems were flies and desert sores. Flies were a curse throughout our entire stay in the desert; even if we camped in the most virgin bit of desert, miles from anywhere and in the depths of winter – when it could be really cold – there would be swarms around in a few hours. Anti-fly precautions were in their infancy; we were hard put to it to devise means of keeping our food fly-free in the cookhouse and we never really managed to design a fly-proof latrine, notwithstanding countless experiments, then and in later months, to construct a portable unit.

Desert sores were quite another thing; there didn't seem to be any satisfactory way of combating them. On some people, every slight cut or abrasion went septic and became a running sore that needed medical attention. If the sores were bad, the sufferer had to be removed to the local Advanced Dressing Station at Bagush for several days. In the workshops, we were particularly exposed to this scourge, since we were always knocking our hands about at work and thus were constantly open to infection. I was fortunate to be immune, like some others, and we could cut ourselves without suffering, but all ranks needed extreme care. This scourge seriously interfered with our work and men went around with their hands encased in dirty protective bandages.

As there were no women this side of Alexandria, the normal conventions of civilised life were not observed. No one wore bathing suits, a fitter might strip off before tackling a dirty job and latrines were seldom surrounded by screens.

About this time, the authorities decided that some things were going too far for the maintenance of good health and an order was issued making it an offence to appear on the public roads without a shirt or hat. The Military Police received instructions to put anyone found disobeying this order on a charge. The edict jarred on the sense of free democracy entertained in certain Australian units in Matruh. They dutifully complied with the letter of the law and wore their unaccustomed shirts and hats, but just to show their distaste of this Pommie interference with their lives, they discarded their shorts instead!

Office work was simple and our combined staff of clerks had little to do except answer the telephone, which seemed to ring incessantly. The phone connected us with the Signals exchange at RHQ in Bagush and, through them and with great difficulty, to the outside world. Communications at this time were complicated by a sudden campaign of security in the WDF wherein every unit in the Force was allocated a code name of four letters, which had to be used at all times under threat of severe punishment, particularly for the offence of linking the code with the actual name of the unit you wanted to speak to. If you didn't know the code name you wanted, no one would tell you. Just to confuse the enemy still further, officers' appointments were each given as a code the name of a tree, and the information that "Oak Wick" wanted to speak to "Cedar Erad" made life difficult. One humourous individual – I think it was the IFC (Instructor of Fire Control) at RHQ, on finding he had been omitted from the schedule, succeeded in persuading the Signals Exchange for several days that he was "Eucalyptus Ponk". Rear HQ of 122 LAA Bty had the code "Wool" and took umbrage at the hoots of merriment on the other end of the line when announcing themselves as "Rear Wool". 'It sounds like the backside of a sheep,' the Battery Captain said sadly to me.

Just to make sure that the enemy didn't know who was facing him, the code lists were changed every month or so and everyone went up or down the list a few places like progressive whist, on receipt of a signal. This meant that you acquired the code name that had hitherto belonged to someone else. Any wretched unit out of wireless range that didn't hear the amending signal was completely isolated and everyone was reduced to tears of mortification. I don't know if any German could have been listening to our intercepts, but if so he must have thought we were mad. We probably were.

38

Spares for use in the workshops were an absolute headache, as the peacetime system was still in use at that time. Theoretically, on wanting some part, you made out an indent in quadruplicate and it was sent back to Base, through the local ordnance system. In due course, if the part were available at the Base Ordnance Depot, it arrived at the Sidi Haneish railhead and you signed the appropriate copies of the indent to say you had received it, and could then replace the faulty one with it. Needless to say, this antiquated peacetime ordnance system was as much use as a hole in the head, since the "turn-round" was often five or six weeks and most folk preferred to deal with the mobile Ordnance Field Parks attached to the Divisions. Various other unofficial methods of obtaining spares were resorted to, such as cannibalising otherwise damaged vehicles and/or switching parts onto a piece of equipment being sent back to Base as BLR (Beyond Local Repair). All these were highly illegal and most units wrongfully, but quite understandably in the circumstances, began to lay in a secret stock of such small spares that they thought would come in useful sometime. This practice was self-defeating, because instead of a few spares being available centrally, where they might do some good, it was usual to find they were in some secret stock of a unit that had only the occasional need for them. However, we as a workshop section held ourselves to be as entitled as anyone to such stock of fast-moving items and speedily set about collecting a supply of what we now saw to be necessary. Estlin knew about this, but professed not to and just looked the other way.

Our greatest troubles were lack of enough welding gases and nuts and bolts. Our equipment scale – devised for some static unit in the UK with an Ordnance Depot just round the corner –- was one bottle of oxygen and one of acetylene. We very soon found that this was pitifully inadequate for the tasks with which we were faced. One had to hand in the empty bottle in order to obtain a full replacement, and we were told that everybody was in the same boat; it was bottles that were short, not gas. No one would authorise any extra holding, so at first we had to stop a job while we tried to get some replacement gas and, since the local Ordnance Depot could be out of that particular gas that

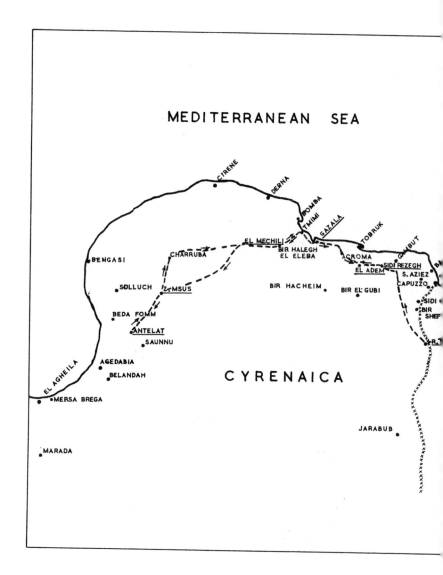

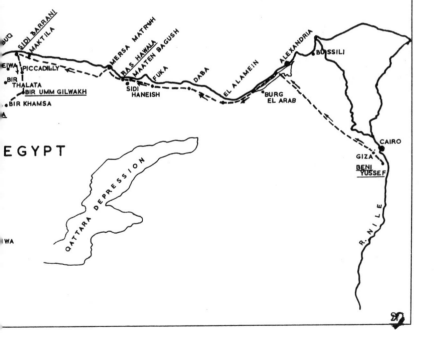

THE WESTERN DESERT ——

2 LAA WORKSHOPS –JULY 1941 – MAY 1942

ROUTE FOLLOWED - — ⇌ — —
WORKSHOP SITES - EL ADEM

Scale

0   20   40   60   80   100   120   140   miles

week, we were obliged to live a very hand-to-mouth existence. The obvious solution was to acquire a spare bottle or two, by fair means or foul, and exchange the empties for full ones in rotation.

Nuts and bolts were almost as great a problem. All vehicles seemed to shed them like rain on the bumpy terrain and, as if that wasn't enough, numerous desert modifications issued from the wise ones at GHQ MEF almost weekly and had to be fitted at once, if not sooner. In all such cases, the Batteries looked to Workshops in childlike hopes for us to produce the goods. The real things were difficult to come by and, since our "customers" weren't parting with their own hard-won stock, thank you very much, we had to revert to the desert for supply. A lot of the modifications were carried out with metric threads from Italian wrecks, and a couple of fitters were on constant patrol in our 15cwt, equipped with a wide variety of spanners, looking for derelict vehicles. As a result of these unlawful activities, we never actually came to a halt for lack of these vital items.

At the risk of being accused of overdoing the technical difficulties, I cannot omit the problems with broken vehicle springs which were to haunt us for the rest of the campaign. Vehicles broke springs on the terrible tracks as a daily routine and we were expected to do something about them. According to the "book", a vehicle with a broken spring was put off the road until a replacement arrived from the nearest Ordnance Depot. At current consumption, this would reduce the Batteries to walking in no time, so we were forced to various tricks to keep the Regt's vehicles on the road. Most sizes of spring proved virtually unobtainable through normal ordnance channels, but spring steel in long flat strips could be obtained occasionally. Accordingly, I set about laying in stocks of as much steel as we could lay hands on (and carry) – which wasn't much – and our blacksmith, Corporal Siddle, made springs and spring leaves in the field on our portable field forge. Siddle proved a positive genius as a smith and I do not know what we should have done in the subsequent campaigns, but for his skill.

However, the supplies of spring steel were not enough to meet all our greater needs, so once again we had to resort to the desert. We sent out parties to search for abandoned and badly damaged vehicles and took the springs off them. Everyone, when driving abroad, kept a lookout for them and I never travelled without a ruler, so that I could decide at once whether the specimen was useful or not. At one time I knew the dimensions of the front and rear springs of all the popular makes and sizes of truck and lorry in use in the desert. By this means, we gradually built up a small stock of the more fast-moving varieties and we were generally able to maintain stocks for emergencies.

It was generally the main leaf that broke – Ford 8cwt trucks were the worst culprits – and we sometimes had to redesign the whole spring and add extra leaves for the pair, front or rear, because there was nothing we could modify as a repair. Very occasionally, later in the winter campaign, we did things that ought not to have worked at all, such as actually welding the broken top leaf together, with a stiffening plate, and, just once, we actually riveted the top leaf together and it stood up to a couple of weeks' battering.

But all this was in the future. At Ras Hawala, we were just learning our job – under the eagle eye of Major Estlin.

3

Although we were attached to the RHQ of an LAA Regt, we saw little of any AA activity during the "shakedown" period I have just described. There was fortunately no trouble from enemy aircraft at Ras Hawala. Occasionally a solitary reconnaissance flight would sail by at a great height and the guns at Sidi Haneish would open up at it, but nothing came over low and we had nothing like the ground-strafing that took place daily further west, according to tales passed back by the occasional visitor from 122 LAA Bty and 1 LAA Regt. In fact, although we didn't like to admit it even to ourselves, we were rather too far to the rear of the Forward Area to be within easy reach of the enemy, who was operating from advanced LGs far away in Libya at Sidi Aziez and Gambut.

Whenever there was a bit of moon, however, Matruh came in for quite a heavy pasting and we avoided the place as much as possible after dark. We could see the barrage going up from the safety of our workshop site, but the night bombers left us alone. Just as well, it seemed.

I heard little of the war "up front". Our informants, again 122 LAA Bty and 1 LAA Regt, were a trifle vague but I was left with the impression that the "fighting", if any, resembled a giant game of hide and seek played over a wide expanse of desert, where neither side spent two consecutive nights in the same place or knew what the morrow would bring them. If we were short of troops in the Forward Area, the Germans seemed very little better off.

One night during the August full moon, Estlin, Hallack and I, with a party of fitters, drove into Matruh in two trucks before the

44

air raid that was a foregone conclusion for that night. I forget what the trouble had been, but we had been asked to attend in case one of the 3" guns misbehaved.

We arrived in Matruh before dark (the road was closed at dusk) and visited Bty HQ in the basement of the ruined Lido Hotel, where, so report had it, the Duke of Windsor and Mrs Simpson had once stayed. Matruh was quite a sizeable little place with white houses and hotels along the edge of a blue lagoon, clustering among the only palm trees for many miles. From the brow of the hill on the landward side, it looked a charmingly unspoilt spot, which in pre-war days had been quite a famous resort and much visited by the Egyptian upper classes, but now it was merely a shell; all the houses were roofless, and otherwise damaged. During the previous autumn, when the Italians were at Sidi Barrani, it had been badly knocked about by heavy air raids and had never recovered.

When the air raid took place, we observed the guns at one of the two sites, on a small promontory near the Lido Hotel. It seemed a rather half-hearted raid by a couple of Italian aircraft, who departed smartly as soon as they were fired on. There was a lull and we moved off to visit the other site, which was located on a spit of land separating the lagoon from the open sea, near the point where it was pierced for the entry to the harbour. It would have entailed a long roundabout drive round the lagoon to reach the site by road, but the gunners said there was a just-submerged ridge of land across the shallow water that they always used as a short cut, and they gave us a guide.

Estlin decided to attempt this short cut, after speaking to the site commander by phone and asking for a small light to be shone along the line of approach. I was in Estlin's vehicle and it was a very eerie feeling driving across a 400-yard stretch of water in the moonlight, aiming at the tiny beam ahead. We reached the other side without mishap – Estlin was always lucky – but Hallack in the second truck deviated slightly and went down with all hands in some five feet of water. His party reached the gun site on foot, to the gunners' great amusement, and we had to salvage the truck the following day.

* * *

By mid-August, the composite workshop was working as satis-factorily as it was ever likely to and I was detailed to make a trip forward to visit 37 LAA Bty at Sidi Barrani on the CO's behalf, to find 1 and 14 LAA Wksps as Estlin's representative and see if they were in need of anything special. I think in retrospect the trip was really to see how I coped with finding my way about in the desert, and Estlin sent my AQMS Harding with me for initial guidance and to be dropped off at 37 LAA Bty for an inspection of transport.

Harding had replaced Holgate as my WO. He was an old Middle East hand, a regular who had been in the area for some years, and I was relieved to have him. Estlin had observed Holgate at close quarters at Ras Hawala and decided a Work-shops under his jurisdiction needed more of a live wire, so Holgate had been posted away and I was delighted with the replacement. Harding was quiet, competent and generally a nice chap and, most important, knew what he was doing. We got on very well together.

We reckoned it to be a three-day trip, for 14 LA Wksps were on the far side of Sidi Barrani, a good 120 miles away, and 1 LAA Wksps were somewhere in the Habata, Sofafi, Bir Thalata area some 40 miles to the south or south-west of Barrani. Where exactly, no one had any clear idea, but Estlin suggested a courtesy call on RHQ 1 LAA Regt would provide the informa-tion. They were at present at Maktila, a point on the coast just east of Barrani and ought to be able to tell me.

So off the three of us went in the 15cwt truck, Harding, me and Cpl Thorne, my driver, on my first excursion into the real "front". Harding volunteered to sit in the back of the truck on his bedroll and we bowled along merrily into Matruh, turned left in the town and climbed the long escarp-ment that sheltered it from the south-west. At the top, the road divided and a battered noticeboard stuck in the ground informed us that this was Charing Cross. The right fork was the coast road to Sidi Barrani and the left track went straight as a die south across the featureless desert. An arrow pointed along it and carried the single word "Siwa", an oasis far out in the "blue".

We took the coastal road and came to an extensive belt of old minefields, laid as the first defence of the Matruh fortress during the previous autumn's "scare" when the Italian army under Graziani was encamped at Sidi Barani and Maktila and was feeling its way gingerly down the road towards Matruh. The minefields had never been challenged and were now a relic of rusty barbed wire and danger boards on either side of the road.

Beyond them, the road went straight on, as straight as if it had been drawn in bitumen across the dusty, scrubby waste that disappeared into the shimmering horizon on all sides. A single telephone line ran alongside, but otherwise the only signs of previous human activity were hundreds of discarded "non-returnable" four-gallon petrol tins, some new and bright, some battered and rusty, lying in a continuous stream along the verge. Occasionally, we encountered a lone vehicle and when this happened both parties drove off on to the hard desert verge for there was little width for passing at any speed. This stirred up a following plume of fine white dust into which the truck to leeward disappeared as into a smoke-screen.

About halfway to Sidi Barrani, the tarmac surface of the road suddenly stopped and we crashed on to a stony foundation of rocks the size of footballs. Harding, the old desert hand, said this was another thing done to discourage the Italians from venturing too quickly towards Matruh the year before. Whatever the reason, it was impossible to drive on it and risk our springs, and we took to the desert verge for preference. If we met a vehicle coming in the opposite direction, a great amount of jockeying for position ensued and the loser was lashed with choking dust. This bad surface lasted some 20 miles and then stopped as suddenly as it had begun, so that we could get back on to the road again. Almost at once we came across traces of the Italian advance; first a broken field gun, then a couple of shattered lorries, a trackless tank, more lorries and so on, the wrecks gradually increasing in numbers until the desert seemed to be littered with them. Finally, as we neared Sidi Barrani, the whole stony desert became a vast refuse dump of shattered lorries, guns and tanks, abandoned piles of Italian shells and shell-cases, petrol tins in their thousands, barbed wire and just oddments of no identifiable use or origin.

About six miles short of Sidi Barrani, we turned off into the desert on our left beside a small British cemetery and headed towards 05 and 05 Satellite LGs which were defended by 37 LAA Bty. LG 05 was the most forward of the landing grounds at present in use by the RAF, although on the road between Sidi Barrani and Matruh (where the road surface had been removed) were the sites of LGs 01, 02, 03 and 04. We had been told that the RAF didn't like the 05 pair very much either, as they were a trifle too exposed and far forward, so that they preferred to use them mainly as refueling bases to give greater range when acting as cover to the barge convoys running up the coast between Alexandria and beleaguered Tobruk. I rather agreed when we got there, a mile or so off the main road, for they lay on a flat stretch of desert, lacking any cover or visible identifying marks, on which two diagonal runways had been graded clear of scrub and stones. The AA defences were nothing to write home about either. On the two LGs 37 LAA Bty had deployed eight captured Italian 20mm Bredas, one at each corner of each LG. The proper British 40mm Bofors, of which a LAA Bty should have had twelve, were so scarce in the ME that, in common with many other units, 37 Bty had had to make do with these eight pea-shooters. Odd though it might have seemed to me, no one appeared particularly worried by this lack of adequate AA defence. Bty HQ received us cordially in the hospitable manner which I learned subsequently was the pleasant custom in the desert towards visitors, and we spread our beds on the open ground and slept the sleep of the just, or at least of men who had driven for a hundred and thirty miles over bad roads in a Bedford 15cwt truck.

Early the following morning, just after we had risen, had wrung the dew out of our clothes and breakfasted in the open, we were treated to an impromptu demonstration as to why the RAF disliked LG 05 and declined to have aircraft on the ground there for long. A large twin-engined black monoplane, flying low and very fast, roared out of the south-easterly sun and, sweeping over the edge of the LG, sprayed the surrounding desert with bright, flickering tracer from its front and rear guns. At the end of the runway it banked in a tight turn, wings almost vertical, and did another run diagonally across the LG, spewing out tracer for all it was worth. Seven Bredas on the two LGs – one was stripped for maintenance – now opened up in a high-pitched crackle of curving, bursting little shells, and rattle of Lewises, Brens and miscellaneous small arms added a lighter background to the mayhem. Now thoroughly awake, everyone dived into the nearest slit trench or under the nearest truck, but the aircraft turned west, after completing its run, and made off at great speed.

As far as we could learn, no casualties and no damage were sustained anywhere on the LG, except possibly for a few holes in the odd vehicle, but it bought home to me as nothing hitherto had done that there was a war on!

Leaving Harding at Bty HQ for his vehicle inspections and to be picked up on our return, we set off into Sidi Barrani to find 14 LAA Wksps, who people said were at Alam Halfa, a map reference between the coast road and the sea, some ten or twelve miles on from Barrani towards Buq Buq, another map reference location. In pre-war days, the road had terminated at Sidi Barrani, which in common with Sollum and Matruh had been a frontier garrison of the Egyptian Army. These garrisons, in particular that of Sollum on the Libyan border, had in fact been supplied by sea. The Italian Army under Graziani, during their occupancy of Sidi Barrani the previous autumn, had laboriously laid the foundations of an extension of the coast road to link up with their own Libyan coast road at Fort Capuzzo, but, at the time of the British attack, hadn't quite had time to finish it and it had been left unsurfaced.

Sidi Barrani, as we drove into it, looked an absolute shambles of rubble. The Egyptian barracks on the higher ground between the road and the sea was a mass of broken masonry, littered with rusting Italian tanks and self-propelled guns. What was left of the little town would scarcely have afforded cover to a rabbit, so completely was it destroyed, as a result of a massive bombardment by the Mediterranean Fleet during the previous

December. A few chipped palm trees leaned forlornly over the churned white dust and fallen walls – inscribed wholesale with the slogans "*VV Il Duce*" and "*Vinceremo*" – and an enormous rusty gas engine brooded starkly over the scene from the top of a mound of rubbish.

We had been warned by 37 LAA Bty to avoid the road west of Sidi Barrani, as this was a favourite hunting ground for German ground-strafing aircraft, and this morning's experience suggested this was good, sound advice. One look at the road surface, however, decided us that we wouldn't use it, for other reasons, for it was massively constructed of even bigger rocks than those we had encountered the previous day on the way from Matruh. It was a pity, someone said, that the Italians hadn't been allowed to finish it.

Lt Purcell had formed 14 LAA Wksps at Hucknall the previous November at the same time as I had 2 LAA, but he had gone overseas in December and I hadn't seen him since. We found the workshop among a range of low sandhills not far from the sea and I was much surprised at the amount of dispersion between individual vehicles; no vehicle or tent could have been nearer than a good fifty yards from its neighbour and many were even more than that. To have made a tour of the work in progress must have entailed an hour's hard walking. Purcell explained to me that, shortly before, a German strafing raid had cost him two or three men killed and he was taking no chances.

I thought he looked very tired and played out and his men seemed listless and dispirited; rather surprising, considering they had only been in the desert since April – five months – but during that time they had been "nobody's baby" until they had been adopted by 12 AA Bde and set to look after the AA units in the Barrani area. It was a small unit living by itself on the edge of the salt marshes by the sea, not under any particular authority, except for the far-off 12 AA Bde, to provide any form of moral or material backing. I was to find in later days that this wasn't such an unusual state of affairs as I had first imagined.

Purcell said he hoped they would soon be going back for a refit; he knew of several fighting formations which had come into the desert at the same time as he had and had "gone back".

50

Like everyone else at that time, he had the idea that one spent only about three months at a stretch in the desert, before getting a bit of a rest in the Delta.

It seemed they had few troubles I could rectify, or really any that could be rectified by higher authority. The morale of the whole unit from top to bottom was apparently just very low and I didn't know how to remedy that. And so, after a brief look round the workshop, I headed back along the road towards Sidi Barrani, where I was to visit the Rear HQ of 122 LAA Bty, if I could find them.

The finding proved quite difficult, for the unit was a small one and had tucked itself away unobtrusively among the sandhills and gorse-like scrub just to the east of Sidi Barrani itself. Whereas 14 LAA Wksps had relied on dispersion for safety, 122 Bty HQ had gone in for concentration and camouflage. Their trucks were dug deep into the sand dunes with hessian-garnished scrim netting festooned above them and the men had constructed deep dugouts by the beach for living, sleeping and office quarters. There were evidently two schools of thought here and I wasn't in a position to judge between them, but I was impressed that these two schools of thought did exist.

The Bty Captain, who was in charge at Rear HQ, received me cordially and produced tea at a moment's notice in the manner I was beginning to recognise as the hallmark of desert hospitality, and we sat and drank it on the hard white sand outside his dugout, shielded from the fierce afternoon sun by a piece of camouflage netting. Not thirty yards away, a glinting blue sea rippled gently and a warm breeze rustled through the spiny sand grass. Once again, the war seemed very far away.

My host was a bit of an amateur botanist and pointed out clusters of little white, bell-shaped flowers set amid long-pointed green leaves which grew in profusion in the sandhills. He called them "desert lilies" and said they grew from a bulb rather like that of a hyacinth. Except for the sand dunes of Sidi Barrani, I never came across them anywhere else. We dug a few bulbs up and I sent them home to my mother, but they didn't seem to like the English climate and never flourished.

After tea, I moved on to RHQ 1 LAA Regt, who I learned

were a little further east among the sand hills at Maktila. Here, again, I was welcomed with instant and courteous hospitality, and empty bivouacs were placed at my disposal and that of my driver for the night. I learned from them that 1 LAA Wksps were probably not at Sofafi, a point on the escarpment due south of Buq Buq, where they had been for the past few weeks. Enemy light armoured forces had been out on the prowl recently in that neighbourhood and 7 Armoured Division had moved all its "soft-skinned" troops some 30 miles to the rear out of the way. They would probably be at Bir Talatha, some miles south of Sidi Barrani, 'but if they're not there, the "flap" is probably over, so just pop along to Sofafi – doubtless they'll have gone back'. Apparently the CO wasn't in direct wireless touch with his Batteries' "B" Echelons and everyone seemed to take it as quite normal for a Commanding Officer not to know the whereabouts of some of the troops under his command.

So the following morning, armed with a map and compass, and with more than a couple of qualms at the prospect of pushing out into the trackless desert away from the friendly road, we set off.

At first we followed a well defined, rutted track which struck due south from Sidi Barrani over sandy, tussocky downland and we rapidly lost sight of the road and the sea. Although the desert is always described in popular speech as "trackless", this is a complete misnomer. Most of the desert we had to deal with over the next few months was only too well provided with tracks, going all over the place. The problem is which one to select, using a combination of map, compass, speedometer mileage and common sense. After a while one develops a sort of feel for the direction and it helps, but at this time I was limited to mileage readings and compass.

We had been advised that almost any aircraft we saw (and any that saw us) would be hostile, so we took down the canvas canopy on the Bedford, the better to keep a good lookout, and got badly sunburnt for our pains, for the August sun struck back from the surrounding waste like the blast from a foundry furnace.

On the rising ground inland from Sidi Barrani, our track

passed through a vast park of rusty, derelict lorries, scattered in huddled heaps and half-buried by the fine, drifting dust or sand. They were vehicles of the defeated Italian Army, captured in the fighting of the previous winter, which, owing to the sudden change-round in the campaign – turning this Base Collecting Area overnight into the front line – it had been impossible to remove. Now, after six months of exposure to rain (it does rain in the desert!), sun, wind, firewood hunters and seekers after spare parts, they had been reduced to battered piles of rusty wreckage. A sad spectacle.

As we drove on southwards and the morning sun rose above us, we began to be plagued by tricks of the desert that later became familiar. On all sides of us stretched a slightly undulating expanse of greenish grey waste of stony gravelly soil, sprinkled with sparse patches of a dead-looking scrub that I learned was locally called Camel Thorn. I don't know what its real name is. There were no landmarks by which to steer or aim at and nothing except the position of the sun that gave any indication of whether one was going straight ahead or round in a giant circle; on all sides the horizon was the same. It gave one a funny "lost" feeling in the pit of one's stomach and I have heard others say that it affected them in the same way, the first time they ventured alone into the desert. One had, one felt, only to break down and one would never be heard of until one's bleached bones were discovered beside the ruins of one's truck!

It was a horrid feeling, but sheer nonsense; we were on a well known and frequented track, I had a compass, and if we felt lost we had only to turn round and motor due north until we struck the coast road, but it seems to be a feeling which takes some fighting down. I firmly oppose the belief that seemed to be held in very high quarters that any fully trained troops armed with maps, compasses and all the necessary adjuncts to navigation, but unused to the desert, can be let loose in it and immediately thrown into battle with a desert-wise enemy, without any acclimatising period to overcome their instincts. The desert is like the sea, for one must navigate its vast expanses of "sameness" with map and speedometer, with compass by day or stars by night, just as if one's vehicle were a ship, and the penalty for faulty navigation is to run the danger of becoming a castaway, waiting for a rescue party.

As the sun grew hotter and the desert air heated up, odd optical effects made themselves apparent. It became impossible to gauge accurately the size, shape or distance of any object more than half a mile away. Dwarf bushes would elongate themselves in the heat shimmer until they looked like an advancing host of men; objects on the horizon would suddenly detach themselves from the ground and seem to float, apparently unsupported, just above it; hollows would appear to fill with water and drain themselves again as we drew near; and across the scene stalked majestically groups of "sand-devils", locally known as "whirling willies", miniature whirlwinds of yellow dust which sprang up unexpectedly in the rising hot air, pursued a wayward course for a few minutes and then suddenly collapsed, equally unexpectedly.

Several times we saw, or thought we saw, groups of stationary vehicles in the distance away on our beam, but couldn't be sure, since our track didn't pass close enough to overcome the mirage effects. Several times, also, we were tricked into confusing the sand-devils for the dust wakes of moving columns of vehicles. During that whole morning, I do not think we actually passed close to more than half a dozen vehicles and three of these were staff cars, which overtook us in line ahead, one, two, three, slightly echelonned to avoid each other's dust, pitching and tossing over the stones like destroyers in a choppy sea.

The further south we got, the stonier the ground became and we were obliged sometimes to slow to a walking pace to avoid breaking springs as we bumped and crashed over the rocks. As we slowed for each bad bit, our own wake of dust overtook us and we would be enveloped in a cloud of fine, stinging grit.

Some two hours after leaving Sidi Barrani, possibly 25–30 miles at the speed we were travelling, we came on ranges of low stone walls and signs of previous human occupation: derelict broken lorries, piles of spent shell cases, splintered wooden ammunition boxes, discarded steel helmets and bent rifles, all gradually disappearing into the slowly shifting dust. Consultation with my map suggested this must be Nibeiwa, one of the Italian perimeter forts of the Sidi Barrani position and the first to be overrun in the battles of the previous December. No one went there now; it was deserted, save for the little green lizards which darted hither and thither among the stones.

Some way beyond Nibeiwa, we came to the first landmark of any sort we had seen so far, a prominent mound by the track, which was crossed – of all things! – by a line of telegraph poles, coming out of the heat-haze on one hand and disappearing into it on the other. It was a silent reminder of man's continued existence in these parts, something we had been beginning to doubt. Where the line crossed our track a signpost had been erected, its left arm pointing to "Piccadilly Circus" and the right to "Straffer's [sic] Wadi", neither of which appeared on my map. Straight on was, it seemed, the way to Bir Khamsa, a location far out in the desert to the south.

Once again, I consulted the map and we checked our mileage recorder, to come to the conclusion that this spot was Bir Enba, not so very far from Bir Thalata as marked on the map. We were nearing our destination. From this point onwards the track grew better and the ground somewhat less stony, so that we made better progress and after a few miles more a vast array of stationary vehicles came into sight, scattered over several square miles of desert. This could only be the "B" Echelon of 7 Armd Div (the B Echelon of a fighting formation consists of the administrative and non-essential men, vehicles and stores, which are kept back out of the fighting) and so it proved to be. The halt seemed to be a temporary one, for among that multitude of vehicles I couldn't see a single tent of any sort. The lorries just stood in the heat at something like 100-yard intervals and in no particular sort of order. Their crews sat or lay beside or in or under them, wherever a trace of shade could be found, and beside each truck was a freshly dug slit trench. A motley forest of Lewises, Brens and miscellaneous light machine guns on AA mountings pointed skyward, their magazines already in position.

After a bit of searching, we found 1 LAA Wksps. Notwithstanding the heat of the sun, the scene was one of great activity. The hand-operated blacksmith's forge was in full blast, trucks under repair were scattered around, and men were working at vices fixed to the tailboards of vehicles. Lt Bentley, a round-faced lad with horn-rimmed spectacles and a battered SD cap on the back of his head, welcomed me with cordiality and we shared our bully and biscuits in the back of his covered 15cwt truck, which he had fitted up with a stretcher type of transverse bed across the front end and with a small table. It was, in one, his home, his transport and his office. It looked a good idea.

Bentley denied that he had any troubles and said he was quite on top of his allotted task. They were all probably moving back to Sofafi or Habata that evening, but it didn't matter, for he could pack up and move out in under half an hour. I solemnly reflected that it would take me the best part of two days of hard work to move out of Ras Hawala. As we talked, various "customers" looked in, asking for his assistance or for repairs and he sent his craftsmen scurrying round to deal with them; all seemed very cheerful and hard-working – so different from Purcell's hangdog crowd.

During our short chat, Bentley propounded several precepts which I was subsequently to find were of great importance and are, perhaps, worth summarising. They were:

- As soon as you arrive anywhere, fill up with petrol, ready to move off again, especially at night.
- Never unpack anything unless you really need it.
- Never accept more tasks in your workshop than you can work on at once. Let the unit the work belongs to keep it and send it in as soon as you have the men to tackle it.
- Never, never have the wheels off a vehicle overnight.
- The more your vehicles are fitted up with vices, etc., for immediate use as mobile workshops, the better.
- Make sure the fitters know their own vehicles and pack their tools with ready access for immediate use.

Good advice, all of it. I was soon to find out by practical experience exactly how good.

A couple of hours sufficed to complete this visit and by mid-afternoon we were again on the hot, stony track, heading northwards. Somehow, the return trip didn't seem to take so long and, although we scarcely saw another vehicle the whole way, I never felt "lost" in the wilderness as I had on the outward journey. The desert was no longer such a trackless waste after all; I had mastered my terrors and had returned "blooded". In fact, as we topped the last rise and saw the white ruins of Sidi Barrani gleaming in the evening sun, I could have burst into song.

Perhaps I have laboured this point overmuch; I don't know. However, this was a significant occasion and one that stands out vividly in my mind – my first real encounter with the Desert with a capital "D" and I had survived.

We spent the night with 37 LAA Bty, picked up Harding and bowled happily back to Ras Hawala the following morning. I reported to Estlin that Bentley seemed to be in command of his situation, but that the morale of Purcell's lot was depressingly low.

4

Work went on steadily at Ras Hawala during the next few weeks. With Estlin's forceful backing, the local RE came and dug and cemented in a large inspection pit for underside examination of vehicles. More useful, they rendered with cement the floor and sides of an even larger pit we had excavated, and over it we erected an EPIP tent. This made it possible to have an almost dust-free instrument workshop in which we could take apart predictors and other equipment, with some small hope of keeping free of the ever-present fine dust. It was the Bde Lt (AOME)'s pride and joy.

Estlin also conceived the idea of a lorry-mounted LAA gun which could be used for convoy defence and fired on the move. From somewhere or other he scrounged a 20mm Breda and an old four-wheel drive Morris portee, of the sort normally used to transport the virtually useless two-pounder anti-tank guns that the powers-that-be had decided were the British Army's answer to the German 88mms. The result was, to my mind, highly successful and we careered about in the desert hinterland, doing all-round test-firing of the gun on the move. The effect on the wretched portee driver, of the fierce little weapon firing at low elevations just over his head, can be imagined!

To this day, I don't know if Estlin had heard something or whether he was gifted with uncanny prescience, but when, some two years later, a lorry-borne 40mm gun was produced officially at Abbassia Base Workshops in Cairo, the vehicle was a Morris portee and the whole set-up was nearly a duplicate of our experimental project. However, on this occasion, the authorities failed to "buy" our idea (no guns or no portees or something) and it got no further. We had ideas of holding on to it as private mobile Workshop AA defence, but Col Helby heard about this and we had to give it up; the gun went back to whoever was its owner, while RHQ, who were perennially short of transport, froze on to the portee.

About this time, I took a trip back to the Delta to do some business for Estlin in Alexandria. The journey that had taken us the better part of a day on the way up was covered in a matter of hours in a bucketing 15cwt. I liked Alex better than Cairo; it was a cleaner, cooler and generally more European city stretching along the seafront. Officers in town on business – as distinct from leave – were accommodated at the Army's expense in great luxury at the Windsor Hotel on the front and I spent a wonderful evening having a monstrous bath, a fabulous dinner, a visit to the cinema, and another even more monstrous bath. Then I popped into a real bed with *sheets* and a bedside reading lamp! It brought home to me how the lads coming back to civilisation on leave must feel, and I made a mental note that sheets and some form of reading lamp were amenities I would have to introduce into my tent on my return.

I knew No 3 General Hospital was at Bussilli out to the east in the Delta near Rosetta, and I would have liked to ring Phyl up and have a word, but I found that the Hospital could only be reached on the Military Exchange and a special code number had to be used to get on to it from the civilian system. I didn't know this number and resolved to obtain it in future.

Part of my official business was to collect a large trailer destined to carry an electric welding set for the South Africans, which they were obtaining from one of the Base Wksps ready to be fitted with their own generator. I found, somewhat to my satisfaction, that the assembly wasn't quite ready and I needed no encouragement to spend another day in Alex. This left me more time to follow up an attempt by Estlin, on a strictly unofficial basis, to obtain a certain amount of priority in the supply of stores for his workshops, before the battle started. As things were at present, the supply situation, using the orthodox channels, was just about able to meet only almost "peacetime" demands and it was painfully obvious, even to me, that when the battle started, the "system" would immediately break down. As indeed it did. Notwithstanding the authorising chit with which Estlin had provided me, I had very little success with this part of my mission; everyone was very friendly and put me off with kind promises to look into the matter and see if anything could be done, within the framework of what the "Book" said.

The rest of my extra day was spent in seeing the sights of Alexandria. Although the city was rather more exposed to the attentions of the enemy, everything was still very civilian and peaceful. There was little to remind me of the war, apart from the hours of darkness, that is, when a highly efficient blackout was rigorously enforced and a few hostile aircraft sailed over at stratospheric heights and dropped the occasional bomb, amidst an orgy of AA fire, in which the Fleet joined. The cafés did a record trade in fantastic ices, sundaes, sweetmeats and drinks; the cinemas were packed – emptying in colossal panic only when the mournful notes of some form of foghorn announced the air raid warning, – the shops were full of all manner of luxury goods; and down the boulevards strolled elegant civilian loungers in great numbers, accompanied by their painted, parasolled and diaphanously garbed "lovelies" in even greater profusion. War had yet to come to Egypt...

Our run back to the desert on the second morning was made eventful only by the behaviour of the trailer, which had no springs and steadily disintegrated. Every few miles would come a loud clatter from astern and Thorne or I, whoever wasn't driving, would alight, gather up the bit, throw it into the back of the 15cwt and climb wearily back into the truck. It became quite monotonous. When we reached Ras Hawala, towing the chassis of the trailer – all that remained in one piece – Captain Stephen, late of the workshop and now attached to RHQ 1 (SA) AA Regt HQ, was quite peeved at the repair work that would have to be done and accused me of over-speeding. My retort, that he ought to have specified something better suited to desert conditions, did little to cement inter-unit good relations.

As August rolled by, rumours began to be heard from cook-house and latrine attendants that we were going to be relieved and were going "further up". These unfailing sources of information were soon corroborated by the official news, supporting the rumour. We were going to be relieved, about mid-September, by 94 HAA Regt Wksps, now fully equipped at Beni Yussef and ready to come up and win the war for us.

This, though we only guessed at it, was part of the overall build-up of forces for the coming great battle of the winter season, which was intended to sweep the enemy from Cyrenaica.

After the retreat the previous spring, the main Western Desert Force had been concentrated in the Matruh area and based on dumps still further to the rear at Bagush and Daba. The terrain forward of Matruh was very nearly a no-man's-land and, although the actual Forward Area of contact with the enemy was on the Egypt/Libya border, the intervening space was lightly held by highly mobile forces. Patrol and outpost operations were the order of the day, and hostile raiding parties on either side might penetrate deeply beyond the contact zone without much let or hindrance.

GHQ MEF decided that this state of affairs must stop. Before the coming battles of the winter of 1941, it would be necessary to build up considerable dumps for the striking forces well in advance of Matruh, without the danger of interruption by freebooting itinerant German armoured forces. As a prerequisite of safety in the desert south of Sidi Barrani, much more air support would be needed, since at present there was an 80/20 ratio between German and British air strengths in the Forward Area. This meant that the Sidi Barrani airstrips would have to be occupied operationally, instead of, as hitherto, being merely refueling points, since the Sidi Haneish LGs were much too far in rear to give any useful time for fighter patrols over the Forward Area. Consequently, the old 02 and 03 LGs were re-occupied and a new landing ground was constructed nearer the sea in place of the old 05.

A reshuffle of AA units was necessary to strengthen the AA defences in the Forward Area, starting with the withdrawal of 1 (SA) AA Regt from Matruh and its replacement by 94 (City of Edinburgh TA) HAA Regt RHQ and two of its batteries, 291 and 292 HAA Btys, initially defending Matruh and Sidi

Haneish. The other Bty of 94th (290) had been detached at Gibraltar on the way out and its place was taken by 261 HAA Bty, a London Transport TA Bty, shorn from its parent regiment, which had gone elsewhere. I don't know what this Regiment was or where it had gone. 261 were located down the line of communication, relieving 23 (HKS) HAA Bty, and 25 HAA Bty was moved up from the Matruh area to Sidi Barrani to stiffen the AA defence in that area. RHQ 2 LAA Regt went with them to command and coordinate all the AA defences of the LGs in the area. This, Stage 1 of the reshuffle, took place at the beginning of September, in a great hurry, to be followed a fortnight later by Stage 2 with the withdrawal of 14 LAA Wksps from the Sidi Barrani area. Their commitments were taken over by my unit and our replacement was to be 94 HAA Wksps up from the Delta.

Purcell's 14 LAA Wksps had by now moved back from their "front line" site at Alam Halfa, and were now somewhere to the east of Sidi Barrani, where we would replace them shortly. Our South African friends were being withdrawn to the Delta for refitting as an orthodox LAA Regt, while Purcell's lot were to do some refitting at Ras Hawala under the wing of Estlin. Quite a switch round and just as complicated as it sounds.

Everyone became very cheerful at the prospect of the impending split of the composite workshop, and Stephen and Hallack sought to build up a massive stock of stores, which they intended to take back with them to the Delta as the nucleus to equip their new workshop. Since the majority of these stores had just been dug out of the Base Ordnance channels by toil, sweat and tears, if not actual blood, they were blatantly appropriated by Estlin, who justified this piracy with the admonition that they were required for use in the Forward Area and there they should stay, under the control of 12 AA Bde. He got his way, of course, and Stephen didn't like it at all, but his CO was over-ruled by the Brigadier.

When RHQ moved up, I sent with them a small party of six men under S/Sgt Dean, with two lorries, to start assessing the work we should have to take over from Purcell and to look after

RHQ. They had quite an exciting time, for the enemy, on waking up suddenly to the realisation that the RAF was now in strength in Sidi Barrani, visited the new LGs in force and shot up the surrounding countryside with great verve. ME 109s and Hurricanes scrapped at all hours and at all altitudes, trucks were shot up on the road, HAA guns shot off over 100 rounds per gun per day and a morning ground-strafing attack wrote off about ten aircraft on 03 LG. There was hell's delight around Sidi Barrani for the best part of a week and then the enemy drew off, somewhat to our surprise, for honours were pretty evenly divided.

Estlin by this time was hopping up and down with irritation, because no one was answering his urgent signals as to the state of equipment readiness with 94 Wksps, as well as their intended date of arrival at Ras Hawala. The result was that he despatched me to Cairo post haste, to meet Lts Cresswell and Marshall, the OC and 2 i/c of 94 and find out what the hell was going on and when he might expect them. Starting about dawn, Thorne and I covered the distance in whirlwind style and reached Beni Yussef in mid-afternoon. Cresswell was out somewhere, but Marshall, a burly, hearty individual, entertained me to tea in his tent and painted a vivid picture of his magnificent workshop, his wonderful collection of stores and equipment, his splendid body of craftsmen and his unsurpassed array of well-found vehicles. He also dropped in a few remarks as to how the war was going to be run, once they were in operation in the desert. The Germans didn't seem to be going to have much of a chance...

After tea, he took me for a stroll round the camp on a sight-seeing tour and I was treated to further eulogies of 94 Wksps. They certainly seemed to have quantities of material that we would have given our eye-teeth for. I drove on into Cairo, to stay at the Continental Hotel at the Army's expense, in a somewhat chastened mood.

On our return to Ras Hawala, the following day, I reported to Estlin. He commented he had heard this one before and that the proof of the pudding was in the eating.

* * *

94 HAA Wksps arrived in Ras Hawala during the second week in September, amidst great flourishing of metaphorical trumpets. Cresswell and Marshall took one look at my camp site, pronounced it "dirty", and settled down about 200 yards away, with a sort of "cordon sanitaire" between us. Niggled by their attitude, I omitted to warn them that the nice flat ground they had selected was "*sabakha*", or semi-dry salt marsh, and came over the next day to commiserate with them, because three of their heaviest lorries had sunk to the axles overnight. After digging and towing them out and moving again, they drove another into my inspection pit – which promptly collapsed under it – and tempers became a trifle frayed. It wasn't a good start.

Cresswell and Marshall were both quite decent chaps really, but they contrived to get on the wrong side of Estlin at once, which was the worst thing they could have done. Cresswell, although on paper slightly the senior of the pair, was a studious, rather retiring type, overshadowed by the bluff, extrovert Marshall. Cresswell should have been a captain, according to the establishment, but somehow this had never occurred and he was still a lieutenant. As a consequence, his authority in the unit suffered. Estlin took a poor view of this.

94 Wksps had come into the desert simply laden to the axles with spares and stores – far, far more than they were normally expected to carry – and Estlin, who had great ideas on the necessity for mobility in a unit, promptly made them disgorge all the hard-won items which they could not justify and impounded them as the basis of a stores pool, on which other workshops could draw, and which would serve as a "float" to cushion the shocks of war on the normal channels of supply. I don't think either Cresswell or Marshall ever quite forgave him for this.

With the arrival of our relieving unit, the Anglo-South African partnership broke up, much to the relief of both parties and amid fulsome farewell speeches on the magnificent manner in which we had cooperated in putting public weal in front of private wishes. The next morning we broke camp, where we had lived for a matter of two months, and moved out on to the road, en route for what we reckoned was the real job we had come to do.

Our small convoy was quite impressive, although not as large as it could have been, since two of our lorries had been sent on with Dean's advance party. Our AF G.1098 (War Equipment Table) for an LAA Regt Wksps Section accorded us the not-very-munificent scale of vehicles, which someone in the War Office in England had decided was adequate for our needs. I need hardly say they were quite inadequate. They consisted of one motorcycle (quite useless in the desert); one 15cwt truck, for which the OC had to bid against the rival claims of ration-drawing, gunsite repair parties and the like; two 30cwt lorries, for "tools and shelter" and "personnel"; one 30cwt light machinery lorry fitted with a small lathe, power drill, grinder, battery-charging board, and auxiliary petrol-driven generator set; and a 30cwt 6-wheeled Morris breakdown vehicle. All except the two 30cwts had been issued in the UK and had come out with us. The two Bedford 30cwts had been drawn in the ME.

To this list, just before we left Beni Yussef, we were issued two 3-ton Karrier lorries. The powers-that-be in the Middle East, rightly scornful of the home War Establishment, had issued these two extra 3-tonners to each LAA Wksps entering the desert operationally. One of these was supposed to be fitted up as a stores vehicle with steel bins, and this we had just been able to complete before we moved out of the Delta; we had, so far, practically no stores to put in the bins.

One 3-tonner and one of the Bedfords had been sent with the advance party to Sidi Barrani. The remainder formed the column that, on this particular day – it was a Friday, I remember, not the most auspicious of days to "set sail" – pulled out of Ras Hawala. I led the way in the 15cwt and the rear was brought up by AQMS Harding in the breakdown lorry. This vehicle, I noticed, was flying the Union Jack from its breakdown jib, an emblem reserved for the GOC in C MEF, although where it had come from goodness only knew.

Purcell's unit was deployed on a wide stretch of tussocky ground on the seashore about three miles on the Matruh side of

Sidi Barrani. A prominent ridge of grass-covered sandhills bordered the shore, which was mainly rocky cliffs reminiscent of north Cornwall, interspersed with steeply-shelving beaches on which a surf broke with a sullen roar and a perpetual flash of spray. A nasty bit of coast to have on one's lee in a storm, or so it seemed to me. The living accommodation was fixed up among the dunes, and the more or less open and level space on the landward side formed the workshop area.

S/Sgt Dean reported to me that the few vehicles scattered round were under repair and would become our responsibility on the changeover, but Purcell's own transport was widely dispersed with barriers of sand-filled petrol tins protecting the radiators. Apparently, the low-flying, ground-strafing German aircraft were making a practice of shooting up the radiators of any truck they came across and could do this with great accuracy.

After settling ourselves in and agreeing we would take over the workshop commitments the next day but one – Sunday – which would allow Purcell good time to pack up and move down to Ras Hawala on the Monday, I went over to report my arrival to RHQ. They were about a mile or so nearer to Matruh, also on the coast. Claud Phillimore suggested I should come over the following morning to the AADC's operational HQ on the edge of the new 05 LG to see Col Helby, who held the local appointment of AADC for the Sidi Barrani area. I should explain that the AADC is the AA Defence Commander and is the senior officer in command of all the AA facilities in the area.

So far, so good. Purcell and I had a chat about old times and we turned in as though there wasn't a care in the world.

LG 05 was about a mile away on the other side of the main road and I found AAHQ amid a welter of RAF operational transport. Claud was already there and seemed a trifle distrait; he asked me whether Purcell had handed over any secret instructions for emergency evacuation of the workshop site in the event of raids by hostile ground forces. I said he had not and Claud then told me that there were rumours that German armoured forces were on the loose in the desert to the south-west, with the apparent intention of disrupting the newly set up

66

airstrips in the Barrani area. Of course, he said reassuringly, there wasn't any danger of them reaching LG 05, for our own forces were out locating them and would see them off, but in case, – just in case, mind – there was any slight danger, 22 Guards Brigade, who were in overall command of all troops in the area, would issue direct to units certain code words implying the degree of seriousness of the situation and on receipt of which certain action would immediately be taken by the recipients.

As far as 2 LAA Wksps, successors to 14 LAA, were concerned, the words were "Wheelbarrow", "Carriage" and "Coach". They would be issued consecutively in that order, meaning, respectively: "Warning, – be prepared to move at short notice"; "Danger, – move out at once on to the road opposite LG 05 and await further orders"; and, lastly, "Urgent, – Move out forthwith with all speed and rendezvous with Bde B Echelon and other "soft" troops at Kilometre 74 from Matruh". Claud repeated that we would receive any such codes consecutively in that order should the tactical situation merit. But, as he explained soothingly to the apprehensive newcomer, there was no reason to be alarmed. It was unlikely that anything would happen; he was just putting me in the picture.

Reassured, but a trifle uneasy beneath the surface, I returned to the camp to find that Harding had taken the opportunity of gathering a work party and had pretty well emptied the stores lorry to repack and re-bin the stores before we had to open the workshop in earnest on the Monday morning. I told him the news and he agreed it was unwise to unpack any more than was absolutely necessary, while there was any danger of a "flap" occurring; accordingly, he set to with the working party, putting the stores back into the lorry with all speed. Concurrently, Dean went the rounds of the few vehicles in the workshop replacing the wheels and ensuring they were reasonable "runners".

Late that afternoon, Claud rang up and, without being very explicit, suggested that I shouldn't unpack too much. He seemed relieved to learn that I had already taken steps in this direction, but was non-committal about what was happening to the supposed German raiding column. As far as he knew, there was nothing to worry about.

Darkness fell with the workshop partly packed, partly unpacked and generally disorganised. 14 LAA were definitely apprehensive and made no bones about being ready to pull out and beat it for Matruh and beyond, a day in advance of programme, should there be the slightest sign of trouble. Purcell explained that they had had things like this happen to them before.

This communicated itself to my lads and they were exceedingly windy. Lights were strictly forbidden and there didn't seem very much we could do until morning, or so we believed, with so much of our gear still "on the deck".

About 9.00 p.m. Purcell and I were idling in the tent which we were still using as a joint office; it was a dark night and most of my lads had turned in. The field telephone connecting us to the local AA Signals exchange on the LG rang and the operator passed over a signal message. It was terse and to the point: "22 Gds Bde to 14 LAA Wksps COACH Message ends."

Purcell got up. 'Well,' he said, 'You can do what you like, but I'm moving out. Cheerio!' And out he went. Within 15 minutes, and with the well drilled precision of an oft-rehearsed exercise, his column of vehicles slid out of the camp and disappeared into the blackness.

Somehow, I got hold of Harding in the darkness and issued orders for a double-quick pack-up, ready to move at short notice. Then, I tried to get through on the phone to RHQ, or AAHQ on the LG, but without success. The exchange operator said that both lines seemed to be out of action, and added the gratuitous information that his lot were packing up themselves.

Our packing up was an undisguised shambles. Most of the men were newcomers to the site and had little idea of where any of the sleeping tents were in the dark, or any of the lorries, either, for that matter. Things were complicated, because some of the stores still had to be loaded, the office tent had to be dismantled and the men's personal kits had to be found and put in a vehicle. I was determined, Germans or no Germans, that nothing should be left behind of our hard-won equipment.

A wild scramble lasting nearly an hour served to get most of our gear on to some lorry or other, but it was too dark to see and no one could rightly say if it was all on board. Then, it was found that most of our vehicles were short of petrol; I had omitted to give the necessary orders on arrival from Ras Hawala and I could have kicked myself for forgetting the most important of Bentley's rules. Somewhere behind the sandhills, 14 Wksps had established a petrol dump and, after some blindman's buff, we located it and began humping heavy four-gallon tins back to the camp through the soft sand.

Whilst we were filling our tanks in the total darkness, more or less by sense of touch, we heard several distant heavy explosions – or were they so very far distant? And from the road, about half a mile away, we could distinctly hear the roar of traffic moving in an easterly, or Matruh-wards direction. Then, quite plainly, we could detect the resonant thump of gunfire, somewhere off to the south. We had all heard AA fire in England and thought very little of it, but, somehow, this distant sound was different; it was a flat sort of "smack" and I realised it must be high-velocity tank or anti-tank guns. Somewhere out there, the Germans were coming! It wasn't a nice thought and I savoured the inexplicable impulse that had made whole civilian populations in Belgium and France move out and take to the roads in their thousands in 1940. If the Germans were coming, it wasn't so inexplicable after all.

Something like this must have been passing through the minds of my lads, too. They were getting panicky and, when Harding reported that he thought all essential items were aboard, I set out for the road, with the Workshop following, together with the two or three vehicles that had been in the "shop" for repairs, with some of my lads detailed to drive them.

We bumped and crashed over the invisible tussocks and stones and reached the road, which stretched away emptily eastwards, just a dark smear of shadow in the starlight amid the faint lightness of the desert on either side. No traffic and not a sound to break the stillness, except the continuously pulsating tremble of gunfire; and except – what was that! It was the sound of a tracked vehicle coming up behind us at high speed from the Sidi Barrani, or German, side. There was no mistaking the

69

metallic clatter of tracks on the road surface, or the full-throated roar of a heavy motor. In something very like panic, we pulled off the road and I shouted to the lads to scatter and take cover; escape seemed impossible – it was on us before we could get right out of sight. Oddly enough my prevailing thought was, what would Estlin say if I were to go "into the bag" on my first independent assignment in the desert!

It wasn't a German tank. In fact it wasn't a tank at all. It was a big, half-tracked grader belonging to the South African Engineer Company that was working on clearing extensions to the new LG 05. It passed us at a speed that I wouldn't have believed it capable of, amid a whirlwind of dust, and making enough noise to wake the dead. I had a brief glimpse in the starlight of a big black man standing hunched over the controls, in order to see past the raised blade, all white eyes and bared teeth, as he struggled to keep his monster on the road. Although we pulled back on to the tarmac as soon as he had passed, we never caught up with him for the rest of the way.

We were very nearly the only traffic still on the road heading eastwards. From Matruh there was nothing, at least at first. Then we met, with almost disastrous suddenness, a long, fast-moving column coming up in the middle of the none-too-wide highway. In fact, it was really two columns: some South Africans in 3-tonners towing 2-pdr anti-tank guns and a detachment of Australian 25-pdr gunners. They had coalesced in the darkness somewhere down the road and were now driving nose-to-tail, hell-for-leather, in one single disorderly mob. We were swept on to the verge and had a brief vision of the gun-crews in steel helmets and greatcoats, hunched in their gun-tractors against the dust, the guns and limbers snaking all over the road, and then they were gone into the night. A little later on, we met further detachments of artillery and lorry-borne infantry, inextricably mixed, all storming westwards towards the Front. All this evidence of frantic stopgap action didn't seem to ease our minds significantly.

We reached the neighbourhood of Km 74 about three in the morning, to find there were a lot of vehicles milling around in the dark and no one knew exactly what was happening, but there seemed little more we could do, so we camped where we were beside the road and went to sleep in our vehicles until daylight. The night was cold and I spent it curled up on the driver's floorboards of the Bedford 15cwt, next to the engine. Surprisingly, I slept very well in this peculiar posture.

Dawn revealed that we had stopped rather short of our correct rendezvous, which was about a kilometre nearer Matruh, but, since no one seemed to know anything or care much about us, I decided we might as well stay where we were; we dispersed a bit more, put up our AA LMG and had breakfast, much chirpier now that the terrors of last night were behind us. The section was apparently trustfully assuming I would get them out of any further trouble; this should have been heartening for my ego, but I wasn't as sure as they were.

As the morning passed, more B Echelon vehicles straggled in, and 122 LAA Bty turned up and went into action positions around the rendezvous area. Then silence reigned and the desert relapsed into stagnation. We had a hot lunch and went on waiting.

Finally, I got fed up and did what, on the face of it, seemed daft, but some instinct prompted me. Opposite us, on the other side of the road, was a Signals Post, manned by the detachment that was responsible for that particular length of telephone line; outside the tent was a noticeboard announcing "You may telephone from here". On impulse, I walked over and asked to be put through to RHQ, using the correct code name and, to my great astonishment, within a couple of seconds I was talking to the Adjutant. It was as easy as that. And we had been supposing them to be nearly surrounded by the enemy and selling their lives dearly!

Claud was pleased to hear from me and to learn that we were no further away. 'There haven't been any orders yet,' he said, 'but the flap is over. You'd better come back to your old site straight away and open up. We need you.'

And so, feeling that it was all an anticlimax, we piled into our vehicles, left the rest of the rendezvous groups to their own devices and slipped unobtrusively back into our campsite, not much more than twelve hours after we had left it.

71

A couple of days later, Phillimore explained to me what he had been told had happened. It wasn't such a shambles as we had thought. Apparently, the day before the flap, a fair-sized German armoured raiding column had crossed the frontier into Egyptian territory and part of it had detached itself from the main forces and begun moving northwards in the direction of Sidi Barrani. They were shadowed by our light forces until darkness fell and then they disappeared. 22 Guards Bde naturally supposed they would continue through the night, as was our custom in such a raid, which would have brought them to LG 05 by first light, and so they hurriedly called up reinforcements from Matruh, telling all their own soft-skinned units to get out back down the road and leave the field free for the big boys. We should have had progressive warning of this and RHQ would have been told about us. Somehow, in the event, 14 LAA Wksps were forgotten and didn't receive the progressive warnings, but in the final count they were suddenly remembered and told to get the hell out of Sidi Barrani. 'Which you did, too, very creditably,' said Claud, with a suggestion of relief.

In actual fact, the column just sat down and "leaguered" for the night not far from where they were last seen and were discovered there by our air patrols the following morning at first light. However, this and other German thrusts towards the coast continued, but no ground battle ensued, for before the defending forces came into action, tactical bombing by the RAF had settled the issue. They bombed, not the marauding armoured forces, but the supporting columns of petrol tankers, coming from Libya to refuel the tanks. Without its fuel, which went up in strings of blazing vehicles miles to the rear, the potential attack petered out and the armoured columns retired without firing a shot. 22 Guards Bde withdrew their warnings and everybody came back. It was a case of "Sorry you've been troubled".

Clearly, the RAF's local air superiority was a thing to be reckoned with, since no further attempts were made by enemy ground forces to disrupt the build-up of strength around Sidi Barrani and the immediate neighbourhood.

* * *

Our site was very such as we had left it, although someone in those last twelve hours had gone over it pretty thoroughly. Luckily, there was little of value to take and all we had really lost were a couple of RD tents which we had left behind. I was told that these were probably pinched by marauding Bedouin, who had a practice of coming out of the woodwork and disappearing afterwards. Good canvas for shelters was very acceptable to them.

We settled down again, better and wiser men, and I may say with some satisfaction that never again, as long as I was with 2 LAA Wksps, were we caught out by a sudden "flap" movement order. Our vehicles were always full of petrol; there was a crew-list and a stores "loading list" for each of them, so that everyone knew exactly who and what went into each; and nothing more than was absolutely necessary was taken from its place and put on the ground at any one time. We were learning how to survive.

After the frenzied excitement of the first couple of days at Sidi Barrani, we settled down to an existence that was hard-working, but dull. Our day began soon after dawn, in order to make the best use of daylight hours, shattered out of our sleep by a few well chosen rounds fired from our Lewis gun by the night sentry. This was an old and effective desert custom and, although it was later banned on the grounds of ammunition wastage, I have yet to meet a better way of waking a sleeping camp. We took a light breakfast and then set about the day's work, until lunch at midday. There was an hour's break and then we worked on until 5.00 p.m., by which time it might be getting a little too dark to see our work properly. This was the end of the working day and the lads were free to do their own thing for the half hour until teatime. Most of them took advantage of a swim in the warm sea, when it wasn't too rough – which quite often it was – and then after tea they played football, until it became really too dark even for this. Afterwards, most of them retired to their tents to read or write letters by the light of a hurricane lamp, or patronised the canteen.

This canteen was quite a masterpiece and was constructed by

73

the lads entirely in their spare time. It consisted of a deep excavation into a sand dune, covered over with a tent sheet and fitted with a bar, tables and a couple of forms. It was walled in with some of the wooden crates in which four-gallon petrol tins were delivered. Outside it was a name board, reading: "The Better 'Ole. Bints served". *Bint*, I should explain, is Arabic for a woman.

Altogether, it was a magnificent effort and was presided over, within my general orders, by our second storeman, one L/Cpl Finnigan, an ex-regular recalled to the colours, whose service was said to go back as far as Agincourt. I don't know how he came still to be in the Army, for he must have been nearly sixty, but he was a useful man to have about the place; he doubled in the diverse duties of caterer, canteen corporal, barman and chucker-out. We didn't have an official "closing time" for the canteen, but Finnigan knew what I wanted and he decided when it was necessary. He was a tower of strength and I relied on him to keep order in the place, which he did without ever bothering me.

He and Sgt Hughes, our clerk and orderly-room sergeant, managed between them to keep up an adequate supply of beer and other NAAFI items, obtained from heaven knows where (I didn't ask), and the place became justly famous in the neighbourhood, so that we had to allow only "known" friends of the unit into its portals. We also drew a radio set from the local comforts fund, one that worked off a six-volt vehicle battery, and the lads, with my permission, even ran concerts of a sort on the occasional half day.

We were rather too far from the nearest other unit for me to be member of an Officers' Mess, so I had a decent dugout near the sea, which just about accommodated my bed and a table; I lined the walls with the ubiquitous petrol-tin boxes as shelves and went in for reading in any spare time 1 had. This wasn't as much as might be expected, because I was frequently out most of the day on inspections and, when I returned and had sorted out the day's office work, there was the censoring of the unit's letters to be done. This was a most exacting task in a single-officer command, if it was to be done so as to impose the minimum of delay on outgoing letters, and an unpleasant one at any time. There were set items I was obligated to look for and, apart from that, I deduced from the gist of stuff I skimmed over that the unit as a whole was pretty cheerful and as contented as men separated from their families could be expected to be.

At first, I tried to keep one day of the week, Sunday, as a shut-down day, but it seldom worked out like that, and when the war really hotted up, we worked seven days a week for weeks on end. At Sidi Barrani, usually something cropped up to bring half the unit in on Sunday morning at least, and so normally the best we got was one afternoon off a week. To fill this we organised football matches against neighbouring units, held athletic contests, went bathing in the sea and at one time I persuaded the CO to allow me to set up a 30-yard rifle range on the shore so that we could practice our military skills.

Our nearest neighbours were the BHQ of 25 HAA Bty, who were some half a mile away on the Matruh side, with our own RHQ about the same distance in the other direction. Occasionally, I visited Bty HQ after hours. 25 were a grand, if eccentric, crowd of Territorials from Northern Ireland, who had been in the ME for some time. They had been raised, almost single-handedly, by the Bty Commander, Major Sir Basil Macfarland, the Lord Mayor of Londonderry, and were a tight-knit community. I believe they were mainly Macfarland's own retainers – gamekeepers, ghillies, personal estate servants and the like. They all knew one another and adored Sir Basil; he called them all by their Christian names, Willy, Sean, John and so forth, and he never seemed to give an order, just a request: 'Willy, would ye now do so-and-so...?' And Willy would knuckle his forelock in a most un-military sort of salute and reply: 'Yes, Sir Basil...' But their gunnery and mechanical maintenance was without parallel for its excellence. Everything that could be polished was glittering and their boots and cap badges shone like stars. One thing I particularly remember was the way they were awakened at dawn by some gunner sounding reveille on a silver trumpet; he was supposed to have been a musician in the Londonderry Symphony Orchestra in peacetime.

Although we considered ourselves to be in the desert, we

75

were surprised at how much bird and animal life there was around us on this coastal strip. Little chirruping birds, rather like sparrows, abounded, and seabirds in plenty; on land there were chameleons of all shapes and sizes; little bright green-and-blue lizards, the occasional desert fox and once a swarm of jerboas, the so-called desert rats invaded the site, to the delight of the lads. One morning I was sitting just outside my tent, and found I was being solemnly studied by a big-eyed, big-eared mouse on stilts, with a bushy tuft on the end of its tail. When I moved, it hopped off like a mini-kangaroo. They seemed so delicate, friendly and unafraid of man that I decided to issue orders that the excited lads should not try to catch them. These delightful little creatures were adopted by the 7th Armoured Division as their mascot and for their badge. The name caught the fancy of the more uninformed newspapers, who incorrectly called anyone who had been in the desert a "Desert Rat".

The sea was full of fish and, until it was stopped, the more adventurous of the lads used to go fishing in the time-honoured style of the Forward Area, using Mills grenades.

The weather, though warm enough by midday, was getting progressively cooler and the nights were quite cold enough to make me glad of a battledress blouse or an overcoat. Occasionally, it rained a little, which surprised most folk very much, for, to them, the idea of *rain* in the desert was unnatural. However, even up to the beginning of November, when we left the coast, it was still warm enough to enjoy a dip in the sea after work.

We saw little of Estlin these days, except for the very occasional visit of inspection. Mostly, his edicts came through by letter and woe betide anyone who didn't jump to obey them at once. Rumours filtered through about what was happening in the rear. Purcell got his captaincy and was transferred to some Armoured Bde Recovery Section; Marshall took his place as OC 14 LAA Wksps, which were suddenly moved down towards Siwa; 94 Heavy moved from Ras Hawala into the old Egyptian barracks at Matruh and were living in great comfort. The tale was that every man had constructed a massive wooden bed for himself, but little work was being done. Finally, we heard that two new workshops were to come up into the desert: 68 Heavy (Capt Cotterill) and 25 Light, commanded by my old friend Bill Volum, who was another who had formed it at Hucknall at the same time as Purcell and I had formed our units.

The move of 14 Light affected me directly. Still doubtful of Marshall, Estlin posted AQMS Harding to him; Harding was an old hand, notwithstanding his youthful appearance, and would provide backbone to Marshall with his desert experience. He had been in the desert for four years, on and off. In his place, I got another young regular, AQMS Spooner, a cheerful, enthusiastic, popular and untiring WO II, who had come out with a draft on another ship in the same convoy as ourselves. He took to the unit like a duck to water and never did I have cause to regret the exchange, good though Harding was. To this day, I am not sure why I got him, for he was so good. Maybe Estlin had had his eye on him for sone time elsewhere and perhaps the attachment was to be of advantage to both parties: for me, as the longest-serving OC Wksps under his command, to teach Spooner in the ways of the desert; or for Spooner to keep a restraining hand on my exploits.

But I am skipping ahead a bit; most of these things happened during late October and, at the beginning of the month, I went down to Alex on leave, as part of a general pattern that the whole unit had had leave one by one. I went down in a new vehicle of ours, a highly unofficial one. On our return to Sidi Barrani after the flap, one of my scouting parties reported that there was an old Ford utility (station wagon) abandoned not so far away which hadn't yet been vandalised. It had wrapped its front axle round a large rock and its occupants had fled. We pulled it in, the axle was straightened by our blacksmith, its engine was swapped for a better one from a Ford 15cwt that was being evacuated as BLR and I took it into use as my personal vehicle, thus releasing the Bedford 15cwt for more pressing duties.

S/Sgt Lewis, Estlin's Chief Clerk, told me that the Major knew of its existence pretty quickly – there was little that went on in the desert that he didn't know about – but he let me keep it for a while, since there was quite a good operational case for our having an extra light vehicle at that time.

Cpl Thorne and I went on leave together in this car, which some time in the past had acquired the name of "Perdita", as much as anything to get further repairs done, for which we couldn't get spares in the desert, in particular a new radiator. No vehicle can be considered desertworthy with a badly leaking radiator and Perdita's leaked like a sieve; in fact our last 100 miles into Alexandria were covered with a water consumption of 20 miles per gallon!

I made a date for Perdita to go into the Base Wksps there and, after dropping Thorne, I motored out to Bussilli to visit No 3 General Hospital and Phyl Ball. She put in for several spaced days of leave and we spent them looking round the city, while Perdita's radiator was fixed. As I have said, Alexandria is a good place in which to have leave and, notwithstanding some very heavy and noisy air raids, the atmosphere was still too peace-like to be believed. Our time was well spent, but I spoilt it on the last evening by mentioning my true feelings about her. She was greatly shaken and went all upstage. I believe we were both being very silly, but we finally agreed that we would continue to write to one another and that we could remain "good friends".

As a consequence, I returned to the desert somewhat emotionally upset, to find that Estlin had become highly active in my absence and had spent most of my leave time at Sidi Barrani. He now weighed in and fairly tore strips off me for lack of organisation, maladministration and general unsatisfactoriness. Again, looking back after several calming years, I still consider his strictures somewhat unjust and uncalled for. At the time, being in a bad mood after my return from leave, I was livid and I told him straight out, in almost as many words, to let me run my show in my own way and judge me by results and, if he wasn't satisfied with me, to remove me and get someone else. However, I didn't get the immediate chop and he left with the dark comment that I was now on probation and, if I didn't come up to scratch, he would indeed remove me. I never heard anything more about it and when we next met, he was as cordial as ever. Perhaps he felt he had been a trifle too niggling, but the posting of Spooner may have resulted from this. I never learned how near I came to being slung out on my ear.

There was no doubt, however, that the unit had deteriorated markedly in standards, as soon as my back was turned; this was a bad thing and indicated that it was not yet fully trained and disciplined. I set out with Spooner, who was with us by now, to remedy this.

The desert was waking up, slowly but perceptibly; a faint smell of impending battle was in the autumn breeze. In July, many folk had confidently predicted that the desert would be held defensively for the rest of the war, and that the main battles in some other theatre would decide it; but now the only difference in opinion was not if, but when, the clash would take place. That it was coming soon was fairly apparent.

Overnight, Western Desert Force became 13 Corps and the HQ moved up to Piccadilly, a map reference and track junction in the hinterland some 30 miles or so to the south of Sidi Barrani. Then, amidst greatly quickening interest, all the forces were placed under the command of a newly created even higher formation, an Army HQ, the Eighth Army, to be commanded by General Sir Alan Cunningham, who had done so well in the East African campaign. Even in the heyday of the Wavell campaign, the highest formation had been only a Corps – 13 Corps, under the direct control of GHQ MEF – so this sounded like something big.

When we came up into the desert, the railway from the Delta ended at Matruh, to which in peace time it had brought its quota of holidaymakers from the hot lands further east. Now, it suddenly developed a side shoot near Qasaba, a few miles short of Matruh, and a line climbed up the escarpment behind the town, ran along beside the road to Barrani for a short distance and then disappeared off into the desert to the south. The speed at which the construction took place was simply phenomenal; one day there would be virgin desert at a particular spot and the next, or so it seemed, a single-track railway was traversing it from one horizon to another. Soon after the formation of 13

Corps, I motored down to visit the DADOS spares dump at Piccadilly; the desert was an empty space, as in the days when I did my trip to Bir Talatha. A week later, when I had occasion to make a repeat trip, just short of the Piccadilly track junction was a railway line, complete with a level crossing, crossing sign, telegraph wires and all. It was uncanny. Where, but a few weeks ago, the solitary truck bumped over the stones and scrub, now a full-sized train passed by, belching clouds of black oil-smoke.

Railhead was at a spot called Mischeifa, not so very far from Bir Talatha itself. The rail line must have been very obvious to the Germans, so two railheads were built, one real and a more noticeable dummy one, visible from the air, which the enemy was free to bomb, if he so wished.

The desert population also began to change. More RAF arrived and opened up new landing grounds at Oxford Circus, a map reference to the south of Piccadilly, and at Bir Umm Gilwakh, some 20 miles further south again. Much of the importance of the Sidi Barrani LGs faded and the centre of gravity of the air striking force drifted away south.

With the RAF went the majority of 12 AA Bde forces. RHQ 2 LAA Regt packed up and moved off down to Bir Umm Gilwakh, leaving the Wksps back on the coast, because it was a more suitable site; 25 LAA Regt arrived to cover Oxford Circus and 68 HAA Regt went through for the defence of Mischeifa railhead. Each of the HQs was accompanied by its respective Wksps, Lt Volum of 25 Light and Capt Cotterill of 68 Heavy.

With the declining importance of Sidi Barrani, most of the AA units from there also went inland. Our old friends and neighbours 25 HAA Bty went "back" and were replaced by 291 Bty of 94 Regt. Both the other Btys of 94th, 261 and 292, also case up and trekked south, leaving HQ 94 Regt in Matruh in command of their own workshops and acting as a sort of Area HQ. Temporarily, the LAA defences of Sidi Barrani devolved on two new units: 82 LAA Bty of 25 Regt and an independent Bty, 274 (NH). The (NH) part of its name stood for Northumberland Hussars, from which Yeomanry regiment they had been formed. Although they were a pretty good crowd and we got on well together, they never quite forgot they were Yeomanry and not like other gunners, and made great play with their silver cap badges and the special blue flashes on their sleeves.

Back at Matruh, Estlin was preparing for the battle. He turned the faintly protesting 94 Wksps into a sort of Advanced Base Workshops and, by some high-handed daylight robbery, he commandeered a heavy recovery lorry from the two HAA Workshops (68 and 94) to run a recovery service from Mischeifa via Oxford Circus and Sidi Barrani to Matruh, where there were facilities for heavier work than in the Forward Area. This ran twice a week, towing back any vehicles that were beyond the local repair capacity, and on the return trip brought up stores. The scheme worked splendidly and the forward workshops were released to concentrate on their proper job of keeping their regimental equipment in good order, without becoming too deeply involved with repairs beyond their capacity.

We heard of other activities of his, too. With the connivance of his brigadier (whose blind eye was second only to Nelson's where some useful scheme of Estlin's was involved, especially where the scheme benefited the Brigade, but, strictly speaking, was illegal), Estlin acquired several 3-ton lorries. These came from one or other of the HAA Wksps or from some Battery. They were fitted up with clandestinely acquired store bins; into these were put a carefully selected range of stores which he had been building up for months, and the 12 AA Bde Stores Section was born.

Lt Wray, his AOME (Instruments), wasn't letting the grass grow under his feet either. When the South Africans went back to refit, they had in their possession – illegally – an "F" type machinery lorry, one fitted with benches, etc., for electrical testing. Tongue in cheek, Estlin confiscated it, pointing out the crime of holding a "buckshee" vehicle. It wasn't much use for its designed purpose of electrical testing, since most of the gear had disappeared long ago, but it had a wooden "box-type" body. Wray now set about stripping it and installing in it a watch-maker's lathe, some further bins and some test jigs. The box body provided an almost completely dust-free environment for deli-cate instrument work, so that it made a very presentable mobile instrument-repair lorry. A further 3-tonner was filched from somewhere, filled with a couple of spare predictors, height-finders and other heavy stores; half a dozen S/Sgts (Instruments) and Instrument Mechanics were "attached to Bde HQ for special duties" and the 12 AA Bde Mobile Instrument Repair Section came into official – actually highly unofficial – being.

October crept on towards its close and, as it did so, the weather changed; the skies became darker and the wind rose. And in the wake of the wind came dust storms. The ground in these parts wasn't pure sand, except for a thin strip bordering the sea: the remainder was a solidly packed top layer of earth, part gravel, part loam. Had there been reasonable rainfall, it would probably have been very fertile – in Roman times, this coastal strip is said to have been the granary of the Empire – and would be capable of supporting a large population. Once there had been forest near Matruh. But, for the past few months, this top layer had been ploughed up by countless lorries, aircraft, and human feet into a fine, whitish dust, anything up to a foot deep. It lay on all sides for miles.

Through some meteorological freak, as long as the sun shone hotly enough, the dust remained static and no amount of wind, it seemed, would move it. But with the coming of the cooler and cloudier weather, things changed. A bright morning would dawn; then the sun would cloud over and the wind would whisper through the camel-thorn, rising, rising. And, as its velocity rose past a certain level, the dust began to move, imperceptibly at first, running in little streams across the road and over one's feet, then rising airborne ankle-high, knee-high, head-high, finally blotting out the sun and the daylight itself. The world disappeared into a yellow half-light of swirling, choking powder; visibility was reduced to five yards or less; men lost their way in moving from one side to the other of a well known campsite; and the rolling, oily-looking sea became covered with a scum of fine mud.

All work had to come to a standstill. Anyone out in a vehicle was well advised to stop and remain where he was until the wind dropped, even if that meant a whole day. In camp, we crouched in our tents, protected it is true from the main force of the steady gustless wind, but not from the dust, which penetrated through the very pores of the tent fabric and settled on men, food, office papers and bedding with the utmost impartiality. During the days when the wind blew from inland, we ate dust, breathed dust and slept in dust, helpless and sweating. If the wind blew in from the sea, we found ourselves in a narrow strip of clear air, cut off from the outside world by a thick yellow fog that rose like a wall a few hundred yards inland and shut out the sun.

I had heard of dust storms interfering with operations; I realised it was no exaggeration.

As the importance of Sid Barrani lessened, our work became less exacting and we had a few attempts at making ourselves a bit more independent and potentially mobile. The water trailer was dismantled and the tank placed on a much stouter chassis with better draw-bar gear and sounder wheels; we also managed to fill it and keep it full, no small feat with water so scarce. We also constructed a mobile office of sorts, fulfilling a long-felt want; setting up an office tent, with which we had hitherto been content, took a long time and the dropping and packing up took even longer. Futhermore, the tent, tables, etc. took up much space in the lorries which we could ill afford. So S/Sgt Dean, after a discussion with me and Sgt Hughes, our chief clerk, devised the Office Trailer. Following Estlin's example, we cut off the back end of a derelict 15cwt truck just behind the cab, then the spare ends were bent together, welded up and fitted with a towing eye. Over the whole a wooden deck was built, just at table height, and in the centre of the four-position desk so formed, were mounted lockers for all our stationery, the typewriter and the office chairs. A couple of tent poles fitted into sockets at each end, and a tent was stretched over these as soon as the trailer was detached from its towing vehicle. Practice proved that the tent could be put up and the office made ready for use in 15 minutes from coming to rest by Sgt Hughes, his two assistant clerks and the driver of the towing vehicle. It took even less time to dismantle.

About the beginning of November, it suddenly dawned on me

that the unit was beginning to run itself and was functioning as a coherent and smoothly working team. How, and for how long, this desirable state of affairs had been achieved, I didn't know, but it was now clear to me that we could face the possibility of a mobile war with some confidence without disgracing ourselves.

I supposed Estlin knew about this. He probably did, for as I have said before, there was little he didn't know about what his workshops were doing. Anyhow, I didn't care.

5

At the end of the first week in November, I received a brief signal from Col Helby to bring my workshop down to Bir Umm Gilwakh at once, if not sooner. We had a fair amount of work in the shop to clear and I was issuing the necessary orders, when S/ Sgt Lewis came on the phone to tell me the Major wanted to speak to me – urgently.

Estlin gave me the same orders and added that my illegally held Ford station wagon would not be taken from Sidi Barrani, but would be delivered to his driver and taken to Matruh. So, to my sorrow, we overhauled Perdita, greased her up – Estlin would have raised hell if she didn't arrive in first-class condition – and said goodbye to her. I learned later that Estlin, on the very eve of the battle, had stripped the crown wheel in the differential of his Ford staff car, and that Perdita, on arrival at Matruh was torn asunder to put this car back on to the road again; a sad, but useful end.

Just to make quite sure that we were complying and were leaving nothing behind on the ground, the Great Man turned up in person that afternoon, while we were tidying up. After ticking me off for packing up at 3.00 p.m., ('You should aim at working up to the last minute, before moving off. That is the hallmark of a good mobile workshop') he sprang another bombshell on us. Our electrical generator truck was to be handed over to 68 HAA Wksps on arrival at Gilwakh.

This needs a little explanation. A LAA Wksp was equipped with a small 30cwt machinery lorry and the power for its machine tools was derived from a small twin-cylinder petrol engine mounted inside the lorry and driving a 110-volt DC generator. We had come up into the desert with all new equipment and we had lavished on our new generator the care of a mother for her first-born. Just before 14 Light had departed for Siwa, their corresponding gen-set had blown up and since these were almost impossible to obtain at the time, we reluctantly transferred ours to them, on Estlin's orders. In its place, as a temporary expedient, Estlin had given us on loan a 15cwt truck on which was mounted a bigger and superior gen-set, to which we were not, of course, entitled. I don't think Estlin was either; he had impounded it from the departing South Africans as yet another illegally held "buckshee" vehicle and was holding it up his sleeve as a Bde spare, against a rainy day, such as this.

We hadn't complained. As we fondly thought, as well as the deal being in our favour, we could use the truck to carry some of our own kit when we moved. Now, however, we were to hand it over to 68 HAA Wksps on our arrival at Gilwakh to replace their own similar truck which had completely packed up. This sad blow was somewhat tempered by Estlin producing a GHQ Authority to draw a small portable gen-set from the OFP (Ordnance Field Park) at Oxford Circus. Since such Authorities were very difficult to get, he must have pulled some pretty influential strings to help us.

That night, we held a final farewell party in the canteen, at which the lads made sterling efforts to reduce the holding of canteen stores in case we were unable to find other room for them. I had to look the other way. The official excuse was that it was the first anniversary of the formation of the unit at Hucknall the previous November. A good time was had by all and, at the crack of dawn the following day, we dropped our tents in good order and set off on what we were pretty sure were the beginnings of our real experience of mobile warfare. We were not wrong...

I had been down to Gilwakh about a week earlier and had no trouble in leading the column there. The country was much the same as that at Bir Talatha, somewhat to the west; that is to say, it grew stonier as we drew inland. At Oxford Circus, a couple of miles after crossing the railway at Piccadilly, there was a group of LGs and the desert for a mile or more around was a vast array of tents, bivouacs and vehicles. I was amused, as we passed it, to see that the track junction at Piccadilly was now adorned by a huge model of Eros constructed out of petrol tins welded together, which could be seen for miles.

From Oxford Circus, the route instructions were simple in the extreme: you picked up a pair of signal phone cables that led south and followed them to RHQ, some 20 miles further on. This may sound daft, but it was typical of the sort of direction that was common in the desert. It was quite infallible; in this case, only one pair of cables on the ground led south and these we followed for another 20 miles, to reach RHQ without bother.

Bir Umm Gilwakh was a scarcely inspiring spot; a place of sun and wide, featureless desert. It sticks in my mind only because this was the place where we had our first real introduction to the "simple life", without any of the semi-civilised home comforts of Sidi Barrani and the coast.

The terrain at Gilwakh differed completely from that further north. Before we reached it, we drove out of the stony country into a wide virgin uncharted plain of gravel flats, powdered with little black pebbles resembling rendering on cottage walls, and great clay-pans of hard-packed alluvial silt. The ground was broken up irregularly by small escarpments, never more than about six or ten feet high, so that it resembled a giant chess board with alternate squares raised above their neighbours. The hollows, at the time of our arrival, were, generally speaking, clay surfaces of untouched smoothness and around them were hundreds of vehicles carefully nosed into the escarpments. In little brown clusters were the bivouac tents of their occupants, erected over a shallow hole that was both a bed and a slit trench. Here and there a larger tent betokened some headquarters office. It was all very simple, shallow-rooted and open-air.

In the centre of the area a much larger clay-pan had been marked off in runways as an airstrip, but so confined was the space available that the tents of the RAF ground staff and the LAA gunsites were inextricably mixed up between them and it was difficult for the newcomer to distinguish what was landing strip, dispersal area, gunsite or camp accommodation.

We were allotted a stretch of clay-pan a few hundred yards away from RHQ and Claud Phillimore advised me, "as a friend" to learn at once the way back to my camp in the dark as the first condition of a happy life. It would seem that Col Helby, in a fit of impishness, was in the habit of calling "unit commanders' conferences" after dark and then letting the unfortunate officers find their own way home. It was a good way of instilling into the newcomers the tracklessness of the desert at any time and particularly at night. On the first occasion that he tried it on, one of the unfortunates arrived, as dawn broke, in the neighbourhood of Oxford Circus, after wandering all night. In this officer's Battery, at least, stellar aids to navigation were now extensively taught.

As a matter of fact, since one clay-pan looked very like another, finding one's way about in daylight wasn't all that easy either.

Just beyond the top of our little escarpment, where we had nosed in our vehicles in the local style, we found Bty HQ of 261 Bty and, since this unit seems likely to figure largely in my account of the next few months, perhaps I should say a few words about them. As I have said earlier, they were not one of 94's original Btys, for they replaced 290 Bty which had been diverted to Gibraltar on the way out. Since the other two Btys of 94 Heavy were from Scotland, 261, a TA unit raised from London Transport and regimented with 94 to fill the vacancy, were rather odd-men-out, not least because 261 were vastly superior to the rest of 94 in equipment maintenance, technical ability and, I believe, gunnery. Now they had got away from RHQ 94 and its repressions they were much happier, for they got on well with Helby, who appreciated their worth.

Major Russell, their Bty Commander, Capt Penn-Symonds the Bty Captain (2 i/c) and the two Troop Commanders, one of whom was a Lt Maitland Brown – I forget the other's name – were charming and I was immediately invited to join their Mess, since we were such near neighbours. This I was glad to do and we formed a firm friendship at once. Like them, I was an English-speaking officer in a wilderness of Scotsmen.

On looking about me at Gilwakh, it was immediately obvious

that the Battle was imminent, only a matter of a few days off, at the most. The whole desert to the north and west was seething with life and returning travellers from Mischeifa, Habata, Bir Khamsa and other more advanced areas spoke of great tank forces in serried ranks, just sitting waiting for the word, their crews living in or beside their tanks, without so much as a tent to be seen from one horizon to the other.

Whatever was about to happen, it was clear that it was to be a cross-desert show and not a thrust along the coast.

These portents made us scurry into action to render ourselves ready for the "party", whenever it should start. The generator truck was delivered to 68 Wksps, who were somewhere forward of us at one of the advanced FSDs (Field Supply Depots – dumps of stores, ammunition and food). Cotterill, OC 68, in his turn, tried to inveigle us into towing several BLR vehicles from their site back to 25 LAA Wksps at Oxford Circus, who had been allocated the task, by Estlin, of acting as a collecting point and ferrying agency for such vehicles on their way to 94 at Matruh, but I told them to do their own dirty work.

Spooner went and collected the new small gen-set from the OFP and we spent two whole days, off and on, trying to make it work, only to find, in the end, that we had been attempting to make it rotate the wrong way round; some casual and doubtless overpaid herb at the British factory having stamped the wrong direction on the casing. When we tumbled to this, the wretched little thing started at the first swing, and roared and rattled away with a noise that must have been audible even to the enemy. Our welder and turner, who would have to work in close proximity to it, looked somewhat askance at our new toy.

We made another attempt to get bivouac tents for ourselves and to hand in our larger RD ridge tents, but without any luck. McKeown, the QM, had refused to get us any when he had got some for RHQ, on the grounds that, at Sidi Barrani, we had no need for them. Now, when he tried again, it was too late; there were none to be had. His quartermaster's soul revolted in horror when I said I would have to cut up the flysheets of our RD tents and make some DIY bivvies out of these. He was even more horrified when we actually did this, and prophesied that I would have to account for the destruction of Army property on my charge before a Court of Enquiry. He nearly had a fit when I said I could write them off as "destroyed by enemy action".

As for work, we were rushed off our feet with it. A further LAA Bty, 149 of 27 LAA Regt, was rushed up from the Canal Zone about two days after our arrival and, needless to say, had broken most things breakable on the way. Just to cap things, no sooner had they deployed round the LG than a Tomahawk fighter overshot the runway and impaled itself on one of their guns, the barrel of which was driven clean through the engine like a skewer, miraculously stopping a foot from the pilot at the other end. The two machines, locked together, bounced over in a cloud of dust and came to rest upside down with the aircraft still impaled on the barrel. The shaken pilot undid his safety belt and then fell out of his inverted cockpit to the ground four feet below and broke his nose.

A flurry of RAF fitters descended on the scene and gently detached their valuable aircraft from the mess, leaving me, with two men and a boy, to right the inverted gun. With the eyes of the whole LG on us, I consider we made a creditable showing. This was the first time I had been called upon to do any tricky recovery work by myself in public and I was complimented by Major Wadley, the Bty Commander, for not damaging his gun. Spooner cane to check it over with the Bty fitters and we were all greatly relieved to find that, even after my robust treatment, it needed little more than replacement of the barrel with their spare.

A night or so after our arrival at Gilwakh, the sky to the north was lit up by intermittent flashes of light. At first, we wondered if these might be the reflections of artillery fire on the clouds, and perhaps that the battle had already started on the coast. The following day, however, news filtered through that the winter rains had started in good earnest with a heavy thunderstorm. To judge from the reports, it had caused a good deal of disorganisation to the rump of our forces still there; we heard of 291 Bty's guns being almost totally submerged in their pits; of 05 LG, now luckily non-operational, being unusable due to mud; and vehicles being bogged down to the axles for days. An anecdote in lighter vein was that of a mobile Field Cashier being marooned in his truck for three days, with no drinking water, food or cigarettes, but with £20,000 in unusable cash!

Sitreps (situation reports) said that the Germans were in an equally parlous state. Their airfields at Sidi Aziez, Gambut, El Adem, Gazala and even as far back as Martuba, near Derna, had been flooded and rendered virtually unusable, so the score was about even. Our own LGs at Oxford Circus and Gilwakh, out in the desert, were unaffected by the rain and the RAF Hurricane and Tomahawk fighters and Blenhein and Maryland light bombers ranged far and wide, without encountering a breath of opposition. We began to see some reason for the apparent madness of the inland airstrips after all.

The tempo of war now began to speed up and events followed hard on each other's heels with ever-increasing speed, like a torrent, swollen with rain approaching a cataract. 12 AA Bde moved from Matruh to "battle positions" near Piccadilly and, following hotly in the wake of 149 LAA Bty, RHQ 88 HAA Regt, accompanied by its Wksps and three Btys, moved up from the Delta. 2 and 25 LAA and 68 HAA Regts were put on six hours' notice to move.

Estlin called a Wksp commanders' conference at short notice at Piccadilly on his arrival, and Cotterill, Volum and I sweated across the desert to attend. At Bde HQ, we met Capt Morton, OC of 88 Wksps, another of the old Hucknall gang, who had come up in advance of his main party to report to Estlin. Bde HQ was even then packing up to move to some more forward location near Mischeifa, and Estlin was sitting in an empty tent on one of the stationery boxes, with S/Sgt Lewis hovering around, seeking to retrieve it and put it in Estlin's car. We retired and all squashed into Morton's car for the conference.

Estlin was brief and to the point. 'The battle will start in two days' time,' he said. 'Today is Day D minus 2. The programme of our attack is being speeded up, because it has been learned that the enemy, notwithstanding the rain, is even now concentrating his forces to assault Tobruk. It is the Army Commander's intention to attack him while he is deploying against the Tobruk position. On Day D plus 1, the RAF intend to open

91

airfields on the Libyan border, near Ridotta Maddelena, and 2 and 25 Regts are to act as AA defence. 88 Regt will take over the defence of Oxford Circus from 25 Regt and the Gilwakh LG will be abandoned. 68 Regt will move forthwith to rendezvous positions near Mischeifa to accompany a force which is advancing into Libya through Sidi Omar and will move to Sidi Aziez or Gambut when they are occupied. All Wksps will forthwith evacuate back to 88 Wksps at Oxford Circus all vehicles and equipment they cannot repair in three working hours and will continue to do so. As soon as the situation clears, the Bde Recovery Service will be restarted to take over this duty.'

We all dispersed to our units as cheerful as larks at the prospect of action at last and the morale of my own lot at least, by no means low at any time, rose to phenomenal heights when the news was disseminated. The idea of catching the enemy on the hop, when he was looking the other way at Tobruk, was particularly appreciated.

(If I may be pardoned for a slight digression, I believe that if this attack on Tobruk had been launched, the enemy would undoubtedly have taken the place. Without wishing to cast any doubt on the courage, endurance and versatility of the Tobruk garrison – who had been set what was probably the dullest, dirtiest, bloodiest assignment of the whole Middle East campaign – the "Siege of Tobruk" was in fact only a siege; the garrison was beset for months, but it was never actually assaulted in earnest throughout. The initiative never passed out of the hands of the defence and Tobruk, famous as it had become, was never really a defensible position, owing its continued integrity to the half-heartedness of the besiegers, who were mainly Italians with little or no desire for glory in battle. Throughout the two years of the Desert Campaigns, Tobruk was seriously assaulted only twice – by the Western Desert Force against the Italians in January 1941 and by the Germans against the demoralised Eighth Army in June 1942 – and each time it fell to determined attackers in a few hours like a rotten apple. That comment, however, is made with hindsight.)

Back to Gilwakh in mid-November 1941. We promptly set about patching up what vehicles were in the workshops for some minor repairs, and bundled them off back to their units; those for heavier repairs were formed into a park and the recovery lorry started on a programme of towing them back to Oxford Circus. There were about a dozen such, and, since our 30cwt recovery could manage to tow only two at any one time, this operation occupied the best part of the two days until Day D; in fact, it only returned from its last trip the evening before we actually moved. About midday, Spooner took the 15cwt Bedford over to see whether 68 had left behind anything worth having. He found they had already pulled out, having abandoned on the site two partially stripped 15cwt trucks and a lot of scrap steel plate. One of the trucks had had its wheels removed, but the other was complete, though lacking an engine; he put as much of the steel as seemed useful into this one and the recovery lorry towed it back to Gilwakh.

Strictly speaking, both derelict wrecks should have gone back to Oxford Circus with the other BLR stuff, but Spooner had looked at the rescued one with an appraising eye. 'We could cut the front end off that,' he said, 'and make a fine two-wheeled trailer out of the rear end. Since it has an all-steel body, we might fix it up as a mobile cookhouse, in which we could mount our petrol cooker, for use on the march.' We looked at each other and I gave orders for it to be concealed behind the escarpment, in case Estlin paid us a last surprise visit. There was no hope of our doing anything to it before we moved, but we decided to leave the steel in it, since we couldn't carry that any other way, and to tow the new acquisition behind the recovery lorry, so as to be able to start the conversion as soon as we settled down for a few days.

The two days passed in a turmoil of last-minute work. The CO and Phillimore had disappeared with a small party, to move up with the advance, and we packed up ready to move at first light on the morning of Day D plus 1. We were to move off as part of the RHQ column under the command of Quartermaster McKeown, although he didn't know for certain whither we were bound, or exactly when we were due to set off.

This time our final packing up was a matter of less than an hour. Our roots were getting shallower; Ras Hawala and even

93

Sidi Barrani were fast becoming a faded memory. Before dawn, we had breakfasted, packed our small personal kits into our lorries, dropped our improvised bivvies, hitched our full water trailer and the office trailer behind their respective towing vehicles and were ready to move as the sun's rays began to colour the dew-spangled camel thorn with a faint touch of pink.

I motored over to the remnants of RHQ, a few hundred yards away, to report my readiness and, to my annoyance, found them only just getting up. It seemed that they had heard from the CO, the previous evening, that no move was likely before midday, but had forgotten to tell us! It had just slipped their tiny minds.

Thinking that they knew we were packed up, and might equally forget to tell us again when the real movement order came, I moved the whole unit column over to the spare ground next door, so that we could keep a good eye on them, and settled down to wait.

This waiting, we were to find, was one of the characteristic features of desert convoy work and, for the rest of the morning, the whole of the RHQ rump and ourselves remained fully packed up and standing by impotently. Some of the lads played football in rather a holiday spirit in the blazing sun; some slept; some read. All were keyed up for something more exciting than they had hitherto been getting and the party spirit began to wear a bit thin.

Then, about 2.00 p.m., just as I was beginning to think we were to be stuck there for another day, a runner from RHQ brought the word to move and we were off. In fact, the RHQ column was actually on the move as the messenger arrived and they had made about half a mile on us before we could get the lads into their vehicles. Morale seemed to soar to fever pitch as we stormed off in pursuit in a ragged line, and Pte Ingham, our welder and tame humourist, stood precariously on the roof of his pitching lorry, shouting through a megaphone – obtained from heaven knew where – 'This way for Tobruk. Derna, Bengasi, Tripoli, Tunis and points west!'

We were off...

For the next hour or more, the problems of motoring across

94

country absorbed our undivided attention. Our convoy movements had hitherto been confined to definite roads or tracks that made a Line Ahead formation the only possible pattern. However, now that we were moving across untracked desert, we were initiated into the mysteries of "Desert Formation" in which we moved in a number of parallel columns. We were to become fairly expert at this before the advance was over.

These columns are usually separated by something like a hundred-yard interval and in each column every vehicle keeps station a fixed distance behind the one in front and level with the corresponding one in the columns on either side. Each column finds its own track, endeavouring to choose as easy a path across the terrain as possible, and the distance between columns varies somewhat from time to time. The normal number of columns is five, as in this instance, since this gives a frontage of about 400 yards, which is not too far for visual signalling from the leading vehicle, but difference in terrain may dictate as few as two or three columns, or as many as ten or twelve. To be able to change from one to another on the move is the hallmark of the really efficient and well trained unit, and we never became as good as that. The clever thing is to be able to halt like a single vehicle, should the signal be given at the head of the column, without gaining on one's predecessor, and to restart without lagging.

Our vehicles formed the two rear ranks of a five-column formation led by RHQ, with the rear party of the Regt Signals Section, commanded by an NCO, in the middle. The signals officer, Lt Overton – who had superseded Travis in the past months – had gone ahead with the CO and had taken an advance party with him. His wretched sergeant, left on his own, seemed to be looking to me for support, as a fellow-sufferer. With the RHQ party which, as I have said, was led by Lt (QM) McKeown, were the doctor (Messent), and the padre (Gilchrist), each in his own truck. Although each of them carried the equivalent rank of captain, as non-combatants they were under the operational command of McKeown, who as an old soldier was highly conscious of the precedence of the RA over all other units and very "Right of the Line".

95

As it happened, all the vehicles in front of us were small and quite lightly loaded at that; whilst almost all of my own lorries were heavy and loaded well beyond the Plimsoll mark. McKeown set a pace of about 25 miles per hour and, although we could keep up with this on hard and flat surfaces, as soon as we came to gradients or patches of softer ground we dropped down to a lower gear and fell behind. This caused friction with the good McKeown, who was all for following the CO's orders to get his lot to wherever he was going as quickly as possible. Being at the rear meant that the surface we encountered had been churned up by the previous vehicles in the column, and our vehicles tended to dig in. McKeown became increasingly irritated at having to make repeated stops to allow Workshops to catch up. He accused me, not without reason, of delaying the advance by overloading my vehicles beyond the legal limit, and I retorted that he was over-driving his trucks and predicted he would suffer for it. Not that I had much hope of this, but I was greatly cheered when shortly afterwards his own truck broke a back spring and he called for our assistance. I had a quick word with Dean, who inserted a wooden block between the axle and the chassis and lashed it all solidly with rope. This made the drive so uncomfortable that he was compelled, out of sheer concern for his backside, to reduce speed to a more reasonable 15mph.

Soon afterwards, one of the RHQ motorcyclists smashed up his machine against a large rock and the wreck was left behind "for Workshops to deal with" and, presumably, carry, for it was quite unrideable. This was grossly unfair, because they had space to carry it and we had not; besides, there was a matter of principle involved: no unit which could carry or tow a broken-down vehicle should leave it behind, just like that, for someone else to do something about. Such behaviour was just sheer avoidance of duty and anyhow Workshops were there to bring along anything that cannot normally be towed. Our own motorcycle, which we weren't such fools as to ride, was being carried in the engineless 15cwt truck containing scrap metal, on tow behind our recovery lorry, so we put the damaged machine and its rider in along with that until we could argue the toss about it.

The country through which we were travelling was open and gravelly, slightly undulating and broken by the occasional clay-pan. Until the previous day, it had been the leaguer area for the forward armoured formations, and several rear parties were still packing up. The place was strewn with rubbish and discarded petrol tins, and unexpected slit trenches made driving a bit tricky. Somewhere away to our right a line of telegraph poles ran parallel to our route.

As the afternoon wore on, all sorts of troubles beset the vehicles ahead and we were forced to experiment with our recovery procedures. I soon realised that our decision to use the recovery lorry as the towing vehicle for the engineless 15cwt truck was a mistake, and that in future it must be kept "free" to tow other folk's mistakes out of the soft gravel. As it was, every time this happened, we had to drop the tow off and then pick it up again, after the unditching was done. Fortunately, we didn't have to do any front-suspended tows.

Once, attracted by frantic waving from a stationary truck on the horizon, I sent the 30cwt machinery lorry to investigate and it returned towing one of Overton's advance party signals trucks which had been there for three days. We towed it to the next halt, where we were able to get it going with a new distributor rotor and it fell in with the column ahead.

Just before dusk, we halted on a deserted clay-pan to brew up an evening meal. McKeown then sprang a surprise on us: we were not going to stop there for the night, but after the meal he proposed to form us into single file, and lead us on through the night on a compass bearing to a rendezvous with the CO, somewhere on the Libyan frontier. I suppose Helby had impressed on him the importance of speed and to McKeown, being an old soldier, this was an order, if not from God, then from His nearest representative on earth. He saw no alternative but to follow this daft course. A year later, I would have refused to risk my unit in a blind trip of this sort, or, if I had been over-ruled, would have quietly dropped off the tail of the column in the dark and leaguered down for the night.

As it was, being still somewhat green, I had failed to extract from McKeown the rendezvous map reference and so, leaving

Spooner to head the Wksps column, I volunteered to travel at the rear, in order to ensure that stragglers weren't left behind. Considering what happened, this was fortunate or ludicrous, according to the way you looked at it.

So, just as the light failed, the long, snake-like string of vehicles, nearly nose-to-tail, pulled out of the staging area. Side and tail lights were forbidden, but we were allowed to use the standard under-body lighting on most WD vehicles, wherein a small lamp illuminates a white patch on the rear differential casing.

I brought up the rear in the Bedford 15cwt with Thorne as driver, immediately behind the recovery lorry (with its tow) and with S/Sgt Dean and Pte Smith and its crew. In front of this vehicle was the 3-ton Karrier driven by Pte Reilly.

For the first couple of hours all went well; there was quite a bit of light left in the western sky and the going was good, hard and flat. From the rear, I could see the faint shaded lights winding away in the distance ahead and everyone kept a steady speed and a good interval.

Then the sky clouded over and it became really dark. This wasn't in itself much of a hardship, but at just about the same time the column entered a stretch of undulating country, cross-seamed with little wadis and small escarpments – much the same country as we had had round Gikwakh – and the convoy discipline, which had been good up till then, began to wear a bit thin, opening up and closing like a concertina. We at the end, as always, had the worst of it. One moment, we almost overran the vehicles in front and the next they were away at great speed, leaving us standing, so that we had to strain to accelerate our heavily laden lorries in the churned-up gravel to keep up.

In particular, the recovery lorry didn't like this sort of thing; as long as it kept going, it could make the grade, but as soon as it stopped and was called on to restart with the laden 15cwt in tow, it began to spin its rear wheels and dig itself in. This meant that its crew had to make a lightning descent, cast off the tow; hitch the winch rope to it; drive forward a few yards on to a harder surface, paying out the winch rope as it went; stop and winch in the tow; connect up the tow rope again and head off after the column, which was fast becoming an occasional faint gleam of light in the distance. Several times I thought we had really lost them, but each time we came up with them after a few hundred yards, again stationary, and the farce would be repeated. The recovery crew began to get a bit mutinous.

This sort of thing went on for about an hour, when it was obvious that McKeown had lost his way, or at least had lost any trace of the track he might have once been on. The column snaked and twisted and, on one occasion, nearly doubled back on itself.

Then we almost ran into the back of Pte Reilly's 3-tonner, stationary with its two off-side wheels up on a small embankment and almost toppling over sideways. Dean jumped out of the recovery lorry, yanked Reilly from the driving seat by the scruff of his neck, with a volley of Tyneside oaths, and very skilfully eased the lorry down on to an even keel. Instead of stopping, however, he shouted to Reilly to take his place in the recovery lorry and disappeared hell-for-leather after the column. The recovery lorry, meanwhile, at once started to dig itself in and we had to resort to our winching drill. By the time we had fastened to the rope on again and both vehicles were moving, everyone jumped on to the nearest vehicle in terror lest we had really lost the convoy this time. In this scramble, I found myself in the recovery and Reilly jumped into the Bedford 15cwt beside Thorne, and in this order we charged off in pursuit.

But this time we really had lost the convoy; there was no doubt of this and, although we zigzagged a bit, not a light could we see; it was as dark as a coal cellar on a moonless night. All we could find was one of Overton's small signals trucks, which had broken down and fallen out. As we drew up beside it, I became fully aware of my own plight – in addition to our being lost, the Bedford 15cwt was no longer following either. Vainly, we sought to attract its attention by blowing our horns and even flashing a torch, but without success. We could hear a vehicle moving intermittently nearby in the darkness, but presumably it was in some fold in the ground and out of sight. Obviously it was a mug's game to try fooling about in the dark any more, so I gave the order to pack it in for the night.

There were ten of us in all: Pte Smith and his recovery crew of four; myself; and the four occupants of the signals truck. Everyone had his blankets except me, but Dean's kit was there. Doubtless he would be making good use of Reilly's in the 3-tonner, while Reilly would be a greater fool than I knew him to be if he didn't use mine. We all had rations in the vehicles – I had seen to it that they were divided in this manner before setting out, against just such an emergency as this. So we spread the canvas canopy from the recovery lorry on the ground to keep the dew off, wrapped ourselves in our blankets and resignedly turned in for the night.

I learned later that the main column went on for another hour or more, before McKeown acknowledged defeat and gave the order to halt also. During this time, they had blundered into a line of telegraph poles and had pulled three or four of them down by running through the stay wires which were invisible in the dark. They remained halted until the small hours, when a bit of a moon rose and then went on to their destination, rather depleted, reaching Helby's lot in mid-morning.

But we slept the sleep of the healthily tired and were awakened by the sun edging redly over the rim of the desert. A brief look round revealed the Bedford some three or four hundred yards away with her crew asleep on the ground beside it. Thorne was an old soldier and had sensibly done what I would have done and waited till morning. I sent one of the signallers over to call them in and we set to to boil some tinned bacon and brew up some tea. Thorne and Reilly joined us, much relieved that they hadn't been abandoned, and we ate a cheerful meal as the sun rose and began to dry off the heavy dew. Our spirits rose. This was something like being boy scouts.

The country where we had spent the night was a bare and slightly undulating expanse of gravel, exactly like any other stretch of desert. Away to the right ran a line of poles carrying signals wire, probably the same one we had seen on the previous afternoon. The only other sign of human existence was a stationary tank about a mile away, with some figures moving about near it.

While the rest of the gang were packing up and making the

signals truck work, I cruised over to the tank in the Bedford, to see if they knew where we were, if indeed they knew themselves. The crew gave me an approximate map reference of the position and told me they had broken down two days ago during the advance on Day D and were waiting for their Bde Recovery Section to pick them up. Their officer volunteered the information that they had been on the Div Barrel Track, the axis of the 7 Armd Div's advance, and that he believed the telegraph line had only been put up the previous day and led to 8 Army Battle HQ near the Libyan frontier. These "axis tracks" were usually marked by small cairns of stones or empty oil drums – hence the name "Barrel Track".

We now set off, three vehicles strong, or three and a half, if you count the towed 15cwt, and struck out westwards along the telegraph line. Soon we came to a party of South African Signals repairing the line where it had been damaged by, their Sergeant told me, some '(asterisk) convoy swanning about in the dark, with no idea where it was going, man!' He just added he would like to get his hands on the person responsible. Apparently the line was the vital link between Eighth Army HQ and GHQ MEF, and the Army Commander was hopping up and down, unable to communicate! I felt I could have told him who it could have been, but forbore. They also told me that the line ran to Army HQ on the frontier.

Moving on, we encountered a Fordson 15cwt stationary beside the track and the occupants waved us down frantically. They proved to be Padre Gilchrist and his driver, who professed themselves much relieved to see us. It appeared that they had broken down in the small hours and had watched the column pass them, waiting hopefully for Wksps to arrive with their recovery lorry and either make the truck work or give them a tow. Their horror on finding the recovery lorry and I were also missing can best be imagined. Gilchrist sadly commented on the commissariat arrangements of the RHQ party: it appeared he had a load of boots, comforts, welfare equipment, and 150 hymn books, but no rations.

By now, our breakfast was beginning to shake down a bit, so we brewed up a further can of tea, while Reilly and I set about

101

tracing the trouble in the Fordson truck, which luckily proved to be nothing more serious than a blocked petrol filter.

As we were so engaged, a flurry of staff cars bore down on us from the rear, or Egypt direction and a gorgeous Being in khaki gabardine tunic and slacks, collar and tie, polished buttons, red gorget patches and the badges of a full colonel, alighted and demanded rather brusquely of the nearest officer in sight whether he could tell him where he was. The "officer" happened to be Gilchrist, unshaven, in shorts, with a mug of tea in one hand and a bully and biscuit sandwich in the other. The Padre eyed him mildly and said he was afraid he was a stranger in these parts.

The Colonel seemed to refrain from the remark about insubordination that was on his lips, by suddenly perceiving Gilchrist's corps emblems, and out of respect for the Cloth, turned and left us in a whirl of dust, travelling westwards. Shortly afterwards, the Fordson responded to treatment and we sped off again in fine style, now four and a half vehicles strong.

We covered about 15 miles in the next hour and then nemesis overtook us. I was leading and was surprised to see a lorry wheel bowl merrily past and make off into the desert. Looking round, I saw the Padre's truck skidding to rest on only one front wheel. Obviously, a front stub-axle had snapped, this being a well known defect with this type of truck.

Thorne went off to collect the errant wheel and the rest of us gathered silently round the victim. Had Reilly's stores 3-tonner still been with us, we could have fitted a new stub-axle, but now there was no option but to sling it behind the recovery lorry as a front suspended tow, and this meant that the engineless 15cwt had to be towed by something else. The only "something" available was the Bedford 15cwt and it would obviously not be able to do such a tow in its heavily loaded condition. So, very reluctantly, we set about jettisoning the heavy, but useful, scrap steel plate that had been the choice of AQMS Spooner and which we had brought so far.

Again we started off, although somewhat more soberly. We hadn't got far, however, before we found that the Bedford was quite unequal to the task of towing even this lightened load and could scarcely get out of second gear. Another halt was called and, after a bit of a conference, we stripped anything usable from the smashed-up RHQ motorcycle and ditched the battered remains. (There was a terrific row about this at RHQ afterwards and I had to issue a special BLR certificate to cover them in writing it off.) We also unshipped our own motorcycle and Pte Reilly very bravely volunteered to ride it.

But even this wasn't enough; with its full load, the Bedford was boiling again before we had done another half-mile and, with our small stocks of water and little prospect of obtaining any more in the near future, this was a very serious matter. There was no alternative left – we must abandon the complete tow which we had brought so far.

In case there might be some chance of returning for it when we reached our destination, we towed it several hundred yards from the main track and removed its wheels to render its appearance unattractive and discourage looters. Since its wheels seemed to be somewhat better than those on the Padre's Fordson, we swapped them over in case we might have to lighten the ship still further.

It was now nearly midday and we were so exhausted that we decided to have lunch before moving on, and consumed a meal of bully, cheese, biscuits and tea out of our shrinking vehicle rations. The Padre also took a photograph of the assembled multitude and never have I seen a more uninspiring collection of roughs than this snap revealed when it finally got printed many months later.

We now entered a land of giant billiard-table-like clay-pans and we careered across them at a good speed for another twenty miles or so. The going was enlivened by occasional treacherous small cross gullies which made driving a matter requiring much alertness. Reilly, on the motorcycle, didn't see one of these and came a terrific purler. He wasn't hurt, only winded, but we replaced him with another of the recovery crew, Pte Crane from the Isle of Man, our reserve motorcyclist, to give him a rest. Almost immediately afterwards, the recovery lorry ran foul of a similar gully and covered several yards in a series of giant leaps. Padre Gilchrist, who had been public-spiritedly sitting in his towed truck to keep the rear wheels down, was much shaken and expressed a willingness to walk the rest of the way. We found that the recovery lorry had fractured two of the four studs holding the twin rear springs on to the intermediate trunnion bearing on one side. This was a known fault on the Morris LAA tractor, which used the same chassis, and once again we were reduced to more strapping with rope, before proceeding a trifle more carefully.

We were now reaching a more populated area dotted with small tents and lorries galore, which became a vast caravanserai of marquees, signals trucks, command vehicles and the like, grouped together with little regard for the dispersion that we had once been taught to regard as essential. Since the telephone line stopped here, we assumed this was Army Battle HQ and bypassed it with care not to raise any more dust than necessary.

Ten miles further on, miles strewn with newly established landing strips and countless RAF vehicles, we arrived at the frontier with Libya. From a slight eminence, we looked down on that landmark of almost legendary fame of which we had heard so much – The Wire – that notorious barrier stretching from the coast almost as far inland as Siwa and erected by the Italians in the 1930s on the orders of General Graziani to prevent the harassed Senoussi tribesmen migrating en masse from Cyrenaica into Egypt and creating an international incident.

It had always been a bit of a puzzle to me, and to others as well, how a "bit of barbed wire" could possibly prove a serious obstacle to any determined Bedouin who wished to be on the other side, but now we saw it "in the flesh", as it were, our queries were answered. This "Wire" was a formidable barrier indeed. Six feet high and twenty feet wide, strung over a serried forest of steel and concrete posts and guyed down on either side, it was a fantastic web of rusty barbed wire which would have given pause to a regiment of tanks. It stretched away on either side to the horizon, like a dirty brown smear on the clean desert and we began to wonder how we were to get across it. However, a track led to a gap somewhere to our left, where we found a tall, white milestone-like pillar of concrete, bearing on the one side the word "*Egitto*" and on the other "*Libia*". On the Libyan side lay a series of tumbled ruins which marked the remains of the famous Italian frontier fort of Ridotta Maddelena.

We had left Egypt which had been our domicile since our landing in May and had crossed over into enemy territory – Libya!

6

We stumbled on RHQ almost at once, merely by picking on the most-used track beyond the Wire and following it until we found someone we could ask. It is something that has never failed to cause me wonder that one could travel about in a piece of desert as big as Wales, and just reach one's destination by guessing the right direction and asking the "inhabitants" one came across.

RHQ was nestling into a small escarpment, in the traditional manner, on the edge of large area of immense activity, where the RAF were obviously operating a new LG. Claud Phillimore was pleased to see me, but wanting to know where I had been all this time, and he was relieved that we had picked up the Padre and the two missing signals trucks. He mentioned almost in passing that we were not to unpack more than was absolutely necessary, since we might be expected to move on at short notice if the battle continued to go well. Apparently it was going well at the moment; our armoured forces had penetrated to within about 40 miles of Tobruk without meeting much opposition and had only now come up against the main enemy forces which had, as expected, been deployed against the fortress. Heavy fighting was now in progress.

My Wksps was deployed at the base of the same small escarpment a few hundred yards beyond RHQ and was already hard at work. Spooner was delighted to see me and reported he had instructed all the Battery fitters to send in a list of their requirements which would be called in rotation as soon as we had men to work on them. The Signals had no wire to lay us a line to the RHQ exchange; and, worse, our water trailer had broken adrift and had been lost the previous night. This was a grave blow for it meant that we would be dependent for our water supply on a few small two-gallon cans of doubtful soundness. It would appear that the trailer had fractured its towing eye and turned over on its side during McKeown's disastrous night drive and its towing lorry hadn't dared remain to do anything about it for fear of getting lost. They had told him about it only on arrival at Maddelena!

The gloom was dispelled when one of my late-arrival recovery gang piped up that he had noticed, about 20 miles back, a small Signals detachment which had a water trailer with a broken tow eye on the ground with them that looked very much like ours. He hadn't given it a thought at the time because he assumed ours had gone on with the main party.

This was enough for Spooner. 'If you agree,' he said, 'I'll go back at once and bring it in. I'm ready now.' And although he hadn't slept a wink the previous night, he was away back on our course with the recovery lorry and the Bedford in just as long as it took to get them filled up with petrol. We gave him such directions as we could for the location of the trailer and also for the now-wheelless 15cwt chassis, for which he took a set of wheels.

He was successful. Just as it was getting dark, the party arrived back, towing not only the trailer but also the abandoned 15cwt. The clouds lifted from my mind.

Pte Smith, the recovery driver, told me afterwards that it had been 'as good as play'. They had spotted the trailer, without any difficulty, in the hands of the Signals party who had obviously picked it up and had brought it along many miles with great difficulty, but were in no position either to mend it or to tow it when full. The detachment was under the command of a lance corporal and Spooner had sailed in with all the majesty and assurance of a Regular Warrant Officer Class II. Ignoring any possibility of "findings being keepings", he claimed it as ours, thanked the unhappy lance corporal for finding it, and complimented him on his skill in bringing it so far in its damaged condition. Then he hitched it up behind our recovery lorry and departed without more ado. The lance corporal had

107

said nothing beyond 'Yes Sir' and 'No Sir' during the entire interview.

Recovering the abandoned 15cwt was plain sailing; it was just where we had left it.

For the next three or four days we were as busy as we had ever been so far. The LGs were defended by three LAA Btys, 81 and 82 of 25 LAA Regt and 149 of 27 Regt, as well as our old friends 261 HAA Bty from Gilwakh. Everyone had broken everything they possibly could, particularly 81 Bty, who had motored straight up from the Delta to Maddelena, with only a couple of stops. In addition to this, we had been trying to get the most urgent modifications done on the guns of the other three Btys during the few days before the battle started and the advent of a completely new unit requiring a whole workshop to itself rather upset our calculations.

One of the worst headaches which we suffered throughout most of this campaign was the way in which the Btys we were supposed to look after were changing almost daily. We seldom found ourselves responsible for the same units for very long; in fact, Claud Phillimore calculated that between September 1941 and May 1942 the Btys under the command of RHQ 2 LAA Regt altered no fewer than 37 times. Many of these changes involved only ringing the changes in the pool of old stalwarts, but all the same, it complicated the job of trying to keep them in good mechanical order if we saw them for only a few days at a time.

One assumed all this was necessary. At least, the reason why we, a LAA Regt HQ, were commanding HAA Btys was becoming clearer. Each defended site required both HAA and LAA protection and the Btys available were roughly in the proportion of one Heavy to two Light. These were parcelled out to the various Regt HQs, possibly somewhat haphazardly at first, and the composite Regt, so formed, proved a neat unit for landing ground defence. Occasionally, odd Btys were lent for other duties outside the Bde and this sometimes led to some luckless RHQ being left high and dry without any Btys at all. This had happened to 94 HAA RHQ at the start of the battle, leaving them back at Matruh and their three Btys all up in the desert, under "alien" command. Although the strength of such composite AA Regts didn't alter much, the swapping of Btys between them hardly stopped as one Regt leapfrogged another in advance or retreat.

Our workshop site at Maddelena lay along the base of one of those small escarpments that we had come to regard as a typical feature of the gravel desert belt which seemed to stretch for hundreds of miles either way at this distance inland from the coast. The escarpment was about ten feet high, cut into by numerous nooks and crannies into which we inserted our vehicles for protection against air attack. The "work in progress" was dispersed on the wide level ground in front and we soon found there was a maximum degree of dispersion beyond which it was almost impossible to keep an adequate check on the work going on over the site.

To our left as one faced the escarpment, lay RHQ, and the LG area was several hundred yards away over the top of the ridge. We seemed to be on the edge of the outer rim of the "inhabited" zone. No one seemed to know what lay on the far side of the LG and it made one feel a bit naked when one reflected that there was probably little between us and any marauding German armoured columns except a light screen of armoured cars some twenty miles out. The story was that our air patrols were keeping a close eye on any traces of enemy activity in the hinterland, but they reported no sign of anything nearer than the battle now in progress somewhere south-east of Tobruk.

We soon found that sleeping at the foot of an escarpment was dangerous, because stray trucks wandering lost during the twelve hours of darkness could drive straight down through our camp like Gadarene swine. No one suffered any harm, but once one of these lunatics drove straight over my camp bed one evening when I was elsewhere and my carpenter had to spend the best part of half a day in repairing the damage. After this we adopted the practice of parking our trucks along the skyline above the camp when dusk fell and moving them down at dawn.

Water was our most pressing worry. The towing eye on our recovered water trailer was replaced with a much stronger one in a matter of a few hours, but refilling it with water to replace what had been lost was quite another matter. We had to collect water daily from a water point near Army Battle HQ on the other side of the Wire and the ration was half a gallon per man per day for all purposes, cooking, drinking, personal hygiene and shaving, cookhouse cleansing and any refilling of vehicle radiators that might become necessary. All this water came in tins by lorry from Oxford Circus, to which a pipeline had been run all the way from Alexandria! By the time it reached us it was valuable indeed. Petrol was far more plentiful.

As a workshop, we were entitled to a small extra quantity of water, seven gallons a day, I think it was, and without this we would have been very badly off indeed. It was no uncommon thing for us to receive damaged radiators for repair and, when the repair was finished, we would test it with a small quantity of our own precious fluid, but couldn't spare enough to send it back to the unit already filled. That was their responsibility and I heard of cases where trucks were towed around for several days before their crews saved up enough water to fill their cooling systems. A leaking radiator was a catastrophe.

I called a conference of the five senior NCOs and put it to them that we must try to build up some small reserve of water, before we moved again; it was decided that we would allow an issue of one half water-bottle per man per day for sips between meals, shaving, washing and "laundry", and the remainder would be at the disposal of the unit QM (Sgt Hughes). It would go for cooking and for building up a small reserve at the rate of six gallons a day. Out of the "cooking" allowance, each man would get two full mugs of tea per day.

Afterwards, I explained it to the lads and said I would have the same ration as themselves and they took it very well. It seemed much better than just issuing an impersonal order and they cooperated loyally to make the scheme a success. Spooner, I heard afterwards, let it be known unofficially that, if the choice was between washing and shaving and drinking, anyone appearing unwashed or unshaven on parade would incur his

110

extreme displeasure and would be found plenty of unpleasant work. Certainly, I never saw anyone in this condition.

I found that washing, shaving and cleaning my teeth in half a mug of water wasn't as difficult as it might sound. The only problem was deciding in which order to perform the operations. We usually found that we even had a few eggcupfuls of our personal issue over at the end of the day and we encouraged each bivouac pair to put their joint surplus in an empty petrol tin. This enabled them, unbelievable though it may sound, to wash their shirts after a fashion every few days.

We also rigged up an elaborate sand filter behind the cookhouse and reclaimed all the dirty water that had been used for washing dishes. It was not, of course, fit for drinking or personal ablutions, but we used it to top up the radiators of our vehicles and it sufficed for this purpose, although it smelt awful if the vehicles boiled, as they often did in the soft gravel.

Our efforts slowly bore fruit and, before we left Maddelena behind us, the tank had been half filled and thus we had the reserve we so badly needed and could relax some of our restrictions.

News of the battle, which was still being waged to the north and north-west, was somewhat scanty. Our two main sources of information were the BBC World Service news bulletins, always a couple of days behindhand and containing little but the official handouts, enlivened by some imaginative and ill-advised interpretations by some London news editor; and the Corps "Sitreps" which were received every 24 hours at RHQ and which I studied and passed on to the troops in the form of a short daily news conference of my own.

Reading between the lines of both these sources, the overall picture didn't look quite all that it should. It would seem that, after some four or five days of fighting, our forward armoured elements had made contact with the Tobruk garrison, only to lose it again and now were strung out halfway across eastern Cyrenaica, with the Germans around Tobruk on one side and the bypassed defenders of Bardia, Sollum and Sidi Omar on the other.

The spearhead was stalled in heavy fighting near a locality called Sidi Resegh, some 40 miles short of Tobruk. Sidi Resegh lay on the Trigh Capuzzo, a secondary track running parallel to the main coast road but several miles inland. The battle for the airstrip there and for the commanding hills of Belhamed, El Duda and Zaarfran had devolved into a slogging match with little apparent result, the initiative remaining with the Germans and probably heavy casualties on both sides. The battle was forcing the Eighth Army into that most unenviable role: a desert attacking force with its wings in the air, reduced to the defensive. We hadn't achieved any of our objectives and hadn't broken through to the coast at any point; this was still held by the enemy, who was sustaining a stubborn defence all the way from Halfaya and Sollum on the Egyptian border back to Sidi Resegh and was entrenched in strength in the desert on our right at Bir Sheferzen and Sidi Omar. For all we knew, he might be skirmishing in the desert on our almost-unprotected left. The impetus of our attack seemed to be slackening and things didn't look so good.

Then there were rumours that enemy armoured forces had been spotted sculling around in the desert south-west of El Adem and the majority of "soft-skinned" units in the Maddelena area, ourselves among them, were put on three hours' notice to move. This restricted the amount of work we could do and, for three nights, we slept in our clothes and boots, ready to pack up and pull out at the first warning.

Then, suddenly, the storm broke. Just before we were due to shut down for the day, Spooner and I were standing outside the trailer-tent, reviewing the work for the next day, when a ragged string of vehicles spewed over the escarpment to our right, going like bats out of hell, and made away towards the Wire in a cloud of grey dust. There must have been fifty of them – mainly RAF – and they came bouncing and sliding down the slope like the riders in the more spectacular sort of Wild West film. One of these lorries was towing a Hurricane on its wheels, with its tail wheel lashed to the tailboard of the lorry and bouncing right off the ground as it hit the bumps.

Now this was not an ordinary convoy, nor was it the way the RAF treat their machines except in some exceptional circumstance; it had the sinister suggestion of panic and rout. Both Spooner and I remembered the advance party of RAF ground staff that had set out a few days earlier to set up a forward refueling airstrip some 30–40 miles further on towards Bir El Gubi to the north-west. With that odd tightening feeling about the stomach, I gave the order to pack up and come down to 15 minutes notice to move.

Shortly afterwards, Sgt Major Bliss came over from RHQ, looking worried. The Adjutant's compliments and would we pack up immediately and move over to RHQ. "Something Unfavourable" was happening out in the desert to the north-west.

Our packing was no longer the lengthy business it had been at Ras Hawala and Sidi Barrani. We were already on three hours' notice and we were moving towards RHQ in about half an hour from my own inspired order. I reported to Phillimore that my unit was dispersed on the flat ground just beyond his camp and what was the trouble?

Claud knew nothing definite, but he was worried and RHQ were also packing up. Something, he told me, had happened up north and, although news was scanty and confused, it seemed likely that German armoured forces, whether heavy or light, strong or weak, – no one knew – were operating unchallenged in the hinterland between us and Sidi Resegh. No one could say for sure whether our fighting troops were still holding out at Sidi Resegh, but the wolves were out among the supporting columns on the lines of communication. We were to remain where we were, post double sentries, report any unusual occurrence and be ready for instant movement.

Reassured that at least the Germans were not about to overwhelm the camp, the Workshop philosophically set about brewing up the evening meal whilst it was still light enough to see.

As the cold December evening faded into twilight, a stream of hurrying vehicles of all types flowed round, through and across the Maddelena LGs. Mostly they seemed to be South Africans

113

and they belted towards the Wire as if all the devils of hell were at their heels. One or two of them stopped to find out where they were, and from them we gathered that the Support Groups of one or two of their Bdes had been overrun the previous evening and dispersed to the four winds by a German armoured force which was now fanning out across the desert and among the soft-skinned columns like a wolf pack among sheep. They were all badly scared, demoralised and had the one idea of placing the illusory protection of the Wire between them and the enemy. One party of them had run into 261 Bty and Major Russell, on learning that they hadn't even seen any Germans for over 24 hours, but were still on the run, fairly tore strips off three majors and told them to go back and fight.

Then darkness closed in and the rumble and rattle of the refugees tailed away into a creepy silence. It was a clear, starlit night and, far away on the northern horizon, we could see, as we had done on the past few nights, the faint blinks of light as the guns fired around the defences at Bir Sheferzen and Sidi Omar. No sound was audible but one could detect a faint tremor from the explosions, if one put an ear to the ground. We turned in fully dressed.

Some time in the middle of the night, the guard commander reported to me that some gunfire had been heard from some-where much nearer than Sidi Omar. As we listened, a burst of star-shells sprang up to the northward, not so very far away it seemed, palely lighting up the campsite and shining on the whitish faces of the lads as they sat up in their blankets in alarm. I sent a man over to the RHQ office to report and we settled down to listening again.

The whole desert was full of little noises which we couldn't identify, but which gave to our anxious ears the impression of men or vehicles moving, away to the south or west, and then flicker, flicker, flicker – that was gunfire not so far away to the north. I remembered to count the seconds and the sound followed fairly quickly: eight miles or so away. Dead silence and then – yes, the faint sound of tracked vehicles somewhere to the north or north-west.

There was no mistaking the sound of tanks; the distinctive

crunch and clatter of tracks, backed by the low, full-throated roar of heavy internal combustion engines. I listened, petrified, while the sound rose from a whisper in the still night air, thrummed in my ears and then died into silence again. The tanks, friend or foe, had passed parallel to us and were, temporarily at least, gone. We didn't sleep any more that night, but there were no further alarms and we were glad when the grey dawn came at last.

The whole morning passed without anything happening and we hung about our vehicles, unable to get down to any work. Phillimore had no news to offer, and he and Col Helby were sitting at a single small table in the one tent still standing at RHQ. Then at about 2 p.m. orders came. We and all the non-essentials of RHQ and the Btys were to move back forthwith through the Wire to a rendezvous some ten miles on the far side of the rearmost RAF LGs about Army battle HQ. Claud told me that the entire German armoured forces had struck across country from Sidi Resegh to near Bir Sheferzen and were starting to move south down the Libyan side of the Wire.

Suddenly it seemed to us, who had but yesterday looked askance at the refugees, that perhaps, after all, the other side of the Wire was a healthier place to be; and, seeing that the Wire was thick and the gaps in it were few and far between, perhaps it would not be a bad thing to get through it and put it behind us as soon as possible.

We found the neighbourhood of Army Battle HQ a vast milling throng of men, guns and vehicles spread over a mile of desert. Individual tanks, odd groups of artillery, carriers, command vehicles, signals trucks, LAA troops, all higgledy-piggledy and intermixed. Whole Divisions, or so it seemed, were in the process of reforming, collecting stragglers and rearming. Groups of scattered formations were continually trickling back through the Wire and a series of report centres and information posts manned by tired-looking, but competent Military Police were sifting them out and directing them on to someone who would deal with them, or knew where their unit was. Forests of hurriedly painted signs on posts and vehicle tailboards called on stragglers from this or that unit to report here.

115

And amid it all, the RAAF Tomahawk fighters took off in clouds of driven dust, went out to strafe the enemy and returned, bouncing and slewing on the cut-up ground as they braked, in more clouds of dust. And amid it all, too, the RAAF ground staffs, miscellaneously clad in boots, khaki drill shorts, battledress blouses, mufflers and broad-brimmed bush hats went stoically about their duties, weaving their way through the chaos with the philosophically resigned expression of adults who didn't exactly approve of the games the kids were playing but were unwilling to interfere with their fun.

Our party was nominally under the command of Howe-Brown, the Assistant Adjutant, as well as being the only RA officer present. He reported at various centres and, at last, found us a dispersal area where we could camp until orders came from the CO or Bde HQ for us to do something else. As we pulled in, I was amused to observe the difference in attitude between my gang of thugs and the remnants of RHQ. We had a petrol cooker out, the evening meal in preparation and the radio set connected and delivering the World Service news almost before they had pulled their handbrakes on and were dismounting and stretching their legs. The teamwork was telling.

(The news, incidentally, was the usual two days old and dealt with the successes our troops were having at Sidi Resegh.)

As the day faded, we were heartened to see wave after wave of American built "Honey" light tanks careering in from the east and pitching and bouncing away towards the Wire. A few of them came quite near our leaguer area and we were less heartened to see that each tank had a sort of canvas "skirt", almost concealed in the bow-wave of dust, and beneath the skirt were the familiar four wheels of a 3-ton lorry

We packed down in the open for the night in a mood that could scarcely be described as over-cheerful. For two or three days, we sat around, while the battle hung in the balance, and then the "flap" seemed to collapse and we were ordered back to Maddelena.

It might be appropriate here to give a short account of what

116

happened in the broader battle during those few days, pieced together from Sitreps, "travellers' tales" and personal experiences.

It would seem that after our unsuccessful attempt to relieve Tobruk, the German general, Rommel, had concentrated his armoured forces and launched them smartly at our forward troops, who were holding out precariously by their eyebrows on the airfield at Sidi Resegh and its surrounding escarpment. This became an isolated pocket for a short time and the enemy tanks, flowing round to the south, fell on and dispersed two South African Bdes which were just moving up to reinforce the Sidi Resegh position. Sweeping on to the south-east, they overran and routed any unarmoured unit they came across; any determined unit that "formed square" and shot them off, they left alone and in 24 hours they arrived at the Wire near Sidi Omar. It is not clear what their original intention had been, but Rommel then turned them south and began to advance down on the Libyan side of the Wire. Then the history of the "September Battle" was repeated; his supporting columns of petrol tankers were attacked by the RAF and the RAAF and left burning; his support infantry was shot up; and, after wavering for a day or so, the Germans withdrew slowly and deliberately back up the Trigh Capuzzo. Again the battle flared up around Sidi Resegh, but by this time the initiative had passed into the hands of the Eighth Army, under its new commander, General Ritchie, of 13 Corps – who had replaced General Cunningham at the height of the battle, because the latter had expressed the opinion that the operation had failed – and Rommel went on to a dogged defensive. A big attack by the reformed Divisions from Maddelena, coupled with a full-dress sortie by the Tobruk garrison, cut the enemy forces in Libya in half again and Rommel withdrew his main forces westwards to El Adem, while the remains of his other wing retired towards Gambut, Capuzzo and Halfaya.

However, I am running on a bit. At the end of the first week in December, we re-crossed the Wire to Maddelena and normal service was resumed. The "flap" was officially adjudged to be over.

117

* * *

Our new workshop position was very nearly the same as our
previous one, but the various units, on their return, clustered
rather more closely round the LG for mutual support. There was
one difference: whereas previously the only protection on the
hinterland side had been an armoured car screen, now 22 Guards
Bde had provided a couple of rifle companies as ground
defence. I hoped their firepower discipline was better than their
appearance, for I have seldom seen a more scruffy set of tramps
than this lot. We learned that they had received strict orders
about ten days previously not to waste any of their water ration
on washing and shaving: it had not been rescinded and, being
well trained soldiers, it was as much as their skins were worth to
disobey.

They were setting a very bad example to my own lads, who
were trying so hard under difficult conditions, and I fairly
chewed up the sergeant of their nearest detachment about his
condition, when he came to me to request a bit of workshop
assistance. I later heard that Spooner had only just finished
tearing him into strips for the same reason and, to cap it off
neatly, Estlin arrived while the wretched man was still with me
and nearly flayed him alive for, of all things, *not polishing his
cap badge*! This detachment moved off a couple of hundred
yards or so immediately to a safer distance and, if they
approached us again, they did it at lance-corporal level.

Estlin had now got his recovery service going again and was
back-loading to 94 at Matruh. This Recovery Section was under
the command of a S/Sgt from 68 Heavy by the name of
Hartshorne, an odd, likeable little Yorkshire gnome of a man,
who rarely smiled, seldom slept, hardly ever saluted an officer
or called him "Sir", but never as long as I knew him seemed to
make a mistake. 25 Light had now moved up to the neighbourhood of Army Battle HQ and was accompanied by the Bde
Instrument Section, so it appeared that 94 was now the only
workshop in the Bde not closely involved in the battle.

With some relief, we got rid of the Padre's Fordson, since we
hadn't been able to replace the stub-axle as I had hoped, and for
the next few weeks Gilchrist was seen visiting his "parish" on

the Morris portee chassis that had once carried our experimental 20mm gun. I never found out how it had got to Maddelena. He had become quite attached to it and it went by the name of "Wilbur".

We went ahead with the conversion of our unit into a really mobile effort. The ex-15cwt truck, now a two-wheeled trailer, which we had brought from Gilwakh, had, after a bit of discussion, been allocated to Cpl Siddle, our blacksmith, to carry his tools, anvil, coke (in a specially constructed bunker), and his ready-use stock of spring steel. It was intended to double as the mobile cookhouse when on the move, on account of its fireproof steel floor, but Siddle must have decided to use it to sleep in as well, since it soon sprouted a canvas canopy from somewhere. We also fitted the other (non-stores) 3-ton Karrier with benches for the carpenter and the welder – a curious partnership – but both of them needed a bench always in readiness when we were on short notice to move.

As the threat of German armoured raiding forces diminished, there was a spate of rumours about "loot", in the form of only slightly damaged vehicles left behind in the region to the south of Sidi Omar. This was enough for Spooner; we needed some extra carrying capacity for our increasing stocks of spares. I gave him permission to carry out an investigative sweep to the north and he departed with the recovery lorry and crew to see what he could find and report back.

He returned that evening to report that there was no sign of the enemy this side of Sidi Omar and he was towing a most remarkable vehicle. It was a German Opel staff car of the sort that I had associated with pre-war news films of Hitler review-ing the Wehrmacht– a squat, vertical-sided tub of a car, with an open five-seater body and a big six-cylinder engine that lacked only some minor component, such as a distributor cap, to make it work. The Afrika Korps sign of swastika and palm tree was painted on the side and there was a bullet hole through the windscreen which matched up with another hole in the back squab of the driver's seat, making one wonder if the car had been occupied at the time.

It took a matter of minutes to get it running and we spent a

119

happy evening trying it out around the neighbourhood. It proved to have no great turn of speed – it must have weighed nearly $2\frac{1}{2}$ tons unladen – but it would climb up inclines that British vehicles then available would have jibbed at, without faltering and with the thunderous growl of a light tank. In addition to its normal four-speed-and-reverse gearbox, it possessed a two-speed auxiliary box engaged with a separate lever behind the main lever and a double-ratio rear axle controlled by a form of foot pedal. The whole, if my mathematics are not at fault, gave the driver the magnificent choice of sixteen forward speeds and four reverses. It also had independent suspension all round with big coil springs, which enabled one to drive over six-inch rocks without being aware of them. Just to complete the tale it had four-wheel drive controlled by yet another lever. Driving the thing was rather like playing an organ.

We called it Brünhilde, after that other Nordic lady who, according to Wagner and others, used to hang around battlefields when the fighting was over. Without asking anyone, I took it over as the OC Wksps' private transport, at least until someone found out and took it away, and Spooner took over the Bedford 15cwt, which, for some reason known only to himself, he christened "Malika Farida" after the Queen of Egypt.

Spooner also reported that there was quite a fair amount of good general pickings to be had and recommended another scavenging party while it was still possible. To demonstrate this, he had brought back a few ingenious pressed-steel 20-litre water and petrol cans with snap-on caps; these later became known as "jerricans" and were copied and manufactured in millions by the Allies. These were the first anyone round here had seen and they were such a great improvement to the British tinware that I was determined to lay in a stock of as many as we could find for the carriage of our petrol reserves.

Accordingly, the next day, I headed a party myself to have a look round, and we made good speed up the Libyan side of the Wire in the direction of Sidi Omar. This required some care and open eyes, because no one could tell me exactly where the

Germans now were and it would have been a pity to have encountered some anti-social armoured cars operating from Sidi Omar or Bir Sheferzen.

The farther north we went the more frequent and varied became the flotsam and jetsam of the receding tide of battle. There were vehicles galore, some British, but mainly German, most of them pretty badly shot up or otherwise smashed. Although we had a good look at the most promising ones as seen from a distance, we found nothing the whole day that was really sound enough to warrant towing back for repairs. It was a derelict scene of stony, rolling gravel-desert, littered with battered vehicles in great profusion; burnt-out, with wheels off, on their sides, with shattered windscreens, torn flapping canopies, splintered woodwork and punctured tyres. Most of them had suffered from air attack and were heavily pock-marked with aircraft cannon shell, and all of them had been hurriedly rifled and looted either by our troops or by the Germans. The desert was strewn as far as the eye could see with bits of paper which lifted and fluttered in the wind. It brought home a feeling of the great wastefulness of war.

My party made a carefully selected collection of jerricans – I will use the name by which they were to become well known – together with a few useful ammunition containers for general storage purposes, while I was lucky enough to come across an almost undamaged officer's folding camp chair and a table with a roll-up canvas top. But the main quarry, a serviceable light lorry with which to augment our slender transport resources, eluded us. Most of the less seriously damaged vehicles were German and scarcely worth the trouble of taking away. They were all about two tons in capacity and were almost unmodified replicas of civilian lorries which must have been turned out in their thousands from the motor plants of occupied Europe. There were Opels, French Fords, Czechoslovak Fords, German Fords; all with light bodies, twin rear wheels with narrow ersatz tyres that would just dig in in soft sand, rear-wheel drive only, and not a patch on the equivalent British vehicle.

Then we had a real find. It was not a whole vehicle, but it was one which, by being hidden in a fold in the ground, hadn't been

121

rifled. It was a stores lorry with 7 Armd Div signs and, although the front end had been badly damaged, its main body and contents were intact. It was found to contain eight bins full, literally full, of nuts and bolts. We called off the rest of the search and spent the remainder of our afternoon sorting it through and making an enormous selection of nuts and bolts of the more useful sizes. We couldn't possibly store all of them, it was obvious, but we filled our truck with them as goodwill offerings to our Batteries and, as a makeweight, we threw in a couple of the most easily detachable bins.

As we drew to the end of this labour of love, we were disturbed by a series of heavy explosions not far off and saw large spouts of desert flying skywards a few hundred yards away. Even as we watched the dust and smoke blowing away in the wind, there came the sound of several more heavy shells approaching from the north, or German, direction, and a further set of spouts of earth sprang up a trifle nearer. There was no indication that we were the target, but there was no assurance, either, that the guns were at anything like their extreme range. It provided an excellent reason why the stores lorry on which we were working had escaped looting. By common consent, we decided that it was teatime and, as unobtrusively as possible, we slid off to the south, keeping off the skyline.

Shortly afterwards, we ran into an RASC column, led by an officer with a tommy gun across his knees, who were much surprised at the direction from which we had come and asked whether the Germans had evacuated Sidi Omar. We replied courteously that, as far as we knew, they were not only still in residence, but rather hostile, and we passed on.

These nuts and bolts, of which we kept all we could possibly carry, and distributed the remainder around the rest of the Regt, just about kept us going through the rigours of the campaign and, by some sawing and welding up, we managed to fit the extra bins into our already full stores 3-ton Karrier. We never had cause to regret that either.

The following day, Spooner made another sweep, this time deeper into ex-German territory, and brought in quite a service-able 30cwt Opel equipped with a plywood box-type body that immediately acquired the nickname of "The Breadwagon". It was in much better shape than those we had seen previously and was quite a good runner. RHQ looked rather askance at us for acquiring these two unauthorised vehicles, but their own hands weren't clean enough to protest officially, so it was a case of "live and let live". We decided to fix the Breadwagon up as a sort of mobile instrument repair shop, à la Wray, in view of its almost dust-proof body.

It might be appropriate here to mention another "party" which didn't come off. A few days after our arrival at Maddelena, and before the "flap" started, Col Helby called us all in to a conference and divulged that a big party was in prospect. Details were somewhat scanty at the moment, but it was nothing less than an attempt to repeat the cross-country assault that had put paid to the Italians in the previous winter when the entire Italian Army was cut off and defeated at the Battle of Beda Fomm. The present operation was called "Benforce" and involved a large-scale advance right across the Cynenaica "bulge" from Maddelena to occupy the port of Bengasi in rear of the Axis forces. A large air striking force would accompany the ground attack and 2 LAA Regt HQ was briefed to command the AA troops which would give the necessary defence to the landing strips. My Wksps would be going with them.

It was a truly noble conception and one wonders what the course of the campaign, and perhaps even of the whole war, might have been, had the operation been carried out at that time and with the original objectives and strength. Conjecture on the possible future course of the war is out of place here, but I cannot help feeling sorry that this particular operation came to nothing, when I think of what the outcome might have been if at that early stage Rommel and the Afrika Korps had been routed and dispersed. However, it might have been a failure and the decision to shelve it may have saved me from three or more years as a POW.

Anyhow, cancelled it was. The "flap" at Maddelena cut across the plans for Benforce and the troops which were doubtless to have formed the striking force were, I believe, thrown into the battle around Sidi Resegh instead and used to sway the fighting there to a successful conclusion.

Life at Maddelena was considerably hampered by the almost daily visits from German fighters and the occasional bomber. They did little damage, but they provided the AA defences with plenty of targets and when the defence really opened up it became quite dangerous to stray from under the safety of a truck body on account of the falling splinters. There was no doubt that LG defence had come a long way since the days of the old LG 05 south of Sidi Barrani, which had had four 20mm Bredas, one at each corner and with which everyone was apparently quite satisfied.

Our Workshop labours were accentuated by the arrival under command of our old friends 274 (NH) LAA Bty, whom we had last seen at Sidi Barrani. They replaced 149 Bty, who were moved out of 12 AA Bde on some other assignment. 274 were a pleasant enough crowd (apart from being ex-Yeomanry), but they were a bugbear to any workshop servicing them because they were equipped with a large number of 8cwt Ford trucks in lieu of motorcycles. These little Fords had a special non-standard section of spring steel in their front springs and we were quite unable to keep up with the breakages they sustained. At first we replaced complete springs; then made new leaves to rebuild the broken ones; and, when our stocks of steel ran out, we were obliged to use all sorts of unorthodox methods to keep them on the road. Several times we welded broken spring leaves, which worked quite well, although technically impossible, and, finally, when we ran low on welding gas, we tried riveting the two halves together, with a fishplate. 274 objected strongly to this latter expedient, but only when they knew of it; if the driver didn't know, the riveted spring seemed to last almost as long as a real one.

Another trial was Estlin's big idea for providing a "universal" spare wheel system for the 3.7" HAA guns and their AEC Matador tractors. It arose because spare wheels, or rather tyres, for the Matadors in that part of the world seemed non-existent. It followed that if a Matador had a puncture – no uncommon thing in the desert – it was off the road, and couldn't tow a gun, until the wheel could be removed and the puncture repaired. However, some brighter-than-usual gunner spotted that the wheels on the gun were almost the same as those on the tractors in diameter and position of stud holes. Matador wheels, in pairs (for the tyre section wasn't the same) could be used on the guns, but not vice versa, since the tractor wheel had to fit on to a couple of bosses on the Matador hub, as well as the normal studs, which the gun wheel lacked. Estlin therefore decreed that all spare gun wheels (one spare was provided with each gun) were to be drilled out, forthwith, with the correct additional holes to fit the Matador hub bosses. Two spare gun wheels could then be used, in pairs, on the front axle of a punctured Matador.

This meant drilling a pair of 3" diameter holes in the web of each gun wheel with some accuracy, and, after a lot of trial and error, we hit upon a method of boring them out on the bed of our small lathe. It was a horrid job and, once started, our turner and S/Sgt Dean, working a shift system for 24 hours, modified all the gun wheels in 261 Bty, not just the spares. It did us a good turn, because Major Russell was more than grateful and there was nothing that 261 wouldn't do for us in return.

One day in the second week in December – the 9th, I think it was – we were instructed to send a lorry with some crates of newly arrived spares up to 291 Bty, who were defending one of the forward FSDs (Field Supply Depots) some miles away to the north-west. I had only one lorry available for the job at that moment, one of the 30cwt Bedfords, and the only driver with enough sense of direction to be allowed out alone into the desert was Thorne. So Thorne and a mate with the crates of stores were sent off into the "blue" with instructions to get back quickly in case we moved.

And, of course, it would happen that, within 24 hours, we got orders to pack up and be ready to move at "first light" the following morning. Our destination wasn't stated, but it was obviously somewhere "up", for we knew by this time that the fighting along the Trigh Capuzzo and around Sidi Resegh was over and that the enemy had begun withdrawing towards El

Adem and Gazala. Col Helby caused me much annoyance late on the evening before the move by summoning a Bty Commanders' conference and I motored over in Brünhilde to attend.

The news, as it affected me, was that we were going to move out on the morrow and that we were all to rendezvous at a trig point on the Trigh Capuzzo (map reference so-and-so) to the south of Gambut. It was probable that the RAF were going to use the extensive LGs at Gambut, but we would receive more definite orders from Helby himself at the rendezvous. He was going with Phillimore and the RAF advance party. My lot would move under the command of Major Russell, since 261 Bty would move off first.

By the time the conference was over it was quite dark and there were no stars. Like a fool, I didn't take a compass with me and when I set out to return I missed the workshop site completely and, driving in circles, I arrived twice outside Tony Overton's tent. He was much amused and, the second time, he suggested I should ring my unit on his phone and ask them to put out a hurricane lamp as guidance.

This they did and in five minutes I found them. Spooner said they had heard me grinding round and round somewhere near, but didn't know who it was. As a lesson on the folly of trying to motor alone in the dark in the desert without a compass and a bearing on which to drive, I do not think it could have been bettered. It was something I never did again.

On the following morning, after a hurried breakfast in the half dark, we pulled down our bivvies and packed up. Thorne hadn't returned, and the best I could do was to leave a message on the top of a pile of stones where his bivouac had been, instructing him to make his way over to one of the various rear parties, who were clearing up and to join one and follow us when they moved.

Apart from Thorne, there was another thing to think of: he had with him one of our 30cwt Bedfords, which meant that several of the gang had no transport. Spooner set about redistributing them among the other vehicles and I finished up with four of them in Brünhilde. This made their day and they rose to their feet, Heiling Hitler whenever we met another vehicle, until I told them to stop or get out and walk, because, without Thorne, I had to do the driving, and, as I have said, Brünhilde needed all the concentration one could give her.

With all settled, we moved over to meet up with 261 and fell in behind them when they started off. It was a fine morning, sunny but cool, and battledress was a welcome attire rather than a burden, particularly at 7.30 a.m., the hour when the column really got going. In addition to ourselves, some LAA troops of guns were moving with 261, making Russell's command quite a large one, but we fell in at the rear, as usual.

At first, I had little to do, except bully the unit into keeping some reasonable measure of Desert Formation and to keep a check on the route we were taking, so as to be able to estimate where we were at any one time. This wasn't as difficult as it might sound, for the desert in this part of Cyrenaica had been pretty thoroughly surveyed by the Italians, who, in the course of their work had erected a network of small stone cairns on prominent points some five or seven miles apart on which to take trigonometrical bearings. All these "trig points" were marked quite accurately on our maps, which were anyway based on the Italian originals, and desert navigation was simple; one mapped out one's route in advance from trig point to trig point and then drove on compass bearing from point "A" to point "B", point "B" to point "C" and so on. With decent planning, even allowing for some inaccuracy of maps and bearings, it was difficult to be so far off one's course that one couldn't see the next trig point.

We had a spot of bother right at the start. Our remaining 30cwt Bedford was towing the office trailer and, on starting from a halt, pulled the complete sprung tow-hook assembly out of its mounting with a noise like a shell burst. We dared not add to the loads of the already over-laden Karriers, Malika Farida was no use for towing, and the 30cwt machinery lorry and our recovery lorry might be needed for recovery work. So the trailer went on behind Brünhilde, and I must say that I couldn't tell without looking round whether I was towing anything or not.

We also had trouble with the Breadwagon, which started

early and went on all day. This vehicle was quite heavily loaded with the gear that should have been in the absent 30cwt Bedford and its thin-section twin rear wheels dug into the gravel like knives whenever it was at all soft. Any doubts about the "desertworthiness" of German vehicles we might have entertained rapidly disappeared. They were not a patch on our own transport.

As we struck north, we began to run out of the gravel into stonier country, and the Breadwagon's ersatz tyres began to give trouble. Punctures occurred at an average of about one an hour and Spooner and Dean devised a novel way of keeping the vehicle, at least part of the time with the convoy. Dean, in the recovery lorry, ranged the desert on either side of the route, inspecting the vehicle wrecks which were scattered fairly frequently over it. Any suitable tyres were removed, wheel and all, and handed over to Spooner who kept a running stock of two or three available for instant use. Every time the Breadwagon had a blow-out, Spooner would stop, heave out a new wheel and stand by while the Opel's crew would hold up the vehicle by sheer manpower and change the wheel. The old wheel had to be abandoned, as there was no time to repair anything, and the Breadwagon would come storming up after the column in a cloud of dust, stones and noise, the latter because its silencer had been holed by RAF cannon fire.

Curiously enough, the crew remained in high spirits all the time, notwithstanding their hard task.

Towards evening we had trouble with the Karrier stores lorry which seemed to have water in the fuel system and dropped behind. Dean passed over to Spooner his remaining stock of Opel wheels, together with the goodwill, if any, of the business, and dropped back with the breakdown. He was a bit worried because he had no compass – Thorne had the unit's compass with the absent Bedford, but said he would follow our wheel tracks as soon as the Karrier was put to rights. The two stationary vehicles were soon specks on the horizon and passed out of sight.

Some fifteen miles further, just as it was beginning to get dark, we pulled up and dispersed slightly for the night. Major

128

Russell gave it as his opinion that only fools would career about in the dark with heavy guns in tow and that he, for one, intended to sleep in his bed. He should have spoken to McKeown! We would start off again at first light.

We brewed up tea and some sort of hot meal in the black-smith's trailer and the total darkness of a moonless and overcast night settled over the desert. There was no sign of the missing two lorries and, as the hours went by, I began to get a little worried. The likelihood of their finding us in this inky blackness was small and I didn't relish moving on in the morning leaving them behind. However, some time after 10 p.m., we heard faint noises to the rear and, by flashing torches, we guided in the little recovery lorry, which was actually towing the fully-loaded 3-tonner! Apparently, the carburettor wouldn't yield to treatment and so Dean, rather than waste any more time, put the non-runner on tow, in an attempt to catch us up.

Forthwith, Siddle was turfed out of bed in the trailer and another brew-up was produced for the newcomers; then a tarpaulin was draped over the offending Karrier to shield the light and the petrol system was drained into spare jerricans, cleared of water and refilled. It was well after midnight before Spooner reported to me that the vehicle was fully roadworthy again and ready for the next stage of the journey.

The next morning was cold and grey, with a hint of rain in the air. All our transport behaved properly and by 11 a.m. the head of the column halted on the lip of a steep escarpment overlooking the plain below. Col Helby, advised by Russell by radio, came up to meet us and called unit commanders forward to a briefing.

It wasn't an inspiring scene; a wild, windswept upland, grey below low scudding clouds, with a featureless grey-green desert fading away to a misty horizon behind us and, at our very feet, a sharp drop to the plain below, also featureless, except for a road or track that seemed to run at right angles to our direction of advance. This was the notorious Trigh Capuzzo, leading back on our right to the German positions at Sollum and Bardia and on our left to Sidi Resegh, Tobruk and the rest of Cyrenaica. On the horizon were a dozen or more stationary British tanks –

129

battle casualties not yet removed. Some of them had lost their tracks, others were more or less shot about, and one or two had that ominous blackening about the upper works that betokened a "brew-up".

It might be appropriate here to say a word or two about the geography of this neighbourhood. In simple terms, north-east Cyrenaica is a low plateau that goes down to the sea in two steps, all the way along the coast from Bardia to Gazala. These steps, or escarpments, are really stony screes, anything up to 100 feet high, and are separated by a shallow valley, called locally a "*sgifet*", varying in width between five and ten miles. Along this runs the Trigh Capuzzo, a narrow secondary road with an original surface of water-bound macadam. It runs as straight as a die from Capuzzo on the Egyptian frontier to a cross-tracks west of El Adem, later to become famous as "Knightsbridge", where it peters out into a mere camel track. All the bitterest and bloodiest fighting of the desert war took place along this shallow valley. On the inland or upper escarpment from west to east lie the vantage points of Bir Hacheim, Bir Bellefaa, Bir Temrad, El Adem, Sidi Resegh and Gazr El Arid, and on the lower crest the eminences of El Duda, Belhamed, Zaafran, Gambut and finally Bardia, where the escarpment cuts the coast. The southern escarpment reappears further to the east at Capuzzo, Sollum and Halfaya (known as Hellfire to the Western Desert Force). These names were to become well known in the desert; they were the names of battles.

Col Helby informed us that our original destination had been the extensive Gambut LGs, but the RAF plan had been changed, after the enemy had made a sortie in force the previous night from his positions in Bardia and had shot up the advance parties with light field artillery. Accordingly, the RAF decided that Gambut wasn't yet all that healthy and instead they would be forced to use the smaller and less satisfactory landing strip at Sidi Resegh further to the west. We were to be in Sidi Resegh before dark that evening.

So, over the top of the escarpment the column spilled, still in its five lines, and bounced and slithered to the foot of the hill in clouds of dust and stones. It was very dangerous, for the guns only had brakes operating on the overrun and tended to take charge of the towing vehicles and turn themselves or the vehicles over. I could liken our progress to the Wild West films in which the sheriff's posse charges down the hill in pursuit of the hero or villain. Had we been obliged to halt, it would have been just mayhem, for no one could stop, but by skilful steering and because there was plenty of room, everyone reached the valley floor in one piece. Then we turned left on the Trigh Capuzzo.

"Heavy fighting on the Trigh Capuzzo" the BBC news bulletins had said, night after night, with little idea of what that meant. We had expected to see some traces of this, but the sight of the battlefield shook us.

For the next twelve miles, up to and beyond Sidi Resegh, the valley was strewn with derelict and damaged vehicles, first in ones and twos, then in dozens, then in scores and then in their hundreds, until finally as we drew near to Sidi Resegh, the desert was virtually carpeted with them as far as the eye could see. They were on the rising ground to our right, in the valley, on the road, in the wadis and chines of the escarpment to our left and silhouetted against the sky on the escarpment edge. They were smashed, shell-torn, bullet-riddled, burnt out; on their sides, without wheels, tossed upside down; British, German and Italian, inextricably mixed and jumbled – cars, lorries, tanks, tracked carriers and guns. The road was broken up with shell-holes and the ground on either side was torn up and pock-marked with craters; tank tracks criss-crossed amid the mangled steelwork, crushing them into the ground. And everywhere the litter of bits: bits of vehicles, bits of guns, bits of equipment and just *bits* which might have once been men; rifles, ammunition, piles of expended shell cases, ammunition boxes, all smashed and crushed into the earth by heavy tanks turning and slewing. "Heavy fighting on the Trigh Capuzzo". There must have been...

The last of the series of battles had taken place only a couple of days before, as the German forces fell back from the sortie that had so nearly defeated the Eighth Army's invasion of Libya; the British casualties had mainly been cleared from the

131

area, but many of the enemy who would never see Germany or Italy again were still there, where they fell four or five days before, crumpled over their steering wheels, twisted over lorry tailboards, prone beside the open doors of the vehicles they had just quitted in frantic haste as the ground-strafing fighter aircraft caught them. Some of the corpses had been partially covered, but some were exposed to the desert sun and were swollen and turning a reddish black.

Over all a dead silence reigned. Except for our column, the little grey wagtails that hopped and chirped among the wreckage, the hosts of bright red butterflies (for all that it was December) that fluttered hither and thither settling on heaven knows what, and the disturbed fork-tailed kites wheeling gracefully overhead, there was no sign of life anywhere as far as one could see. It was a place of the dead.

And it smelt. Spilt diesel fuel, burning wood, and the sweetish stink of decaying human flesh. Once again, the main impression was the utter futility and wastefulness of war.

The airstrip at Sidi Resegh lay on the top of the southern escarpment and had to be reached from the Trigh Capuzzo at this point by a narrow, exposed track that zigzagged up the steep slope. It was here that the Support Group of 7 Armd Div and a Bde of New Zealanders had held off the violent German attacks from the valley below. The whole face of the escarpment was pocked with little stone-rimmed rifle pits, commanding the approach from the Trigh, and the men who had died in them had apparently been buried by hastily heaping earth and stones over them, so that occasionally a hand or foot protruded. At the escarpment top, where the track took a sharp bend, there was an absolute chaos of stone breastworks, rifle pits, shell-holes, wrecked machine guns, broken rifles, bayonets, hand grenades, stick grenades, shell cases and thousands upon thousands of rounds of ammunition of all sorts, British, German and Italian. All around again were the little mounds of stones that marked the hasty burials. Burnt out British carriers lay in whole groups, some still with their dead crews in them, other vehicles also burnt out and various brewed-up British "Crusader" cruiser tanks. Fire seemed to be the keynote of the whole scene.

Commanding the bend in the track where it breasted the escarpment, was a 20mm Breda anti-tank gun in a little stone emplacement. One of its wheels was missing and its barrel was cocked in the air where it had received a direct hit. Beside the entrance of this shallowly dug little sangar stood a pair of boots, placed neatly side by side, as their owner might have put them outside a hotel bedroom door at night. Except that in this case he had omitted to remove his feet.

We had to wait in the unpleasant valley for quite a time while 261 hauled their guns up this frightful hill. There was a welter of abandoned vehicles about and, as we had nothing better to do, we set out carefully to examine some of these, avoiding those that still had their owners in them. One of the best of the untenanted ones was a German Ford staff car, generally similar to my Opel Brünhilde in appearance, except that it had four-wheel steering as well. All it seemed to lack was a battery and, since no workshop worthy of the name has ever been short of spare batteries, one was produced and fitted while we waited. Forthwith, the engine started and Spooner, who had discovered it and had impounded it at once as his personal vehicle, drove it up to the top of the hill with zest when his turn came.

It was getting dark by the time it was our turn to reach the top of the escarpment and after I had found and reported to Claud Phillimore at RHQ, who were in a steep-sided gully nearby, I gave the order to bivouac for the night where we were, for everyone else was up. We would find a site for the workshop in the morning. No one felt like exploring much in the dark, so we chose as open a spot as possible and set about brewing a hot evening meal in the blacksmith's trailer. As we did so, we became conscious, by sense of smell alone, that the place we had chosen for the trailer could have been a better one, and, after a glance at the ground in the vicinity, a party of rather white-faced cooks and fatigue-men hastily manhandled the trailer to a more salubrious spot some 50 yards away. No one was really hungry for his supper after that.

And so we turned in after a long and disturbing day. I doubt if my youthful team got to sleep very quickly; the realisation of what war was really like, after their happy-go-lucky start from

Maddelena, was being slowly absorbed. Nowadays, after being exposed to such scenes, the public conscience prescribes "counselling", but there was nothing like that available in December 1941.

I lay awake for a while on my camp bed in the open beside Brünhilde, looking up at the deep-blue sky studded with very bright stars and watching the sparkle of little lights away to the north-west where the AA defences of Tobruk, 30 miles off, were dealing with a night bombing attack. I remember the guard coming to tell me that a wrecked carrier, just visible in the gloom, contained two dead bodies, and giving him instructions to call me if the wind shifted. But, after that, I think it would have taken a full-scale air raid to rouse me.

A brief reconnaissance in the morning after an early breakfast convinced me that the top of the escarpment was a quite unsuitable place for the deployment of the workshop. It was too confined, too bestrewn with wreckage, too insanitary and much too dangerous on account of the quantities of unexploded ammunition dotted about. So we packed into our transport and motored down the hill again to the flat land below, where we found a place where we could nose our vehicles into the escarpment and spread out a bit.

Here we found a large workshop trailer, abandoned by the retreating Germans, and not yet looted. It was a mobile armourer's shop and must have been brand new, because all the tools were in their proper shelves and drawers, wrapped in greaseproof paper. There was no sign of the towing vehicle among those around, but we examined the very handsome instruction book which was in one of the drawers and deduced that it was customarily towed by an enormous omnibus-like machinery lorry. Since nothing else was big enough to shift it, I supposed the enemy had been forced to leave it behind.

The equipment in it was beautiful and we got permission to abstract anything that was required to make up our own deficiencies, before handing it in to the nearest vehicle park. We had quite a lot of deficiencies, it seemed.

Our stay at Sidi Resegh lasted for between a week and ten days, and I cannot say that we enjoyed it very much. The site was dusty and indescribably insanitary. The weather warmed up and in a couple of days the hygiene problem became so acute that Doc Messent, accompanied by the Padre, commandeered parties from the Btys as burial squads in respirators and anti-gas clothing and buried the dead of both sides decently and deeply. I was told that, several weeks later, when the official burial parties appeared on the scene, they raised hell because we hadn't established properly laid-out and marked cemeteries.

Sidi Resegh was unhealthy for other reasons, too. Unused bombs and grenades lay around in great profusion to be trodden on, and the face of the escarpment, in places, was a maze of trip wires and mines. Booby traps had been left behind in fair quantities by the retreating enemy and the RHQ Sergeant Artificer was blown to pieces by one as he investigated a tent in an abandoned Casualty Clearing Station a little nearer El Adem. It was found later that every tent in this "hospital area" was ingeniously mined. This death cast a shadow over the Workshop, for the sergeant had been a popular member of RHQ, and we made a special little white wooden cross when he was buried in the cemetery in Tobruk.

We lay, as I have said, among the stony wadis at the foot of the escarpment. From here the ground sloped away in a gentle, green, camel thorn-covered depression to the Trigh Capuzzo, about a mile away, and then on up to the low hills of Belhamed and Zaarfran. To our left, we could pick out the little white dome of the sheik's tomb that gave Sidi Resegh its name, and beyond, on the height of El Duda we could faintly see the line of telegraph poles which marked the Tobruk perimeter road. The whole of the valley in front of us was littered, just littered, with wrecked vehicles, probably a couple of thousand, most of them German or Italian. Had we not been so busy and, anyhow, chary of booby traps, it would have been a most entertaining pursuit to have examined them.

However, we were much too busy for such entertainment. Every tradesman in the unit was worked almost to a standstill as the stream of damaged vehicles and guns requiring modifications came in. Just to enliven matters, Estlin, who hadn't troubled us for a week or more, suddenly turned up from Bde

HQ, now somewhere near Bu Amud where the perimeter road branched off from the main coast road which ran straight on into Tobruk. He gave me instructions to collect any enemy AA weapons we could find on the LG, make them work and send them to stiffen up the defences of Tobruk, where they were getting a first-class pasting every night. We could see the "fireworks" from where we were, some 25 miles away.

I had no men to spare for the job, so I borrowed a couple of plain gunners from 261 and scoured the neighbourhood in Brünhilde. We found five in all, 20mm Bredas, and I stripped them, with my unskilled knowledge and the help of the equally unskilled gunners, made sure they worked and towed them back to the workshops one by one behind Brünhilde. I cannot say I knew very much about how they worked before I started, but I did by the time I finished. I had them taken into Tobruk and I hope the Garrison found them useful.

Before we had been a couple of days at Sidi Resegh, some driver reported that right opposite us on the Trigh, only about 1000 yards away, there was a large covered Italian lorry with water tanks inside. Dean and I went out to investigate and found a big shot-up Lancia with two 1200-litre tanks in the back. One of them was holed and empty, but the other was nearly full. The lorry had all its wheels intact, but its brakes seemed to be locked solid and it was quite immovable. We retired to the workshop for a huddle as to what to do about it.

While we were discussing how we could bring it in, we observed one of the RHQ 15cwts stop by our prize and investigate it. This incensed Dean and he rounded up the nearest ten men and disappeared in the recovery lorry and a cloud of dust.

Bringing in the Italian monster caused a great deal of sweat, toil and tears, if not much blood. To get the thing to move at all, they sawed through the brake rods and, since it was too heavy to tow, began to winch it back in 100-foot stages. This took a long time and it was quite dark when they got it back, but it was worth it. After filling our own tank to the brim, the water worked out at a ration of something like six gallons per man and, after the self-imposed short commons of the past few weeks, it was like the answer to a prayer. I, for one, got out my

136

canvas bath and "blued" five gallons straight away; there may be pleasanter ways of getting clean than crouching in four inches of cold water in the open at 8 p.m. on a December night, but really I don't know when I have enjoyed a bath more.

Most of the lads were doing the same thing and morale rose to unprecedented heights. RHQ, the following morning passed somewhat snooty remarks about lack of public spirit, but we couldn't have cared less.

On the second day of our stay, Thorne turned up with the rear party of 261. Apparently, he had arrived back at Maddelena only a few hours after we had left; he had found our note and had then to wait, fuming at the delay, until the RA party moved. I was glad to be up to strength once more, both in men and vehicles.

As soon as the first inrush of work had abated somewhat, the lads were complaining that they hadn't received any home mail for over a month, since leaving Sidi Barrani, in fact, so I took a trip into Tobruk in the ration lorry, to see if I could raise any information about what was happening to it.

The route led circumspectly across the shell-torn valley and up the gentle rise of El Duda, between serried ranks of burnt-out British tanks, little green German bivouacs and broken Italian guns. All around, the ground was churned to dust by tank tracks, and it was obvious that a fairly sizeable armoured battle had taken place here, probably during the short-lived initial link-up with the Tobruk Garrison. Although any number of British tanks were to be seen, I could pick out only about two or three German ones, and they were very badly smashed. The reason for this, we came to learn later, was partly because the heavier guns of the German Mk III and Mk IV tanks greatly outranged the 2-pdr pea-shooters of the Crusaders with which our armoured forces were equipped, and partly because the Germans remained in command of the battlefield afterwards, thus enabling their very efficient recovery service to clear away all the moveable casualties for repairs.

On the top of El Duda ran the perimeter road, the "Achsen-strasse", or "Axis Highway" to give the English translation of its German name, and called locally "The Tobruk Bypass". Before the war this road didn't exist. The main Italian coast road had run straight from Bardia down into Tobruk and then on up to Derna. This part of the world was then undeveloped desert, served only by a minor road running out from Tobruk to the Italian airfield at El Adem. However, when the Axis forces had been obliged to bypass Tobruk in the spring, it had been necessary to build this road, skirting the Tobruk defences, just out of artillery range, to maintain communication between the eastern and western portions of Cyrenaica. Like the road from Sidi Barrani to Sollum, it had been built by the Italians and, for much the same reason, it had never been finished and lacked its final surface, since our advance had interrupted their programme.

Notwithstanding this lack of a final surface, it was paradise after our desert wanderings and the Bedford 15cwt bowled down it at a good speed. This road had also been somewhat shot up and the burnt-out tanks were fairly evenly mixed with shattered German and Italian lorries. At one point, too, we passed three large German siege guns and their limbers, brought there for the aborted attack on the Fortress and at another a very dead mule, lying on its back with its four legs sticking vertically into the air and blown up like a large balloon. Everywhere along the road were scenes of great activity; dressing stations set up; supply depots inaugurated; petrol dumps formed; and the whole process of transforming the place into a forward base well under way.

We drew out of the battle area and came to El Adem, once a prosperous civilian airfield before the war. Now it had been reduced by successive bombing attacks, first British, then German, and then British again, into a waste of shattered concrete and twisted steelwork, covering several acres.

The Axis Highway went straight on at this point towards Acroma and Gazala – both still under enemy occupation – but opposite the entrance to the airfield the spur road to Tobruk turned off to the right and we went down it. Very shortly, we came to the perimeter defences: tangled and indeterminate mazes of barbed wire, dugouts, breastworks, rifle pits, field gun emplacements and minefields, all the typical signs of trench warfare.

Since the ground here was so flat, it was difficult to see where the German lines ended and the British lines began, and I was left with a certain lingering surprise that it had been possible for so long to hold this featureless plain against any sustained attack. Away behind the lines on both sides, and presumably beyond local mortar range, tall mast-like structures had been erected, bearing observation posts at the top like crows' nests. So flat was the ground, that the observer in one of these OPs must have had a view stretching for miles on a clear day. It was a depressing view to have to survey – a dreary desolation of shell-turned earth studded with smashed vehicles.

It was only as we approached Tobruk itself that we realised that, unlike the country around Sidi Barrani and Ras Hawala, the immediate hinterland was several hundred feet above sea level, for Tobruk lay in a hollow. The road from El Adem descended in three steps, the last two near the coast and at the top of the middle step, the old coast road from Bardia came in from the right and then dropped down two steep winding hills in succession, losing several hundred feet in a mile or so. The actual town of Tobruk lay on a whalebacked promontory between the open sea and a harbour that was really a long flooded valley running westwards into the rising ground.

From the top of the escarpment, the valley floor seemed to be speckled with black dots amid a gentle haze of shifting sand and the dust kicked up by moving vehicles. We drove down a series of steep-sided chines, resembling gaps between slag heaps and about as desolate, and on coming out on the valley floor I saw that these "specks" had been vehicles and bits of vehicles; casualties of the siege. They were mainly Italian and they stood or lay, rusty and derelict, half-buried in the sand and stripped of anything useful which might have served to keep on the road others of Tobruk's fast-dwindling stock of transport. All around, the ground was littered with refuse and wreckage, all eaten away with rust and getting covered with the gently blowing and running sand.

The little town stood out against this sordid background as a

139

white haven, looking remarkably undamaged, considering what it had been through, and at the foot of the hill stood the Tobruk cemetery, the only thing within the whole perimeter that seemed clean and properly cared for. Each grave had some form of rough white cross or headstone and was outlined in whitewashed petrol tins.

At first sight, the harbour appeared to be full of shipping, but, on closer inspection, it was clear that most of the vessels were sitting on the bottom with only their upper works above the surface. On the side of the harbour facing the town, two fair-sized wrecks of cargo ships were burnt out and beached, while opposite them were the remains of the Italian cruiser *San Giorgio*, half-submerged and on its side in the mud. All around the blue unrippled surface of the harbour projected the masts and funnels of invisible ships. Navigation into and out of the harbour must have been a tricky business, considering that for a matter of several months all traffic to Tobruk had been exclusively at night, but somehow it had been managed.

We drove across the valley to the Derna Road and turned right at a T-junction, where a military policeman was controlling the traffic from the top of what looked like a tank turret. Opposite him were two relatively undamaged white buildings, labelled respectively "Hamburger Joe's" and "Hotel Ack Ack – WAAFs, WRENs, ATS and WASAs welcomed".

The major portion of the town stood on a bluff overlooking the harbour and we drove up a double hairpin, past the "Scoula Benito Mussolini" (which had been flattened by a direct hit of something heavy) and into the main square. Compared with Matruh, Tobruk seemed relatively undamaged; most of the buildings still had their roofs on and it looked as if some civilians were still living in them. At one side of the piazza was a beautiful little cathedral, quite untouched – at that time, that was; some months later it was severely damaged when a bomb-loaded Stuka was shot down on to it.

There was some tremendous bustle and activity all around. The Eighth Army was in the process of taking over from the erstwhile Tobruk Garrison, who were reforming and concentrating prior to being withdrawn to the Delta. All except the Polish

Carpathian Bde, that is. These doughty warriors had but one object in life, namely to kill as many Germans as possible; relief with the rest of the Garrison would have seriously interfered with this work and, in fact, a lot of potentially productive time was already being wasted, now that the battle front had swept on beyond Tobruk. Having been brought in by sea, they had insufficient transport to keep up with it. This sad, but temporary, deficiency was being alleviated slowly by issues from the Advanced Vehicle Parks, but not quickly enough for the Poles. We were warned to keep a fully armed guard on any stationary truck in the town, as otherwise it would have certainly been "nicked".

The Army Post Office knew nothing of any mail for us, nor, for that matter, for most of the thousands of Eighth Army troops that were pouring in, but were coping manfully. They told us, however, that 13 Corps had taken Acroma that morning and the Germans had fallen back to positions at Gazala, 20 miles or so further west. So much for my first visit to Tobruk. I was to get much better acquainted with it before another few months were out.

Sidi Resegh was now being cleaned up. Burial squads arrived, together with ammunition disposal parties and recovery detachments to remove or destroy the tank casualties. When we first arrived, in the words of Padre Gilchrist, 'The battlefield wasn't quite cold yet'. Now it was being thoroughly cleaned up; proper cemeteries were laid out and some, at least, of the miscellaneous ammunition which lay scattered dangerously about was collected into piles. The non-British material was detonated in thunderous explosions that brought the loose stones sliding down the screes for hundreds of yards around.

We had now got on top of the worst of the work that had faced us on our arrival and Tony Overton, the Signals Officer, came over for advice and help. His problem was that his section was required to lay thousands of yards of signals cable on arrival at each site and to collect it up again whenever we moved; since such wire was always in short supply, it was unacceptable to leave it as it was on the ground, and this meant that it had to be collected undamaged against time by an overworked squad of linesmen after the departing host had gone, and then rushed frantically to meet them at the other end. The task was made more complicated by the manner in which other signals lines had been laid haphazardly over them in profusion.

Laying the wire was easy. A drum was mounted on a horizontal spindle in the back of a 15cwt truck and the wire was pulled off the free-turning drum by the friction of the ground as the truck motored at speed from A to B. For reclaiming laid wire, the textbook method was for the truck to follow the line, while a little man walked in front with a sort of pitchfork, guiding the wire off the ground, away from the truck's wheels and on to a drum in the truck wound by a couple of sweating signalmen turning a handle. To keep in step with the drum turning and the pacing of the pitchfork man, who had to unravel any knitting of overlaid wires, meant that the truck had to proceed at a veritable crawl.

I called in Dean and the three of us went into a huddle from which the Great Idea resulted, which was subsequently copied throughout the Bde Signals and beyond. Each Signals Section was equipped with two small cable rewinding sets, consisting of a drum and spindle driven by a $1\frac{1}{2}$HP petrol engine; these were intended for use in reeling cable from one larger drum on to another when stationary. We mounted each of these sets in the back of a 15cwt truck and the wire being picked up was threaded on to the drum through two guide eyes, one on a triangular strut standing up from the front bumper and the other on the cab roof. Once the cable had been threaded through these and on to the drum, all the driver had to do was to drive at speed down the line of the wire whilst a man in the back kept the drum running fast enough to wind in the wire and keep it taut. Any "overlaid wires" were scooped up by the rising "own wire" and flipped back over the truck's roof. We modified all the Sigs trucks like this so that any of them could be used with the powered winder sets.

Dean attended the acceptance trials and reported soberly that it worked like a dream but looked highly dangerous. The man in the back had to keep his head down as the truck drove along at 35mph and any "overlaid" wires whipped by as the truck went underneath them, nearly decapitating the drum operator. Overton's delight at the easing of his task knew no bounds and our stock stood very high in Signals circles. From then on, we were provided with two telephones, one for the office and a private one for me in my tent.

We also, at RHQ's request, transferred their 250-gallon water tank from its 15cwt truck on to another 15cwt, which seemed more reliable. As things turned out, this was just as well.

Then our old friend "Benforce" suddenly resurfaced and we were under orders to be prepared to move again. The Germans were expected to be able to hold out for quite a time in the Gazala position and "Benforce Mark 2" involved 22 Guards Bde making a left hook round them and fighter airstrips being set up far down in the Solluch area to the south of Bengasi, on the enemy lines of communication. With the Guards Bde were going an immense force of assorted auxiliary troops, an RAF advanced ground party and appropriate AA defences. The latter was to be commanded by – guess who? – 2 LAA Regt HQ and serviced by 2 LAA Wksps.

By the evening of 18 December every detail had been laid on and we were all set to move off at dawn on the following morning. We would rendezvous, for the first night, at a place in the desert to the south-west of El Adem, which we would reach by travelling along the Trigh Capuzzo to a cross-tracks – later to become better known and infamous as "Knightsbridge" – from which we were to turn left into the desert to Bir Hacheim. Here we would receive the final details for the dash across the Cyrenaica "bulge".

One sad preliminary to the move was the loss of our captured German transport, since all units, to conserve fuel, were limited to their bare scale of vehicles. We hung on to the newly acquired German Ford car, which we hadn't declared officially, but we had to part with Brünhilde and the Breadwagon. We offered the latter to RHQ as a mobile office lorry, for which they had a vacancy and for which the Breadwagon's closed body seemed ideal, but they had already acquired another, similar Opel with which they were satisfied and our offer was turned down. As it

143

happened, this was just as well, but we weren't to know that at the time either, and we saw our two vehicles off into the Returned Vehicle Park in Tobruk with such sorrow that we failed to notice that the Breadwagon's engine sounded a trifle woolly.

We packed up in the gathering dusk, fixed up the proposed convoy routine for the next day and retired to bed somewhat weighed down by the importance of the morrow's implications. After all, as Claud Phillimore put it, we were setting off into the unknown on a very serious undertaking, which, to say the least, was likely to involve some risk.

7

We were up before dawn the following morning, and after a hurried cup of hot tea and some boiled tinned bacon on biscuits – we had been issued with hard rations for the next few days in advance – I motored off up to RHQ for our final instructions for the move.

RHQ seemed to be in a strange state of suspended animation, all packed up but showing no sign of moving off. Everyone was looking unhappily at one another in hushed silence and the impression given was that of a sudden death in the house. This was correct, I soon found out – Benforce Mk 2 had passed peacefully away that morning! Phillimore told me that the operation had been cancelled without prior warning in the small hours and Col Helby had gone across to Bde HQ at Bu Amud to look for fresh orders. It would seem from a telephone conversation he had had with the Bde Intelligence Officer that the front had suddenly broken up the previous evening and the Germans had retired from the Gazala position and appeared to be in full retreat across the Cyrenaica "bulge", rendering the Benforce attempt too late to cut them off. The war in the desert had opened up in a big way and there was no saying what might happen now.

Everyone at RHQ was feeling very much in a "we-must-go-somewhere-now-we've-taken-the-trouble-to-pack-right-up" mood. No one fancied the anticlimax of having to unpack again at Sidi Resegh. That would be just too much. Doc Messent remarked apprehensively that, unless they were away by 9.30 a.m., he supposed he would have to hold his morning sick parade as usual!

145

The Workshop took the news philosophically and, as I might have expected, another brew of tea appeared from somewhere.

However, halfway through the morning, an urgent summons for me came down from RHQ on the plateau, and I arrived to find the whole party moving off. We had been ordered to move forward forthwith to El Mechili, an airstrip in the desert somewhere in the hinterland of the "bulge", which the RAF had picked as the next fighter base, and we were expected to rendezvous by that evening at a map reference, Bir Halegh el Eleba, somewhere between Mechili and the coast. Since Eleba was anything up to 100 miles away from Sidi Resegh, the chance of our getting there before nightfall seemed to me to be pretty remote.

Such news was, however, momentous. It could only mean that the enemy was pulling right out of western Cyrenaica and going back to the coast beyond Bengasi. Such indeed proved to be the case; and, if I may be pardoned for digressing again, these events only went to support the theory that the Cyrenaica "bulge" was not really defensible. A defensive line of sorts could be held on the eastern side at Gazala, but if an attacking force were to penetrate these defences, the next defensive position was at the western end of the "bulge" in the El Agheila-Marada salt marshes, after a retreat right across Cyrenaica, and the attacking forces would need to penetrate these marshes if they wished to proceed further. Similarly, any force defending Cyrenaica from attack from the west must seize and hold the Agheila marshes or retreat to Gazala, at least. This had been the problem for the WDF in the winter of 1941.

But back to Sidi Resegh. We were instructed to bring up the rear of the regimental column, behind 82 LAA Bty, who were, even now, moving towards the escarpment at the western end of the LG. I wasn't too sanguine about finding Bir Halegh el Eleba from the directions provided, so I decided it would be desirable to stick to the rear of 82 like a leech and we charged off along the foot of the escarpment, to catch them as they descended from it to cross the valley toward the perimeter road.

The scene here was just plain chaos. Practically the entire Sidi

146

Resegh ground staff must have moved off within half an hour, and a solid column, two or three vehicles abreast, was roaring across the valley and up the El Duda slope to the road, AA and RAF ground staff intermixed. As this horde struck the road, it was joined by a fair amount of traffic already proceeding west and the congestion was terrific, but eventually it seemed to sort itself out. Things weren't helped by the fact that most units seemed to have three or four illegal captured vehicles over and above their establishment, whilst every other man in the RAF had now a private BMW motorcycle, which he rode with great verve until it broke down or crashed, and he was forced to abandon it. The roadside to Mechili became littered with derelict BMWs and dismounted RAF "erks" trying to thumb a lift.

Everyone was now acclimatised to the pious hope of covering the 100-odd miles between mid-morning and nightfall and the chaos increased, if that were possible. Unlike most traffic queues which proceed at a snail's pace, this lunatic procession stormed along at the startlingly dangerous speed of 30–35 mph. Well disciplined units like 82 Bty and ourselves endeavoured to keep our official convoy speed and vehicle interval, but wave after wave of RAF beat over and around us, until we were caught up in the mob and, for sheer safety's sake, conformed to the average speed. As the road was wide enough for only two vehicles abreast, the disintegrating surface of the verge kicked up into clouds of thick grey dust, and there was a constant fast-moving stream of returning RASC lorries coming in the opposite direction, so overtaking by anyone was something to be discouraged.

In the general melee, we lost contact with 82 Bty and I adopted the practice of drawing off the road every ten miles or so to allow my own stragglers to catch up. If we couldn't travel as part of the RA column, it seemed only sensible to make sure that we were, at least, undivided amongst ourselves.

It was a marvel that the Germans didn't make any attempt to bomb or strafe this 40-mile-long moving traffic jam on the Derna road. One or two well placed bombs would have brought it all to a dead halt and made a sitting target of it. We were not to

147

know that the day of the Luftwaffe's air supremacy over the desert had temporarily ended and that, from now on, although we were to see quite a lot of enemy aircraft, they were never really seriously to bother us during this advance.

From El Adem the perimeter road swept round in a northerly direction to Acroma, where the Trigh Bir Hacheim branched off to the left. Just beyond El Adem there was quite a steep little hill and then it was open, downland country devoid of any vegetation and rising steadily to the northern "step" near Acroma, where the road dropped over the edge of the escarpment to the coastal plain.

Between El Adem and Acroma, there didn't seem to have been much recent fighting and the only signs of the departed enemy were neatly painted little signboards pointing off the road towards the former site of this or that German HQ or base installation.

Just short of the Acroma escarpment, someone ran forward, violently waving us off the road. It was Gunner Beale, Col Helby's driver, and behind him on the verge was the Colonel's staff car, empty and stationary. I waved the column on, under the leadership of Sgt Hughes in the second vehicle, shouting to him to stop after about another five miles and wait for me, and pulled off, followed by Spooner. Shortly afterwards S/Sgt Dean with the recovery joined us from the tail of the column as it passed. Beale told us that the car had broken a rear spring and the Colonel had left it behind for us to deal with. Beale unwisely suggested a rear-suspended tow.

Spooner quelled him with The Warrant Officer's Look and opened the boot, to find, as we had surmised, a perfect mountain of kit. This we chucked out on to the ground, amid feeble protests from the unhappy Beale, and the rear of the car rose visibly about four inches, so that the rear mudguard ceased to rest on the tyre and the car became reasonably driveable. Dean produced a length of signal wire and threaded through the rear shackles, tying them together to prevent the spring spreading out any further. As an extra corrective, he also wedged a block of wood between the axle and the chassis and bound it firmly in place. We stacked the displaced kit in the front seat and on the bonnet. 'Just to keep the rear wheels off the ground, Beale,' Spooner explained. Beale was unwise enough again to murmur about a tow, but we said 'Will we hell!' or words to that effect, placed him in the driving seat, closed his fingers about the steering wheel and bid him drive.

'Now you fall in behind the OC and let's have no more of this waiting for Workshops over trifles,' said Spooner. Definitely not a good day for Gunner Beale.

While this was going on, the rest of my Workshops was presumably heading steadily for Gazala, with only Sgt Hughes in command. So the four vehicles – my Bedford, the Colonel's car, Spooner's German Ford and Dean's recovery, in that order – belted off down the escarpment in pursuit, weaving our dangerous way in and out of the already fast-moving traffic. I had a vivid vignette of the wretched Beale peering unhappily through a breastwork of luggage as he zigzagged after me at anything up to 40mph.

At the foot of the escarpment, the perimeter road met the old coast road from Tobruk and the spot was marked by a large obelisk commemorating some Italian achievement or other; each of its four faces was liberally adorned with bas-relief carvings of bundles of *fasces* and noble-browed, stern-jawed young gentlemen in steel helmets. Some of the brutal and licentious soldiery that had preceded us had added their opinions of it in basic monosyllabic English.

Shortly afterwards we came upon the Workshop drawn off behind 82 LAA Bty, who had stopped for lunch, and Hughes had followed suit. They were in the courtyard of a large single-storey white building that was somewhat the worse for fire. It was one of the modernistic roadhouses which were dotted along the whole length of the Strada Littorianea Libica every 30km or so from Tripoli to Capuzzo, and it had obviously been in use as a field Dressing Station, for it was liberally adorned with red crosses. Opposite was a large cemetery with little wooden crosses in neat rows and one couldn't help feeling that the view from the ward windows was hardly likely to engender much confidence in the medical staff among the wounded within.

When the combined column restarted, we held on to the tail of 82 Bty almost as far as Gazala, where once again we lost them in the melee. This stretch of the road lay through open and undulating country with the sea just visible over to our right, a mile or two away. Just before Gazala, the plateau rises in a couple of steps, to dominate the coastal plain and after some five miles, the road drops down another fantastic hill to the plain. This latest escarpment formed the backbone of the "Gazala Line" of the following spring. The German position at Gazala had been on the two steps facing the road to Tobruk.

On the top of the steps and on the plateau between them and this dreadful hill, had been the LGs from which the German bombers had raided Tobruk, only a few minutes' flying time away, and they had suffered very badly from the great rains of mid-November; the Eighth Army had forced their hurried vacation, with field artillery fire and they presented a dreary picture of desolation and dried mud as far as one could see. All around were wrecked aircraft embedded in the mud and riddled with gunfire, possibly a couple of hundred of them. We learned that the November rains had caught the enemy unprepared, as the storms turned the coastal LGs into quagmires, while our bombers from their airstrips in the rainless desert had stamped them flat on the ground, without a single aircraft being able to take off to oppose them. These wrecks were now being raked off the LGs by clearance parties with tractors and bulldozed off the edge of the escarpment.

And so we came to the top of the great Gazala hill, which marks the boundary between eastern and western Cyrenaica.

Someone, rather later in the campaign, referred to the Eighth Army's frantic advance across the Cyrenaica bulge as a "hunt" and it caught on. Certainly, it was quite an apt description of the way in which for about a week the miscellaneous assortment of troops under General Ritchie's command poured westwards at high speed in pursuit of the swiftly disengaging German and Italian forces. They never quite caught up with the quarry, which managed to keep one skilful jump ahead of their pursuers all the time and finally went to earth in the Agheila salt marshes, with the pack snapping at their heels.

On the Derna road, a few solitary civilians – "Arabs", for lack of a better description – prodded lackadaisically among the wreckage and refuse left behind by the retreating Axis forces and scarcely spared a glance for the roaring traffic stream that surged by only a few yards away. They seemed quite apathetic about the whole business and didn't seem to care that the white soldiers now wore khaki instead of grey or green. Their feet, I noticed, were well shod in new Italian boots and some of them were carrying German rifles.

Although I have just said that the soldiers were clad in khaki, that is an exaggeration; the man fully and correctly dressed in battledress stood out from his companions, who were arrayed in a varied assortment of KD slacks or shorts, battledress blouses, corduroys, brown pullovers, RAF tunics and even a sprinkling of ex-German and Italian uniforms. They were doing this, not, as has been said so many times since, to demonstrate their abhorrence of rules and regulations, but simply to keep warm. The British Army in the MEF was issued with a scale of "tropical kit" each summer and, at a certain date, this was withdrawn and serge battledress substituted. The ordinary soldier was prevented, by reason of weight limitations on his kit, from retaining his battledress during the summer, and the start of the battle had just beaten the date for issue of winter clothing, so the majority of the Army had missed it and was now heading away from Base at a greater speed than the vast stocks of winter clothing following them through the "normal" ordnance channels.

As it gets very cold in the desert in December, one can hardly blame the troops for putting on anything they could scrounge or pick up in order just to keep warm. No warm battledress from the orthodox ordnance channels? Well then, out with the woollen scarves, the welfare pullovers and the rest! The RAF were particularly ill-served by this lack of supply, because, in addition to the troubles just described, they were the victims of a wrangle between GHQ MEF and HQ RAF Middle East as to whose was the responsibility for clothing them at all. All stocks of the official RAF winter "blues" had become exhausted and the RAF was trying to sell the idea to the Army of clothing their

151

charges in battledress to make up the deficiency. Eventually, the Army gave in and khaki was issued to the disgusted "erks" who resented being turned from natty "Brylcream Boys" into rather scruffy "brown jobs".

But back to the Derna road and its curious high-speed population of semi-soldiers and quasi-airmen. At the farther side of the Gazala plateau, at the top of the notorious Gazala hill, stood another of the Italian roadhouses, once white, but now badly smoke-blackened and somewhat lacking in plaster. In its courtyard, did we but know it, was the RHQ 15cwt Morris from which we had recently transferred the water tank. The 15cwt Ford to which we had transferred the tank had originally been used by Doc Messent and the Doc had objected very loudly and bitterly at receiving the other, less reliable, vehicle in exchange.

I was to learn afterwards that, after leaving Sidi Resegh, this Morris had gone steadily downhill mechanically. First the steering had developed half-a-turn of play and the truck was taken on tow. Then the brakes faded out and, after the Morris had run violently into the rear of the towing vehicle a couple of times, it was decided that it was probably safer after all, or at least less absolutely dangerous, if it were driven. Some half a dozen folk had had an attempt at driving it, with potentially frightful carnage, and eventually it was Messent himself who brought it, battered but still just a runner, to the top of Gazala hill. One look at the hill decided him, and his nerve cracked. Swearing frightful medical oaths at Ordnance, Quartermasters, Workshops and Lord Nuffield, he gave the order to abandon ship; the truck was driven into the roadhouse yard, or, more correctly, since it had no brakes, slam into the roadhouse wall; then all its load was distributed among the other two trucks, and the Doc and its crew stormed off with them in pursuit of the rest of RHQ.

Gazala hill descended four or five hundred feet to the coastal plain in less than half a mile. It was narrow, little over two vehicle widths. On the left as we went down, the shoulder of the escarpment rose up almost vertically, and on the other side the ground fell away at the same angle without any retaining wall;

most of the descent was at a gradient of about one in seven and, to complicate matters, the retreating Germans had had a try at blowing the outside of the road away at a point where there was a bit of a tight bend. Just to make things worse, an ex-Italian lorry, full of Poles, had rammed the bank on the "landward" side and turned over exactly opposite the demolition, leaving just enough room for a following vehicle to get by with its wheels resting on the very edge of the precipice. I was extremely glad to see that all my Workshop had got through to the bottom of the hill.

From the bottom, the road ran over a causeway for about half a mile, bordered on either side by some very treacherous-looking salt-marsh, and then wound its way up on the seaward side of a gently rising escarpment bordering it on the left and with the sea on the right, across broken moorland covered with what looked, from a distance, like gorse and brambles. This moorland and the crannies in the escarpment were littered with tented camps, bearing every sign of pillage, probably by the local Arabs. Rags fluttered from every "gorse" bush, and papers and the Army Forms of German and Italian Base-life rose and fell like flocks of birds with every gust of wind. The roadside was littered with broken-down or stalled ex-Italian lorries carrying loads of armed Poles, that had got so far from Tobruk, and Dean, with the recovery crew gained a lot of goodwill by giving them tow starts. Most of them were big diesel-engined Fiats or Lancias which had no self-starters and were set running normally by cranking, through gearing, a giant flywheel in a casing in front of the radiator. It took three men on a long handle to work the flywheel up to speed and, when it was really up to speed, everyone stood back and some brave herb threw in a dog clutch connecting it to the crankshaft. There was then a frightful convulsion and the engine started – if the settings were all right – or, more usually, it didn't and the whole process had to be repeated.

The Poles were immensely pleased and pressed flasks of some Eastern European firewater on the recovery crew as payment; this was wasted on Dean who was a lifelong abstainer, but greatly appreciated by the band of thugs that

153

always seemed to form the recovery crew. Every so often, one of these rejuvenated juggernauts, stuffed with Poles all armed to the teeth and liberally bedecked with red and white flags, would come thundering up from behind and pass us dangerously, the whole mob waving to their saviours and shouting thanks, to disappear in dirty clouds of blue smoke, stones and dust.

Our instructions were to turn off the main road at a rather indeterminate side track, so many kilometre stones beyond Gazala. When we reckoned we must be about there, we came across 82 Bty pulling off the road, with the obvious intention of calling it a day while there was still light enough to have a decent brew-up and a hot meal. I went over to find the Bty Commander and agree where we were to turn off and found that he didn't know either. He said he wasn't going to be such a fool as to press on across uncharted desert in the dark, Colonel or no Colonel, and advised me to do the same. Since the sun was setting, it seemed sensible advice and we pulled off among the gorse-like scrub beside them and to hell with the likes of McKeown.

As we turned in to sleep in the open, we heard the slowly pulsating drone of German aircraft passing overhead, and presently, far away on the horizon, we could see the flicker of AA fire and the sparkle of shell bursts as the nightly raid on Tobruk took place.

Early the following morning, we pulled out in the wake of 82 Bty and turned along what the Bty Commander decided must be the correct track. He afterwards admitted that it wasn't; in fact, after a few miles any semblance of a track disappeared and we were forced to spread out five abreast across virgin desert. However, since we were in about the right place and driving on the right compass bearing for the rendezvous at Bir Halegh el Eleba, it was reckoned that we would make out all right.

It was tough going. The country was undulating and covered with thick camel-thorn, three or four feet high, with here and there an occasional stunted and unhappy-looking tree. Moreover, the ground was criss-crossed with steep-sided small gullies containing stony dry watercourse beds, some of which required a bit of reconnaissance on foot before attempting to cross. Some time later, we found that the Bedford's frame was a trifle bent and we came to the conclusion that it must have occurred when crossing the worst of these wadis.

As we left the coast behind, the country became more open, the camel-thorn thinned out and we came to the gravel belt, with the clay-pans we had known at Gilwakh and Maddelena. In the far distance to the north we could discern the faint shapes of hills: presumably the fertile Jebel Akhdar that filled the nor-thernmost portion of the Cyrenaica bulge.

Round about midday the column halted in the sight of a couple of prominent little hills, which we reckoned must be Bir Halegh el Eleba, and the Bty Commander went off to look for the rendezvous, while the rest brewed up a midday issue of tea, bully, biscuits and jam. After a couple of hours, the Bty Commander returned with the news that we were to follow him on to Mechili and we set out along a track that came in from the right and must have been the one we should have been on in the first place.

As we moved off, the wind rose and the rest of the journey was achieved in a dust storm. Hitherto, these dust storms had always been accompanied by unbearable heat; this one was the reverse. A bitter wind made us glad to wrap ourselves in our greatcoats and huddle down behind whatever cover we could find in the trucks, out of the way of the stinging sheets of grit.

Mechili appeared through the murk and a section of reason-ably flat desert, bounded on all sides by blinding dust clouds, was suggested by Claud Phillimore as the site for the Work-shops. Col Helby's compliments and could we give top priority to his car, which was urgently needed. Since it was now late afternoon, I gave instructions first that everyone should get his bivvy down and dig himself in a bit before starting work.

Soon afterwards, the wind dropped, to reveal that we were six hundred yards from a large group of airstrips on which a lot of aircraft appeared to be completely grounded by the dust. RHQ were some distance off and I motored over to find out what the form was, because all sorts of units we had never heard of were coming in and claiming workshop assistance. Claud admitted

155

that he wasn't very sure either what Batteries he was supposed to be commanding. It seemed that in the turmoil after the break up of Benforce and the substitution of the move to Mechili some bright herbs at Bde HQ had issued two sets of conflicting Operation Orders, with the result that 2 and 25 RHQs were both now at Mechili and each was commanding, on paper at least, the Btys previously commanded by the other before the move. Bde HQ was coming here and all would be clear later.

I then sought out Helby to ascertain how long it might be before the next move took place, to give me time to deal with his car. He reckoned about four days on present information, but it appeared that the RAF were fed up with Mechili already on account of the dust, which must have been why the Germans had made so little use of these LGs. Anyhow, RAF parties were now out looking for some alternative site from which they could see to operate.

That being so, I propounded a scheme that Dean and I had worked out for his car; it involved rebuilding the whole two rear springs with new thicker main and second leaves and forging new clips to accommodate the increased thickness. This would mean having the car out of action for a day and a half while the blacksmith did the work, but it would be a great improvement on the present poor springing. Helby thought that was a good idea and told me to get on with it. We were not likely to move quite as soon as that!

The following morning, Spooner instituted a system to cope with the work that flowed in from all sides. Only the faulty part was to be brought in for repair; the removal and refitting would be done by the Bty fitters concerned, thereby ensuring that the workshop site was not inundated with a mass of vehicles we hadn't the labour to deal with. It also threw back on the Btys the responsibility of ensuring that their transport was ready to run after repairs; we did the skilled work and they did the dirty work of stripping and reassembly.

While we were getting down to this, a couple of one-time German vehicles came careering over from 25 LAA Wksps – sheer joyriding I thought. I hadn't seen anything like them before. They were tiny open-bodied cars with rear engines and

156

minimum equipment; I was told they had been picked up after the German retreat and Volum's men had hung on to them. They were also said to be called the "People's Car" – Volkswagens – which had been designed to be sold to the masses, and these were the military version.

Just after they had gone, Estlin turned up to see how we were getting on and to sort out what we should be doing and to whom. From what he said, Estlin must have been making himself somewhat unpopular with 25 Wksps. Volum had developed measles on the way to Mechili and had been whisked off back to Base in an ambulance. Estlin had just paid them a visit and had found they had about a dozen assorted captured vehicles, including these Volkswagens, about which he had known nothing. Volum must have been pretty successful in keeping them on the other side of the sandhills whenever Estlin had visited him in the past, for there was little of this sort that escaped Estlin's eagle eye. Anyhow, the fat was in the fire and he confiscated the lot, putting his AOME, Wray, in command of 25, until Volum was released from hospital. Wray, one gathered, was now endeavouring to decide what to leave and what to take in the way of stores, now that the unit transport had been about halved. I don't think Volum ever quite forgave Estlin for this.

About a quarter of an hour after he had gone, Spooner came in looking rather perturbed and asking if I knew anything about an imminent move. Gunner Beale, the CO's driver, had just appeared in a great flap to find out if the car was ready yet – which, of course, it wasn't – and had said the Colonel was leaving right away, while the rest of RHQ was packing up preparatory to moving before dark.

I got on the phone to Estlin, to find out that he had just got back. He said it was correct, and that whether I moved with RHQ or later was a matter between them and me. He sounded somewhat peeved and admitted that the decision had been made by Bde that morning, but that no one had condescended to tell him. Once more, I trundled over to RHQ.

They were in a first class flap. It seemed that the RAF had decided overnight to wash their hands of Mechili and were moving forthwith to some dust-free site further west, where they could also be nearer the battle. Phillimore was busy dictating the Regt Operation Order and, until this was finished, was little help. He seemed to think that we should pack up at once and come with them, and it was quite a bit before I could get it across to him that the Colonel had told me only that morning that I had possibly four days at Mechili, and that it would take us eight hours of solid work to clear the shop and be ready to move. Finally, it was agreed that we would start at first light the following morning and come after them, towing anything we couldn't repair in the time. He gave me a copy of his Operation Order and I scrounged two or three copies of a 1:250,000 map of the country between Mechili and El Agheila from McKeown.

The flap was in full swing in the workshop, when I got back, for all the units that had brought work in were now clamouring on the doorstep, howling for it to be returned to them – finished, of course! Spooner had organised a sort of queue and, as each workshop job was finished, some Bty fitter snatched it up and fled home with it, as if the devil himself were at his heels.

To keep the flow of work moving, we served lunch in two shifts and just afterwards Tony Overton's Signals Sgt came in, very worried, to ask if we could do anything about one of their 3-tonners which had just packed up in its transmission. We found that the vehicle would drive all right in any gear in which it could be coaxed to start, but no amount of clutch work could enable the driver to change gear. Dean diagnosed a broken clutch plate, which was very nearly a Base Workshop job, to which it ought to be consigned. The nearest workshop to do the repair was at Tobruk and anyhow there was no means of getting it there, not in this flap situation. So we decided to take it with us and told the sergeant to get it emptied, so that it could be driven in second gear, or, if necessary, towed. Its driver should stay with us. Five minutes after he had gone the other 3-tonners of the Section thundered in and there was a very hectic half-hour as the load was transferred and they groaned off with springs effectively reverse-cambered under the load of four and a half tons.

During the afternoon, as we slogged away to get mobile, the troops and vehicles round the LG gradually melted away until only a bare sprinkling remained. I saw RHQ move off, with some misgiving, because my directions for the next day's trip were sketchy in the extreme. The Bde was to rendezvous at a map reference about 80 miles to the south-west and as the space between there and Mechili on the map was a stretch of virgin whiteness, broken only by some vague dotted lines that might have meant anything from mountains to footpaths, my uneasiness can be understood. In addition, McKeown had told me a rumour that the rendezvous wasn't the final destination but merely the place at which we were to receive final instructions.

Towards evening, the last of the outstanding jobs, Col Helby's car, was completed and the Workshop set about packing up ready to move at dawn in the traditional manner. By now, there was considerable activity on the LG nearest to us and a bulldozer squad was busy lengthening the runway that pointed in our direction. I got chatting to the subaltern in charge of the squad and he told me that the extra run was for the benefit of some Wellingtons that were expected in for refueling some time after dark. Glancing at our encampment, he commented that bomb-loaded Wellingtons needed all the run they could get, especially after dark. The tip seemed a good one and I gave the order to shift our camp forthwith. We straggled several hundred yards from the danger zone, dug ourselves in and settled down to a belated tea. As the meal finished, it began to rain heavily, just to increase our miserable lot.

I can think of few more cheerless sights than the view of the almost deserted Mechili airfield in the gathering dusk, with heavy lowering clouds obscuring the sunset and swathes of fine driving rain stalking across the wilderness. But, like magic, the atmosphere cleared with the advent of the rain and, between the rainstorms, we could see the black foothills of the Jebel Akhdar away to the north.

Before it got really dark that night, who should arrive on foot at the Workshop but Howe-Browne, the Assistant Adjutant. His truck had broken down some five or six miles out much earlier that afternoon and, after all attempts to make it go had failed, he

159

had walked back to Mechili, to find we had moved from our old site. It was only by sheer good fortune that he had found us at all.

So Dean rustled up a crew for the recovery lorry and they went out into the dust to bring the truck in. I cannot say I had much faith in their return that night, but there must be some guardian angel that looks after the fortune of recovery crews, for, well after dark, we heard the familiar sound of the recovery grinding along in low gear and we shone a torch to guide them in. It was still pouring with rain, but a sheet was thrown over the front of the truck and a tired and somewhat blasphemous party set to work on it. I forget what the trouble was, but by 10 p.m. they had set it to rights and it was agreed that H-B would make the rest of the journey as part of the Workshop convoy. This was the result of a bit of acrimonious discussion in which I put my foot down and said he would come under my command and no nonsense about the RA being senior to the RAOC – "Right of the Line" and all that – and, anyhow I as a lieutenant outranked him as mere 2nd Lt. I was getting mildly annoyed by the airs some RA folk were adopting.

H-B had certain further information about our destination, which it appeared was likely to be a spot on the map called Zawiet Msus, some five or ten miles beyond the rendezvous. Msus, as it was more usually called, was on the far side of the blank area on the map, where the topographers had started committing themselves to something a trifle more definite than dotted lines, but H-B added gloomily that the RAF recce parties had reported the map was highly inaccurate. A poor prospect for me on the morrow, with my small-scale maps, tiny celluloid protractor and single compass.

Everyone went to sleep that night under the best shelter he could find from the steady, driving rain. The following day dawned fine and bright, with a clear sky, and the early sun and a brew of hot tea thawed us out somewhat after a most uncomfortable night. The rain seemed to have blown itself out and a clear day promised.

When we came to move, we found that the RHQ truck had gone back on us and again refused to start up. Dean tried towing it round at high speed in an attempt to get it going, but without success; there seemed to be some obscure electrical fault, so, saying harsh things about RHQ vehicle maintenance in general and Bdr Bennett, their motor mechanic, in particular, which must have made his ears tingle away down at Msus, or wherever he had got to, the truck was hitched up behind the machinery lorry and towed. Howe-Browne elected to travel in comfort in the CO's car.

Thus we set out. Our instructions had been to follow the main track which led westwards from the south-west corner of the airfield, but the airfield had been so completely evacuated that this corner wasn't easy to find. We moved in single file, since H-B had heard some talk of scattered minefields, and before we had gone half a mile, it was quite plain it wasn't the right track. The western side of the LG ran on the edge of a low plateau which overlooked lower ground and this was covered by a vast expanse of water, stretching away as far as the eye could see. H-B said it hadn't been there yesterday afternoon and it must be flood water that had collected in the night; this was most disconcerting. So, exercising the full authority of the OC Unit with a 2/Lt, I instructed him to go out and find the right track, and shortly he returned with the news that he had found the correct track somewhat to our right, but that it also seemed to go straight into the lake. Even the spot where he said he had broken down the previous night was submerged.

We appeared to be near the northern end of this lake, so I decided to follow its shores until we came to the track where it emerged on the opposite side, and this we did; we found the track, or at least *a* track, after about a two hours' delay, Once on this track, which seemed to lead in the right direction, we trundled off in a generally south-west direction into the heart of Cyrenaica.

This heart of Cyrenaica was a very odd and unexpected place. We had left behind the dust bowl of Mechili and journeyed all morning through rolling country carpeted with green grass and scattered with shrubs rather like rhododendrons; past lakes and lakelets surrounded by banks of vivid green rushes; over ridges and rock shelves garnished with mosses and lichens through

161

which little streams of water trickled; and over billiard-table-like stretches of white, hard alluvial clay-pans which had once been lakes. The country abounded in wildlife: kites or buzzards sailed overhead, water birds bobbed up and down the meres, and once I was sure I saw a couple of gazelles scurrying in and out of the tall grasses. There were lizards; and hordes of hopping little desert rats everywhere. It was all as unlike the "desert" to which we had become accustomed, as one could imagine. But nowhere was there the slightest sign of the existence of human passage, except for the little track we were following. It all brought it home to me that Africa was a very big place.

About midday we had a distant view of a column of HAA guns on the horizon, going in the same direction as ourselves – to my secret relief – and I sent Howe-Browne off to find out who they were. He reported that it was a troop of 261 Bty, who had started the previous evening by a slightly different track, and that Penn-Symonds, who was in command, was confident that we were going aright. Much cheered, we stopped and brewed up lunch, confident that we could catch up with the HAA column in an hour or two.

That afternoon we were faced with the most shocking piece of country yet struck; we had come out of the fertile grassland into a stretch of rocky terrain which slowed us down to a walking pace. I suppose it was about 15 or 20 miles across, over endless successive transverse ridges and hollows of stony desolate desert, but it took about four hours to get to the other side, during which we saw not a vestige of green. Giant weather-worn boulders lay around in tumbled profusion, while under our wheels stretched a neverending succession of jagged rocks, some the size of footballs. Our track climbed painfully to the top of each ridge, we slithered to the bottom and then essayed the next climb, wondering if we were ever going to come to the end of it.

From time to time we saw other columns going in the same direction, either on our track or on parallel ones. All were crawling along in bottom gear, except an RASC convoy of 10-ton six-wheeled Macks that didn't seem to feel the rocks beneath their giant wheels and rumbled along at their steady governed speed of 20mph, passing 3-tonner and staff car alike with equal ease.

The strain on the steering and suspension of the vehicles that had to drive over this going was severe and it claimed its casualties among the older trucks. We came across one of 274 Bty's old 30-cwt Fordsons, which had broken the ball-joint of its track rod clean off – their fitter sergeant, who had stayed with it, was trying to tie it up with a baulk of wood and some wire. Our arrival was hailed with enthusiasm, and as luck would have it, we had a spare ball-joint readily available in our stores that we were able to throw to them. They were loud in our praises and we left them busily fitting it.

Shortly afterwards, we encountered yet another of 274's Fordsons, and this was a more serious case, for the damage was a snapped steering drop-arm. We hadn't a spare that would fit, but after rummaging beneath the mounds of kit in the stores lorry, we found another drop-arm that was something like what we wanted. Spooner had the machinery lorry sufficiently cleared, so that the turner could work and the socket was enlarged and given nearly the correct taper, so that it could just be tapped on to the tapered drop-arm shaft and the retaining nut tightened up over it. The new drop-arm was shorter than it should have been, but the truck was a runner again, although with an odd steering lock, and the reputation of the Workshops rose even higher in RA circles.

During these repairs, I halted the whole Workshop column, because I was determined not to lose anyone. With such a small unit, the absence of even one truck might impair our ability to do some job and I was determined to arrive at the other end intact but possibly a trifle late, rather than on time but with half of the Section left behind on repair jobs and thus unable to do our proper work. Howe-Browne rather hinted that perhaps we ought to press on and leave Spooner to deal with the casualty, but he was told politely that no one was stopping him if he wanted to push on, although to be careful with Col Helby's car. He remained with us, however, because he had no rations left, for, as I have remarked before, the RHQ system of dishing out vehicle rations left a lot to be desired.

163

Night overtook us as we drew out of the stony country into the undulating gravel-land that we had encountered so many times before in the past few months, and we leaguered down in a small wadi, sheltered by low escarpments. We had very little idea where we were, but I was quite sure that we weren't anywhere near the only track that was marked on the map, which ran due west from Mechili for 50 or 60 miles and then turned south for Msus. All that day we had been heading steadily about south-west and by my calculations, based on speedometer readings and compass checks at intervals throughout the day, we ought to be very close to the only name-place marked on the blank part of the map – Bir el Gerrari.

While supper was being prepared, Spooner and I took the German Ford car, which was still with us, not having been declared at Sidi Resegh, and motored up on to the higher ground beyond us to see if we could espy anything that might be Bir el Gerrari. We couldn't, for it was growing too dark, but on our way back we encountered a broken-down RASC water tanker lorry and we jointly did a Good Samaritan act in putting it to rights. I forget what the trouble was; it was something that any reasonable motor mechanic could have diagnosed, but the RASC men were so delighted that, in return, they presented us with four jerricans full of beautiful clear, sparkling water they had brought all the way from the water pipeline head at Oxford Circus, back in Egypt, – about 20 gallons, that is. They had very little idea of where they were, but said they were on the 7 Armd Div Axis Track, which was supposed to lead to Msus.

Very early, on the following morning, a further quick recce disclosed a large encampment a mile or so further on. Investigation proved this was Main HQ 13 Corps who were spending the night here at Bir el Gerrari – to my relief and satisfaction as a navigator.

This day the going was easier, we bowled along in good style all morning over open, undulating gravel country and after about 40 miles we came up with a concourse of HAA guns dispersed on the horizon. It was 261 Bty who were waiting at the rendezvous for instructions as to where to go from there. I reported to Penn-Symons, and Howe-Browne departed with the CO's car to find RHQ. Eventually, guides arrived to conduct us to Msus, which incidentally proved to be 10–15 miles on and not the six shown on the map!

The LG at Msus was on the highest point of a low plateau, bounded on the north, west and south-west by a wadi about 100 feet deep and some 200 yards wide, quite the biggest I had seen so far. Overlooking the wadi was the rubble ruin of an old fort – Turkish, I was told – and radiating from the LG, shallow wadis ran out like the spokes of a wheel. Well defined tracks ran north-east towards the fertile Jebel Akhdar, west across the wadi to Sceledima, Solluch and Bengasi, and south-west to Antelat, Agedabia and the almost-mythical El Agheila.

Our workshop site was in one of the shallow wadis to the south of the LG, with RHQ on the higher ground just above us. A good deal further down the same wadi were RHQ 25 LAA Regt, and 25 LAA Wksps were on the flat ground beyond again. Bde HQ was somewhere a little way off to the north-east on the other side of the big wadi.

Our arrival at Msus was on the afternoon of 23 December and, as it happened, we were to stay there for some three weeks until the middle of January 1942, a longer time than we had spent anywhere since leaving Sidi Barrani. We weren't to know that, however, and we plunged into the welter of work just as soon as we had partially unpacked, in fear lest the fiasco of Mechili be repeated.

Everyone confidently predicted that we would be moving on before many days were out. We found, on arrival at Msus, that the enemy had already run through and out of Bengasi and were now falling back, rather more slowly in the region between Antelat, some 40 miles away and Ghemines, on the coast south of Bengasi, towards Agedabia. The Germans, in particular, seemed rather more inclined to "bite" a bit when jostled by our advanced elements, who were now in full contact again, but were now so spread out, under strength through casualties and short of supplies and armour, that the original hopes that we might be able to "bounce" the enemy through the Agheila position were fading daily in favour of an alternative plan of a lull until the port of Bengasi was opened up and supplies available for a full-scale attempt to force the Agheila position somewhat later.

I do not think that the supply position was ever fully appreciated by the majority of the folk who watched the desert warfare through the medium of the British newspapers. A glance at the map will serve to clarify the situation. At the end of December 1941 the Eighth Army was deployed on a broad front south of Bengasi, and all its supplies were still coming by "road" from the railhead at Mischeifa in Egypt, as it had done when the battle started. From Mischeifa to Bengasi, as the crow flies, is nearly 300 miles and a great deal more by the winding tracks on which the RASC convoys were obliged to travel. Every tin of food we ate, every gallon of fuel we put into our armour and every round of ammunition that was fired at the enemy had to come to the forward area in RASC lorries across the 300 miles or more of this appalling intervening desert. Later, by almost superhuman efforts of the railway construction companies, the railway was extended some time in January to Capuzzo, where a new railhead was established and, at about the same time, the harbour at Tobruk was cleared sufficiently to allow its use as a supply port. But Bengasi was never properly cleared and the long overland route had to carry up to 90 percent of all supplies.

At Msus, where we were at the sharp end, one could sense how tenuous the link was with our supply bases. For a month or more, we got our barest battle ration of tinned meat or fish, tinned milk, biscuits, tea, margarine and sugar; we didn't actually starve, but we were perpetually hungry, our heavier manual workers began to lose weight and we felt the cold very much. I, for one, got into the habit of saving some of my daily ration of half a dozen biscuits to eat before I went to bed, otherwise I was unable to get to sleep. The whole workshop was rationed, in common with all other units, for petrol, and we had to make do with 15 gallons per day for all purposes. As our machinery lorry generator was running from dawn to dusk and for lack of any other fuel, we were obliged to rely on our petrol cookers for all cooking; this left very little for any other

166

purposes. One thing I insisted upon was that all vehicles must have full tanks at all times.

I was told that over two-thirds of the petrol that set out from the railhead was lost through leakage before it reached the forward area. It is interesting to speculate what would have been the situation had the British Army been equipped with stout containers on the jerrican principle at that stage of the desert war, as they were later, instead of the flimsy "non-returnable" tins that were then the only container available.

We had no mail, no cigarettes, and no drink to cheer us up. It was cold as if we were in a Scottish winter, and a biting wind swept over the bare gravel flats, so that we worked in overcoats and mufflers and snuggled down in our bivouac tents, pitched in the hollows of the wadis, as soon as the day's work was over. Either it rained intermittently in swift stinging showers, or else a Scotch mist covered the sparse camel-thorn with sparkling droplets for the greater part of the day. On several mornings there were patches of white frost in the hollows and odd pans of water round the cookhouse had films of ice on the surface. "Till the sands of the desert grow cold", runs the song, implying eternity. Well, believe me, it does get cold, very cold, in the desert, every year.

Notwithstanding the many discomforts and shortages, the unit remained cheerful and put in some grand work. After some time, there was a slight improvement in our lot, as some NAAFI stores were received at Bengasi and were distributed on a strictly "all share alike" basis, so that everyone got a few bottles of beer and some cigarettes. But still there was no mail.

The authorities were none too happy about the location of the LG at Msus. It was rather up "in the air" on the extreme left flank of the Army, which flank, incidentally, rested on nothing more solid than the wide open spaces of the desert, where a raid carried out with determination by highly mobile light armoured forces could do immense damage to the parked aircraft. The sole defences were a screen of armoured cars which could be easily penetrated, particularly if the raid were mounted at night.

The Germans, at that time, were showing a most regrettable

167

degree of uppishness, too, and were still only about 50 or 60 miles away. So the AADC, Col Helby, received instructions from on high that all units on the perimeter of the Msus LG would forthwith prepare defensive positions, to which they could retire in the event of a raid and collectively hold off the attackers until relief came.

This was all right for relatively underemployed gunners, but we were still working all round the clock. As part of the general scheme we set about digging two large V-shaped trenches, each capable of holding twenty men, on the bluff above the workshops and commanding the approaches to our small wadi. So as to get this extra work in as well as our main workshop activities, we had a cup of tea at crack of dawn, hacked and hewed at the stony ground until breakfast and then continued with the normal work of the day. I turned out with the rest and, with the large number of picks and shovels we had acquired over the past months, we soon had a pair of workable trenches completed. Just to make a good job of it, we decided to build a stone breastwork in front as additional protection, and were doing this quite well, as I thought, when Pte Crane, our motorcyclist, a Manx carter in civilian life, suddenly upped and said that that was no manner of way to build a stone wall. I was considerably surprised and put down my pick; Crane had never been known to say more than two words at a time in the presence of an officer and a giggle ran through the trench. I quelled the incipient laughter with a gesture and said we were always ready to learn something new and would Crane show us how to build a proper wall. Rising to the occasion, Crane divided us up into small squads and set about teaching us how a proper drystone wall was built in the Isle of Man. I gathered that it was the only place in the British Isles where the art of wall building was properly understood. From then on, the squads vied with one another at wall-building and Foreman Crane moved from squad to squad, criticising and instructing. I learned a lot and I doubt if anything short of a 25-pdr shell would have penetrated our finished breastwork.

I recall that when Estlin came round to view our fortifications, he remarked with a smile that, if we did have to use the

168

trenches, we were well placed to pick off RHQ 25 LAA Regt further down the wadi, should they start to retreat without orders. Fortunately, we never had to use them.

Meanwhile, the enemy, possibly because he was intending all the time to do so, and possibly because we just managed to fetch up enough strength to compel him, retired gracefully and, without any undue hurry, into his prepared positions in front of El Agheila. The Army followed him gingerly to the very threshold of the position at Mersa Brega, and came to a halt, too. The quarry had gone to earth, and both sides crouched panting and awaiting reinforcements for their battered forces before taking any further initiative.

It might be reasonable, at this point, to give a few details about this "Agheila position", so as to indicate what we were up against. El Agheila lies on the coast at the southernmost extremity of the Gulf of Sirte and was on the boundary between the Italian provinces of Cyrenaica and Tripolitania. At this point, a vast area of *sabakha* (salt marsh), dried salt-pan and seawater lagoons, stretches inland from the coast for 40 miles or more. This *sabakha* is quite impassable to vehicles and is treacherous in the extreme, for it forms a hard, deceptive crust that will often bear the weight of a man, but will engulf a vehicle. It was traversed by a number of stony ridges, where some substratum rose to the surface, notably at El Agheila on the coast and at Marada some miles inland; south of Marada, it merged with a northward arm that projected from the "Sand Sea" of the northern Sahara. To add to the difficulties facing the 8th Army, there was a wide and indeterminate area of soft sand on the Cyrenaica side of the Marada marshes and a deep and almost impassable wadi, the Wadi Faregh, ran north and south through this sandy area. This sand was also traversed by hard ridges as with the salt marsh, but all the known ridges that were marked on the map were held by the Germans and, although it was suspected there were many more ridgeways not mapped, they were not fully reconnoitred until later. In fact, I think I am right in saying that this mapping was done by the LRDG (Long Range Desert Group) and kindred spirits like Col Stirling's SAS

169

(Special Air Service) the following spring and summer, when the front line was at El Alamein in Egypt.

There was little hope of scooping the enemy out of this bolt-hole without a good deal of preparation, and so the war in the desert quietened down, with our advanced forces lobbing the odd shell into Mersa Brega and the Germans lobbing the odd one back.

8

I do not think we had ever worked so hard as we did during our first couple of weeks at Msus. We thought we had been extended before, but we had known nothing. This was the real thing.

Christmas Day passed almost as another day. Owing to the amount of work, we were unable to have any sort of celebration, even if there had been anything with which to celebrate. Of food we, in common with almost everyone else at Msus, had little but our bare battle rations, and our Christmas fare consisted of a double portion of boiled tinned bacon, for which we would have to go short later, fried sausages and dehydrated potatoes, two tins of sliced apricots (three slices per officer and other rank), fried bully beef in crushed-biscuit batter, biscuits, margarine, a spoonful of jam, and tea. We had thought, as a special treat, to have put on a supper of hot cocoa, with more biscuits and jam, at a camp sing-song, without campfire of course, on account of the blackout regulations, but it came on to rain and we were obliged to retire to our tents and celebrate alone in silence. When I finally went to bed, I swore a solemn oath that, if it was my misfortune to spend another Christmas on Active Service, I would see to it that the lads had as fine a day and as filling a meal as could possibly be devised, even if we had to start saving up in January.

Later that evening, I squelched over to RHQ in the rain to wish them the compliments of the season. Helby had gone over to the RAF for the night and Phillimore, McKeown, Messent and Gilchrist were crouched over a small spirit stove in Claud's tent, trying to boil up a few fruit drops into a sort of cordial with which to drink the last half-bottle of gin their Mess possessed. That and a couple of litres of dark-red wine, optimistically described as Chianti by the Padre – who had been sold it in Bengasi, where he had been trying, without success, to scrounge a few comforts for the troops – was all the liquid cheer available.

The gin and cordial made one small tot for each of us and the "Chianti" had the consistency, taste, and alcoholic effect of black ink. I squelched back to my bivouac in the savage squalls of fine rain, feeling thoroughly low.

But the amount of work to be done didn't allow time for us to feel low-spirited by day. Fortunately the rain stopped after the first two days, although a bitter wind swept across the gravel flats, so that everyone was glad to work in mufflers and greatcoats. It was quite a sight to see Cpl Siddle, our blacksmith, swinging his hammer while wearing greatcoat, balaclava helmet and mittens.

But, *per ardua ad astra*. Little by little, we began to see light at the end of the dark tunnel and the mountain of repairs resulting from the move from Sidi Resegh dwindled. At the end of ten days of solid application, we were about on top of the job and could look around to pick up work that wasn't absolutely essential. I don't know what we would have done without the stocks held in the Bde Stores Section, which was temporarily located, with the Bde Instrument Section and a detachment from 68 HAA Wksps, with 25 LAA Wksps down the wadi.

The orthodox procedures for obtaining stores had completely broken down and, although it was a dreadful crime to strip parts from abandoned vehicles (orders were that they must be evacuated whole to Base for repair), we had to have recourse to it, since there was no other way, in many cases, of keeping our regimental transport on the road. Estlin, who should have enforced the order, chose tactfully to look the other way, if ever he was unfortunate enough to come upon our recovery lorry removing the springs from some abandoned wreck.

'I don't mind what your lads do, within reason,' he said to me, 'as long as they keep decorously out of sight. If you must

172

savage some wreck, don't do it by the highway, where some public-spirited Brigadier can see you and report you to me, because then I would have to take official notice. Tow it away into the desert out of sight first.'

Our biggest job, one we had postponed tackling and of which ultimately we were justly proud, was the Signals 3-tonner which we had towed from Mechili. We stripped the clutch and gearbox down and found, as Dean had forecast, that the cast-iron clutch driving plate had fractured right across. For this there were no spares available nearer than Tobruk and if we were to condemn the vehicle as BLR, there was little chance of Overton getting a replacement for months. So we set about welding the pieces together, on a "kill or cure" basis, little thinking we could do this with the rough and ready methods at our disposal, without distorting the plate. However, our welder, Pte Ingham, managed it and the surface looked pretty true when set up in the lathe. Then Cpl Siddle case-hardened the driving surface in his furnace, as well as he could and again set it up in the lathe. Our lathe hadn't a grinding attachment, but Dean mounted a small grinding wheel on the lathe's tool-carrier and Ingham wound this back and forth by hand for hours across the face of the rotating disc, until he was satisfied it was dead flat and smooth. All was put back into the lorry and Dean gave it a trial. Nothing snapped, so he slammed the vehicle about until we were satisfied that the repair seemed to be standing all he could give it and then gave it back to the marvelling Signals Section. When I last heard of it, the following September, Overton said it was good as ever. Dean purred for days at the thought of this good work.

Another heavy job we had to tackle was the shifting of the complete body and upper works from one Morris LAA tractor to another. One of these tractors had gone out into the desert on a scavenging expedition and had run over a bunch of Italian "Thermos" bombs. These were small devices the size and shape of a small thermos flask which the retreating enemy was wont to scatter over the ground near anything that might be expected to attract our troops. They were detonated by the vibration of a passing vehicle and would often set off neighbouring bombs. In

173

this case, the driver had lost his life, his front-seat mate had been badly wounded, but a third man in the back of the vehicle was unharmed. This man had run several miles for help, but the rescue party was too late to save the life of the driver's mate.

The wreck was towed in to us. The front end was a complete write-off, beyond our powers of repair, but the body was in good shape, and we were asked if it was possible to exchange the body with that of another tractor, shot up some time previously, which had a good front end but was badly damaged from the driver's seat rearwards. The magnitude of the task we were being set can be judged when I say that we had no crane facilities that would lift the complete body from one to the other chassis and we were obliged to jack up both bodies and manoeuvre the two chassis out and in below them. It was a sickening job because, in addition to the technical difficulty, the bonnet and the driver's cab were a mass of torn steelwork and there were pools, literally pools, of congealed blood on the seats and floor.

From time to time, alarms out in the desert made Col Helby keen to use the 3.7" guns in an anti-tank role, like the German 88mm, should such an emergency arise. It was easy to say that, but it would have involved designing and making a special bracket and sight bar for the gun and someone (not us) deciding what sort of forward area sights would be needed. The existing gun had no forward area open sight, so it would have been a major design and construction job and, as soon as Estlin heard of it – which was almost immediately, for Estlin had his ear pretty close to the ground – he prevailed upon the Brigadier to pronounce against it, on the grounds that it would prevent his workshops from carrying out their proper task of First Line repairs. This was, of course, true, but I think in this case Estlin was wrong and subsequent events underlined his error.

We did, however, after considerable discussion with Helby, Claud and the LAA Bty Commanders, devise and produce in great quantities an enlarged and improved pattern of LAA fore-sight which enabled the guns to take on low-flying, high-speed aircraft, moving at speeds considerably in excess of that per-mitted by the standard sight, which was designed some ten years earlier, when the ME 109F was still on the drawing board. Our modification took the form of a large oblong frame which bolted on the existing sight-bar and was fitted with two extra vertical sighting wires on each side. This enabled an incredible amount of "aim-off" to be used, and the Btys were delighted with their performance. We knocked them up out of thin, square-section steel rods which we had picked up in great quantities from the nut-and-bolt lorry we had discovered back near Bir Sheferzen, months ago. Helby was very pleased and put the design up to AAHQ MEF as a proposed modification. Subsequently, it was adopted as the standard Middle East forward area sight and was manufactured in great numbers at Base Workshops to exactly the dimensions of our prototypes. It is an interesting thought that, had we not found this nut-and-bolt lorry, this standard ME sight might have had quite different dimensions. I never got much credit for my part in it from Higher Authority, but Helby was very bucked with us and sang the praises of "*his workshop's* cleverness" to other COs.

As the New Year came in, it brought with it rumours of big changes among the troops in the forward area. 7 Armd Div was being pulled out, lock, stock and barrel, for rest and refit, and its place was being taken by a completely new armoured formation, 1 Armd Div, recently arrived in the ME from England. 1 Armd Div had had battle experience already – of a sort – with the BEF in France in 1940 and whispers went round of the wonderful completeness of their arms and equipment. Certain old stagers were heard to recall the situation at the same stage of the previous campaign, when, having reached El Agheila, 7 Armd Div was withdrawn in the same manner as now and replaced by 2 Armd Div, just before the first assault by the newly arrived Afrika Korps. These comments were dubbed "partisan" and pessimistic. 'You won't get that sort of thing happening, or being allowed to happen, twice,' said the "experts". 'There's no Greek campaign to divert our troops this time.'

From time to time, columns of sturdy new vehicles rolled through and past Msus, all bearing the Divisional badge of a white rhinoceros on a black oval background. Many lorries, many guns, many tanks on transporters, and the dust columns rolled wide across the desert in their wake, as they passed towards Antelat, Agedabia and the enemy.

They passed out of our ken, it is true, but from the desert to our front came back little uncoordinated whispers of whole convoys of lorries getting lost through bad map-reading, field batteries completing their basic training on the ground, tanks getting hopelessly bogged down in soft "going" and steadily a small cloud of doubt and disquiet, "the size of a man's hand", hung over the southern horizon.

7 Armd Div began to flow back through us, a battered, weary, but highly cheerful crowd in battered and worn-out vehicles, their blackened brew-cans dangling from the undersides of the chassis, all heading hopefully towards the Delta and its Base camps, its fleshpots and its prospects of leave.

On 13 January, an unlucky portent, we packed up and moved down to Antelat. The RAF had found Msus was too far from the forward area for their fighters to have much of an operating range and had decided to move the extra 40 miles or so to get nearer the action. We were told that the airstrip at Antelat was still a bit too far away to be ideal and that our stay there would be only temporary, until a new airstrip was opened up at a place called Belandah – "Belinda" to the troops – some 40 miles further on still and inland from Agedabia. Belandah was only about 50 miles from El Agheila, so this looked pretty encouraging, since the RAF was well known for its objections to exposing its ground staffs so far forward, if the Germans were to show any signs of getting tough.

Our unit's move to Antelat was even more ill-starred than the unlucky date merited. A party under Sgt Hughes had been to Bengasi some days previously in an attempt to raise some NAAFI supplies. In this they had been unsuccessful, but they had come back with a large quantity of tinned Italian food, with which we had thankfully eked out the "bully and biscuits" of our battle rations. We had finished the last tins the night before and – alas – we found that one of the tins must have been "blown". Many of us suffered the most unfortunate internal disorders during the night and, after a highly disorganised and tardy departure, during which numerous members had virtually to be torn from the latrines, we proceeded to our destination in bad order, with vehicles dropping out periodically as the internal needs of their crews demanded.

The desert between Msus and Antelat was stony and camel-thorn covered, seamed with numerous cross-tracks, but I followed a broad and well defined one, marked out with barrels by 7 Armd Div. This track kept to the higher ground of a long ridge and we eventually arrived at another of the old and totally ruined Turkish forts on a bit of a bluff overlooking a broad plain. This was the Antelat fort which had been our destination and the airstrips were down on the flat below. Accordingly, we left the main track, which went on towards Agedabia, and descended to the plain, where we found RHQ already ensconced on a broad stretch of clay-pan between the fort and the airstrip.

Claud said that the rest of the clay-pan was ours and advised us to make good use of the soft soil to dig ourselves in. He said that the enemy had taken a delivery of the new ME 109F fighter and, since Antelat LG seemed to be their main target, it was a good thing never to be far from a slit trench at any time. Accordingly, we spread out beyond RHQ on the flat and properly dug our bivouacs into the ground.

He was right about the 109Fs. Three or four times daily there would be a warning shot from one of the HAA guns and everyone would leap for the nearest cover. LAA guns would open up on all sides and sweep the approaches to the LG, fighters would scramble into the air in all directions and a rattle of small-arms and LMG fire would crescendo. Somewhere in the midst of this Mad Hatter's tea party, two or three slim 109Fs would weave their way at nought feet across the LG, shooting at anything that crossed their line of sight. Thirty seconds of hell let loose and then they would be gone, ineffectively pursued by the slower Hurricane and Kittyhawk fighters, leaving a few burning vehicles in their wake. Once they shot down one of our Hurricanes returning from a patrol, just as it was coming in to land, and it crashed in flames, but we never heard of a 109F being seriously hit. All this was rather wearing and it definitely interfered with our work.

177

The first two or three days at Antelat were distinguished by the arrival of mail in great quantities – the first we had received since leaving Sidi Barrani over two months before. Every man had a dozen or more letters and morale rose to fantastic heights.

We also had the laugh on Doc Messent. It was the custom to supplement the meagre official ration of "safe" water with any other water we could find; this latter, if pronounced unsuitable for drinking, could be used for washing. Consequently, at every new camp site, we and others put out scouting parties for "birs" (rock cisterns), and similar local natural or artificial sources of water. At this time of the year, after the autumn rains, there was usually a fair quantity of water in them. On this occasion we and one of the Btys each found a rock cistern and, according to regulations, took a sample to Messent for analysis. The Doc approved the Bty's sample but threw ours out with contumely as unsuitable for any sort of human use on account of "animal life". To everyone's joy, it was later found that both samples had been taken from the same source within half an hour of each other and Messent had his leg pulled for days.

There were no definite rumours as to when we might expect to move on, although Claud remarked disconsolately that he had been issued with maps of the country around Marada, well to the south of El Agheila, and he feared the worst! However, it was obvious that something was in the wind and folk began to talk optimistically about "Tripoli by Easter". But there looked an awful lot of desert between us and Tripoli on the map. And then it began to rain...

It started with a downpour of almost tropical intensity just after lunch one afternoon and it lasted for about an hour and a quarter. In that short space of time something like three or four inches of rain must have fallen and its result was startling in its immediate effect and its dire potentialities. I have said that we were encamped on a flat clay-pan and so was everyone else on the surrounding plain. Under the influence of the heavy rain, this beautiful hard-packed surface went soft under our eyes and under our very feet. I happened to be in the office trailer when the storm broke and was forced to remain marooned there until it was over. In full view before me, the stores lorry, about a hundred yards away, began to sink slowly at the rear, or heavy end, as though performing a curtsey, until it came to rest with its tall-board nearly touching the ground. Further afield, the other Karrier 3-tonner tilted slightly and went down by the head, until it had the semblance of resting on one knee. It was ludicrously fantastic and there was nothing one could do except watch impotently.

When the rain stopped and a fitful sun broke through the scudding clouds, we came out from our various shelters to view the scene of damage. The plain was a waste of vast pools of water, from which rose gauntly tents, vehicles and aircraft like small islands. Around them milled a sodden throng trying to salvage their personal belongings or unit equipment from the morass. And over them a Kittyhawk fighter from some Australian squadron belatedly sailed in to land, all unwitting, touched down on the mud and came to rest violently on its nose in the glutinous mess with its tail helplessly vertical in the air.

My first thought, as was that of almost everyone on the site, was for my tent and I splashed over to it, only to be appalled with what I found. Like everyone else, I had made a good job of digging in to the soft ground and the hole was now two feet deep in water in which my bed was floating and my steel trunk was submerged. Frantically, I dragged them out with the help of Thorne who happened to be nearby and dumped them in my 15cwt Bedford, where, if not dry, they would at least be out of the water. Then I collected Spooner, who had been doing the same thing, and we made a tour of the Workshop to assess the situation.

Even the most casual observation confirmed that the present site was useless. Some parts of it were not so bad as others, but probably as the surface water drained away they might go soft for about two feet down. We had to move to harder ground while it was possible to do so. Spooner's four-wheel-drive German Ford was at hand, so we piled into it and skated off over the mud, looking for a place from which the water was draining

179

away and we could judge whether it had possibilities of a hard surface.

About 400 yards away, we came upon a slightly raised plateau of rock and stone big enough to house the whole unit; we wouldn't be able to dig ourselves in deeply, it was true, but at least there would be solid ground under our feet and wheels. As daylight was now fading, we decided to use the remaining couple of hours to pack up and get somewhat organised, ready to move over to the new site first thing in the morning.

Back at the site, something like chaos reigned and it was several hours, rather than two, before we had sorted out all the equipment on to the lorries and winched these out of the worst of the mud. Matters weren't improved by a little Dingo scout car from some 1 Armd Div unit which blundered into our midst and promptly got bogged. We got it out several times, using the winch on our recovery lorry, and each time the driver, who had as much idea of driving in mud as of flying, would move a few yards and then bog himself down again. Finally it was decided to leave it for the night and the other occupant, an RAMC Captain, confidently asserting he could find the unit he was bound for up by Antelat Fort two miles away, set off on foot, leaving his driver and the vehicle to follow in the morning. I tried to dissuade him from such a foolish step, for he had no compass and there were no stars on this pitch-black night to guide him, but he knew better and splashed off into the darkness. I often wondered whether he reached his objective before dawn, or if he got there at all.

Our cooks responded nobly to the difficult conditions and, after a scratch hot meal and some even hotter tea, we turned in uneasily on any coign of vantage we could find. Notwithstanding the hardness of the boards in the back of my 15cwt and my wet bedclothes, I for one slept very well.

Moving to our new site and setting up took most of the following morning before we were fully operative. Almost all the vehicles had to be winched out of the embedding mud again, but it was done at last and I was glad to see them all on hard standing. After that, we resumed the task of keeping the Regt mobile.

180

In spite of the chaos caused by the rain, the business of the war went on. 1 Armd Div had come up into the desert without a Div LAA Regt and so 25 LAA Regt was detached from 12 AA Bde and transferred to them, lock, stock and barrel. As only 81 and 82 Btys of their original complement were at Antelat, our old friends 274 (NH) Bty were given them to make up the deficiency. 274 were hurriedly equipped with guns with the Mk 1 mobile platforms, replacing the Mk 2 semi-mobile pattern, some of which they already held, and they joyfully handed in their hated No 3 Predictors, which they had never used when out of sight of the Brigadier, to a Bde dump.

The temporary departure of 25 Regt affected us in two ways, one indirect and the other direct. 274 Bty was under-strength in officers and Howe-Browne was seconded to them from RHQ 2 Light; we were all sorry to see him go. Also, since 25 Wksps were leaving the Bde, the various extra men and vehicles previously attached to them by Estlin were transferred to my command. Three parties were involved: a detachment from 68 HAA Wksps, who were now no longer in 12 AA Bde, being in Bengasi under 1 AA Bde, but somehow Estlin had hung on to the useful party he had detached from them; the Bde Stores Section; and the Bde Instrument Section. I was glad that my new site was large enough for the newcomers, who arrived on the afternoon after our move and when we were still at sixes and sevens.

These folk were to be with me for the rest of the winter's campaign, so it seems desirable to give more details about them. The 68th detachment consisted of QMS Neath, S/Sgt Butcher, S/Sgt Hartshorne – of the former 12 AA Bde Rec Sec – and about twelve men. They brought with them an "A" type, 6-wheeled Leyland machinery lorry, possessing a most useful big $9\frac{1}{2}$" lathe, an "I 30" type similar Leyland battery-charging lorry and a 3-ton, 6-wheeled Leyland recovery lorry. This last had been the property of 25 Wksps until the move and the 68th detachment had a 30cwt Morris similar to ours. These had been exchanged, because the Leyland was showing signs of a cracking chassis, rendering it of doubtful use in a mobile armoured division.

181

The Bde Stores Section had a 6-wheeled 3-ton AEC lorry, also ex-68 Wksps and three four-wheel-drive Fords with their drivers, pinched from various units before the battle began and now almost a unit on their own, together with full complements of stores. I now became responsible to Estlin for the issue of these stores.

S/Sgt Morgan and four instrument mechanics comprised the Instrument Section. They had with them the stripped and modified ex-South African "F" type 6-wheeled Leyland machinery lorry and a four-wheel-drive 3-tonner, now almost empty. Wray was, of course, still in charge of 25 Wksps in the absence of Volum.

This all augmented my gang to some 70 men, quite an impressive assembly, much more than a normal lieutenant's command. Maybe I was the only or the nearest unit that could take them but it seemed to imply that Estlin's opinion of my capabilities had altered since the previous autumn. This thought heartened me and I was determined not to let him down.

However, all these extra men and vehicles couldn't have come at a more convenient time, for everyone's vehicles at Antelat were hull down in the mud. For the next three or four days, before the plain slowly dried, every gun tractor and recovery lorry that possessed a winch was in almost constant demand from dawn to dusk dragging bogged vehicles and aircraft on to firmer ground. The whole system of communication on the plain came near to breaking down, as the tracks across it were turned into ploughed-up furrows of liquid mud about the consistency of brown treacle. First they became too deep for two-wheel-drive vehicles, and for a time only four-wheel-drive lorries were able to traverse them, before they themselves became bogged down in the ever-increasing depth of slime, and even men on foot were unable to cross them without wading almost knee-deep. As each track became impassable, another one was started close by and, within half a day, this too was almost unusable. The whole area surrounding the airstrip deteriorated into a criss-crossing network of wide rivers of mud separating unit from unit and even tent from tent. The Bde Staff Captain's car became isolated on a small island amid the sea of mud and remained there for three days simply because no one could make up a cable long enough to bridge the gap and enable us to winch it out.

Our Leyland ex-68th recovery lorry, going to the help of a bogged-down 3-tonner, got itself stuck and remained there for four days, unable to move. We could see it across the intervening mud "strait", but were unable to drive anything near enough to act as an anchor to enable it to winch itself out, and we had to ration its crew on foot.

Life degenerated into a maniac's dream, and, if the enemy had taken it into his head at that time to attack us, we couldn't even have run away. Fortunately, he didn't.

We sat on our rocky outcrop for the next five days, a trifle aloof from the general mêlée on the plain and laboured like slaves. We were obliged to work mainly in the open, because there was no satisfactory means of putting up proper shelters on the rock surface of our eyrie, and the wind and rain swept over us in biting squalls. By night, we huddled in our small bivouac tents or bedded down in any space in lorries and slept in damp blankets that no amount of exposure to the wind seemed to dry out. But for the continuous employment of mind and body, I suppose we should have been thoroughly miserable, but somehow there didn't seem to be time for that.

How we failed to qualify for rheumatic fever or something similar, I just don't know. Perhaps it was because we were all fit and hardened, for no one went sick. Or perhaps it was the rum issue that the Brigadier authorised for us at the request of Estlin, to whom we were eternally grateful. He knew, as no one else did, what we, "at the sharp end", were up against and he never let us down. The rum enabled us to turn in, internally warmed at least. I believe that even Dean was persuaded to forget his habit of lifelong abstinence.

On 21 January, the RAF decided that the Antelat farce had gone on long enough. Part of the runway on one airstrip had now dried sufficiently for aircraft to take off and, accordingly, the squadrons, with their attendant ground crews, the AA defence and ancillary forces would move back to Msus and operate from there, unsuitable though it was, until the new airstrip at Belandah was ready. The move was scheduled to be completed the following day and, as far as the AA defences were concerned, all guns, except a troop of 261 Bty and a LAA troop would go with the RAF. These troops of HAA and LAA, together with my Workshops would remain behind for another 24 hours, respectively to defend the rear parties and to complete the recovery work and to ensure that nothing was left behind that would need to be ferried back to Msus.

Just to make life more difficult, a Matador tractor of 261 broke something in its gearbox that penultimate afternoon, whilst hauling a particularly recalcitrant aircraft out of the mud and they towed it in for us to see if we could do something about it, so that the Bty would be able to use it to tow its gun away the next day. Dropping a Matador gearbox was a heavy job, but we set about it right away, hoping against hope that the problem might be something simple to correct. Otherwise we would have to tow it back to Msus, and it was a heavy load to tow 40 miles.

Life was lightened late that evening when S/Sgt Hartshorne, returning from the day's recovery work, came across a YMCA lorry stuck in the mud and hauled it out. The YMCA people were exceedingly grateful and, although they were really not supposed to dispose of any of their stocks until reaching 1 Armd Div, they let us have 100 cigarettes and some chocolate and biscuits through the back door.

On the following morning, everyone but a few rear parties and ourselves cleared out and departed, in bad order, for Msus. We also set about clearing up; the wretched Matador was still with us, unrepaired and with its gearbox on the ground, and the Brigadier's car had been brought in with a broken front spring. To add to our worries, a frantic message came from the remaining LAA Bty that they were unable to get one of its guns to stay on its wheels, owing to a mechanical fault in its latching gear. I sent S/Sgt Hartshorne with the Leyland recovery, (now back in the fold after its few days' separation in the mud) to seek to repair it, or if that wasn't possible on site, to bring it back into the workshop. Later that morning, Tony Overton's Signals Sgt came in to report that one of their small Signals trucks was broken down about 15 miles out on the track to Agedabia with a suspected fractured front stub-axle. Cursing their, and our, bad luck, I detailed the other 68th recovery lorry to go and fetch it in. It looked as though we were in for a hard afternoon's work.

At 1.00 p.m., I retired to my tent for a bit of well-earned lunch. At 1.15 p.m., Tony Overton rang up from RHQ at Msus to say that, on the CO's orders, I was to pack up at once and move forthwith to Msus. I protested that I had been left behind on Bde orders as Recovery Officer, but got no change out of Tony, who just repeated that Helby considered it operationally vital that I should move to Msus without delay, so I had better get my skates on, and he brusquely rang off.

At 1.20 p.m., the RA/Air Liaison Officer from RAF HQ arrived in a great flap to collect his truck which was in workshops for some minor repair. 'Didn't you know that the Germans have taken Agedabia?' he asked. 'You'd better get out, quickly. When last spotted, they were some 15 miles this side.'

He was in a great stew, because one of his two lorries was away and he was quite unable to move all his valuable "classified" equipment in the remaining one. After a few moments discussion, Spooner, who was present, and I decided to lend him the German Ford car temporarily, just to get him back to Msus, and he drove it away. He never showed up at Msus and I can only hope that the Germans were satisfied with our standard of maintenance on the Ford.

We now started to pack up, with a horrid sinking feeling in the pit of our stomachs. This was Sidi Barrani over again, but with a difference. This time there was no actual panic; training and experience told, and every man went about his alloted tasks in the pack-up without confusion.

There was a great deal to do, because of the work still in the shop. We had to hoist the gearbox back up into the broken-down Matador and make it towable; we had to drop all shelters and stow them; to pack up the blacksmith-cookhouse trailer and stores; dismantle and pack the office tent on its vehicle; stow our personal kit; and quickly patch up and clear the site of the few other vehicles which would run or tow, handing them over as they were to the impatiently waiting parties that had rushed to collect them. There was no time to fix the Brigadier's car and so we tried to run it up on one of the light 6-wheeled recovery trailers (the 68th detachment had brought two with them), but it was too long to go right on and we had to be content with hitching the front end of the car up on the rear of the trailer and leaving the rear wheels on the ground. There were also six crated engines to be manhandled on to the other trailer, because the Leyland recovery was out on a job. It was muscle-testing work, but I was determined not to abandon anything we could possibly bring with us.

As we were doing all this, a sort of ripple began to spread over the Antelat plain as everyone arose and frantically started throwing things into lorries as fast as they could. Main HQ 13 Corps, who were encamped on the flat to the south-east of us, began to trickle back as individual vehicles were packed and ready to move. Two miles away, on the ridge where the track from Agedabia ran past Antelat fort, we could see long, ant-like columns of vehicles all streaming hell-for-leather northwards, as though the Germans were already snapping at their heels.

At 2.30 p.m., the Bde Staff Captain motored in, almost wringing his hands. He had the 12 sets of predictor equipment handed in by 274 Bty still in his dump and only one 3-tonner with which to shift them; it would take only four sets and he wondered whether I could help, since I was the only unit left on that part of the plain. The 3-tonner of the Bde Instrument Section was almost empty and was now coupled to an empty lorry of German origin, which seemed to have been abandoned by its owners, so I packed the pair off with the Staff Captain to salve all it could. It returned in half an hour, laden to the axles, with the whole eight sets of predictors piled on board.

About the same time – 3.00 p.m. – the Leyland recovery came in with the 40mm gun on suspended tow. Hartshorne had been unable to rectify matters on site with the equipment available locally, so he had brought it in for the workshop to deal with. He was quite unaware of the flap that had started whilst he was away and was expecting his lunch!

Spooner and a gang set about wedging the swivelling axle

with wooden handspikes and rope, so that it could be towed without folding up, as it was trying to do at this moment, and I was confronted by Major Russell who was looking for his broken-down Matador, to tow the fourth gun of the rear-party troop. The guns had been frantically dug out of their emplacements and put on their wheels, ready to move and I had his Matador. What could I do to help him? he asked. The only vehicles that were heavy enough to tow a 3.7 were the four Leylands. Of these, I couldn't spare the recovery lorry, but the Leyland "A" machinery lorry, with S/Sgt Hartshorne and its crew of three was already packed. I ordered it to follow the grateful Russell back to the gun-site and act as a temporary tractor to tow the gun to safety. They went off in a flurry of mud, with Hartshorne on the front seat, an infuriated little gnome of a man whom the war had deprived of his lunch.

On such small things as efficiency in packing a vehicle do the fate of the men depend. I never saw them again...

Meanwhile, around us, the tempo of the evacuation of Antelat was speeding up. The remaining troops on the LG were rapidly thinning out and a long column was winding its way up the hill to Antelat fort. Away on the southern horizon I noticed, with an uncomfortable feeling in the pit of my stomach, half a dozen plumes of black smoke, obviously from burning vehicles.

At 3.45 p.m., the 30cwt recovery lorry came in with the 8cwt Signals truck on suspended tow. They reported having been passed by streams of vehicles travelling north and they were shaken to the core when told the reason, of which they had been blissfully ignorant. Dean suggested that we should be well advised to dump the six crated engines on the recovery trailer and put the Sigs truck on it instead; the engines, he pointed out, were old ones which had just been exchanged for new replacements, but I was determined to leave nothing for the enemy that we could possibly get away with, and therefore we would have to take the Sigs truck away as a suspended tow.

At 4.00 p.m., Spooner reported that we were completely packed up. We had left nothing on the ground, except a pile of empty tins by the cookhouse site with some bits of broken spring where the blacksmith had been. It was about time we

187

were off; the plain was nearly empty; a wide, dreary expanse of mud in the greying afternoon, with here and there an abandoned tent flapping free or a single moving vehicle. And, drifting silently through the wrack, like patches of brown smoke, were little bands of Arabs, grubbing and picking among the refuse left behind by the retreating Army. Where they came from so quickly in such numbers, I don't know, for we had scarcely seen one all the time we had been at Antelat. They just seemed to have sprouted from the desert as though some seed of war had germinated and they had sprung up unnoticed from the very ground at our feet.

To the south came the sound of gunfire – the quick, sharp thud of anti-tank guns that we had heard months ago under similar circumstances at Sidi Barrani – and more plumes of smoke sprang up. Definitely, it was high time to be going.

There were two ways out of Antelat towards Msus. One was on the far side of the plain from where we were now, and the other lay past the fort on the track by which we had arrived. The first was less likely to expose us to any brush with the enemy, but I didn't know the way; so I decided to take the route I knew, or thought I knew, past the fort. Getting lost in the desert in the dark in a flap like this didn't appeal to me.

We wound up the rise to the fort in a long thin line with me leading in the Bedford and Spooner and Neath bringing up the rear in Neath's 15cwt. We passed some Coldstream Guards at the fort, with their Bren carriers splayed out in a little defensive screen of stone sangars built out of the rubble from its walls. They were gazing intently down the track to the south and their Boyes anti-tank rifles had their breech covers removed and their magazines in place.

There were still some odd bunches of vehicles coming from the south in disorderly confusion, remnants of the great stream of transport we had seen in the distance pelting back from Agedabia earlier that afternoon. They were mainly RAF trucks, probably from Belandah, and their crews had the appearance of badly frightened men. They were just individual vehicles, belonging to no organised unit, which were "getting out" to some safer place and they were driving like bats out of hell.

They spread out over a large number of parallel tracks, covering a frontage of half a mile or more, crashing from rock to rock, without heeding the possibility of damage, in their flight to Msus and the safety it represented. The Germans were coming!

My own lads were probably windy enough in this mayhem, so to keep them from panicking, I deviated onto a parallel track well to the left of the madding herd and let the herd sweep by. After a mile or so, I instructed Sgt Hughes in the second vehicle to carry on slowly, while I drove back to the rear to make sure that all the party had followed us.

I came to Spooner and Neath stationary on a bit of a rise, about two thousand yards from the fort, which was still just visible on the horizon. They reported that the platform of the gun they had been towing had completely broken up and had collapsed on the ground. They were just about to abandon it as I came to them. It did indeed look a wreck, so Spooner removed the breech-block to make it useless to the enemy. The orthodox way was to push a live round down the flashguard and then stand back and fire the gun with a lanyard, but there was no time for this. Spooner also reported that one of the Bde Stores Section 3-tonners was missing. It appeared that it had somehow attached itself to another column and was last seen by someone travelling at high speed out into the desert south-east towards Saunnu. There was nothing we could do about that; one could only trust to the driver's good sense to stick to the column he had adopted and try to rejoin us later on.

While we were dealing with the gun, the Guards in their Bren carriers roared over an intervening rise and passed us in a splatter of mud and stones. Spooner said that he had spoken to them when passing the fort and had been offered a large mug of rum. It seemed that the local ration dump had been abandoned late that afternoon and the Guards had removed the liquor stores "to prevent them falling into the hands of the enemy".

All the fleeing vehicles appeared to have passed us, and we seemed to be alone in the desert. The short winter's afternoon was dimming into a grey twilight over the Antelat plain and the dusk was rolling up behind us. The fort stood out, clearly silhouetted against a light band in the darkening sky, and among

189

the ruins we could see one or two vehicles moving and the tiny figures of men. Beyond the ridge on which the fort stood the rattle and crack of anti-tank fire rose in a crescendo in the plain. Then, little twinkling lights sparkled by the fort and the air near us was filled with odd little chirruping sounds I had never heard before.

Spooner nudged me. 'I think we're being shot at, Sir. Time to make tracks.' And he pointed to a spot a hundred yards away where stones and dust were leaping into the air, kicked up by machine-gun bullets falling at extreme range and ricocheting in all directions with that queer little bird-like note.

It wasn't healthy. I looked at my watch, as we piled into our two 15cwts and sped off into the darkening eastern horizon after my vanished column. It was about 4.20 p.m. Behind us, the burning vehicles glowed like beacons in the gloom and the thud of the anti-tank guns echoed among the stony hillsides.

We caught up the column about five miles on and I moved into the lead again, while Spooner and Neath brought up the rear. Under Hughes's control, the unit was still all there, but in the fading light, we seemed quite alone and the sense of being in "no man's land" gave me an uncomfortable feeling. I was somehow assuming that this sudden arrival of the Germans had been a raid such as we had been expecting when we were at Msus, and that our own fighting troops which were well the other side of Antelat would close in behind us and drive the raiders off. Nevertheless, the very unexpectedness of the attack, when we had been assuming that the enemy was on the point of retiring to Sirte, was disconcerting.

Before we had gone very such further, we encountered two Matadors with 261 Bty plates on them, coming down from the direction of Msus. I was half-expecting them, because I knew that Russell had wirelessed Penn-Symonds, who was with the other troop at Msus, ordering him to send two Matadors at once to tow the gun which my "A" lorry was now towing and the broken-down Matador our "F" lorry was bringing along. I sought to detach one of them to take on our broken-down Matador, but they had orders to report to Russell first. It seemed to me that Russell's party would be unlikely to still be in their gun-site north of the LG, so I advised the bombardier in charge of the party as to the situation and suggested he cut to the right to approach Antelat from the north, away from the enemy and in a direction which also might bring him across Russell's line of retirement to Msus.

They went thundering off into the dusk and they didn't return to Msus. Somewhere that night or the next morning, they must have fallen in with the enemy and that was that. They didn't find the missing troop of 261, either.

Subsequently, almost a year later, I did indeed come across one of these Matadors again. It was distinguished by the name "Mary Hill" painted in very large letters across the top front of the cab and, during our advance through Cyrenaica after Alamein, we saw it by the side of the road from Martuba to Barce. It was adorned with black crosses and was burnt-out in the ditch together with the 88mm gun it was towing.

Msus was between 40 and 45 miles from Antelat by a track on which I had travelled only once before. This had been on our way down to Antelat, but apart from being in the opposite direction, that was in daylight. I was now going the other way in the gathering dusk and I fancied that Hughes, during the time I had been away to find Spooner and Neath, must have deviated, and we were no longer on the original track. The thought uppermost in my mind now was that I was in command of some 65 men who were relying on me to get them to safety and I must not let them down. It would have to be basic map and compass navigation and I think I was praying that I would get it right...

A quick look at the almost blank map – you will remember that Msus wasn't in the exact place shown on it – determined the compass bearing I should need, regardless of the maze of criss-crossing tracks. I told Thorne, who was driving me to keep an eye on his speedometer mileage reading and tell me at once when we had done 40 miles; meanwhile, I transferred myself on to the front wing of the 15cwt and sat there with my compass continually in action and with a loaded Tommy-gun across my knees for emergencies. This uncomfortable stance was adopted after a short stop to tell each vehicle in the column individually to close up and keep nose to tail. I also told Spooner, now at the rear, to see that all vehicles were in their correct order. From my "front" seat, the track beneath the wheels was faintly visible in the darkness and every time another track crossed it or branched off, I called to Thorne to take the one that led in the direction nearest to my chosen compass bearing. Looking round, I saw that the faint pinpoints of fire from the burning vehicles behind us had disappeared from sight in the distance and the sound of firing had died away, to leave an eerie silence over the desert.

Thorne was calling out the mileage we had travelled, every few miles and when we were about ten miles, according to my reckoning, short of Msus, we suddenly ran into a couple of armoured cars, who brought their turret guns round to bear on me with disconcerting rapidity. After I had identified ourselves, an officer got out of one of them and asked what the hell was going on, down there. Everyone was very much in the dark and he said he was part of an armoured car screen deployed across the approaches to Msus from the south to give early warning of a possible German night attack. I told him that, as far as I knew, the enemy had taken Antelat before dusk and might well be somewhere on this side of it by now. This information didn't cheer them overmuch and I was told to get on to Msus quickly and not foul up their line of fire. Msus, I was relieved to be told, was on this track about eight or ten miles straight ahead. I hope I offered up a short prayer of thanks for our deliverance, but I don't remember.

Ten miles on, we suddenly overtook the "F" lorry and the Matador stationary by the track; somehow they had managed to get in front of us. S/Sgt Morgan, after I had sworn at him for giving me such a fright at the thought of losing him, said he reckoned we were now in the wadi at Msus where 25 Wksps had been. A bit of recce confirmed this and we moved further up the wadi to our own site; there was no one about, but then we came on some more armoured cars, which upped with their guns very menacingly when they saw us. They too knew nothing of what was going on, except a report that the Germans were supposed to be out on the loose on a wide front in the desert to the south. We could camp behind them for the night, if we wished to, as long as we weren't in their field of fire.

It sounded a good idea, so we brewed up some hot tea in the blacksmith-cookhouse trailer and issued some cheese and biscuits. Very welcome it was, too, since we had had nothing to eat or drink since midday and it was now getting on for midnight.

The Signals operators in the towed wireless 8cwt had opened up their set and tried to contact RHQ, but couldn't get anyone to answer their call sign. They reckoned the codes had been altered in case they had been compromised in the flap and that RHQ were probably receiving them somewhere, but not answering in case we were the enemy. They also reported a lot of enemy RT speaking in "clear". This was not encouraging; the enemy was said only to talk in clear, when on the warpath. We turned in and spent a rather disturbed night.

As soon as it was light enough to see, I went out scouting and located RHQ on the rising ground to the north, a couple of miles away. Col Helby was greatly relieved to see me. He thought he had really lost me that time, because I had reported our departure from Antelat, just before uncoupling our telephone and bringing it along, at 4.00 p.m., and the Bde Intelligence reports had put the Germans in possession of the fort at 4.20 p.m. I think that was about right, too.

We were all, it seemed, on 15 minutes notice to move, so I brought the Workshop over to sit by RHQ, where we could keep an eye on them, in case they departed again without telling us. Then I went out to seek rations and petrol. There was no petrol and everyone was jittery and on tenterhooks; rumours flew around of heavy fighting to the south, and one of these was that Antelat had been retaken by our armoured forces. But there was no news of Major Russell and his guns, nor of my "A" lorry, who seemed to have disappeared into thin air and no one really *knew* anything.

On my return to the workshops, I ran into Estlin, who was also glad to see me, although characteristically he first ticked me off for not having shaved. He wanted to know how I had got away in the flap and I told him about having to offer 68th's "A" lorry to tow one of 261's guns ('Don't see what else you could have done. I won't hold that against you') and the missing Bde Stores Section 3-tonner that had joined some other column ('Oh, he'll be all right'). I gathered, from something he said, that he had reckoned I would get my unit out of trouble and he commended me for leaving nothing behind and for bringing away all the predictors ex 274 Bty and the dud Matador. Warming to the situation, he said he had been down to Antelat with the Brigadier and Col Helby in the latter's car as late as 4.45 p.m. on the previous afternoon and that the enemy didn't seem to be there in great strength. On the way back, however, they had got completely lost, had been fired at by the armoured car screen, and then, just to cap things off when they were almost home, Gnr Beale, Helby's driver, had bogged the car down in a slit trench and the three senior officers had had to "foot it" back to Bde HQ, following a telephone cable on the ground.

On hearing that we had been put on 15 minutes' notice to move, which of course precluded any sort of real work being done, Estlin said that was nonsense and he persuaded Helby to extend the notice to two hours, so that we could open up a bit. This enabled us to get rid of the Brigadier's car and we had another slam at dropping the Matador gearbox to try and free it, so that we could make the wretched vehicle a runner under its own power.

At about 6.00 p.m., when it was nicely dark, Phillimore rang up to tell me that the RAF had decided to move out of Msus, to clear the ground for a big tank battle that was about to be fought in the neighbourhood to drive the Germans back to El Agheila for good and all. Unfortunately, this meant going back as far as Mechili, because there was no intermediate LG before that. However, Claud said, Army HQ were confident that the Germans were only making a grand-scale sortie to disorganise us and so permit them to retreat from El Agheila towards Sirte. Since the half Bty of 261 that was now at Msus lacked two Matadors – the ones which had been sent to Antelat – could I find two heavy vehicles to tow the two guns and go with 261? So I reluctantly parted with the Leyland recovery lorry and the six-wheeled AEC stores lorry belonging to the Bde Stores Section. This move was due to take place at first light the following morning, and so once again we packed up and heaved

194

the Matador gearbox back into place so that we could tow the damned thing.

S/Sgt Morgan viewed the possibility of having to tow the Matador back to Mechili with great disfavour, because, he said, it was doing the "F" lorry's engine no good and made it a swine to drive in convoy. All the way from Antelat the previous night, he had had a lad with an axe, ready to cut the tow rope if they were caught by the enemy and a quick getaway became necessary. Also, the Matador, having no engine power and therefore no compressed-air braking, had to be slowed by the driver frantically hauling on the hand-operated parking brake. It was accordingly in the habit of ramming the "F" lorry up the backside. To counter this latter fault, we gave him one of the two solid "T"-shaped tow-bars from the Leyland recovery and let Morgan use that for the tow, so that it couldn't overrun the towing vehicle. We allotted the other "T"-bar to the 3-tonner with the predictors that was towing the grossly overloaded German Ford. Since we had got rid of the Brigadier's car and the Signals truck while at Msus, our situation was that much easier.

Petrol was the paramount problem. There was none to be had through the normal channels, so we drove down to the RAF petrol dump, searching for motor spirit, but there were only stacks of hundreds of full 40-gallon drums of 100 octane aviation spirit, unattended, and we just helped ourselves. We were only too aware that this aircraft fuel, if used for any length of time in a car or truck engine, would be liable to burn away the valves and valve seatings, so we diluted it with some of our small reserves of motor spirit in an attempt to mitigate the danger, and filled our tanks with that. The amount of fuel our heavily loaded vehicles used in convoy and when the ground was soft, was just nobody's business. The "F" lorry, towing the Matador, was managing only three miles per gallon, so, mindful that there might not be much fuel at Mechili either, I decided to take enough 100 octane in drums on the recovery trailers to get us to Tobruk, if pushed. Not that I was expecting to have to go back as far as Tobruk, but, well, you never knew...

I wondered afterwards what happened to that RAF petrol

dump. I am certain that no one could have taken it all away in time; in fact, even then it had the appearance of being abandoned.

We were due to pick up the tail of the regimental column the following morning, immediately behind the rump of 261 Bty, and we were a trifle early at the rendezvous, which was by the big wadi where the track went across to the west. It was a cold, misty dawn and every one about the LG was packing up to clear out, too. All the aircraft had already gone and there were symptoms of extreme agitation in what was going on – which in the less disciplined units bordered on panic – that I couldn't help noticing and didn't like. Various broken-down vehicles were being abandoned and set on fire, while columns of smoke were going up over in the FSD, also in a manner I didn't like. I let Spooner go over in his truck, mindful of what had happened at Antelat, to see if he could help them in removing any pickings to be had, but he returned empty-handed. Most of the more attractive stores had already gone and the remainder were being thrown on waiting RASC vehicles, just as fast as men could load them.

Another disquieting sight was the endless column of vehicles which poured in single file across the wadi from the direction of Scelidima, Solluch and Ghemines in the coastal area to the west. They at least were orderly but were driving off towards Mechili and the east, with a swift and expeditious urgency that gave one faint qualms. It made one wonder what size of space was being "cleared" for the envisaged battle.

And still no one had any news of Major Russell and my "A" lorry.

The track by which we were to return to Mechili was not the one by which we had travelled on the outward journey. That had been adjudged to be too severe, and the main return supply routes to the east from Msus now ran due east along the Trigh el Abd, the "Slaves' Road" of the old camel caravans, directly to Bir Hacheim and Tobruk, or northwards to Charruba and then eastwards to Mechili and the coast at Tmimi. This latter route was the one on which we now found ourselves.

We bowled along at a fair speed over endless stretches of clay-pan, overtaking on the way many isolated groups of RASC, RAOC and the like, who had been rudely "shoo-ed" out of Antelat, Belandah and Sannau when the flap started and were now sitting down by the track-side, waiting uncertainly for further instructions. No one knew much of what was going on down in the south-west, but there were various vague and disquieting rumours. All had been surprised and somewhat shot up while getting away; it was clear that the enemy had mounted a very robust and extensive sortie from the direction of Marada along some hard track through the southern marshes which they knew of but our forces did not. The Germans had made this sortie in the dark and were among our forward troops before they had any inkling that anything was amiss, largely because of the wholesale grounding of our reconnaissance aircraft in the mud. There were also faint, but rather dispiriting, suggestions that 1 Armd Div had been somewhat mauled and that the enemy was now out of the Agheila position in some force and was coming up the coast road in the direction of Bengasi as well as across the desert. Two and two seemed to make four here, for that would explain the wholesale retirement of troops from Solluch and Ghemines. What *was* going on? It was all most depressing and where news was scarce, rumours proliferated.

Then our troubles began. Ahead of us, our Leyland recovery lorry towing one of 261's guns had come to an abrupt halt and Penn-Symonds ran out to flag us down. The lorry had run over a concealed cross gully and had broken its front spring just behind the front fixed mounting, so that the broken blade was now resting on the underside of the front dumbiron. Worse; the frame was now markedly more bent at its weak point and to our horror we found that a full Matador load of 3.7" ammunition had been put aboard, without us knowing. More in sorrow than in anger, I told Penn-Symonds exactly what I thought of this; he tore strips off his Troop Leader and doubtless *he* took it out on some unfortunate gunner. The ammunition was hastily redistributed among a couple of already overloaded 3-tonners or partly ditched. I whistled up our remaining Leyland, the "I 30" battery-charging lorry over to the gun, hitched it up and told my driver to beat it after the remainder of the column. Meanwhile, we set to and blocked and lashed up the broken front spring on the recovery so that it could still run after a fashion, and limped off as well in pursuit.

We caught the guns up about nightfall, somewhere about 20 miles east of Charruba, and leaguered down for the night with them beside the road, listening to the faint whisper of gunfire to the south-west. There was no news on the Signals net or on the BBC.

After supper, I strolled over to 261's camp to find out when they proposed to move off in the morning and found that six officers had squeezed themselves into a single tent, with quite a lot of whisky they had scrounged from somewhere. They made room for me somehow and invited me to join in their drinking. Apparently, they had some news of the lost troop of 261 which had come in just as they were leaving Msus that morning. It appeared that a light truck had come in from Major Russell to try and locate RHQ and learn the revised Wireless code, which, as I have said, had been changed in a hurry when the flap started as it was believed to have been compromised.

His news was that Russell wasn't trying to get to Msus at all. They had got all the guns out of their pits and had started off back to Msus on the alternative track that I had considered and discarded. Here the ground was still pretty soggy and my "A" lorry pulling the gun made very heavy weather of it, with a tendency to dig itself in as soon as they came to any soft stuff. I reflected that it had probably got a Matador-load of ammunition on board and that this wasn't exactly surprising. They had devised a drill for hitching an extra 4-wheel-drive laden 3-tonner on in front whenever the ground looked suspicious, but the pace was so slow that Russell had decided to give up the idea of a direct move to Msus and instead to keep to the harder ground to the west, where a fairly good track ran off to Beda Fomm and joined the Bengasi to Agheila road at Ghemines. One of Overton's Signals trucks was with them but hadn't been on listening watch at the crucial moment when the codes were changed. As a result, it hadn't been possible to communicate the change of plan to RHQ, and the truck had been detached to find

RHQ and tell them verbally. It had been delayed by a petrol stoppage and thus had been 24 hours late in arriving. It was accordingly assumed that the missing troop was now somewhere in Bengasi and, if any further retirement was envisaged, would move back down the coast road.

One of the officers present was Maitland Brown the Troop Leader (2 i/c and Admin Officer) of the troop. At the time of the flap, he had been returning from Bengasi whither he had been sent in search of NAAFI stores or something. On his return to the Antelat area on the evening of the flap, it was after dark and he had been unable to locate the gun-site, which, although he didn't know it, had already been evacuated. Consequently, to his great annoyance, he had had to pack down and sleep the night in the back of his truck with his driver. There were quite a number of other vehicles about him, dim shapes in the dark, and he turned in without bothering to ask them where he was. This wasn't so unusual as it might sound, because no unit in the desert ever seemed to know where any other unit was and asking the way was generally a waste of time.

He had awakened early, just as the first tinge of pre-dawn made its appearance in the sky and, to his horror, he saw that all the surrounding vehicles were adorned with black crosses and that the majority were armoured cars. He aroused his driver quietly and the pair of them sidled off unobtrusively, without even waiting to put their boots on. 'It didn't seem very polite to depart without saying goodbye to our hosts,' he said, 'but it seemed to best thing to do.' No one seemed to notice their departure and, when they had recovered from the shock, they found that they hadn't, by some massive miscalculation, overshot the front line, but were still in the vicinity of Antelat. Circling round to the west, they traced the tracks of the guns heading towards Beda Fomm and, not knowing what sort of catastrophe had occurred in their absence, they wisely turned round and beat it for Msus, arriving just as the remaining troop started out that morning.

In the morning a couple of our lorries refused to start for some time, with some form of obscure electrical trouble, and we were a little late in getting away. The guns moved off at such a pace that, although we were away very shortly after them, they vanished into the distance and we, who were towing something on every tow-hook except my 15cwt, were swiftly left to come on alone.

All that day, we drove over endless rolling downland country of rock and stone thinly covered with scrub. Overhead hung grey skies; to the west, south and east the grey-green desert merged into an indefinite horizon; while to the north the land grew hillier and hillier, row on row of dark, jagged lines and, in the far distance, the ridges of the Jebel Akhdar brooded blackly under lowering rain clouds. No other vehicles were going in the same direction as ourselves, but we met numerous columns of 10-ton Mack and White lorries loaded to bursting point with petrol – always a sign of action somewhere – all heading west. They passed in strings of ten or a dozen with a small truck flying a blue flag at their head and a long plume of swirling dust behind.

Dotted about on either side of the track were the rusting wrecks of derelict and burned-out tanks and vehicles, mainly Italian, but some German, marking the trail along which the Italians in January 1941 and the Germans a couple of months ago had retreated.

Just after we had re-started after a stop for lunch, a real calamity occurred. The patched-up spring of the Leyland recovery snapped in another place and the front axle slewed back until the off-side front wheel was nearly under the chassis. There was nothing for it; either we abandoned the vehicle as no longer towable, or a new top leaf had to be fitted to the broken spring. It wasn't really a choice, if a choice there was, and it was easily made; Spooner, Neath, Cpl Siddle, our blacksmith, and a party of fitters with their vehicles, were detached to do the job and the rest of us moved on, leaving a small cluster of men round the group of vehicles, busily starting to jack up the front end of the Leyland and setting up the forge and blacksmith's kit.

There was a faint grumble of gunfire far behind us as they started work. We learned later that what we had heard must have been the Army rearguard being shelled out of Msus, but perhaps it was just as well we didn't know then. I had some qualms

200

about leaving such a valuable party behind, but I was conscious that I had an obligation to get the others to safety in Mechili, so leave them we did. Anyhow, they came to no harm. They stripped the complete spring from the Leyland, dismantled it, forged a new top leaf from our stock of spring steel, tempered it after a fashion, rebuilt the spring and, after replacing it on the lorry, rejoined us at Mechili that evening. It had been a very good show and I heartily commended all ranks.

Fifteen miles or so further on, more trouble occurred. The Leyland "F" lorry, towing the Matador, ran over a projecting rock and knocked a piece out of its rearmost differential casing, spewing oil over the camel-thorn. Since we had nothing else left with which to tow the Matador and we refused to abandon it after bringing it so far, there was nothing for it but to effect a patch-up repair on the spot. S/Sgt Morgan took charge and I agreed to leave our original 30cwt machinery lorry with him to help in the job. I took the small remainder of the Workshop under Dean on with me to report to RHQ.

Morgan also did a most commendable repair. He had the machinery lorry's power generator started and personally drilled a couple of dozen holes round the hole in the base of the differential casing and tapped them for 2BA screws from his instrument stores; this meant working upside down under the lorry in a most confined position. Meanwhile, one of his mates was cutting a piece of plate to approximately the right size from an old petrol tin and beating it to the contour of the casing with a hammer over a rounded rock. The bit of tin was placed over the hole, tapped gently into final shape and then screwed home with a specially cut gasket of langite or cork. The axle was then refilled with oil, the Leyland once again took up its tow and the party followed us on to Mechili. A masterly bit of repair, which I noted to remember to tell Estlin. Although not one of my Workshop proper, Morgan was an acquisition to any unit he graced.

Our pitifully small party, so critically reduced, made good time towards Mechili, throughout that afternoon, for I deemed it imperative that I should get in touch with RHQ before dark and find out what was expected of us. The track was good but hard and stony, rising and dipping over endless successions of small transverse wadis running from the Jebel Akhdar in the north towards the desert in the south. This track was now shared with numerous other columns, some overtaking us and coming from the west and others coming up out of the desert from the south. And all the time, we could hear, with a certain uneasiness, the faint but persistent grumble of gunfire to the rear.

As evening approached, the Mechili wind rose and the notorious dust brought down visibility to a few hundred yards. I was glad to see the old fort loom up out of the murk, because I remembered that it stood at the north-west corner of the LG area. I had qualms about being able to locate RHQ, for the plain was simply covered with vehicles, none of them unpacked, with their crews brewing up over petrol-and-sand fires, or just hanging about waiting for orders of some sort. There were no tents anywhere and everyone looked ready to move on at a moment's notice.

Luck was with me, however, for I found RHQ pretty quickly and reported to Claud, who was crouching with a couple of his clerks in his office tent, trying to get some order or other out and muffled to the eyes with a scarf to keep the dust out of his mouth. Dust was drifting over all his papers on the table and his sergeant clerk was trying to keep them from blowing away, using large lumps of rock as paperweights. It was bitterly cold.

Claud, when he could give me his attention, wanted rather brusquely to know why I was so late and where the rest of my unit was, anyway. I answered, equally shortly, that these were all I had left at the moment; the others were behind, doing recovery work, and anyhow where did he want us to deploy, what was going on and what about rations and petrol?

He said things were somewhat disorganised; at the moment there were no rations and no petrol, but McKeown was out trying to raise some from the RASC, who were said to be setting up an FSD on the track somewhere on the Gazala side of Mechili. We could camp down anywhere we liked within a hundred yards, but, until the situation became somewhat more clarified, we were all on half an hour's notice to move, which would considerably curtail the amount of work we could attempt – although, as we were now getting pretty practised, there was quite a lot we could tackle in half an hour, if we didn't unpack anything unnecessarily.

We deployed and I sent two trucks with guides in them back to the fort to bring our stragglers in, should they manage to reach Mechili. As I have said, they all arrived before it became completely dark and very glad I was to see them.

What news there was, was far from encouraging. Army Sitreps were still taking the old line that the enemy was making a last disruptive fling before his final retreat, but this source was now thoroughly discredited. Everybody at Mechili was aware that whatever was going on was something big, not just a raid, and the Army didn't seem to be doing very well in it. The news on the wireless spoke of "heavy fighting in the desert" and spoke lightly of "small tactical withdrawals". But, since it mentioned our evacuation of the "town of Msus", it was clear that the BBC reporter didn't know what he was talking about. Signals communications with the west seemed to have broken down, but there was a persistent unquenched rumour that the Germans had retaken Bengasi. A dense and disquieting fog blanketed the battle area, as dense as the dust pall that enveloped Mechili.

One definite piece of news was that the remnants of 261 Bty, now with us, had been judged too badly mauled to be operationally effective and had been sent straight through Mechili to Gazala, "out of the way". An ominous way of phrasing it. There still was no news of Russell and his missing troop and a belief that they were now "in the bag" was becoming widespread.

Somewhat truncated, for our two lorries on loan to 261 had gone back, at least to Gazala, with them, and thoroughly dispirited, we pitched camp where we were, brewed up a hot meal and crawled into our bivvies to escape the howling wind and the stinging dust that filled the air.

The following morning, the wind and dust continued unabated and, as aircraft were unable to take off, we remained at half an hour's notice. Another flap occurred in the late morning, when the RAF began to send all that was surplus in the way of ground staff back to Gazala, and RHQ and ourselves packed up, ready to move. However it was a false alarm and, shortly afterwards, things apparently calmed down and we were put on to two hours' notice. This meant that we could do quite a lot more work and I moved the workshop over to a more sheltered site, where we could open up again. We considered having another go at the Matador, but Dean turned it down as something we couldn't tackle unless we had at least six hours' notice of any move.

Estlin breezed in about lunchtime and made some remark to the effect that he was pleased we had got out of it all in one piece. Not that he had ever had any doubts on our ability to do so, but he was glad he was right. He seemed fairly confident we would be remaining in the Mechili neighbourhood for some time and was motoring off back to Tobruk to raise all the gun spares he could, for we and the Bty fitters reported some of the guns were beginning to show the results of their sustained pounding over heavy going. These stores would be sent back in the vehicles with 261 which would be returned to us straight away.

We had a hard afternoon. Our Karrier stores lorry was found to have broken the main leaf of one of its rear springs; we had no spare and the leaf section was one for which we had no spring steel, so we were obliged to strip it and make a patch-up repair, all the time with our hearts in our mouths, lest we were ordered to move before the vehicle was on the road again. Also, one of the LAA guns had broken its axle; this wasn't a job to be tackled on two hours' notice, so we reluctantly had to dump the unserviceable engines which we had brought back all the way from Msus and run the damaged gun on to the recovery trailer in their stead. I had set my heart on getting these old engines away, but there was nothing else to do.

Towards dusk, we had effected patch-up repairs to most of the ailing vehicles of the RA at Mechili – there was some doubt as to whom we were now actually servicing – and they were all in a position to move off again, if called upon. We called it a day and sat down to brew up.

After dark, lorry-loads of Polish troops were decanted on the surrounding ridges and commenced to dig in. Some of them spoke a few words of English and tried to find out from us what was going on, but we didn't know anything either. They had no vehicles of their own in which they could move should it become necessary to retreat, for the transport in which they had come had gone back for reinforcements, but they seemed to say they didn't propose to retreat anyway.

At 10 p.m., just after our official "lights out", Claud rang me to give movement orders. We and 283 Bty (of 88 HAA Regt), who were on the LG and had come under command of 2 LAA Regt in place of 261, were to move out within the hour and go back to Bir Halegh el Eleba, where we were to wait for further orders. It was probably only a precaution, Claud said, but, just before dark, aircraft reconnaissance had spotted a German column moving eastwards along the Trigh el Abd to the south of Mechili. The heavy, slow-moving transport was therefore being moved out of Mechili – "just in case".

The twin horns of my 15cwt Bedford were blown (our accepted signal for an immediate "fall-in") and I explained to the parade all I knew of the situation, endeavouring to make it sound that it was all right, really. I doubt if they believed me by now, but they packed up speedily and efficiently in the darkness, even remembering to smash up the abandoned engines. We moved out in single file to the rendezvous exactly 55 minutes after the message came through and I reflected on this with satisfaction, for we had been on a nominal two hours' notice and had been asleep into the bargain. Undoubtedly, we were getting pretty good at this, and it was a far cry from that September night in Sidi Barrani on which we had started to learn.

On seeing us packing up, the Poles near us were pretty worried that we were clearing out in the middle of the night. As I have said, they were without transport of any sort.

We tailed on to the rear of 283 Bty as they came past and headed off eastward on an ill-defined track. There was a fitful moon, partially obscured by clouds, which enabled each driver to distinguish the dim form of the vehicle ahead, but lights were forbidden, except the standard concealed one on the rear axle, and it was all too easy to drop slightly behind and lose the column. Several times we nearly did this, for 283 Bty set out

205

like bats out of hell, being relatively fresh – they had been doing nothing in Mechili a day longer than we had been there – whereas we were dog-tired and almost nodding over our steering wheels as we drove; we had been at it for 16 hours a day for about a week. It was all we could do to keep up with them, but somehow we did it and we arrived in the vicinity of the rendezvous, just as the moon set and left us in total darkness. The lads all collapsed in their trucks and fell asleep where they were, and, after checking with the Bty Commander of 283 that we were there for the rest of the night, I retired to the Bedford and curled up in the passenger's footwell, right beside the warm engine. I fell asleep at once and only a German attack would have wakened me.

All the next morning, we sat there, widely dispersed, on the rolling grey-green moorland at the foot of the hillocks of Eleba. The winter sunshine was warmer than of late and we relaxed in it, stopping only for a brew-up and to carry out such small repairs as we could do for the Bty without much unpacking.

I kept contact with the Bty Commander of 283, Major Cotterill, who was in touch with RHQ by wireless, and he undertook to pass on to me in good time any orders that might come through. But there was no definite news and rumours spread again, mainly originating from what the Signals personnel could pick up from coded messages they half heard while on listening watch.

It was whispered that the enemy was advancing rapidly up the coast road from Bengasi towards Derna, that the remains of 1 Armd Div were falling back on Mechili and that whole columns of RASC petrol lorries and tank transporters had fallen intact into the hands of the enemy, simply by motoring on through an indeterminate "front line" without precise orders.

At Eleba, however, we might have been in a dead world; nothing moved and there was no sign of life, except the wheeling kites above and the little green lizards that scampered through the camel-thorn.

Then, just after midday, columns of transport began to stream past us, all heading eastwards, and we received orders to move back to Gazala.

I remembered the country between Eleba and Tmimi on the coast; it was stony and intersected by fairly deep transverse wadis. The "track" was really half a dozen paths over a frontage of half a mile or so, and all afternoon these were thronged with countless vehicles in desert formation, battered, scattered and dust-covered, crawling eastwards uphill and down dale. And, meeting them, going the other way, came endless streams of six-wheeled Mack and White 10-ton lorries carrying petrol, petrol, petrol.

Near the top of the coastal ridge by Tmimi, we encountered groups of huge Italian lorries flowing towards us over the rise in open formation; these appeared to be the reinforcements coming to support the Poles we had left at Mechili. They seemed surprised at the amount of traffic in retreat, but they waved to us and thundered on. Then, just where the central plateau ran down to the coastal marsh, there were formations of more fighting troops, bivouacking beside their dispersed vehicles. They were Free French – the first we had seen in the desert – and they also appeared to be moving up towards Mechili. They were a motley crew: all colours from white to ebony, clad in a hundred varieties of uniforms, much of that in rags, and armed with a bristling and varied collection of weapons. All of this force was unspeakably dirty, incredibly unshaven and magnificently cheerful, after, as we subsequently learned, a forced drive from *Syria*! White, black or yellow, miscellaneously armed and mounted in a wonderful assortment of vehicles, they were alike only in their forest of tricolour flags with the superimposed Cross of Lorraine, and their terrific enthusiasm and eagerness to come to grips with the enemy. Like the Poles, they had but one mission in life, and that was to kill Germans.

One of our 30cwt Bedfords developed what appeared to be valve trouble at this point and had to be taken in tow. Doubtless the trouble was accelerated by the aircraft fuel we had perforce been using in increasing proportions since leaving Msus.

Our first sight of the coast road came as a bit of a shock. As I have said, it was little over two vehicle widths from verge to verge and it was now crammed with transport pouring back from the direction of Derna. They seemed to be in no organised

207

columns, just hordes of individual vehicles batting along, nose to tail – 3-tonners; 8 and 15cwt trucks; cars; Bren carriers: HAA and LAA guns – all inextricably mixed and all heading for Gazala, Tobruk and anywhere east that offered safety. It was as though behind them some giant force was squeezing them out like toothpaste at high speed on to this one narrow strip of tarmac. It was more than a shock; it was frightening, because it seemed to bear out all the worst of the rumours that we had light-heartedly dismissed as so much exaggeration. *What on earth was happening to the Army?*

Against this stream, and occupying the other half of the road, the Free French were coming up, driving like madmen to get to the battle, their lorries packed with singing men and bristling with AA machine-guns.

Once on the road, we were carried away in the stream towards Gazala. Nominally we were under the command of OC 283 Bty, but they, like us had been swept away perforce and had disappeared in the wrack of vehicles ahead. We saw them no more that day and had no option but to abandon ourselves to the current and hope that we could reform later.

There was no doubt about it, now. The Army was in full retreat out of the Cyrenaica "bulge", and no amount of hopeful talk or wishful thinking about German "raids" could disguise the bitter fact. This was no retirement at leisure to previously prepared positions; something pretty far-reaching had happened "up there" and the Germans were now calling the tune.

We climbed the hill at Gazala just as it got dark and I must say that I felt a trifle more secure with that precipice between us and the enemy. Flight is rather catching . . .

Two or three miles on towards Tobruk, I pulled off the road and counted my flock in. Then I gave the order to bivouac for the night as several other groups seemed to be doing. In the morning I would find someone to whom I could report: RHQ or 283 Bty perhaps. We had just got a brew-up going in the blacksmith/cookhouse trailer, when Estlin, of all people, came motoring through our lines, wanting to know what the hell we were doing there, in advance of the majority of the Regt. His idea of the workshop's role in a retreat was following up the last of the rearguards and doing recovery work in no man's land, you see. I explained I had received a direct order from RHQ and he told me that he had just left a small party of RHQ, who must have come on another track to us and was now only 200 yards off, and he gave me a lift over to see them. It seemed that he had been met by the retreating Bde HQ, while coming back from Tobruk, and his only worry was that the Bde truck with S/Sgt Lewis and all his belongings on board hadn't clocked in yet. He had left my two lorries, after collecting them from 261 Bty, with Bde HQ and would see I got them back.

His news of the war was somewhat more reassuring. The Army, it was true, had had a rough handling from the enemy, who had turned a large-scale probing expedition into a full-dress assault, when it became apparent that we had been caught badly on the wrong foot. The retreat was now over, he was glad to report; a line would be stabilised somewhere in front of Gazala, where the Polish Bde and the Free French now were, and, coming up fast from the east were 150 Bde of 50 Div – a battle-hardened formation – and 1 SA Div. On the whole, it sounded pretty encouraging.

The "B" echelon of RHQ had only just clocked in a few hours before and consisted of McKeown and his QM clerk. McKeown was in touch with Helby at Mechili by wireless and told Estlin we were all still on about 15 minutes' notice to move, including the workshops. Estlin said this was nonsense and asserted that if RHQ didn't know the proper way to employ their workshops, he did. There followed several polite but firm conversations over the RT with Helby and with the Bde Major, with the result that I received orders to go on to two hours' notice and to set up shop somewhere on the Tobruk side of Gazala under the direct command of Estlin. From there we would run a recovery service back up the Mechili track as long as required and set about repairing all the damaged vehicles we could collect.

9

McKeown at last had news of Major Russell, the missing troop of 261 and the crew of my "A" lorry. They were all in the bag. The tale had been brought in by the Signals truck that had been attached to the troop and had just rejoined the Regt at Mechili.

As we knew already, Russell had struck out north-west on the harder ground towards the main coast road, after sending off a light truck to Msus in an attempt to get the new signals code. They had nearly reached the road near Ghemines, when they had encountered some armoured cars and were fired on. This was on the morning after leaving Antelat and opinion at HQ Bde was that these cars were almost certainly 4 Indian Div's outer screen in front of Bengasi and the firing was the result of mistaken identity. Russell wasn't to know that and he naturally assumed they were hostile, so he sheered off eastwards with the intention of reaching Msus through Sceledima. The very fact that the armoured cars made no further attempt to intervene supports the contention that they were from the Bengasi screen and were not German.

The troop slogged on throughout the day and in the late afternoon armoured cars were seen to the southern flank, dogging them. The pace speeded up, but the wolves gathered and closed in. Russell, game to the last, tried to form his guns into a ring to shoot it out over open sights with his HAA guns, and there was a quick mêlée as they struggled to get the guns into action with the armoured cars charging round in line ahead, like Red Indians in a Wild West film, firing into the centre of the circle. But the guns took too long to get into action on the ground – there was no accepted drill for that – and the Sigs truck just managed to slip away by virtue of its superior speed as the Germans overran the troop. As far as they knew, everyone – including S/Sgt Hartshorne and his party – had been captured.

This news sobered and depressed me. Major Russell had been a good friend and I recalled Hartshorne's annoyance at missing his lunch because I had selected him for this duty. I hoped the enemy would find him something to eat.

On Estlin's instructions, we moved out to a site on a breezy upland between the road and the sea, opposite Kilometre Stone 135 from Derna, or about five miles on the Tobruk side of Gazala Hill. The sea was only a mile away and it was bleak and windy, but the ground was hard and, after our experience at Antelat, I was chary of operating anywhere in a hollow for fear of flooding. The recent rains must have been fairly severe, for the valleys were all full of green grass, sprinkled with little yellow and blue flowers like buttercups and forget-me-nots. There were also clusters of pink and yellow night-scented stock which smelt delightful in the evenings.

However, we were not there for nature study, because we had plenty of work to keep us busy. In addition to several broken-down vehicles, a whole spate of troubles with the 40mm guns took our major attention. These were with the unsprung Mk 2 platforms which were replacing the sprung Mk 1 variety, on account of being cheaper and quicker to manufacture; their springing was reliant on large, fat, low-pressure tyres to take the shock of uneven roads and rough terrain. This Mk 2 platform might have been good enough for transport between sites on an English road, but it was definitely not good enough to take the hammering over the rocks of the desert and faults appeared on every second gun. Mainly, the trouble took the form of the wheel and axle-drum assembly snapping off from the main beam, as had occurred on the gun we had brought in on our trailer from Mechili, and, during the next week, we had to tow in from the Mechili track some ten guns with this type of failure.

Hitherto, our main work had been with vehicle troubles, mainly springs, and this was the first time we had to concentrate men on repairing guns. We soon found the quickest ways of dealing with this problem: where the fractures occurred on opposite sides of two different guns, it was possible to make one good one by sawing the two axles in half and welding the two separate halves together, with a stiffening spigot made out of an old lorry halfshaft down the centre of the tube; one or two of the others we repaired by turning up complete new stub-axles out of old halfshafts. This kept our turner, Cpl White, busier than he had been for most of the previous campaign, and he did well. Then we found that the platforms manufactured by the Nuffield shadow factories used stub-axles similar to those on the Morris 8cwt truck and we got quite a number of guns back on the road, with Estlin's approval and connivance, by stripping this part off the more seriously damaged Morris trucks in the Tobruk Salvaged Vehicle Parks. One way and another, I think there was only one gun that was so cannibalised of all its useful parts that we had to evacuate as beyond our capacity.

For another couple of days, the stream of transport continued to pour back from Derna and then the torrent dwindled to a trickle and ceased. Col Helby and the rest of RHQ returned from Mechili and set up at Gazala, and it was rumoured that the Army intended to hold some sort of flexible line running inland from Tmimi to the desert to the east of Mechili. It still sounded a trifle insecure.

Before we had been at Gazala for a day, we got rid of the Matador and predictor equipment we had brought from Antelat, respectively to the Base Workshops in Tobruk and to the Base Ordnance Depot there. I accompanied them into Tobruk, to make sure that we were not refused, and found the place in a turmoil. Tobruk had until recently been an extensive base and the forward area had suddenly and unforeseenly, swung back in little more than a week from 200 miles away to a paltry 40 miles. Everything that could be moved was being packed up, dug up or wrenched up and whisked away down the road to Bardia and Capuzzo. All the big RASC columns that had been based in Tobruk for the long-distance supply of the forward area were on the move back, loaded with ordnance stores, and the static 3.7" HAA guns were being carted off on transporters as fast as tractors could be provided. Replacements for the port defence were being found from the mobile guns from Bengasi, Derna and Martuba.

They seemed very windy in Tobruk about the possible course of the fighting, and people were going about saying quite openly that we were not going to hold Tobruk this time and were going straight back to the Wire. It was said that the Navy was unwilling to undertake the supply of the town by sea in the event of a further siege. It all left an unpleasant taste, and I decided not to pass it on to the lads.

Back at Gazala, during the next few days, it became apparent that the forecast of a stand on the Tmimi–Mechili line had been over-optimistic and that the real defensive position was the Gazala escarpment itself, only about half a dozen miles from the workshop site. In front of it, our forward troops were gradually falling back on a general line Tmimi–Bir Hacheim. The enemy was definitely in Mechili, Eleba, Martuba and Derna and was still coming on, although with slackening momentum.

We were a week at Gazala, days of fantastic overwork at all hours and disturbed nights as the enemy bombers came over and dropped ragged strings of bombs at the LGs nearby, raking the area with machine-gun fire. This was something new to me and, although the aircraft were seldom nearer than a couple of miles away, it gave me an odd, naked sort of feeling to watch the two little squirts of tracer diverting downwards from some invisible spot in the blackness above. Little damage resulted, but for some reason the AA guns at Gazala seldom opened up on the intruders.

Tobruk, on the other hand, had some sort of air raid every night, sometimes two or three a night, and the sky was transformed into a weaving pattern of LAA tracer, and spangled with the flickering bursts of HAA fire. In accordance with the Tobruk tradition, anything that could be elevated or propped up so as to project high explosive into the sky was brought into action.

During the few days we were at Gazala, ASM "Bill" Smith, Estlin's WO I was granted a commission as Lieutenant (AOME) and there was considerable jollification, for Smith was very popular in 12 AA Bde. I remember providing him with some "pips" to complete his uniform, to wear on his first night in the

Mess, because Estlin had been a major for so long that all he could raise were three odd ones which didn't match each other.

Then on 3 February, when we were just beginning to see a bit of daylight through the cloud of work, we received orders to pack up forthwith and move back to El Adem, 40 miles or so further to the rear. Apparently the RAF fighter squadrons had decided that Gazala was a bit too exposed and near to potential ground fighting and were being withdrawn and redeployed at El Adem, from which the bomber squadrons were being moved to LGs still further to the rear. 2 LAA Regt, of course, moved with the RAF and I heard from Estlin, who now released us from his direct control, that we were to take over the workshop site and general commitments at El Adem from 88 HAA Wksps, who were moving out and going back to Oxford Circus in *Egypt*! This last bit of information had a horrid sound and I kept it from the lads, who were speedily mustered at the sound of the twin horns of my 15cwt Bedford. The Workshop swore gloomily and proceeded methodically to pack up with its customary efficiency.

It was a filthy day. A strong wind was blowing which whirled the dust up in blinding clouds, bringing visibility down to 20–30 yards. Through this thick, yellow fog, a packed stream of traffic surged back from the Gazala area. In retrospect, I think the snap decision to evacuate Gazala could have been taken that day on account of the unexpected dust storm, enabling the operation to be completed without the knowledge or interference of the enemy, who would not be aware of the move. We were due to leave Gazala in the next few days anyhow, but the dust was a heaven-sent bit of camouflage.

It was, however, bad for morale. Retreating is always bad for morale and this foul weather brought it down almost to zero. All Gazala – RAF, AA and supporting troops – seemed to be coming back down the road at the same time in a long unending column, a not very disciplined column, either, for the dust made that well-nigh impossible. Vehicles pulled out from the verges and belted eastwards more or less individually in the murk and by the time the gaunt ruins of El Adem loomed out of the dust, I was feeling almost suicidal.

At El Adem, the chaos was worse, if anything. The only

approach to the LG was a single track off the main road and this track was already filled spasmodically by the rear parties of the RAF bomber ground staffs moving out, as at the same time the incoming replacements were trying to gain entrance. Somehow, we managed to squeeze ourselves in and set off across the empty field towards the escarpment which ran along the further side of the LG from the Trigh Capuzzo. I knew that Morton had the 88th on a site opposite the LG and under the eaves of the escarpment, and it was a bit of a job to locate him in the bad visibilty, but, at last, we were successful.

Most of Morton's heavier transport had already left under the command of his 2 i/c, Greening, and there was little for us to do but accept the various jobs that he had been forced to leave unfinished on account of the sudden move. He was highly blasphemous at the short notice he had had to move – an HAA Wksp is about the size of three LAA Wksps put together – and rather gloomy as to the state of the war generally. In particular, he deplored having to move back into Egypt, adding that the RAF seemed to have got the wind up in no uncertain manner; the bomber ground staffs were burning anything they couldn't carry away as though the enemy were ten miles away instead of fifty.

And so we arrived at El Adem, where the Workshop was to remain for four and a half months, although we didn't know that at the tine. With this final retirement, the battle seemed to have blown itself out and an uneasy peace descended on the desert, with the combatants stretched out in a somewhat tenuous line facing each other rather loosely from in front of Gazala on the coast to Bir Hacheim out in the desert.

The airstrip at El Adem had been an important one in the pre-war build-up of the Italian colony of Libya and consisted of a very large expanse of flat and hard desert, scrupulously levelled and cleared of all surface rocks and stones of any size. The Italians had garrisoned it with air force and ancillary ground troops, comfortably accommodated in big, low barrack buildings round the perimeter and large hangars, workshops and repair bays were available for the aircraft. I was told that the aircraft were mainly military, although there was some small use of the airfield by civilian craft of some Italian airline.

In peacetime it must have been a flourishing establishment, but two desert campaigns of advance and retreat had altered that pretty effectively. The hangars were now gaunt and roofless ruins of battered concrete and twisted steelwork, and the less solidly built barracks were now as nearly demolished as they could be. Graveyards of smashed enemy aircraft had been bulldozed together in piles on every side as if with a giant rake – hundreds of them, it seemed – in fact, everything about El Adem was on a gigantic scale, its planning, its pre-war magnificence and its ultimate ruin.

The airfield lay on the "step" between the two parallel escarpments I have mentioned before. Beyond it, to the north, between it and the second escarpment, ran the Axis Highway round Tobruk and on the hither side, between the LG and the escarpment, ran the Trigh Capuzzo along the step, some half a mile in front of the escarpment. This latter was steep and rocky, cleft with numerous gullies, like Sidi Resegh, which afforded good protection from possible air attacks. Anyone who was anyone, including ourselves, was tucked into these gullies as inconspicuously as possible, for the received knowledge was that the enemy, in particular the Italians, knew their way about El Adem very well even in the dark and it behoved one to treat this seriously.

RHQ had established themselves some few hundred yards off to the east, and the air defence of the airfield complex was by 283 and 292 HAA Btys and by a constantly changing succession of LAA Btys, none of whom remained very long but all of whom were old friends and at some time in the past had been under the command of 2 LAA Regt. 292 Bty had achieved the distinction of reaching Bengasi, as part of 2 AA Bde where they had taken part in the defence of the port; 291 Bty, we heard, were now at Gambut after retiring from Derna and 261 were now reforming in Tobruk. RHQ 94 HAA Regt, it seemed, was still in Matruh, where reports said they were still acting as a sort of transit camp staff.

HQ 12 AA Bde, after a few days at El Adem, had retired to

Gambut, which was about 40 miles to the east, whither the RAF Fighter Group HQ had gone. Gambut, in fact, was now the main base for the fighters and El Aden was only a forward airstrip, where aircraft were not generally retained after dark. As the weeks passed, its importance dwindled, making it an emergency LG and finally the squadrons kept it only for refuelling. In the initial stages, however, a fighter wing was stationed there and there was a Gun Operations Room (GOR) with Wing HQ.

This particular GOR was the mobile one which had moved down to Msus and back with 2 LAA Regt. The officer in charge was a friend of mine, but I had seen little of him during the later stages of the flap. He walked into our office a few days after our arrival at El Adem, asking if we had ever owned a box-bodied Opel lorry. I admitted that we had, but it had been taken from us at Sidi Resegh in December, and I hadn't heard of it since. He said sadly that *he* had. Our ex-breadwagon had been issued to him as a mobile ops room a couple of days later and somewhere around Gazala on the way out it had split its cylinder head. Since spares for German vehicles were unobtainable, they were forced to tow it all the way to Msus and part of the way back. Somewhere between Mechili and Eleba on the return journey, its rear axle had collapsed and they had poured petrol over it and set it on fire. Perhaps it was just as well we had been forced to give it up!

Enemy aircraft were quite frequent visitors at El Adem, usually around dawn when they used to sail over the escarpment and drop strings of small bombs on the LG, the Trigh Capuzzo and any other target that presented itself. Lots of assorted AA guns opened up and the enemy aircraft felt obliged to ground-strafe them with machine guns and tracer. Anyone not actively involved prudently retired into the relatively safe upper reaches of the crannies in the escarpment and let the main parties fight it out. I said something to this effect unthinkingly to Estlin on one of his visits and he replied disapprovingly, pointing to our AA Bren, that we were there to fight a war, not to take cover, and commented on the devastating effect on low-flying aircraft of a concentrated fire from several of such guns. End of homily . . .

He never raised the matter again, but there was a sequel

which S/Sgt Lewis gleefully told me in confidence later when Estlin was absent. Some time a little later, an enemy aircraft started a night shoot-up in the neighbourhood of Bde HQ, but not actually aimed at the HQ itself. All the Bde staff – gunners to a man – took cover in their slit trenches, but Estlin, bursting with enthusiasm, routed out Pte Smith, his (somewhat unwilling, Lewis said) batman driver – who must have reckoned that the danger of being shot by the enemy was less than having to brave the anger of the Great Man – and the pair of them took over one of the HQ AA Brens, whose crew had, very wisely, gone to ground. The cheerful madman thereupon fired at the next aircraft to come over and several brisk engagements ensued, with the aircraft raking the HQ camp with both front and rear guns and with Estlin firing back as fast as Pte Smith could load the magazines. Eyewitnesses said that he undoubtedly scored some hits and the battle was called off solely because, they thought, the enemy ran out of ammunition before Estlin. The rumour was that the next morning the Brigadier called Estlin into his tent, commended his on his fighting spirit, emphasised the virtues of prudence and economy in ammunition and forbade any repetition of the event without his express orders. Estlin retired, bloody but unbowed, and it became a joke that the RAOC (Workshops) had shown these RA types how to wage a war; we never heard, however, of anyone else seeking to emulate this behaviour.

Before we had been a couple of days at El Adem, the missing 3-tonner from the Bde Stores Section, last seen going the wrong way at Antelat, arrived at the site and reported to me. The driver said that they had become separated from us in the departure from Antelat and they had joined on to a retreating RASC column, with whom they had eventually reached Tobruk. Here they reported to the local AA Bde – 4 AA Bde was in Tobruk – and found we were at El Adem. They had had a bit of trouble with the enemy near Saunnu during their first day of separation and had been hit by a small explosive shell from an armoured car, 15mm probably, while they were running away. It burst on the steel store bins in the front of the lorry without doing very much damage, although I don't doubt it fairly put the wind up the driver and his mate. They were lucky, because, had it penetrated the bin, it would have gone straight through a full 30-gallon fuel tank and burst in the driver's cab. A very nasty end, too, for 30 gallons of petrol, scattered by a shell-burst, would have set the lorry on fire from end to end in a couple of seconds.

The Bde Stores Section had by this time been withdrawn by Estlin, to operate under his special eye at Gambut, so I congratulated the crew of the missing lorry and sent them on.

Our greatest worry at this time was to get ourselves mobile again. The high-octane aircraft petrol which had been almost solely responsible for getting us away safely from Msus, had done no good to the valves and cylinder heads on one of the Bedford 30cwts, my Bedford 15cwt and QMS Neath's Ford 15cwt. All were stripped down for inspection as soon as it appeared that we were halted for more than a few days and, although we got spares for the Ford relatively easily from Tobruk, we needed two cylinder heads for the Bedfords and none were available anywhere. As a temporary measure, we made one reasonable engine out of the two and put it into my 15cwt, and downgraded the 30cwt to a non-runner to be towed. Our office trailer was showing signs of its recent hard life, so we converted the Bedford into a mobile office, complete with tables covered with army blankets, electric light and a steel filing cabinet that someone had found in the desert. We offered the old office trailer to RHQ who were delighted with it. I heard it finally gave up the ghost at a highly inconvenient moment during the new flap in May, but that was an RA matter and not our fault.

In the Big War, the contestants were pausing for breath, along a somewhat indeterminate line running between Gazala on the coast to Bir Hacheim in the desert hinterland. Both of these strong-points were highly fortified and heavily garrisoned and, between them, were hastily erected a number of entrenched defensive positions, generally described as "boxes", forming individual redoubts about which our armour could theoretically manoeuvre as pivots. Apart from the well-nigh impregnable Gazala position, there were "boxes" at Acroma; at the newly-named "Knightsbridge", where the Trigh Capuzzo crossed the track from Acroma to Bir Hacheim; at a point to the south of this, usually just called the 150 Bde Box; and at one or two smaller points whose names I have forgotten. In the extreme south lay the considerable position of Bir Hacheim, held in strength by the Free French, and beyond that the desert was patrolled by aircraft and an armoured car screen.

To give protection to Tobruk from a possible sudden out-flanking movement round our left wing, the powers-that-be decided to construct another box on the southern escarpment at El Adem and the first we knew about it was when the engineers of a New Zealand Bde Group appeared on the escarpment above the workshop and began to carve trenches and gun emplace-ments out of the rock with high explosive. They told us politely that we were in a "crook spot" there and advised us to move somewhere else, for our own safety. This we did and watched from afar as large lumps of escarpment sailed through the air and landed where our site had been. Our new position was about half a mile further along the escarpment, where it was a good deal lower and had fewer gullies in which we could take cover from air raids, but the compensation was that we were further from the LG and the air raids.

The New Zealanders certainly made a very good job of the defence. The more commanding section of the escarpment was very heavily fortified and there were mazes of subsidiary trenches and minefields. Although attacked many times during the mad days of early June, when it was a famous outpost of the fast withering Tobruk defences, it was never taken by assault, garrisoned by 22 Guards Bde and 292 Bty right to the end, when it was abandoned at night as part of the general withdrawal.

When the box was complete, the New Zealanders withdrew back into Egypt, whence they had come, and various miscel-laneous formations: South Africans, Free French, and British, garrisoned it for short periods. Then it lay deserted for weeks, except for a small caretaker party.

All this information didn't come to me just like that, for the situation during our stay in El Adem was pretty obscure and my knowledge was collated from Sitreps, maps, "travellers' tales" and the like, enabling me to build up some fairly complete pictures of what was going on around us. I kept the Workshops in the know, as well as I could, in order to sustain their interest, and held a sort of "press conference", with Claud's permission, every three or four days as the Army or 13 Corps Sitreps came in. Since there was no official handout for the troops, I think my Workshop had a much better idea of what they were doing and why, than most troops around them.

For a short while 68 HAA Wksps came back into the Bde and sat beside us at El Adem. Estlin returned to them the detachment that had been with me since Msus, less, of course the "A" lorry and crew that had gone into the bag with the troop of 261 – Cotterill, who tended to be a gloomy so and so, although a good engineer, perpetually bellyached to Estlin and to me about the way we had lost it for him. Neither of us gave him much sympathy and I was quite glad when they packed up and moved on into Tobruk, under the command of 4 AA Bde, who had just reconstituted 68 HAA Regt from its component parts and put them to the defence of the port. I was sorry, however, to say goodbye to Neath and his merry men who had been such good colleagues.

As soon as 68 was safely out of the way, Estlin produced, as if from out of a hat, a brand new "A" lorry and a 15cwt generator truck and attached them to us, but remaining on 12 AA Bde strength. I suspected he had drawn them against 68's deficiency, but had kept them concealed somewhere, in the knowledge that 68 were only birds of passage, and, with Estlin, charity began at home. To do otherwise was unthinkable.

I still had the Bde Instrument Section with me and it left us somewhat stronger than when we had started from Maddelena, although much reduced compared with our inflated numbers during the immediate past.

Having demonstrated the great value to 12 AA Bde of the hastily-conceived Bde Stores Section during the recent campaign, Estlin decided to go one better. He took a high-speed trip to the Delta and badgered some form of authority out of GHQ MEF to form a small Ordnance Field Park of his own from within the resources of the Bde and to hold stores against some scale that he argued out with them. Lt Col Humphreys, who was to be my ADME in Force 686 later in the war, and at that time the major at GHQ in charge of such matters, told me much later that Estlin had been so intrusive and importunate that they had given him the authority he was asking for so persistently, simply to get him out of their hair, doubtless reckoning that 12 AA Bde would be unable to do much with the authority, since it would involve equipping this OFP from scratch with the necessary quota of stores vehicles and storemen, as well as stores.

They were probably unaware that Estlin went straight from their presence, authority in hand, to the appropriate section of GHQ 2nd Echelon at Abbassia and had an Ordnance Warrant Officer Class 1 posted with immediate effect to the unborn OFP on the strength of that piece of paper. Which all goes to show how careful you must be in giving out such authorities...

Raising the necessary vehicles from within the Bde resources was, of course, just child's play for Estlin. His connivance with the Bde Commander, who lent a sympathetic ear to anything which improved the efficiency of his command and a large-scale vehicle reorganisation within the Bde – of which more presently – produced all the stores vehicles he required. Some essential gun and vehicle stores had already been acquired from the Base Ordnance Depot in Tobruk before the flap had fully subsided, for the authorities there had been only too pleased to find anyone willing to take these away to prevent them falling into the hands of the oncoming enemy. In this manner, practically all the 3.7" and a lot of the 40mm gun stores there fell into the hands of 12 AA Bde instead, greatly to the annoyance, I was told, of 4 AA Bde who were right on the doorstep, but nothing like as quick off the mark.

For staff, Estlin seconded a clerk or storeman and a driver from each of the workshops under his command and, before anyone but those in the secret were aware of what was going on, the 12 AA Bde OFP was in full operation as a viable unit.

It was an admirable example of foresight and planning with sheer self-interest, coupled with a bit of downright piracy, winked at by Authority, and justified by the end at which it was aimed. I submit that the formation of this OFP must stand alone in the annals of the desert war. As the Bde Commander realised, in a far-seeing moment, it was the best thing that could possibly be done for the Bde, if it were to continue in its mobile role, and I do not think 12 AA Bde would ever have been able to put up the show in the subsequent campaign that it did, without the priceless aid of this brainchild of Estlin's. For, once formed, the OFP wasn't disbanded until after the fall of Tunis over a year later.

As March drew on and the threat of a German thrust receded, all the life that had drained away back into Egypt during the great flap began to flow back into eastern Libya. Tobruk ceased to pack up and reopened in a more moderate style as an advanced base; the RAF returned, stiffening up their forces at Gambut, and bringing up light and medium bombers to Gasr el Arid and Baheira LGs, some ten and forty miles respectively on the "safe" side of Gambut. With the latter came 88 HAA Wksps to set up at Baheira and, to cater for the AA defence of the Gambut area, RHQ 94 HA Regt was dug out of Matruh at last. With them to Gambut came 94 Wksps, for the first time entering the operational zone, a move which caused more than a little quiet amusement in workshop circles, when it was remembered with what flourish they had arrived in the desert.

The Gambut commitment was considered too big for a single AA Regt, so, to assist 94, 15 LAA Regt, with their associated workshops came up from the Delta. 15 LAA Wksps was now commanded by our old acquaintance, Marshall, formerly of 94 Heavy, who had been posted there from 14 Light and replaced in 14 by Cresswell. To command 94 came Purcell who had come back from his Armd Bde Rec Sec, and he was assisted by two lieutenants new to the desert.

Thus, by mid-April, there were five AA wksps under Estlin's jurisdiction, namely, reading from forward to rear areas: 2 Light (myself) at El Adem; 94 Heavy (Purcell) and 15 Light (Marshall) at Gambut; 88 heavy (Morton) at Baheira; and 27 Light at Capuzzo railhead. I forget the name of the OC of 27 Light, but he does not come into my story.

All of us were very much under the thumb of Estlin, and he

made numerous visits to all of us in turn to see, in that order, first that we were not doing wrong and second that we had all the tools, spares and assistance we needed for doing right. If there was anything he considered essential for the proper functioning of the Bde, he spared no pains and wasted no time in providing it. We all worked as a coherent team to get and maintain the Bde's equipment in good trim again after the strains of the recent campaign and, to this end, he allocated to each workshop a steady stream of work according to its capacity.

Perhaps I am labouring rather overmuch Estlin's importance in the Bde's functioning, although, in retrospect, I don't think so. The discipline, training, standard of maintenance and efficiency he instilled into us stood us all in good stead in the coming months and, even when he was replaced by a "Pharaoh who knew not Joseph", his spirit lasted on with us for nearly a year after his departure, before it faded away.

There was another useful activity worth mentioning, which he instigated. After our return to Gazala and beyond, 1 LAA Regt came temporarily under command of 12 AA Bde for a few weeks, before withdrawing to the Delta for reforming and refitting. They had missed returning with 7 Armd Bde due to the flap and had now been over a year in the desert. Bentley was just the same, possibly browner even than before, his SD cap more battered and his spectacle frames now mended with insulating tape, but otherwise little different. We had some long talks in the evening, swapping stories of our adventures and pooling experiences and suggestions for maintenance. I was sorry to see him depart.

1 LAA Regt in departing did us a good turn, for GHQ MEF decreed that they would return to the Delta by train from Capuzzo and instructed them to hand over all their transport to a 12 AA Bde pool before leaving. From this pool, the Bde had authority to equip all the Regts under command to their correct scale, where necessary by exchanging worse vehicles for better and then handing in the surplus transport to the Returned Vehicle Park in Tobruk.

Estlin promptly got the ear of the Brigadier and propounded a very far-reaching but eminently sensible idea, which he was given authority to carry through, although the actual orders were signed by the Staff Captain, to give them the fullest majesty of RA authority in forcing any changes.

At this time all the Regts had a pretty motley collection of vehicles, which they had been issued piecemeal through the past year or so. Everyone's vehicle states indicated that all held a mixture of Bedfords, Fords, Chevrolets, Morrises and sundry lesser makes, such as my two Karriers. Furthermore, each Regt was holding quantities of spares for one or two vehicles only and all repair work was complicated by the diversity of types held by different units.

Estlin's Grand Design was simply to institute a grand re-allocation of the transport within the Bde, so that each Regt would finish up with the same make of vehicle throughout. Using the monthly vehicle strength returns, he and the Staff Captain did a paper redistribution of the transport, published "postings" between units and fixed a date by which all movements were to be completed. Each vehicle was to be properly handed over and all spares were to be handed in to the Bde pool, to be reissued to the proper first-line scale to the homogeneous Regts.

For two or three days chaos reigned as the transfers took place, and it was lucky that the enemy didn't do anything during that time; and then, out of the ashes of reconstruction arose Regts completely equipped with Bedfords, or Fords, or Chevrolets and so on. It was quite remarkable; there were of course a few slip-ups, as units found the vehicles they had been returning for months as Fords were really Chevrolets, or the so-called 3-tonners were really only 30cwts, but it was all sorted out amicably within a week, very much to the advantage of efficiency. As a result the Bde OFP benefited by large quantities of surplus or unnecessary spares, over and above the first-line scale and Estlin was able to equip the OFP with the necessary vehicles that it had hitherto lacked.

Out of all this, I acquired an extra light truck. We had handed in our motorcycle to the local Returned Vehicle Park at Maddelena the previous December, when it became apparent it was no good in the role we were being set, but was in good condition, and we had a proper receipt for it, which entitled us to a replacement as soon as we wanted one, since there were motorcycles and to spare in the vehicle parks at present. But I didn't want a motorcycle; they were no use to us, but we had a great need for another light truck which would have been a godsend in enabling us to do our proper job of work, – we couldn't all use the 15cwt Bedford at once!

When the great sort out was over, Estlin came over to see me one day and offered us a water trailer "in lieu of a motorcycle". I gained the impression that we might be rather his favourites. Anyhow, I said that we had made ourselves a good enough trailer, but if he could see his way to letting me have an 8cwt truck for my personal use, so that I could get around the gunsites and do my proper job of inspections, I would be very grateful. He replied that I should be grateful for smaller mercies than that, but agreed that I could be rather hampered by a tussle with the ration corporal every time I wished to visit a Bty. Nothing more was said at the time, but a couple of days later he rang up and asked if a Dodge 8cwt would be any good to me and, if so, could I send my driver over to collect it. Brushing aside my grateful thanks, he said it was the best motorcycle he could produce. A few minutes after and before the hastily summoned driver had set off, Lewis rang up and told me that the Major in fact had three Dodges to dispose of and that, if the driver were to be S/Sgt Dean, he would be able to pick the best one, rather than taking the next on the list. I gathered that Estlin was out of the office!

So off went Dean and he returned in due course with a very well preserved little truck, almost in showroom condition in fact, except for several bullet holes in the windscreen – a relic of some recent night-strafe, I was told. The Dodge was a most useful breed of 8cwt truck, the only 8cwt in the desert to have four-wheel drive, but was eyed askance by the average unit on account of its unnaturally soft and bouncy springing, calculated to reduce the average driver to travel-sickness after several hours of cross-desert travel, if he wasn't first brained by bashing his head against the roof. However, the one Dean had chosen had been modified – probably by 1 LAA Wksps – by the fitting of tougher springing, so that it was quite comfortable to ride in. It promptly became my personal vehicle and the Bedford was released for other general duties.

I had an emergency collapsible canvas bed mounted across the front of the body, intending to live in it all the time when the mobile war restarted, and, in accordance with the latest GHQ MEF instructions, an observation hatch with a lid was cut in the roof over the passenger's head, so that I could stand on the seat whilst on the move to look out for hostile aircraft and to control the convoy. The vehicle soon acquired the name of "Little Audrey".

The practice of giving names to vehicles and painting these names prominently on the front was an old desert custom and one of which I personally approved, although some commanders objected to it as facetious. The name was usually the product of the driver's imagination and there were three main classes:

(1) The frankly humorous, such as "Packet o' Trouble", "Squibs", the inevitable "Dorcas", "Beelzebub", and our own 30cwt recovery "Otta Zadees".

(ii) The "Home Town", such as "Govan Cross", "Peckham High", "New Cut", "Auld Reekie", "Plymouth Hoe", "Sheffield Wednesday", "Heart of Midlothian", "Maryhill", etc.

(iii) The "girlfriend" variety in which the name of the driver's consort appeared above his windscreen and that of his normal mate's on the other side. Examples were "Elsie-Grace", "Winifred-Jane", "Betty-Joan" and so on. Most officers I knew entered into the spirit of the game and, if I remember aright, "Elsie-Grace" was the car of Major Sir Ian Macpherson Grant (OC 292 Bty), Elsie being Gnr MacTavish's "steady" and Grace being Lady Macpherson Grant.

We had some discussion about whether the name Spooner had given to the Bedford 15cwt, "Malika Farida", fell into Category (i), as he himself maintained, or Category (iii) as I tried to convince him, Queen Farida being a very personable wench.

I have mentioned the formation of Free French who occupied

the El Adem box for a short time, while staging on their way to the forward area. One of its battalions had its HQ and Officers' Mess just uphill from RHQ and we came to see quite a lot of them from time to time, particularly Messent, who spoke fluent and idiomatic French, having spent much of his civilian life in France before the war. They were a unit of the Battalions des Marins Pacifiques, and I can only assume that the "Pacifiques" was intended to be an indication of their place of origin, rather than that of their demeanour, for it would have been difficult to envisage a more warlike crew. Their officers were the only white men in the battalion, and the latter had come a long way, since, although we were led to believe they had been brought from Indo-China, the majority of the ORs were full-blooded Senegalese blacks. Their Colonel was a tall, courteous man with a little clipped moustache and faultless képi and khaki drill – straight out of the novels of P.C. Wren – who ruled them with a rod of iron. His "Adjutant", a sort of super Regimental Sergeant Major, over six feet tall, with a gigantic red, spade-shaped beard, a jovial smile and a voice like a thunderclap, had powers of punishment over "*les noirs*" including ten days in solitary confinement on bread and water, and accordingly indiscipline scarcely existed!

The remainder of the officers were not regulars, but had escaped from France somehow or other, during the past couple of years, and were now prepared, coldly and unflinchingly, to fight their way back. From their talk, it seemed likely that there would be as much bloodshed, when they got back, among the "*collaborateurs*" as with the execrated Germans. I came to appreciate that we British seemed to be the only nation among the Allies out here in the desert that didn't hate the Germans very strongly, regarding them rather as soldiers who, like us, were only there because some politician had "posted" them to the desert. To the men whose countries had been invaded and squashed flat, the Germans were vermin to be attacked and exterminated.

All the officers, except the CO, were young, and the youngest of them was their Medical Officer, whom they called the "*Tubibe*" – I don't know how it is spelt – but it was French slang, Messent explained, for an unqualified medical student. He was a rosy-cheeked lad of nineteen or twenty who frankly admitted that, although the war had prevented him taking his finals, he would be able to give a good account of himself when the battalion went into battle. The most unexpected member of the Mess was a woman ambulance driver-cum-nursing orderly-cum-dispenser, the only female among a thousand men. She was fortyish, small, neat and greying slightly at the temples. Her name was "Margie" and she was treated by "*les gosses*", as she called the young officers, as a sort of good-natured elder sister, who sewed on their buttons and looked after the Mess catering.

Messent took me over to lunch with them one day and they put on the most remarkable meal from ordinary Army issue that I have ever tasted, and that without any suggestion that it was other than their normal fare.

They were a pleasant, light-hearted crowd and I wished them well when they moved out a week or so later to join their compatriots at Bir Hacheim in the south-west. I often wondered what happened to them in the mad days of early June. No doubt they gave a good account of themselves, but none of us ever heard.

Although Margie was the first woman we had seen in the desert since our arrival in the previous July, she wasn't the last. Shortly afterwards, rumours spread about a whole hospital unit with *Women* arriving to support the Free French and setting up somewhere between El Adem and Bir Hacheim. It turned out to be our old friends of *Otranto* days, the Hadfield-Spears Ambulance Unit – Mary Borden's Chorus – who had previously been operating in Syria. Whilst there, in 1941, Lady Spears and some French general had managed to get themselves captured by the Vichy French and the pair had been confined together in close quarters, until the enemy authorities, wholeheartedly supported by the general, had decided that she was a pain in the neck and released her. A scandalous story and one which gained credence when the good lady appeared in person in Tobruk and tackled the medical authorities there to ensure that her unit got the best of everything. This it did, at least as far as comforts for the sick were concerned, because it was difficult to tell Lady Spears what she could do with herself, both on the grounds of courtesy towards a female and because Gen Spears was a great power in the ME, whom no one wished to annoy. As a result there was considerable ill-feeling towards the Chorus in the forward areas, which tended to obscure the very good work they were doing for the French.

I had some of it for, before long, one of their ambulance drivers broke down on the Trigh Capuzzo near my patch and was towed in by our recovery lorry which was out on a "sweep" looking for vehicles to cannibalise. The appearance on the site of a real live and, needless to say, highly photogenic (that being an essential characteristic of the Spears unit girls) *white woman* in our midst, brought the Workshop more or less to an open-mouthed standstill. It was, as Spooner told me afterwards, somewhat disorganising in other ways, because we had long since dispensed with such trifles as latrine screens. Spooner immediately decided that it would be my job to look after the female in the office where the worst of our indiscretions were out of sight, and landed me with her to entertain until the spring of her ambulance had been repaired, at least to a state which would hold until she was sufficiently out of range not to return to us. I had been on the point of leaving for a gunsite inspection when she arrived and the repair took nearly an hour, by which time I would happily have left her to the care of Sgt Hughes and his pay clerk and gone on my way to the inspection. Anyone who has endured the conversational performance of a member of the Spears Unit will understand. I wasn't interested in anything about the hardships she and her friends were undergoing, together with the problems of her transport, and wished she had remained in the fleshpots of the Delta.

The only member of the unit who remained completely unmoved by her presence was the unit dog, Michael, commonly known as "The Perp", who was now an experienced desert warrior, having been acquired the previous July at Beni Yussef by Sgt Clarke, our instrument NCO. At the time of joining us, Michael couldn't have been more than a couple of months old and it was quite surprising that he survived at all. But survive he did. He was a sort of cross between a fox terrier and dachshund, so the experts asserted, with a roughish coat and rather bandy legs, possibly as the result of improper feeding as a puppy, that affected his "wrists" and "ankles", so that he walked with a sedate and splay-footed, Chaplinesque waddle. Somehow he managed to survive the periodic purges that were directed at dogs in that rabies-infected country, this largely due to Estlin, with whom he was rather a favourite and who gave us warning when Authority was contemplating a purge. A dog of great character, he ambled round with a perpetually worried, preoccupied expression, as though he carried the cares of the whole world on his shoulders. Separated from life in an Egyptian community as a puppy, it was probable that he had never seen another of his species since earliest puppyhood and Estlin was once heard to remark that he wondered if Michael had any idea what sex was.

His chief dislikes were wandering Bedouin, whom he missed no opportunity of biting, and German aircraft who unfortunately were out of biting range. The regular bombings and ground-strafings used to drive him into a frenzy of vocal objection, but someone always remembered to yank him down into a slit trench in time. His chief likes were bully beef out of the tin and very stale Army biscuits.

Air raids on El Adem were maintained at a fairly steady, but not intensive, level. Mostly they were high-level bombing attacks, with the aircraft well out of LAA range, although the HAA guns round the airfield opened up with great verve, but little result. However, one afternoon, when I was sitting in front of my tent having my hair cut by Pte Crane – who was expert at cutting hair in addition to building stone walls – we watched a single aircraft sail in un-attacked at about three or four thousand feet. As we gazed upwards there was a sort of flicker beneath it when it was just overhead. This must have been the sun's reflection on the bombs turning over as they left the bomb-bays and the first intimation of any trouble was the sound of them coming down very fast, their note rising in pitch to a thin scream. Crane left in one direction, still bearing the scissors, and I fled in the other, clutching the towel and only partly shorn.

No damage resulted and the bombs landed in a string of dirty-brown fountains of displaced desert some 300 yards off. This was our nearest miss.

Ground-strafing was more spectacular; on two occasions in particular. The first occurred at 7.30 a.m. on 28 February 1942 – my birthday – on a coldish grey morning, just as I was settling down to a late breakfast at the mouth of my tent. The roar of a large number of aircraft engines made me draw aside the tent flap, and I saw, without paying much attention, a dozen or more low-wing monoplanes apparently coming in over the escarpment to land on the airstrip. I was just about to return to my breakfast, when the "air raid warning" gun was fired and simultaneously the aircraft fanned out and began to shoot up anything and everything in sight with cannon shell. We all made a dive for the nearest slit trench and, after a moment's stunned delay, pandemonium broke loose among the AA defences of the LGs. Anything that would fire was fired at low elevation; spent projectiles whizzed past; shell splinters flicked down about us; LAA and LMG tracer came horizontally across the valley, all rules of dead zones ignored; HAA shells burst on the escarpment above us, bringing down showers of stones and rock chips; while the guns on the escarpment above us, firing in depression, or so it seemed, retaliated in their turn, blazing away into the valley, more or less equally at the aircraft and the other HAA defences. During all this, the enemy aircraft sidled away. I was told later that they were Italian G 50s, not Germans.

Shortly afterwards, we had another unexpected ground-strafe attack. It was early afternoon and this time the warning gun went off before anything appeared. Whilst everyone was scanning the skies for some high-level stuff, a grand shoot-up started on the escarpment behind us and half a dozen slim ME 109F fighters hopped over the rim, heading for the LG. A few of our fighters had scrambled in the meantime and a series of very low-level dog-fights ensued. Most of us opted out, and lay down under any sort of cover out of the way of all the friendly and hostile cannon shells that were spraying around pretty indiscriminately, and, just as it seemed over, a lone ME 109F sailed over the escarpment, just above us, going relatively slowly.

Fired by Estlin's example, Pte Reilly and I, who were lying beside our AA Lewis gun, leapt to our feet, banged a magazine on and were just about to open up as a Hurricane popped in sight in pursuit of the intruder, which seemed to be somewhat damaged. Our chance went by and the 109F, which was going quite fast really, beat it for home with the Hurricane right on its tail. The Hurricane must have been out of ammunition, or else its guns had jammed, because it didn't fire, and the pair of them hurtled off westwards, separated by what seemed to us to be only a few feet, with the Hurricane weaving from side to side, apparently trying to slice off the ME's tail with its propellor. They were out of sight before we could see what happened, but I believe the ME's engine perked up a bit and he got away.

About this time we welcomed our old friends, 149 LAA Bty, temporarily back into the fold. They had been in Bengasi at the time of the enemy offensive in February, where they had been deployed round the LGs at Berka and Benina to the south-east of the town. The RAF retired in no small flap when the news of the advancing Germans burst on them, but 149 had no orders and stood its ground. It had held the Benina LG unsupported for the best part of a day and a night, thereby contributing in no small way to the safe withdrawal of many other units. Standing almost in the open, one troop in particular had stopped a German light armoured column and, firing over open sights, had knocked out three or four light tanks and set on fire the half-tracked troop-carriers that followed them. The troops the latter were carrying were forced to take cover behind their burning vehicles and were shelled out with HE, causing quite considerable casualties. For this whole operation, Major Wadley, the Bty Commander, and another officer had received an immediate award of the Military Cross and a gunner the Military Medal.

Since Bengasi was now virtually surrounded, the Bty joined an Indian Bde and with them broke out to the south, finally rejoining 8th Army forces near Gazala, after an extraordinary sweep through enemy-held territory by way of Msus and the desert south of Mechili. They had returned with all their guns intact, but had been obliged to abandon and destroy all their heavy non-essential equipment and stores. I could visualise the pleasure with which they must have set about the task of smashing up their detested No 3 predictors.

10

Tobruk wasn't a place I wished to visit often; it acted too much as a focus to enemy attention and received a lot of air raids during the weeks we were at El Adem. If we were relatively untroubled in our work, it was only because the enemy was much more interested in the target presented by Tobruk. The port was only some 20 minutes' flying time from the LGs at Martuba and three or four air raids a day were by no means uncommon, to say nothing of nights. We heard little of these attacks, unless the wind was from the north, but often, particularly, for some reason, if one was in a tent, the transmitted "thud" of big explosions could be felt. Once, I remember, we both felt and heard a dull roar in the middle of the afternoon and saw a great mushroom of dense brown smoke rise slowly and majestically above the northern horizon, its lower surface tinted by an unseen fire. It was probably an ammunition ship or dump; anyway, it burned all the rest of that day and most of the next.

Although we tended to go into Tobruk as little as possible, we couldn't avoid sending the daily truck in for rations, water and mail. In these sorties we took great care not to be anywhere near the Free French, who had a short answer to German aircraft. Their ration/water lorry was escorted by two 15cwt trucks each mounting a twin-barrel Hotchkiss pom pom. There was always a long string of lorries waiting at the water point and, when fired on by these vicious little guns, the aircraft didn't hesitate to fire back. Accordingly, the French were unpopular neighbours there for the inoffensive ration gatherers who just wanted water and a quiet life.

I saw a close-up of these raids on two occasions. The first occurred in the Returned Vehicle Park on the top of the hill just outside the port. We had been having a lot of trouble with the air-brakes on Matador tractors, which were operated from a small compressor driven off the vehicle's gearbox. This hard-worked piece of equipment managed to suck in all the dust and grit that was going and therefore had a very short life. Replacements were very hard to come by through the normal channels, so Estlin gave me an official chit and I went with our recovery lorry to see if I could scrounge a compressor from a very badly smashed up Matador reported to be in the RVP and replace it with a worn-out unit, since the vehicle was going to be evacuated to the Delta anyhow. The officer in charge of the RVP pointed out that it was a serious sin to cannibalise a vehicle in his park due for repair, but, mollified by Estlin's chit, he admitted it was a reasonable suggestion and strolled off, so as not to be a witness to the crime. Pte Smith (recovery) and his fitter mates got on with the exchange and, while they were prostrate under the vehicle on this exposed spur overlooking the harbour, a dive-bombing attack started.

All that has ever been said of dive-bombing is quite correct, so I will content myself by saying that the feeling of absolute nakedness has to be experienced to be appreciated. You and you alone seem to be the Ju 87's sole target. I joined the others under the Matador and peeped out to see whether this was true. Although we must have been a full half mile from the harbour, it indeed felt as though the Stukas were singling us out as their special target.

As the first Stuka came screaming down out of the clouds, the Tobruk AA defences opened up with a roar that shook the very ground on which we lay. Tobruk was very proud of its barrage, consisting as it did of everything around the port that could be elevated or propped up to launch an explosive missile into the air, ranging from the orthodox Heavy and Light AA artillery of 4 AA Bde, with the guns of any warships that might be present in the port, to a motley and uncountable array of relatively "private" weapons operated by the Tobruk garrison from its backyards. These included the former Italian harbour defence

236

guns, augmented by the AA armament salved from the water-logged cruiser *San Giorgio*; Italian 20mm and 13.2mm Bredas; 2cm German flak; a solitary captured 88mm in AA mode; sundry odd weapons of about 75mm; hosts of machine-guns of all sizes; several very odd pieces of ordnance, such as field guns on improvised AA mountings and the gun of at least one trackless Italian L6/40 light tank lying on its side in a ditch in somebody's back garden, with its barrel cocked in the air. As it was possible to cover a limited arc of sky with this last, a couple of enthusiasts used to add their bit to the general barrage whenever an aircraft happened to enter into their sights. I was told that the gunner had to lie on the rear wall of the turret, with the gun recoiling viciously in a vertical plane just above his ear.

This particular air raid lasted less than five minutes and the firing died down as the last Stuka skated away across the sea, almost skimming the surface. We waited under the Matador, however, until all the fragments should stop falling, for they were coming down like the patter of raindrops, and we were just edging our way out, when we heard the whistle of something much larger heading down. I must confess I thought it was a bomb and that our number was on it, but we had no more time than to burrow into the ground with our noses, when something fell on the Matador's steel roof, exploding with a noise like a thunderclap, and bits of Matador roof flew in all directions. The vehicle bounced on its springing, dislodging the dust of months of desert travel from the nooks and crannies of its underframe which fell on us as from a bursting bag of flour. We crawled out from underneath looking like ghosts, to find that the "bomb" must have been an unexploded 40mm shell. We finished swapping the compressor and left for home, before we were accused of this further damage to the Matador.

The other air raid was a couple of days later. I had of necessity gone to visit the Field Cashier in Tobruk to collect money with which to pay the unit. The Field Cashier's office was in the former Banca d'Italia, a noble edifice of marble, fronted by a colonnade of the same material. I was in the queue within, awaiting my turn at the counter, when the air raid warning sounded and aircraft were heard. Those of us nearest the door poked our heads outside to be met by the head-on view of a Ju 87 apparently diving straight at us. We immediately retired to the safety of the solid marble halls of the bank, considering these were the best Stuka-protection available. Seconds later, there was an almighty bang and we were thrown to the floor, covered in falling material, which proved, as soon as we recovered, to be fragments of the "marble' facing of the roof, which was now reduced to the wooden lattice to which it had been attached! My opinion of Italian architects was as severely dented as the building. We were lucky; the explosion had been that of a Stuka's whole bomb-load when the aircraft was shot down on the former little cathedral across the street.

When I had been to Tobruk on our way to Antelat, Tobruk had seemed only a bit chipped, notwithstanding several months of siege, but now it was getting pretty seriously damaged. If there had been some civilians left there before, there were certainly none now.

The intensive air activity increased in the following weeks and a visitor counted himself lucky if he got in and out of the port area without getting mixed up with an air raid. To cut down the number of unnecessary "visitors" – usually just plain sightseers – to a minimum, the Garrison Commander set up roadblocks on the approach roads to filter out the sheep from the goats, at which all vehicles passing through had to enter the driver's name, rank, unit and reason for visit in a record book.

It was a good idea, but a mistake was made in allocating the manning of the blocks to ORs of 5 Indian Div who couldn't read English handwriting. The first, and last, time I passed through and was handed the book by the smiling Indian junior NCO, I was confronted with the information that I had been preceded that day by A. Hitler L/Cpl; H. Goering, F. Marshal; Col Bogey; Major Road Ahead, Corporal Punishment and Private Parts, with various destinations of "Home", "Berlin", "Bengasi", "Oswaldtwistle" and "Mary's House" (a well known high-class brothel in the Delta). Units included: 8th Clodhoppers; Short Range Shepherd's Group; Berlin Harriers; Rec Sec, Water Zeppelin Regt and the like. Suppressing my urge to follow suit,

238

I signed my name, unit and destination properly and was waved on by the smiling NCO. The one thing one didn't do was drive straight through, because the Indians were somewhat inclined to forget how to count up to three, when challenging, before shooting.

To combat this, the Military Police were called in and erected a roadblock of such complexity at the junction of the coast road and the spur to El Adem, and maybe at other places, that driving straight through was impossible. Here my vehicle was brought to a full stop and confronted by a Warrant Officer Class I of Military Police – almost a mythical being in these parts. No one below the rank of brigadier stands much chance against such a personage!

As OC Unit, I didn't have any problem with this Olympian Being, who, it was said, regularly breakfasted on fried lance corporals. Apparently, he was an old Wavell's Army man and, seeing I had a bunch of Bersagliere cocks' feathers on my radiator (the closely guarded, but unofficial, insignia of the old Western Force, gathered in vast quantities at the battle of Beda Fomm in 1940) my interrogations were purely perfunctory. Every soldier of the Bersagliere must have lost his cockade at Beda Fomm, for there were lots about. I wasn't in the 1940 push, but I reckoned that I qualified for one, as a member of the Western Desert Force.

Air raids troubled us much less than other forms of flying things: flies and bugs. We were now in a part of what had once been virgin desert, but had been occupied by one side or another spasmodically for quite a considerable time, and these temporary lodgers had had varying and inadequate standards of hygiene, mainly with regard to refuse and latrines. The attitude seemed to have been: I'm only here for a couple of days, so why take particular care in disposal of waste? I'm all right, Jack, or Heinz, or Giovanni. The problem was much worse than had been our lot for months. All sorts of measures had to be introduced to cut down the fly menace, but in spite of them "gyppy tummy" was rife among the troops and the occasional cases of real dysentery made their appearance for the first time, involving removal to Base Hospital.

239

Other forms of assorted insect life abounded, particularly in Tobruk, which became alive with fleas. Out in the desert, we had the usual hordes of large black scarab scavenger beetles, scorpions, and peculiar whatnots strongly resembling wood lice, those articulated creepy-crawlies to be found under upturned stones, but nearly an inch long. It was said they had large quantities of waving legs, wiggly whiskers and "a sardonic expression".

We had to look where we were putting our feet down, too, for there was a sudden spate of small tortoises, varying in size from an inch in diameter to about four inches. These caused a lot of amusement and the troops held tortoise races with their "fancies" painted distinctive colours for ease of identification. Often tortoises wandered into the Workshop with RAF roundels or German black crosses enamelled on their shells and at least one had been buffed up until it shone with the brown glow of the tortoiseshell used in high-class dressing table accessories. One other came into our hands with the words in white paint: "Recd 20 March. Forwarded 21 March" on its shell. I was told that someone in the unit had added: "Passed to you for action", before sending it on its way. I wonder what its subsequent history was! Then, quite suddenly, the tortoises disappeared, as inexplicably as they had arrived.

The weather was now getting warmer and it was apparent that spring was just around the corner. This was a mixed blessing, because the ORs had only their winter battledress to wear and, anyhow, the early spring months in this part of the world were distinguished by the arrival of the "khamseen", a hot wind that blows spasmodically from the south for about a month and contrives to make life very unpleasant.

The arrival of the khamseen in El Adem this year was most spectacular. It had been an ordinary sort of day, warm but not particularly sunny and by late afternoon it became quite overcast. I had been doing some work in the office lorry, and came out to find everyone around looking at the sky to the south-west. Right across the horizon was a dark bar of what appeared to be billowing brown smoke and it was clearly coming our way at no small speed. For one moment my mind ran on a gas attack and

240

then I realised that this wasn't man-made, but a large dust storm, similar to the dust storms we had suffered in Sidi Barrani the previous autumn, only bigger. I sent Spooner round with instructions for the lads to knock off work at once and cover up the machinery lorries and anything that would suffer from an excess of dust and to tie down anything that might blow away.

This dust wall took about ten minutes to reach us and we had time to appraise it from the mouths of our bivvies, whither we had retired. It really was most spectacular; a clear-cut vertical wall of churning, billowing fog, several thousands of feet high, as we realised when we saw a lone aircraft disappear into it, stalking across the empty desert. There was no wind, but along the ground a movement of dust trickled towards the foot of the wall, sucked by some change of pressure. The sun came out from behind the clouds just as the edge of the wall was a few hundred yards off and vanished into the brown whorls of rising dust; a great shadow swept across the plain as it disappeared and a premature dusk sprang up in the wadis of the escarpment behind us. Then it reached us; vehicles on the further side of our site disappeared as though wiped off with a sponge and then, with dramatic suddenness, we were in the midst of it. One moment the air was flat calm and we could still see the buildings of El Adem a mile away, and the next, with a shrill scream, a wild wind tore at the canvas of my tent and objects a few yards away became invisible. Around us howled half a gale, the hiss of airborne grit on tent surfaces blanked out almost every other sound, and although I made a swift attempt to seal off my own tent, a cloud of fine, brown fog drifted in through every minute aperture and settled on my bed, table and person in rapidly thickening layers.

This uncomfortable state of affairs lasted for some two hours, then the gale seemed to have blown over as suddenly as it had arrived and we emerged from our shelters to find appreciable "dust drifts" on the lee side of any upright object and our tea just about ruined by the fine grit that had infiltrated into the cookhouse trailer. It was then nearly sunset and the sun went down in a welter of blood-red clouds that I do not think I have ever seen bettered for sheer spectacle.

From that day on, for several weeks, we had the usual strong and blustery winds associated with the khamseen, but the weather remained unexpectedly cold and was inclined to rain. Not until May, in fact, did the sun really make the heat of the day oppressive.

About the time we were at El Adem, we first really began to encounter various troubles with the 3.7" HAA guns, which haunted us for the next twelve months, bulking larger and larger in our work. They were undoubtedly caused by the amount of travel over the shocking terrain which the guns were being forced to endure, although we didn't realise for some time that we were uncovering a series of unrelated design faults. The design might have been satisfactory for bumbling along the Watford bypass in the UK, but the desert soon showed up the weak links. A few words of explanation are necessary to understand the problems that were turning up.

An HAA gun consists essentially of three elements: the *Piece*, the *Mounting*, and the *Platform*. The Piece comprises the barrel and a fixed portion holding the barrel in which it recoils and runs out after firing; this fixed portion includes the hydraulic recoil-absorbing mechanism to absorb the shock of discharge and return the recoiled barrel to its normal position afterwards. It has a pair of trunnions projecting near its rear end which rotate in bearings on the Mounting about which the barrel pivots, enabling it to be elevated or depressed in a vertical plane by means of a large toothed quadrant on the underside of the back end of the Piece, which engages with a pinion gear wheel on a horizontal shaft in the Mounting. The gun layer alters the elevation of the gun with a large handle, rather like winding a bucket up from a well, which rotates the pinion through a worm drive. Since the trunnions are at the rear of the Piece, the barrel assembly is enormously "head heavy" and to balance this a set of heavy coil springs are provided, accurately adjusted to counterbalance the barrel's weight and allow the Piece to be run up and down in elevation with a minimum of effort by the layer.

The Mounting rotates on a vertical axis, "traversed" by a

vertically mounted traversing pinion, driven through gears by another gun layer. This pinion meshes with a fixed annular rack on the Platform and goes round with the Mounting as the gun is traversed. The weight of the rotating part of the gun is taken by a massive bearing in the bowels of the Platform, which allows a small amount of adjustment in two planes at right angles, so that the gun can be levelled accurately when finally in the firing position. There were types of Mounting in use in the desert at the time: the Mark I* and the Mark III which replaced it. The Mark I* had a clever little friction clutch in the drive from the elevating and traversing handles to their respective pinions, to minimise the possibility of any shock from the discharge transmitting back to the layers' handles. The Mark III was a simpler and cheaper wartime product which dispensed with the clutch and relied on a specially designed non-reversible worm and worm-wheel gearing. The whole assembly was prevented from slewing round when travelling by a pair of adjustable stays bolted to the Platform.

The third element, the Platform, is a two-axle, four-wheeled horizontal chassis, shaped like a capital "A" with the apex forward. At the apex, a projecting shaft, the pintle, fits into the pintle bearing in the front axle beam, allowing the front wheels to accommodate themselves to the contours of the terrain. A rear tubular, non-pivoting axle hooks on to the legs of the "A" frame. Both the axles and wheels have to be removed when going into action.

Four stout legs project star-wise from the middle section of the Platform with screw jacking pads on their outer ends, to be lowered and locked to form a broad base for the gun in its firing position, and to prevent it overturning when firing. When travelling, these legs have their locking pins removed so that they can be raised to the vertical and the locking pins replaced in a second set of sockets, to hold them up. The Mark I* Platform had rudimentary springing on each wheel with heavy coil springs, whereas the Mark III had no springing at all, other than that provided by the massive super low-pressure balloon tyres. The drill for bringing the gun into action differed with the two Marks; with the Mark I* gun, the entire Platform was lowered bodily on heavy chains from davits operated with hand wheels, after a securing pin was removed from the axle beside each wheel. Lastly the legs were swung out and secured in the "action" position, before the Platform finally "bottomed" on the ground, when the wheel and axle assemblies were detached and rolled away.

On the Mark III gun, however, the chain-lowering gear was omitted for simplicity and cheapness and all the work was done with the leg jacking screws. The drill involved swinging down and locking the legs, then winding down the jacking pads until they lifted the entire gun off the ground sufficiently to remove the axles, after which, the sweating team lowered the gun on to the ground, again with the jacking screws.

The gun layers, or "numbers" sat on little seats attached to the Mounting and rotated with it, facing away from the gun's muzzle, and they laid it in bearing and elevation by matching pointers on small dials above their operating handles with another set of concentric pointers moving in response to signals transmitted electrically from the predictor, some 30 yards away. The predictor calculated where to lay the gun in elevation and bearing from the information fed into it about height, change of angular direction and distance of the target aircraft and the chosen fuse setting.

Of all the gun team, the layers, who sat facing the rear, saw least of the action, spending all their time subscribing to the pious hope that the rest of the team knew what they were doing, and becoming cross-eyed in the process. It was said that they saw pointers in their very sleep.

These guns started to break things as soon as they entered the desert. The first to go were the devices intended to hold the barrel firm while travelling. The barrel lay on a steel saddle, projecting up from the Platform some three-quarters of the way back from the muzzle, and was held there, theoretically, by a pair of steel straps, tightened with a turnbuckle. However, the whip of the unsupported length of the barrel was such that these straps broke with unfailing regularity whenever the gun was moved (clearly a design fault by some herb who had never been anywhere outside the UK) and their repair at every stop was a pain in the neck for the Workshops. The gun crew sought to minimise the strain on the straps by lashing large quantities of rope round the end of the barrel, to hold it down on the strapless saddle as far forward as possible and secure it to the rear axle (the gun travelled with the barrel pointing to the rear). These makeshift lashings were tightened up, Spanish-windlass fashion by inserting an axe handle into the rope and twisting it round and round as far as was physically possible.

This makeshift reduced the barrel bouncing but didn't prevent it trying to swing the whole Mounting to and fro when traversing uneven ground. The result of this was that frequently the two small traversing stays between the rear of the Mounting and the Platform, put there specifically to cope with this, took all the force of a couple of tons of gun seeking to rotate about its axis and they snapped, or, if they didn't snap, they pulled out of their fixings in the Platform, which was worse. Manufacture of these traversing stays was a staple task of any AA Wksp and, in the Regt's more mobile moments, was a losing battle. As an added precaution against the Mounting breaking loose on the move, the thoughtful designers had provided a spring-loaded plunger in a gunmetal block on the side of the Mounting, which could be dropped into a corresponding socket in the Platform below. The idea was that this would prevent the gun from swinging in the event of a traversing stay breaking. It did not; either the gunmetal block broke, or its securing bolts broke, or the tip of the plunger sheared. Sometimes all three. And, if the plunger tip came off, the likelihood was that it would fetch up in the traversing rack and jam it. The standard gunner's remedy, by inclination or necessity, was rope and more rope, if the barrels were to be prevented from bouncing against the elevating gears or the whole Mounting slewing. A sad business...

So far these relatively minor ailments had been our only worry, but soon after their arrival at El Adem, 283 Bty reported something else. Something happened on one of their guns, when everyone was busy firing off HE at hostile aircraft and no one saw exactly what it was. The elevation layer was thrown off his seat by the elevation handles spinning violently, and he suffered a sprained wrist. Someone else took his place at once and the action went on, and the trouble did not recur. The man said that when the gun fired the handles "went wild" and he was told he should hold them properly.

This was reported to me and, after some consultation with Major Cotterill, the Bty Commander, it was decided to keep a watch on the gun to see if there was really some trouble, or if, as most people were inclined to think, the layer was at fault. Meanwhile this gun was looked on askance by the rank and file of the troop.

Nothing happened for the next half a dozen actions and then the same thing recurred twice in one action with the same gun and once with another gun. Obviously something was drastically amiss, so the Troop Commander took the two guns out of action to prevent mutiny among his layers. So fast does bad news travel, that in half an hour Col Helby was on the telephone to me with urgent instructions to do something about it at once, if not sooner.

Spooner and I charged over to the gunsite to have a look, but we could find nothing wrong as far as we could see. Eye-witnesses said that, as the particular rounds were fired, the gun-barrel seemed to kick up a bit. Both were Mark III guns and there was no doubt that the so-called non-reversible worm and worm-wheel wasn't as non-reversible as it should have been. The transmitted shock had fairly spun the handles out of the layers' hands. They had been holding lightly and so had got off with bruised fingers.

We didn't like the idea of looking for the trouble with a ring of gunners breathing down our necks and getting in the way at every turn, so we condemned the gun as dangerous (the only way of preventing Helby from insisting on keeping it firing) and had it brought into Workshops. Here we set a party on to stripping the worm drive gear and we were gratified to find at once that the worm was assembled incorrectly(?) – well, not according to the book diagram anyhow – on its shaft, with its two thrust washers both on the same side instead of on opposite sides, so that it seemed to be out of proper meshing with its worm-wheel. Incidentally, we found the same assembly error present in the traversing gears.

246

While we had it out, we took a good look at the worm itself and, after a lot of measuring and study of Moulsworth's Engineering Pocket Book, belonging to Dean, Spooner and I came to the conclusion that the angle of the teeth of the worm and the pitch of the thread was much nearer the critical value than we should have thought permissible for a so-called non-reversible gear. Almost borderline, in fact, so that any untoward factor, such as incorrect assembly, might just possibly allow it to drive backwards. I reported this to Estlin, who was somewhat sceptical, saying that, although I might well be right, he somehow preferred to put his money on the designer of the gun. He would file my report until I could support it with some more evidence. There, the case rested...

Now, to get the confidence of the gunners back, we needed to test the gun, to see if it really had been cured, and that meant actually firing it under properly observed conditions. This presented difficulties. The days of freedom, such as had prevailed at Ras Hawala the previous summer when a gentleman could fire off a Breda into the sea without as much as an eyebrow being raised, were over and it was necessary to get permission from the Gun Operations Room (GOR) on the site, before firing a HAA gun into the blue sky. They made a lot of difficulties about it, but popular opinion was behind me and eventually permission was accorded to us to fire twenty rounds of HE on bearing two three something, as long as the RAF confirmed that they, at least, had nothing in the air at the time.

So we got a team of spare gunners over from 283 to put the gun into action on the edge of the Workshops site. Major Cotterill and his troop commander came along to view the revels; the entire Workshops knocked off, for "safety", had thronged in the background to watch, and as soon as the RAF reported that they had nothing in our bit of sky at the moment, we fired the first round at maximum elevation. All went well, so we began to come down in elevation five degrees at a time, firing a round at each stage, until we had to stop, when the wind from the passage of the shot stirred up the dust on the edge of the escarpment behind us. At each shot, a team of observers watched, from a distance, the behaviour of different parts of the gun. I should mention here that the handles were left free on each occasion and the gun was fired from a distance with a lanyard. It behaved with perfect deportment throughout.

Greatly cheered with the result and entering into the spirit of the scientific investigation like a schoolboy on holiday, Cotterill produced more ammunition from his nearest gunsite and told the GOR we were continuing with the test. This time we fired at elevations intermediate between the previous ones, thus calibrating the gun for every $2\frac{1}{2}$ degrees of elevation. The elevation handles remained rock steady, and the watching ranks of Tuscany applauded. It must be recorded that someone said he thought the gun tried to kick a bit somewhere about half elevation. We noted this, but since the handles never moved, which was the main consideration, it was decided to pass the gun as "safe". It was the Biblical "cloud the size of a man's hand" and we attached no importance to it at the time.

Some time later, someone with his tongue in his cheek casually asked me if I knew the map reference of Rear HQ 13 Corps. I did not and he told me it was at map reference so-and-so, with a twinkle in his eye. This proved to be dead on the bearing of two three something we had been given by the GOR for our shoot, but a couple of miles beyond the supposed maximum range of a 3.7" gun. We never heard if the Great Ones had observed the air bursts near them, but the GOR preserved a dignified silence over their part in the affair when we tackled them.

One night soon after the great dust storm, I was awakened by the patter of rain on the flysheet of my bivouac and soon there was a regular downpour. My bivvy was well dug into the side of the escarpment away from any watercourses, so I didn't worry and I went to sleep again.

When I emerged in the morning, however, I received a bit of a shock. A small wadi to my left had overnight become a foaming torrent some three feet deep, and, in conjunction with many similar streams, had conspired to form a vast lake down the centre of the shallow valley, three hundred yards wide by about a mile long. The edge of this lake reached up to within a

The author in 1941

Phyllis Ball in 1941

S/Sgt Dean and Cpl Benoit (storeman) find a bundle of blankets in the desert, 1942

The workshops dispersed at Ridotta Maddelena, 1941

My 8 cwt Dodge 'Little Audrey' and driver, 1942

The flooded workshop site, Antelat, 1942

Machine Shop Assembly, El Adem, 1942

Welder at work, El Adem, 1942   The office lorry, El Adem, 1942

The author and Phyl Ball on leave in Palestine, 1942

The author and Lieut Reg Phillips on convoy halt, 1942

Lieut H. G. Farbrother, 1942

A mine casualty, west of El Alamein, 1942

Italian prisoners driving themselves into captivity near El Alamein, 1942

In convoy on the Libyan side of 'The Wire' (right), 1942

The author and Reg Phillips lunching while on convoy, 1943

The author tests the 'LRDG Jeep', 1943

few hundred yards of the workshop site, which was on harder ground. We had escaped any repetition of the Antelat fiasco and the only casualties were two tentsful of my unit who had taken the line of least resistance and had dug their bivvies into the nice, soft alluvial soil of the (then) dry wadi bed. They had been rudely awakened in the small hours by the torrent and had had to escape at speed on to higher ground, clutching their belongings. Their small tents were dug out of the mud thirty yards down the little valley.

Then the familiar troubles began. Had no one remembered Antelat, but me, I wondered? Everyone in the neighbourhood, from Col Helby downwards, motored gaily too near the edge of the lake, which rapidly began to be absorbed into the porous soil, and churned themselves down to the axles in a matter of seconds. Every few minutes, we received plaintive calls for help and we became quite unpopular because we only had two recovery lorries, so our immediate first reaction was to tell the majority they should try and fill in the time before we could deal with them in rotation by having a go at unditching themselves, with judicious expenditure of muscular energy, assisted by their sand-channels and the common or garden spade. By the time we reached the bottom of the list, the Colonel had ditched himself again and we started to see the programme through a second time. I have dealt somewhere before on the way the Morris recovery used to dig itself in soft going and, as for the old 3-ton Leyland – ex 25 LAA Wksps which Estlin had somehow managed to retain when the 68 detachment had left us – one might have more profitably tried to skate on butter. A great deal of time was wasted in driving round the lake searching for harder ground from which to approach within winching distance.

One particular case baffled and infuriated us for two whole days. Some ass of an officer, driving a Dodge 8cwt, had actually motored halfway through the lake in the dark on some for-tuitous hard ridge and had then sunk right down to the chassis between the centre of the lake and our camp. It was a challenge to our skill and equally a reflection on it if we couldn't get the fool out. Notwithstanding all this and also all our efforts, we

249

failed for two whole days to get him more than a few feet nearer hard ground and he was forced to live a Robinson Crusoe existence on his vehicle reserve rations. Every couple of hours, as the recovery lorry passed though our site between jobs, we had another stab at reaching him, but with sickening regularity, it foundered itself. Thoroughly browned off, during one of the latter sorties, I was ill-advised enough to step back without looking behind me and submerged to the waist in a water-filled slit trench. This circus turn greatly lightened the life of the recovery team, who were as fed up as I was, and the neighbourhood resounded with the plaudits of the onlookers and exhortations to 'do it again, Sir – I wasn't watching that time'. One couldn't blame them and I retired to put some dry clothes on without any desire to take anyone's name for "conduct prejudicial to military discipline".

Finally, as the ground dried off a little, we made a supreme and well prepared effort. There was a Matador in Workshops for some minor trouble and so we ran it as near to the mud as we dared, afterwards paying out its winch rope to the full. The old Leyland was then accelerated like a bomb across the intervening space, until it "bellied" near the end of the Matador winch rope. The Leyland winch rope was then laid out and the Morris, with Pte Smith grimly crouched over the wheel, charged across the hard ground past the Matador, skated past the Leyland, finally coming to rest near the end of the Leyland's winch rope, more or less submerging in the mire the while. Spooner, I think it was, made some scholarly Shakespearean quip about the "Nine-mens' Morris being filled up with mud". The Morris's own rope was then carried to within twenty feet of the wretched Dodge. Three tow ropes bolted together in series bridged the gap and a mighty cheer went up from the assembled multitude.

The real recovery process then started. The Morris winched the Dodge up to itself, put the winch gear into neutral and was winched back to the Leyland, leaving the Dodge where it was on the end of its paid-out rope. The Matador then winched the Leyland back and itself retreated a winch-rope's length towards safety. The whole process was then repeated and in three stages the Dodge was deposited on hard ground and the officer was advised to get the hell out of here before he got lynched by the recovery team. It was quite a nice little exercise in recovery tactics, from which we all learnt something, even the officer, I hoped.

When the lake dried up, the place where it had been grew a wide expanse of bright green grass adorned with clumps of sweet-scented little blue and yellow flowers, which lasted for weeks before withering in the harsh sunlight.

Soon after this, Spooner departed from us. Estlin had approached me a little earlier and said that there was a vacancy on his establishment for a Warrant Officer, Class 1, which had been unfilled since Sgt Major Bill Smith had been commissioned. He asked me how I viewed the prospect of Spooner getting promotion in his place. Of course, I said, I would be very sorry to lose him, but I wouldn't wish to stand in the way of his promotion; in my belief, he was well capable of "holding down" the higher rank. Estlin said this confirmed his own opinion and that Spooner was an exceedingly competent young Regular Warrant Officer, on whom he had had his eye for quite a long time. He proposed to put Spooner up to GHQ MEF for promotion and instructed me, as his OC, to put in the confidential form of recommendation to Bde HQ without delay. He added that he was sorry to have to break up such a successful team, but he reckoned that I was quite capable of training another in his place. For Estlin, who was never in the habit of handing out bouquets, this backhanded compliment was praise of the highest order.

So in the recommendation went and Estlin must have pulled some strings pretty rapidly, for within a fortnight the authority came through and Spooner was wafted away from our midst, to be addressed as "Mr" Spooner, to wear a highly-polished Royal Coat of Arms at his wrist and an SD peaked cap on his head, to dwell amid the great ones. As a regular soldier, he appreciated his great good fortune, but was, nevertheless, somewhat saddened to leave the unit in which we all had got on so well and which was now working so efficiently. In the months to come, however, he always saw to it that, whoever else went short, 2

251

LAA Wksps never did so, if it lay in the power of Bde HQ to prevent it.

Estlin replaced him with us by S/Sgt Butcher, a senior NCO from 88 HAA Wksps who was due for promotion – much to my chagrin, for I had been trying to get Estlin to authorise the promotion of Dean into the vacancy, Dean being of equivalent seniority to Butcher. Estlin had somehow never thought much of Dean, quite unfairly as he later admitted, and said no, Butcher it would have to be. Butcher, however, wasn't my cup of tea; I had nothing against him either as a man, or an Armament Artificer, for he was a quiet, steady and painstaking, rather middle-aged Yorkshireman and a very good tradesman to boot, but he was completely lacking in the sort of team leadership that I considered necessary for Spooner's successor. I kept gently plugging away at Estlin and, as luck would have it, a vacancy occurred in 27 LAA Wksps very shortly afterwards. S/Sgt Lewis at Bde HQ put me wise privately that the OC of 27 Light knew Butcher and had asked for him by name, so I went to see Estlin again. He called me a something persistent so-and-so and said he would look into the matter. He did, and Butcher was transferred to 27 Light and promoted, while a junior S/Sgt was posted to us as his replacement This left me in the dark for a few days and then I was summoned to Estlin's office, where he viewed me with heavy disfavour, real or assumed, and demanded to know why 1 thought this wretched man Dean was so hot anyway?

I replied as best I could, giving my considered opinion of Dean's enthusiasm, powers of organisation and qualities of leadership. Estlin heard me out in silence and then, after remarking that although I was a bloody nuisance I appeared to know my own mind, he announced that he would leave the WO II appointment in 2 Light unfilled for a month or two, during which time he would observe Dean a little more closely.

To jump ahead of my story a little, shortly afterwards 1 went on 17 days' leave to the Delta and Palestine and passed over the running of the Workshop to Dean in my absence, giving him an inkling of what was in the wind, before 1 went. On my return, Estlin called me, announced with heavy humour that the unit seemed to run much better in my absence and said that if I still wanted to recommend Dean for the vacancy, he would support me.

So in went my recommendation and Estlin was as good as his word; in quite a short time the authority came through and a beaming AQMS Dean was writing home to tell his wife the good news. I don't believe that Estlin ever had cause to regret his decision. But, as I have said, that was later in the spring and it was now only early April.

It was now generally reckoned that the battle must be due to restart before long, or at least the lull wouldn't last all through the summer as it had last year. It gave us all a sort of "Journey's End"-ish feeling as the Day of Reckoning crept slowly up on us. All "administration" was quietly draining back from the neighbourhood of El Adem and this lent colour to the entirely erroneous belief, but one very widely held, that the ground was being cleared for the battle.

All this time, the railway construction companies were putting in stupendous efforts and the railway had been pushed forward from Capuzzo, which was still the official railhead, in the direction of Tobruk. It had now reached the flat ground between the heights of Belhamed near Sidi Resegh and Bu Amud, where the "Achsenstrasse", or the "Tobruk Bypass", left the main road from Bardia and circled inland. The railway was intended to go on to Tobruk, but on this flat ground there grew up an enormous forward dump of rations, ordnance and warlike stores and parks of reserve vehicles, all in readiness to support the coming battle and to provide the necessary wherewithal for a drive through to Tripoli, should the battle prove decisive. This dump extended over several square miles of desert and was quite the biggest thing we had seen in this part of the world so far. It certainly looked as if the Authorities meant business this time and the thought was a comforting one. And there was no more loose talk of abandoning Tobruk.

The hot weather, now that it had started, was really hot and several people, including myself, succumbed to a mild form of heatstroke. The symptoms were a sudden high temperature, a skull-splitting headache and a general feeling that the grave awaited one. 1 wandered over to the RHQ medical tent to see Doc Messent and we had an entertaining but abortive attempt to determine my temperature with his clinical thermometer. The temperature in the tent was very hot – of the order of 110 degrees F – and the mercury, instead of remaining stationary when the instrument was taken from my mouth, went on climbing steadily. The first attempt, when the Doc was a trifle dilatory, indicated 108.5°F and Messent pointedly sent his orderly out to get the fire extinguisher from his truck. I was not amused. He then watched the mercury in the instrument as it stuck out of my mouth and decided that it was showing 102. He gave me something for the headache and advised me to go home to bed. The following morning, I had completely recovered, which all goes to show how wonderful Army medicine is.

I had put in for leave commencing on 26 April and Phyl and I had decided to spend it in Palestine. This, I found, entitled me to two or three extra days for travelling there from the Delta, so my actual absence from the unit was about 17 or 18 days. What with the oncoming battle getting nearer every day, I had hardly expected to get this leave, but The Day arrived with peace still in force and I motored off down to Capuzzo, which was still the personnel railhead, burdened with a small suitcase and a large bedroll, which I couldn't do without, in view of the several days' travelling before I reached the comforts of the Delta where I could park it somewhere while I went on to Palestine.

Thorne was with me to drive the Dodge back after dropping me at the Officers' Transit Camp at Capuzzo, where I had to spend the night ready for the train of the day which was supposed to leave at something like 6.00 a.m. on the following morning. As we neared the frontier, we turned left off the almost deserted main coast road (most traffic now went by rail to Bu Amud), to visit Bardia which was only a few miles off our course. The little town lay in a deep chine where the northern escarpment fell sheer down into the sea in massive cliffs. We drove down through a couple of hairpin bends on a road cut out of the cliff face. The houses were virtually undamaged and nestled among clusters of date palms and other greenery, while the harbour, if one could dignify it with such a name, was only a small stone quay with a breakwater at the entrance to the inlet protecting it from the open sea. Bardia could never have been the important supply port that it had been described as in the BBC news bulletins and now housed one or two base area units and some form of rest camp. Up on the flat ground at the top of the hill, there were traces of old Italian minefields and other defence works, but as in the case of Tobruk, the whole place looked highly indefensible and it was no surprise to recall the ease with which it had fallen to the Australians a year earlier.

The transit camp at Capuzzo lay down the Sidi Omar track, some distance from the Railhead proper; very trim and well laid-out in neat lines of large EPIP tents and flower beds edged with white stones round the administrative blocks of tents. I was shown an empty tent in which to spread my bedroll, and Thorpe departed to look for 27 LAA Wksps, for we had discovered on arrival at Capuzzo that Little Audrey had broken a spring nearly off.

I turned in early that night, after arranging for an early call in time to catch the shuttle truck to take me and half a dozen others to the railway "station". I awoke, somewhat jaded, after a series of German air raids on the railhead, shaved in cold water in semi-darkness, scrambled down some breakfast and was bumped away to the railhead in a 3-tonner under a paling dawn sky.

The "personnel train" was standing engineless in a siding. It consisted of a long line of four-wheeled steel box wagons with sliding doors on either side and no other fitments at all. They had probably been shunted down from the stores railhead where they had just discharged stores. The passengers consisted of some ten officers and several hundred Indian ORs. The officers gathered together and selected one of the best and cleanest of the trucks, dumped their kit on board and sat down to await the arrival of the locomotive.

At that time, the enemy had started showing an undue interest in the desert trains and there had been several cases of alarming ground strafes, involving quite a number of casualties one way and another. To counter this, a measure of AA protection had been provided in the form of two balloons tethered to trucks, one at either end of the train; this was to discourage the enemy's practice of flying down the length of the train. Also, two twin 20mm Bredas were mounted on open 3-tonners strapped to flat cars and manned by our old friends 1 LAA Bty, now reforming in Tobruk. They thought the job beneath their dignity and loathed it. There had been one or two entertaining skirmishes when the new scheme was first inaugurated; several enemy aircraft had been damaged and almost 100 percent of the balloons had been shot down by the fire of one side or the other. The attacks had then ceased by day and were transferred to moonlit nights. Consequently, trains carrying troops were run down from the desert by day and back either by day or on moonless nights. The balloons were carried whether it was daylight or not and the trains could be marked from afar off on the featureless desert by being between and below the two silvery shapes in the sky that followed one another in line ahead on the horizon.

After half an hour the locomotive turned up, manned, of all things, by an Egyptian driver and fireman (which seemed odd, but it was in order to provide for the final run of eight miles or so into Matruh on the official State Railways system).

For the rest of the day, we chugged slowly across the desert at what was probably the maximum speed that the Egyptian rolling stock with its innumerable octagonal wheels would travel, on a track laid on virgin gravel desert with a minimum of proper ballast. The journey seemed interminable and the sun made the steel trucks almost too hot to touch, even though we opened the two doors as wide as they would go. Sometimes we would stop for about a quarter of an hour, for no discernible reason and everyone would get out and stretch his legs, whereupon the train would restart without warning and there was a mad scramble as the passengers sought to climb back into the slowly moving cars. We sat on our bedrolls, ate our rations, played pontoon and slept.

About 6.00 p.m. that evening, or nearly twelve hours after leaving Capuzzo, the train rattled down the escarpment to join the so-called main line from Alex to Matruh at Gahrawla and we were shunted back the eight miles or so to Matruh itself, where we spent the night at the transit camp. This was a magnificent affair of wooden huts on the outskirts of the town near the point on the lagoon where Hallack had so nearly drowned himself nine months ago. The Officers' Mess at the camp was famous in the desert for its magnificent, life-size and highly artistic murals of the chorus at the Windmill Theatre in varying states of undress from a bunch of feathers to a couple of beads. Sad to report, it got burnt down a couple of months later, during the German assault on Matruh.

On the following day, we continued our journey in the more orthodox, but much less sanitary and highly bug-ridden coaches of the Egyptian State Railways, passing through the deserted defences of Ma'aten Bagush and Sidi Haneish, where the sand was steadily filling up the anti-tank ditches, Daba and Burg el Arab, where the local inhabitants had flowed back among the date palms on the old transit campsite. After a halt at Amriya, where the train was split into the Cairo and Alexandria sections, we crawled into Alexandria Main Station in the late afternoon.

I took a room at the Windsor Hotel, phoned Phyl and confirmed we would be going by train to Jerusalem the following morning. I will not dwell long on the events of the next couple of weeks. The first stage of the trip took us to the Egyptian station at Kantara on the west side of the Suez Canal; we crossed over in the ferry and joined the waiting Palestine Railways train on the other side. The slog along the dusty eastern coastal strip in the gathering dark went on and on and we got hotter and hotter. There were ten of us in the compartment and we were bitten by bugs and covered with fine blowing dust, in which Phyl's official "whites" became thoroughly soiled. Dawn found us at Rafah, the frontier post of Palestine and we trundled slowly on to Gaza, where the line to Jerusalem branched off to the right and climbed up into the hills to the Holy City. Phyl had been given the address of the Scottish Hostel, a sort of YMCA/YWCA establishment catering for Service personnel on leave, which took us in and provided us with rooms and a much-needed bath.

We spent the next ten days sightseeing, travelling from place

257

to place in six-seater shared taxis, which was the cheapest form of transport, but a bit hit and miss, since the drivers wouldn't start until they had a full load. We didn't care; we were on holiday. One way and another, we saw Bethlehem, Nablus, Capernaum, Nazareth, Jericho and Haifa; and, of course, as much of Jerusalem as was available in wartime. The folk we shared our taxis with were a highly mixed bunch: Service personnel, Jews, Arabs and other Levantines of various types; men and women alike. They were all charming and all wanted to talk to us in English. It was a very happy time. There seemed to be no animosity between the different races. After all, you can't have violent disputations, cooped in a six-seater taxi!

We arrived back in Alex on what should have been the last night of my leave and Phyl joined me at the Windsor, before returning to Bussilli on the morrow. That evening, we became engaged to be married. I had been diffident about how to take my hopes further and I think it was she who gave me the lead. (She told me afterwards that she would never have dared to go back to No 3 "unbespoken" again. Our joint activities had been too obvious!) We drove round the seafront at Alex in a horse-drawn gharri for about an hour, letting the idea sink in, and I decided to take another 24 hours before returning to the desert, without care for what anyone might say on my return, since there was some important business to attend to – the purchase and presentation of the ring.

That night in the Officers' Club, we were sitting near an RAF type who was talking loudly to a group of ATS officers who were obviously newly out from the UK: '...right out in the forward area – Sidi Barrani, you know...' Phyl nudged me, 'Are you going to tell them that Sidi Barrani isn't in the forward area?' I shook my head. 'Wouldn't be kind. Let him have his little fun.' She said, 'Well I'm not going to let him get away with it.' And, when a gap came in the conversation, she piped up in clear and dulcet tones, 'How are you going to get back to El Adem, tomorrow, Monty?' and there was a sudden silence. Unthinkingly, I said, 'I guess I'll be able to hitch a lift to Tobruk and hope I can find someone to take me on from there.'

The RAF type gave us a look that would have curdled milk

and the ATS girls heard no more of his "forward area" line-shoot.

As a matter of fact, it so happened that I took nearly two days extra, for the desert train schedule had just turned over, during my leave, from the daylight service to that of the moonless nights and the next train was not 24 but 36 hours later. So, after seeing Phyl off back to her hospital after a well spent "buck-shee" day, I had a mad scramble with only 50 piastres left to my name to board the night train to Matruh, and reached there in reasonable comfort at 10.00 a.m. the following morning.

By rights, I should have gone to the transit camp and waited for the 8.00 p.m. train for Capuzzo, but I was running so late that I didn't like to do this and canvassed the drivers of the vehicles in the station yard, until I found an RAMC 3-tonner that was going the furthest – to Halfaya. I pitched my bedroll into the back and continued my journey with a cheerful crowd of fellow-hitchers, all ORs, who were trying to get to Sollum and Halfaya. I reached Halfaya in the middle of the afternoon.

Here I was decanted with my bedroll, to make my way onwards as best I could. So I chalked "TOBRUK?" on the bedroll and proceeded to thumb every likely-looking vehicle that approached. Before long, an officer leading a convoy of 3-tonners stopped, my kit and his driver were dumped in the back of the truck and he invited me into the cab with him. It appeared he was from 1 LAA Regt, now back in Tobruk and he had been down to Matruh to collect vehicles to re-equip his Bty to scale. He knew Bentley and several other of my acquaintances and we had plenty to talk about. He reckoned that the battle would be starting during the next week or two and that I had got back only just in time.

We staged the night in the yard of a roadside NAAFI, somewhere past the Bardia turn-off and bedded down in the back of the vehicle. They insisted on my sharing their breakfast, in true desert fashion, the next morning and dropped me off at Bu Amud. Here, I picked up a truck going past El Adem without difficulty and he took me as far as the Tobruk turn-off. I had hardly set foot on the ground, when I was hailed by Padre Gilchrist, who took me all the rest of the way to my camp. I arrived soon after noon, or at just about the same time that I should have done, had I not taken the extra day's leave and come back the orthodox way. A very satisfactory leave in all respects!

The situation at El Adem had changed somewhat since I left, and the LG was now not being used by the RAF at all, although a Bty each of LAA and HAA guns were still emplaced there. All other AA defences had been progressively withdrawn towards Gambut, leaving HQ 2 LAA Regt feeling its command a trifle exposed to the draught. Great precautions had been taken to conceal the fact that any of the defences had been removed from El Adem; all moves had taken place on moonless nights at short notice.

This had started before I went on leave, with 292 Bty who had been whisked out at about four hours' notice on a filthy, rainy night. We had been modifying some of their gun parts in the workshop, and we had to work overtime to get them ready for the move. My Dodge was the only four-wheeled-drive vehicle we had, so I took the bits over to the gunsite personally after dark and I must say that the gunners had a rotten job in the pouring rain and ankle-deep mud, manhandling and winching the massive guns out of their waterlogged pits. Orders were that no lights were to be shown, but Major Macpherson Grant swore fierce Scots oaths about Bde HQ for trying to make his men work in the dark, asserting that no German worth his salt would be such a fool as to be out on a night like this. So the guns were being brought out of action in the light of lorry headlamps, which lit up the waves of stinging rain and the labouring, sweating gunners in their glistening groundsheet capes, like a scene from some wet inferno.

After the Btys had gone, each of the gunsites was then taken over by camouflage teams who erected dummy guns out of telegraph poles and oil drums to fool the enemy reconnaissance aircraft and, for days afterwards, whenever there was an air raid, smoke bombs were set off to give the impression of gunfire. It didn't look very realistic from ground level and we never learned if the enemy was taken in.

260

But back to El Adem at the time of my return from leave. Everyone was now quite openly counting the hours, awaiting the start of the battle. It wasn't "If the battle starts" but "When the battle starts", and there was a growing feeling that we might be losing the race in building up stocks and that accordingly the Germans might bite first. Bde HQ had issued orders that every unit in the El Adem area should practice packing up and getting on wheels, ready to move. Helby was taking this seriously, but Estlin told me to ignore this and concentrate on getting the regimental transport in good condition. It didn't seem to me to be a safe thing, however, and I organised a series of practice "pack-ups" of one vehicle at a time, so as not to disorganise the work too much. With Dean, we worked out revised vehicle loading lists, such that everything of any particular kind wouldn't be lost if we lost one vehicle, practised the stowing of the gear and allocated the crew to it again who would be responsible for loading it. As much stores as we could we kept permanently in the vehicles and, with Estlin's consent, we gave to the Advanced Base Workshops in Tobruk all the things we couldn't repair in eight working hours. The unit fell back smoothly into its "battle technique" as a well-knit team.

There was considerable disquiet in Higher Circles about the possibility of parachutist attacks, because a number of JU 52 troop-carrying aircraft had recently made their appearance on the airfields at Heraklion and Maleme in Crete. So every unit was obliged to prepare an all-round defence scheme and work with steel helmet and rifle at hand, so that each man could go into action stations if the alarm – two HAA bursts in quick succession – were to be heard. Hardly had the order been issued, when this signal was given, albeit unintentionally. An enemy recce aircraft came over and the usual single warning round was duly fired; before the warning gun had finished recoiling, some clot on another gunsite "pulled the chain" with "one up the spout" and a second shot followed close on the heels of the first, causing great alarm and despondency for miles around. Everyone was convinced from the drone of aircraft and the two bursts to the AA fire, that a parachute attack had started and leaped to his half-completed weapon pit, to wait there for a couple of hours, loaded rifle in hand, because, although there was a signal for starting the alarm, nothing had been said as to how it was to be called off.

Morale was, however, excellent and health even more so. The latter was perhaps the result of a common knowledge that anyone going sick would be evacuated to 62 General Hospital in Tobruk about which terrible tales were rampant. Not, I may say, without foundation, for 62 was an all-male unit without the brightening and cheering presence of Nursing Sisters in the old, dark and partly ruined former Italian hospital. I had occasion to visit someone there once and, although I admit they had their work cut out in keeping the place going, it seemed to be the gloomiest and dirtiest place I had been in. The wards were largely windowless, as the result of the almost incessant bombing, which had forced the boarding up of the glassless frames, and a perpetual shower of loosened plaster fell from the walls and ceilings. The beds were crowded together in the long, dimly lit rooms, with dark Army blankets and few sheets; the cement floors were bare; and the place smelt as only a building long occupied by the Italian military can smell. Near the middle of May, or about the time of which I write, a Matron and a covey of gallant Sisters did arrive from the Delta and I believe they played merry hell with the set-up, so that, after a week of superhuman effort, the hospital was 95 percent clean and 100 percent respectable.

Very soon afterwards, however, the battle started and when things began to look bad the girls were withdrawn – only just in time. All the male staff remained and, with their patients, went into the bag.

But I digress. After I had been back five or six days, I received a call from Estlin. Purcell had gone sick with some form of chest trouble and was being evacuated to Base; I was to take over 94th Wksps temporarily and Greening of 88th would hold the fort at 2nd Light in my absence.

Although I didn't know it, my time with the unit that I had brought out from the UK and commanded throughout the recent campaign was at an end.

262

PART TWO

BACK AND FORTH

I'm a lousy son of Ordnance and I'm living in Matruh,
  and I'm sleeping on a bed of petrol tins.
The War has gone and left me and I've bugger all to do,
  and I'm doing it as penance for my sins.
Oh, the walls are stuffed with paper
  and the doors with four by two.
I'm as snug as any lizard in the Zoo.
You can hear that blasted Jerry as he circles round and
    round,
in my flea-bound, bug-bound dugout in Matruh...

Song of the 94th HAA Workshops RAOC

11

94 (City of Edinburgh) HAA Regt RA TA had been embodied in 1939 and had served in Air Defence of Great Britain (ADGB} for sone considerable time, but since the AA Regts in ADGB were served by the static workshops of the AA Division they happened to be in at any particular time, the Regimental Workshop was not brought into being until the Regt was warned for overseas service. It was raised and equipped in Scotland, where the parent Regt was at the time, I believe with the intent to accompany it to Norway or France. When both these campaigns collapsed, 94th Wksps remained mobilised but not employed for nearly twelve months, without ever operating as a corporate unit.

During this time, it lived and messed in some barracks or other in Edinburgh, did regimental training, undertook guard duties and its tradesmen were hawked round the local RAOC Wksps to help out with their deficiencies and to prevent them forgetting all they had ever learnt about their trades. This, however, provided little opportunity of finding out how its members would operate as a team. Promotions were made to fill the WO and NCO vacancies on the establishment as best could be judged by the two officers, Lieuts Cresswell and Marshall, and, in my opinion, their judgement was sadly lacking, although I must admit, in extenuation, that opportunities for assessing potential leadership capabilities in the ranks were almost nil in the conditions under which they were forced to exist. The men were there and the vacancies in the establishment existed and these vacancies were filled from the material at hand on little better evidence of suitability for the appointment than seniority of service (Buggins' turn), or a well turned salute and a brightly polished cap badge. This might not have mattered, if they had been in service as a workshop, but in the long subsequent period of inaction, they became War Substantive in their new ranks, so that they couldn't be reduced to a more suitable level without a Court Martial. And you cannot push an NCO or WO in front of a Court Martial just because he is a misfit in the unit through somebody else's mistake, so there they were.

Moreover, the officer situation had been wrong from the start, with two lieutenants of almost equal seniority, Cresswell and Marshall, when one should have been a captain. Cresswell was slightly the more senior, but Marshall was the stronger character and they never settled down as a team. Since their arrival in the desert, there had been several rapid changes of command. First, both Cresswell and Marshall had been replaced by Estlin when back at Ras Hawala; then there had been a brief interregnum when no officer had replaced them; then Purcell had come in as a captain and a certain Lt Andrews had acted as 2 i/c; then Andrews had been posted away and there had been only one officer, since, back at Matruh in a thoroughly non-combatant area, there were no officers to spare; and finally, as the unit became potentially mobile again, two very new subalterns, straight out of the UK, were posted in, one to fill the appointment of 2 i/c and the other into the newly created vacancy of Radio Maintenance Officer.

One of the peculiarities of the Cresswell–Marshall dual control had been the way in which these two, not content with the already filled War Establishment of NCOs, seem to have gone in for a widespread practice of granting Local Unpaid rank, one step up, to a large number of NCOs. There was Sgt (local WO II) This, and Cpl (local Sgt) That and hordes, or so it seemed, of Local Lance Corporals, all unpaid in these ranks. I suspect that it was all in some attempt to redress the incorrect promotions made previously and the men concerned honestly believed that they would shortly be confirmed in their ranks.

When he had been at Matruh with 94th the previous autumn, Estlin had waded into Cresswell, so S/Sgt Lewis privately confided to me at a later date, about this highly unorthodox and

266

unfair practice. Apparently, there had been quite a dust-up about it and the departure of the two of them for other workshops was probably in no small measure due to the hard words that were said on this occasion. Estlin believed, very rightly, and said so forcefully, that no man should be given a rank unless he was awarded the pay of the appointment and if the men concerned could not be given the appropriate pay, as of course they could not, then they should, in all fairness, revert to their proper ranks. For a senior NCO to "take down his stripe" and then remain in the same unit was bad for authority, as well as being grossly unfair to the man, and so one by one the unfortunates were posted away from 94, to reappear in some other unit in the Bde with a clean sheet and in their proper ranks.

Unfortunately, the procedure, necessary as it was, still further weakened the unit, for the locally promoted types had been the best of the bunch.

Such was the can of worms into which Estlin was plunging me. I suppose I should have taken it as a sort of compliment that he should think I could be capable of bringing some order into this mess. It didn't please me to think that the battle was now imminent and I would be responsible for the safety and well-being of nearly a hundred men of somebody else's unit.

94th's recent fame – notoriety, perhaps, – included something else. They had spent the previous winter back at Matruh, performing the functions of an L of C (Lines of Communication) Wksp and developing an inferiority complex. This had led to their becoming something of a quiet joke among the other more experienced and battle-hardened workshops of 12 AA Bde and the joke was in no way diminished by the reports that filtered through to the forward area of their move, early in March, from Matruh to Gambut. It was reliably reported that the Workshops had closed down for three whole days before the move, in order to pack up their stores and that they had taken the incredible time of three and a half days to traverse the 150-odd miles between Matruh and Gambut, a journey that any competent unit would have managed in a day and a half. To this must be added a couple of days recovery work back down the road to fetch in the vehicles that had been unable to stand the pace and the two or three days that it had taken to open up and get going in the new site. It was generally admitted among the forward Bde workshops that residence close to the astringent presence of Estlin would surely be good for their souls and might conceivably save them from complete mental decay.

Such was the background of the unit to which I had been temporarily moved. I suppose that I should have been flattered that Estlin had selected me out of all his workshop commanders in the Bde to undertake the task of bringing it to operational efficiency, but I could have wept. The battle was said to be due to commence in about a week's time and 94th was still exhausted after its gruelling recent move from Matruh.

Thorne ran me down to Gambut in Little Audrey. Mindful of how one could lose things not immediately under one's own eye, I packed all my few belongings and brought them with me. In actual fact, it was just as well that I did, because the opportunity for returning for them was denied me for quite a time.

The LG at Gambut was situated between the steps of the escarpments. The main east-west road ran half a mile to the seaward of the lower escarpment and there, stretched out in a vast caravanserai on either side of it was Rear HQ Eighth Army. A roughly metalled and now very potholed track led off inland by one of the ruined roadhouses through a scattered array of RAF admin and technical units and up on to the escarpment whereon lay the landing strips. We picked our way across the dusty plain to the foot of the further escarpment, where RHQ 94th HAA Regt and 94th HAA Wksps were sited within a few hundred yards of each other.

As courtesy demanded, I first reported to RHQ, where I met the CO; the 2 i/c, Major Jones (a HAA Regt, unlike a LAA Regt, had such an appointment); the Adjutant; and the Quartermaster. The CO doesn't figure in this account any more, because a few days later he was taken to hospital with the delayed after-effects of a diving accident he had sustained in Cairo some months earlier and from then on Major Jones took over and carried on for several months as CO without any superior officer being posted, or getting the rank himself.

They were all very pleasant and, I sensed, considerably relieved that the officer coming to hold the fort for Purcell had had an equivalent amount of experience in the desert and was not brand new to the game. I saw and mixed with them socially frequently during the next ten months, but I must say that the Happy Family feeling that had been so noticeable with RHQ 2 LAA Regt was lacking and, throughout my stay with 94, I got on better with my old friends in the Btys than with RHQ.

94 Wksps were situated some four hundred yards to the westward of RHQ and between the two lay 15 LAA Wksps – Marshall's unit – tucked into the nooks and crannies of the escarpment. 94, by contrast, was widely dispersed in the Purcell tradition on the flat land at the base of the escarpment, and we drew up by the Officers' Mess, which consisted of two RD tents end-to-end half dug into the ground. Here, my kit was off-loaded, I took my leave of Thorne and was left with the new unit whilst he returned to El Adem. Purcell greeted me cordially and took me in to meet his two junior officers. He himself looked pretty fit, but he explained that he had recently developed a bad cough and had finally started coughing up small quantities of blood, so that the doctor, fearing tuber-culosis, was sending him back to Base for examination and treatment. In actual fact, I heard that it was some pulmonary problem arising from breathing in an excess of dust and grit; he was downgraded medically for some months and then posted back to duty, this time to a unit on the Canal – 2 HAA Wksps at Port Fouad.

He introduced me to his two subalterns. His 2 i/c, Ardis, had been for a short time in 2 LAA Wksps at Hucknall after our mobilisation, but had been pulled out to join an OCTU instead of sailing with us. He was a tall, lanky, red-haired Ulsterman from Belfast, whose father ran an electrical contracting business there. He was a cheerful character and I was to discover that he had an almost unlimited repertoire of near-risqué jokes about two elderly Belfast washerwomen named Mary and Bridget.

269

Having recently arrived from the UK, he was also highly regimentally minded and very keen to make a good impression in his new unit.

Farbrother, the Radio Maintenance Officer, was, like Ardis, newly out from home, and proved to be a large and cheerful youth of about twenty-three, with a round, red face and thick horn-rimmed spectacles. He prided himself on being a technician and, having little or no use for the disciplinary side of soldiering, tended to treat the common soldier as a man and an equal. But so popular was he that his unmilitary requests – one could hardly dignify them with the name of commands – were instantly obeyed by the troops. He spoke with a rich drawl and lived in a more or less permanent state of war with the Authorities who could not, or would not, provide him with all the necessary parts or tools to keep his wretched radar sets in the condition he considered they should be kept in. He had been in the Army ever since leaving Bristol University, after taking an Honours BSc in, of all things, botany, and had been trained and commissioned as a Radio Officer at the time when the authorities in ADGB were having a comb-out of young men with good degrees in any discipline to train in the maintenance of radar.

The Mess was palatial compared with my tiny quarters at 2 Light. One of the two tents was arranged as sleeping quarters and the other of the pair housed a table, several basket chairs, a side table or two and a wireless set. Three batmen drivers waited to command and the whole place had the smoothness and polish of a camp in the Delta. It was hard to believe that my previous unit, some thirty miles westwards, considered itself in the forward area, and another thirty miles on lay the enemy.

After a most creditable lunch, Purcell took me round the site and at my request introduced me to all the senior NCOs. 94 Heavy was so much bigger than 2nd Light, being over ninety strong when fully up to strength. There was a Warrant Officer Class I, ASM Jakeman, two WOs Class II, Harris (Instruments) and Pratt (MT) and half a dozen more S/Sgts and Sgts.

270

For transport, the unit had some twenty vehicles and was actually entitled to several more. The OC, Purcell, had a four-seater Humber staff car as his personal transport; there were two Morris 8cwt trucks, in lieu of motorcycles, used by Ardis and Jakeman, and Farbrother's subsection boasted a very battered and decrepit Humber utility fitted out for radio repairs. In addition there was an AEC stores lorry; two recovery lorries, a 30cwt Morris and a 3-ton Leyland; four six-wheeled 3-ton machinery lorries – "A", "D", "F" and "130" – together with a 15cwt generator truck. The remaining transport consisted of two 8cwt Dodges, a Chevrolet 30cwt, and several Ford or Chevrolet 4-wheel-drive 3-tonners. It was an impressive array, even allowing for the fact that the unit was actually short of four or five more 3-tonners for stores and general transport purposes. While at Matruh, they had attempted to fill this gap with an immense ex-Italian trailer of the type that they used to tow behind their 8-ton Lancia lorries. This trailer had about that same capacity, but, with its thin section twin wheels, it dug itself in on soft ground and needed to be considerably lightened before any of the workshop heavy vehicles could pull it out. Apparently, it was normally towed on the move by the Leyland recovery lorry, an arrangement of which I strongly disapproved. I regarded this trailer with considerable misgiving, especially since no one had thought it necessary to provide a spare wheel or even spare tyre, but it was better than no vehicle at all to carry all the kit that had to be transported somehow.

The Leyland recovery lorry was nothing to write home about, either. It wasn't the original vehicle the unit had brought up into the desert. This had been irreparably damaged during the runs of the "Bde Recovery Service" before the November advance and had been evacuated as "Beyond Local Repair". In its place had been issued, greatly to the disgust of all concerned, the present inferior vehicle, which was continually breaking down and was always more a liability than an asset. It gave us such trouble as soon as the battle restarted.

Purcell left the following morning for Capuzzo railhead and the Delta, leaving me alone with my new command. I made no attempt to initiate any changes, since I had little idea how a unit

271

of this size was supposed to operate, contenting myself with watching how it ran itself on the lines on which it was presently organised. However, I inspected very thoroughly the site, the living lines, the stores, the "work in progress" and the condition of our own unit transport.

What I found disquieted me very much. I had just come from an admittedly smaller unit which had earned the tacit approval of Estlin for its mobility and work, and his approval on such matters was hard to come by. We had thought nothing of being on two hours' notice to move for days on end and, if really pressed, we had found it quite possible to carry on a lot of our workshop activities on 30, or even 15 minutes' notice.

94's approach differed completely from all this. I got out my little notebook and noted down the things I was sure that Estlin would disapprove of as much as I did:

- The workshop was laden down with much too much kit of all sorts, both personal and public. Piles of unloaded stores were heaped beside the stores lorries and for which there was no room once the vehicles were at rest. Lots of the stores were without proper bin cards and no one seemed to know what they were for except that "they might come in useful one day".
- Enormous quantities of individual property were being carried. Nearly everyone seemed to have brought a massive wooden bed up from Matruh and heaven knows what other creature comforts as well!
- The condition of the Workshops' own transport was unsatisfactory and ill-maintained and could not be relied upon not to break down on the most trivial journeys; three times in subsequent days, I took one of them out by myself, as I had been accustomed to do with 2 Light, and was forced to walk back, fuming, in the heat.
- The workshop site was particularly ill-chosen, being on the flat ground much too near the churned-up surface of the LG, so that after a week or so, any breeze from the "wrong" direction enveloped the site in drifting clouds of yellow dust.

- As a result, it was apparently the accepted practice to knock off for the rest of the day when this happened, regardless of what urgent work was in hand, and everyone seemed to regard this as normal desert practice. On knocking off, the majority of the men retired to their bivouacs, mostly dug several feet into the ground, to play cards, write letters and so forth, to emerge only at mealtimes, or when the wind changed. Now that the khamseen season was on us, the effect of this state of affairs can be imagined on the increasing amount of work required on the equipment arising from 291 and 292 Btys' hard campaigning the previous winter.
- Furthermore, the whole geographical layout of the workshop was, to my mind, interfering with the amount of work that could be done. Its dispersion was so vast that it was quite impossible properly to supervise the work in progress and this left immense openings for shoddy work out at the back of beyond.
- On first sight, the "technical" discipline seemed poor. Engines were casually being opened up in the dust; stores were left uncovered to rust in the overnight dew; and tools and equipment were kicking about on the ground and doubtless in danger of getting lost.
- Most important of all, the whole unit seemed to require the most thorough disciplinary shake-up to rid itself of its lackadaisical, fed-up-with-the-desert attitude and make it get down to the essential things of life.

In short it was a right mess. An accident waiting to happen. But, first of all, it needed to become much, much more mobile. The memory of Antelat gave me cold sweats as I pondered what might happen if the battle went the wrong way again.

However, the unit was Purcell's, or had been until a few days ago, and there was no indication as to when it might be Purcell's again. He was hardly likely to welcome, on his return, the changes his *locum tenens* had seen fit to make in his absence. However, the present state of affairs was intolerable and, if the battle came our way, might well result in casualties, from sheer lack of battle-worthiness. So over I went to Bde HQ, seeking an interview with Estlin, to get my own position straightened out.

Estlin seemed to be mellowing somewhat these days, or perhaps, after our joint activities in the recent campaign, I was much more *persona grata* than last autumn, and he heard me out in attentive silence. Then he put a few searching questions, very much to the point, which brought out other matters on which I myself hadn't touched – was it possible that he already knew most of what I was telling him? – and asked me bluntly what I proposed doing about it.

I countered by asking whether I was justified in chucking overboard most of the organisation of someone else's unit and seeking to substitute something else in the short space of time that I might be with it.

Estlin regarded me calmly and I remember his words clearly: 'Purcell has been invalided to the Delta and may be there for weeks, maybe months. I have put you here in his place meanwhile, and if the battle were to start tomorrow, those ninety men, who are as green as grass through no fault of their own, would be looking to you to keep them out of trouble. It is up to you to decide how best to do that, but unless you make a complete hash of it you may count on me to back you up in anything you deem necessary to do.

'As regards the fancy beds and other private furniture,' he continued, 'I suggest you instigate a massive bonfire. The Army doesn't provide scarce transport and even scarcer petrol to enable people to cart these things around. In fact there's a Middle East GO that covers this sort of thing... Lewis!' He called to his Chief Clerk in the outer office. 'You remember that MEGO about heavy beds and the misuse of stretchers? Do a copy for Mr Montgomery and put a note on it from me, which I'll sign, instructing him to make sure it's being observed. Now! He'll take it with him when he leaves.'

And with that he changed the subject and went on to discuss the programme of anti-tank practice – of which more later – that the Bde was about to embark on.

I returned to the Workshop, in somewhat better spirits, realising that it was all up to me and not to the problematical

Purcell on his return. I had a long discussion with Ardis and Farbrother on what I thought ought to be done immediately to hoop up the unit and bring it into something like reasonable shape. Neither of them had been very long with 94th and so were not in any way rooted in the present way it ran; consequently, they were immediately ready to assist me in anything I thought necessary. The deference with which they treated any suggestion made by one who had been in the desert for nearly a year and, moreover, had come unscathed through two mobile battles, to boot, was heartening, although almost embarrassing.

Our first absolute priority was to make our own vehicles reliably mobile. The Btys – 291, 292 and 283 – of 88 HAA Regt, temporarily under command of 94 RHQ, were all hardened and battle-trained and would probably be able to look after themselves for a few days without raising hell about our lack of assistance, but unless we were equally mobile and capable of doing our job in the longer term, their efficiency would suffer. I don't think that at that time I had ideas of making 94 Heavy as highly mobile as 2 Light had been – that was to come later – but we could do what we could to prevent it relapsing into complete immobility.

That afternoon, since there seemed to be no time like the present, I had the entire unit on parade and addressed them, explaining what I had in mind, so that they knew what was coming to them.

As an introduction, I dwelt briefly on the traditions of the Corps and on the trust that the Btys would be putting in us and how we must not let them down. We must make sure that we could move in less than the ridiculous number of days that it had taken them to come to Gambut from Matruh and must be able to operate as a workshop as soon as we arrived somewhere else. A decent unit in the forward area should be expected to be able to move off at two or three hours' notice; less when it got accustomed to working in the manner in which I had been trained. (Subdued gasps of concern all round.)

From my own observation, we were carrying around vast quantities of junk that were not sanctioned by the Army and for

275

which we had no room in our transport. I intended to get rid of
it. At the moment, the enemy was only 60 miles down the road,
but if he mounted an armoured thrust he could be in amongst us
in a couple of hours and, unless we were better organised, we
couldn't even run away. I wished to be able to do that, at least.
(Titters from the ranks.) All the useless junk that weighed us
down – heavy beds, for example – was inappropriate in the
forward area and ASM Jakeman would make a list on my behalf
of all the unauthorised furniture the men were holding. (Jakeman,
I reckoned, was going to be unpopular over the disposal of
these unauthorised beds, but he was responsible for the state of
discipline among the ORs and should never have let things get
this far. He would just have to lump it.) They would be weeded
out in the course of the next week or two, but, rather than have a
gigantic bonfire now, when we next moved we would move
light; and I meant *light!* Anyone illegally holding an Army
stretcher should hand it in at once, or face disciplinary action.
The lives of every man and his mates might depend on the
ability to pack his personal kit into the lorry allocated to him in a
few minutes. Preferably less than five. And we must be able to
operate as a workshop as soon as we arrived at our new location.
Always remember that this wasn't Matruh and a very dangerous
and mobile enemy was altogether too near to permit mistakes.
Otherwise we might all find ourselves "in the bag". Any
questions? No? Then all ranks would make an early start the
following morning.

At the crack of dawn, amid subdued murmurs of dissent, we
set to on our own transport. Reluctantly, I gave orders not to
accept any but the most urgent emergency repairs into the
workshop from the Btys and collected all our own fitters (MT),
motor mechanics, driver mechanics and drivers in groups under
the supervision of QMS Pratt to organise a full overhaul of all
our own vehicles and to bring them up to adequate condition,
without going as far as replacing engines or other major
assemblies. Pratt was as keen as I was, but hitherto hadn't had
much opportunity, because the necessary backing hadn't been
forthcoming, and he set to with enthusiasm.

That was one thing under way. The next thing was to get rid

of all the piles of useless, or possibly surplus, stores that littered the place and this I entrusted to Ardis. He went to work with enthusiasm and some most peculiar things were revealed. I have mentioned the magpie instinct of the Cresswell–Marshall set-up and this spirit had rubbed off on the two storemen. We were found to be holding gun spares for the 3" 20cwt HAA gun, which had once been at Matruh in the South African days, but had long since been superseded by the standard 3.7"; we were also carrying spares for vehicles I had never heard of and vast quantities of them that the storemen did not know to what they belonged. Ardis even found some spares for the Sperry predictor, but I didn't think there were any Sperrys this side of Alexandria.

Ardis had a sorting squad working on the job for two full days and the best part of one night and by the end of that time we had separated out nearly two full 3-tonners-full of stuff which might come in useful to somebody else but was no earthly use to us. On Estlin's instructions, we sent it in to the AOD in Tobruk without delay and even then the remainder still filled our stores lorries quite conveniently full. At the same time, we took the opportunity of stowing the stores conveniently to hand and made out proper bin cards so that we knew what we had got and where it was to be found.

Concurrently, we also despatched to the AOW in Tobruk 94th's "Aldershot" shelter, a sort of miniature aircraft hangar, which we would never use, since it took the whole unit three or four hours to erect and dismantle. It was designed for a semi-base or port-defence role – I recalled that Cresswell or Marshall had had it erected at Ras Hawala – but it stood out like a young cathedral in the open desert and for that reason alone would have been unsuitable in a mobile role. Since it was being carried around on the recovery trailer, it was preventing that useful piece of equipment from being put to its proper task. It seemed reasonable to voucher it over to the Tobruk workshops "on loan" and they were exceedingly glad to take it off our hands.

This cleared the air, or rather our transport, a lot and to improve things further, we dismantled most of the kit in the "F" machinery lorry and stowed it under the benches, so that the rest of the vehicle could be used as a mobile instrument workshop in the manner that Estlin and Wray had done with the Bde Instrument Section. The idea pleased AQMS Harris very much indeed and he too was my man from that day onwards.

During all this, a change of wind blew dust over from the LG. Harris and his gang shut themselves into the "F" lorry and the rest of the men suggested they should knock off until the weather cleared, according to the previous practice. Pratt came to see me and I replied that they should cover all exposed machinery with tarpaulins and keep on with their work, feeling as I did so like Captain Bligh with the crew of the *Bounty*. Pratt kept them at it, secretly pleased to be doing so, and there was no more trouble about minor dust. I do not think my stock could have sunk much lower, but it was a good opportunity to demonstrate the discipline I wanted.

This made me think of how to make the workshop site more manageable and susceptible to supervision. I would have liked to move the whole unit somewhere out of the dust-laden wind, but gave it up for the time being, because that would have caused too great a state of chaos and – heaven knew! – I was disorganising it enough as it was. We compromised by moving the machinery lorries closer together with the generator truck for common supply, and shifting the "F" lorry and the vehicles under repair, so that it was possible to traverse the site without the need of a motorcycle. This brought everyone much closer to my eye, and we had a meeting of the senior Warrant Officers and NCOs with a long discussion as to how a workshop could and should operate under such difficult desert conditions.

While all this was going on, the proximity of Marshall was an embarrassment. His workshop was only a few hundred yards off and he was inclined to drift in and breathe down one's neck, offering well meant and friendly advice. I suppose it was only natural, since 94 had formerly been his own baby, and Marshall hadn't liked Purcell and the way Purcell ran a workshop.

He soon found out, however, that my methods, although differing from Purcell's, also differed from his and we reverted to a cordial, but more distant relationship. This is not to say that Marshall was wrong because he ran his unit differently to mine. Very few officers commanding AA Wksps ever saw eye to eye as to how the running should be done, but that didn't stop the war. We all had our own methods and stuck to them. Marshall, for example, seemed to have acquired a good name for the amount of work that his LAA Wksp was capable of turning out. Estlin was the first to admit this, but retained a sense of proportion by pointing out that Marshall had pulled all the Bty fitters of 15 LAA Regt into the workshop and was operating with 103 men instead of his War Establishment of 37. I preferred to make sure that the Bty fitters concentrated on their proper task of maintenance and first-line repairs and that any equipment coming into the workshop was accompanied by the driver or limber gunner only, as the case might be, to assist my fitters on the job.

One result of my transfer to 94 Workshop was that I got my long-delayed third pip and could look all other captains in the eye with equanimity.

Slightly before this, however, we had a new Brigadier in 12 AA Bde. Brig Campbell had been moved up to be Brig (AA) at HQ Eighth Army and was replaced by one, Calvert-Jones, who had hitherto been the CO of 57 LAA Regt somewhere else in the Eastern MEF.

Campbell had been a relatively mild-mannered man, but a good gunner, and the impact of Calvert-Jones was like a tornado. Six feet three in his socks and broad in proportion, round and red of face, with iron-grey hair and a bristling moustache, he looked the complete fire-eater he proved to be. He had been in Syria earlier in the War, where he had been captured by the Vichy French through getting too far ahead of the front line and now, in the western desert, his name became a byword for relentless activity and efficiency. Woe betide any wretched gunner who told C-J that such and such a thing could not be done!

His predecessor had been content if his regiments had attempted to excel at AA gunnery, but nothing would satisfy C-J but that they should be efficient in anti-tank gunnery as well. He seemed to have a self-imposed mission in life to convert the AA Regts under his command into dual-purpose units after the style of the German 88mm Btys, and he set out at once to make the entire Bde anti-tank minded. There was the excellent precedent as regards the usefulness of the LAA 40mm as a light A/Tk weapon in the recent performance of 149 LAA Bty in the defence of Benina LG in February of that year, but doubts were privately expressed about the ability of the 3.7" gun to do a job for which it wasn't designed. No one dared say this aloud, of course, but the belief was summarised in a crude joke to the effect that only the Almighty had succeeded in designing an efficient dual-purpose weapon and if C-J was aiming for Higher Command, the post was already filled and he was on a losing wicket!

However, if one needed evidence of the damage such a gun could inflict, one need only consider the performance of the German 88mms. The 3.7" was fitted with a very rudimentary set of forward-area sights, whereby the gun team was supposed to be able to take on ground targets in an emergency, but these were crude and inaccurate, except when used almost point blank, whereas the 88s could do their damage at up to 2000 yards and there was nothing at that time which would enable the 3.7" to match this. (149 Bty's guns at Benina, incidentally, had been equipped with the improved forward area sights that had been produced by 2 LAA Wksps!)

C-J had succeeded in selling his ideas to GHQ MEF and the depths of the Base Ordnance Depots had been successfully plumbed to turn up a quantity of small dial sights for which no one had any immediate use. C-J promptly obtained permission to fit them to some AA guns in his Bde, if he was able to get satisfactory results from them. Apparently, these sights had been destined for the Persian Army, before the recent troubles in that country had caused Allied armed intervention. Their dials were calibrated in weird oriental numerals, different even from the local Arabic ones, but they were otherwise a very beautifully made little job. Because of their origin, they were always referred to from then on by the designation of "Persian sights".

Estlin was set forthwith to produce the necessary sight bars with which to mount them on the guns, one troop of which – four guns – from 292 Bty, were to be equipped experimentally with all possible speed. Bde Wksps were also set to collect all available knocked-out German tanks in that part of the desert and deposit them near the sea at a place where it had been decided to hold the necessary trials.

88 Wksps were deputed to manufacture the sight bar sets in double-quick time and 94's instrument section, since they were not affected by my vehicle reorganisation, would overhaul the actual sights. We were also set the recovery task. To assist us in this, Estlin handed over to us a spare Matador which he had impounded from 88 Regt, who had been concealing it up their sleeves very wrongfully for some time. I was despatched post haste into Tobruk to see Col Ralphs in command of the AOW there, armed with credentials from Estlin, to borrow and bring back a 40-ton "Rogers" recovery trailer. With its help, we were able to amass about a dozen German tanks in the required position for the testing, opposite the Gambut roadhouse. Some of these tanks were the semi-heavy Mk III and IV editions with thick armour and either 50mm or 75mm guns.

When we had done that, Estlin told us that the Brig's intention was to use these tanks only for ranging and to ascertain for himself the effect of 3.7" solid shot on tanks with this thickness of armour and, after that, the real fun would begin. 94 Wksps would construct a running target and arrange for it to be towed, while the troop equipped with the Persian sights tried to hit it.

We got hold of an old lorry chassis, locked the steering gear, welded on a towing eye and built up on it a simple sort of superstructure rather like a sail. With this monstrosity trailing at the end of about a hundred yards of stout rope, we found it possible to pull it behind the 30cwt Morris recovery over rough ground, without it turning over.

Meanwhile the chosen troop was practising laying and aiming their guns, which were now fitted with the prototype sights and sight bars, and accustoming themselves to sitting the "wrong" way round on their seats, facing towards the enemy, instead of looking backwards, as when firing by predictor. There were no instructions with the Persian sights, so Estlin and the Bde IG (Instructor in Gunnery) went into a huddle and burned much midnight oil in the production from first principles of suitable range tables for the new sights.

All this sounds as though it must have taken quite a long time, but actually, through the push and drive of C-J, it was, I think, only the third day after the arrival of the first batch of sights from the Delta that the tests took place, before a massive audience. The best part of the Bde, or so it seemed to me, had turned up to view the demonstration or to participate in it, or just for instructional purposes.

The ground chosen for the range sloped gently downhill to the line of tanks at the edge of the sand dunes bordering the sea and the troop initially deployed at about 600 yards from the targets. A few chosen senior officers took up positions by the guns, so as to observe the revels at closer quarters, and the remainder of the spectators, official or unofficial, sat or stood in ragged arrays on the stony ground above and behind the gun position.

Each gun in turn was allowed two or three rounds of armour-piercing shot at selected target tanks, so as to accustom the layers to the novel experience of taking on a target slightly *below* them. These shots were most impressive; the guns were well staked to the ground to preclude any horizontal movement on recoil, and as the round left the barrel an immense cloud of yellow dust leapt up from the ground like a jack in the box, completely enveloping the gun team and the surrounding senior officers and slowly drifting away in the gentle morning breeze. The heavy shot went bucketing off down the slope with the sound of a departing express train, and on the ground beneath it a straight trail of dust leapt up to mark its invisible passage. Then there was a heavy "CLONK!!" and the sound of the distant express train was cut off as though a soundproof door had been slammed to, followed by an almost eerie silence.

All the four guns calibrated their sights satisfactorily for elevation and range in this manner and it was decided to do a further check on the range table by going back to 1000 yards and repeating the operation. While the guns were coming out of action and moving back further up the slope, the majority of the onlookers piled into their trucks and motored down to the targets to view the results of the shoot.

These were most impressive; there was no doubt in the minds of the observers that a German Mk III or IV tank, if hit by a 3.7" solid shot was no longer usable as a tank. They had all been very severely damaged and would have been knocked out even by a single shot. One of them – a Mk IV – sticks in my mind as having been struck at a very favourable angle; there was a clean four-inch diameter hole in the side where the shot had entered and the whole further side of the tank was forced out in tatters of steel. The remains of the engine, which had been carried bodily through an armoured bulkhead, were dangling through the hole. Little was left of the entire interior structure.

The shoot at 1000 yards was also satisfactory and now we came into the picture with our running target. The recovery crew were a trifle dubious about the prospect of being as much in the firing line as this. I couldn't very well detail them for the duty and so, with the redoubtable Cpl Brittain, our recovery NCO, as a volunteer driver, I went along myself as the observer, to report on the results of the shoot.

The scheme of things, as explained to me, was that we should do a number of runs at about five or six hundred yards at right angles to the guns and that on each run one selected gun would fire one round. They didn't tell me at first that, in order not to waste the more expensive solid shot, ordinary HE, admittedly unfused, would be used. At the end of each run, the observer, myself, would go to a field telephone at either end of the course and report the presence of any hits, or if none, where I thought the shot had gone.

So, after hooking up the target and getting the "OK" on the telephone, we started off on our first run, with Brittain driving steadily at the prescribed 20mph and with me sitting up on the rear of the recovery observing the behaviour of the target, which notwithstanding the one hundred yards of tow rope, looked awfully close. I hoped the gunners by now knew what they were doing.

The firing began. Being at the receiving end of one of these shots was even more impressive than being at the despatching end. I saw the flash of the discharge and the associated puff of dust and smoke, and then the line of dust rushed headlong down at us, or so it seemed, springing up just as though a giant subterranean paperknife were slitting the surface from below. The first time, I found myself uselessly ducking – as though that would do any good – as the express train roared towards us; somewhere during its travel came the report of the gun; a violent air-pulse passed over me; and then a loud "smack" out to sea and a plume of white water collapsed back into the blue.

We came to the end of the run and examined the target, which appeared still in its pristine condition; nor were there any marks on it after the next three runs and by this time we were becoming almost accustomed to the sensation of being shelled. At that point, the authorities called a halt and asked me where I thought the shots were going. I said I didn't know, but that they seemed just too close for words, and we were told to stand down and await further instructions. There was a lengthy pause and then Estlin came through and asked me much the same questions. He said that from his end some of the shots looked pretty close and added that I would be in order in running out the winch rope and towing from the end of that, as it would give us another 40 yards of clearance. If we didn't like doing this, of course we need not, because towing on the winch rope was bad practice anyhow, but it would be a pity to lose a good recovery lorry by getting it hit. A typical Estlin remark, but he seemed to be telling me something.

We ran out the winch cable to its full extent, reattached the tow rope proper to the end of that and chocked the winch drum, feeling a trifle more at ease. Then the troop commander at the gunsite came on the phone and he also wanted to know where his shots were going. He was a friend of mine from the collaboration in the past campaign, when I was servicing his Bty in my 2nd Light days, and he told me privately that there was a bit of a huddle in Bde circles about the deflection tables. It seemed that there might have been a bit of a balls-up, and in his calculations in the wee small hours the IG was believed to have added the date or something. This was now being recalculated and it was hoped that he had now got it right. In a friendly way he advised me on the procedure for the next runs: 'Whatever you do, old boy, keep the tow rope taut. Don't slow up! We've been laying off on the last runs and at the speed you were going I reckon we were aiming dead at your vehicle. Good luck. He hopes he has got it right this time!'

Very amusing, to be sure. Funny, ha ha...

The IG's new calculations seemed to have had some success, for, when we started another series of runs, two or three shots went slap through the sail of the target and the next hit the chassis fair and square, writing it off. This put an end to the demonstration, because there was no spare target, and the assembled multitude dispersed to their respective units.

Estlin told me that the Brig had apparently been very satisfied with the general performance of the sights and was sending forthwith to the Delta to keep GHQ MEF to their promise to supply as many pairs of sights as would be needed to equip every HAA gun in the Bde. Certain modifications were needed to stiffen the sight bars and he deputed Morton of 88 Wksps to deal with the bars, recognising that my unit was still in the throes of unit vehicle reorganisation, but, since this latter didn't involve my instrument section, my lot would tackle the actual sights and suitably overhaul them ready for fitting to the bars. For this work, he would reinforce my instrument mechanics with 88th's, which he would take bodily off Morton and put under my command for the duration of the exercise.

Morton stalled a bit over this last arrangement and, in actual fact, the attachment was never implemented, because events on the larger stage claimed attention.

By this time, QMS Pratt considered our unit transport was in adequate running order and we were now able to take in work from the Btys. I was getting to know the faces of the lads and felt that things were settling down and I would be able to see daylight if the battle didn't start for another week. The capabilities of the senior NCOs still had to be properly assessed: Harris and Pratt had what it took and the only one I had faint doubts

285

about was ASM Jakeman. He didn't seem to have the leadership qualities and control of men I would have wished and to which I had been accustomed with Spooner.

The battle was now obviously imminent and there was doubt as to which side was going to get its blow in first. Betting was about six to four on the Germans, and a semi-official rumour was going round to the effect that this would suit the Army Commander, since after the attack had been broken up on ground to our own choice, it would be possible to launch a full-scale counterattack and destroy the enemy before he could get away.

Maybe there was some grain of truth in the rumour, but anyhow the average soldier in the desert viewed the oncoming clash with equanimity and all were very much heartened by the sight of the enormous build-up of stores and equipment that was taking place around stores railhead, which had now advanced from Capuzzo to the Belhamed/Bu Amud area. There were also large numbers of the new American-built General Grant heavy tanks that were coming up as reinforcements on trailers towed by huge Diamond T tractors. This was quite a radical innovation, because it meant that the tanks arrived at the forward area in new condition, instead of half-worn after motoring up from railhead on their own tracks.

These Grants in themselves inspired confidence, too, because they were equipped with a 75mm gun in a side turret as well as a 37mm 2-pdr in a top rotating turret. This surely meant that at last our armoured forces would have a tank that could take on the German Mk III and IV tanks on equal terms, although some carping individuals, mainly in the armoured forces themselves, pointed out that the big gun would only fire forwards over a limited arc and was placed so low down that the turret was in danger of being shot off before the tank could come up sufficiently from its hull-down position to enable the 75mm gun to be fired. However, the desert as a whole was inclined to invite General Rommel to come up and have it.

Air raids on Tobruk were stepped up in an obvious attempt to render the harbour unusable and the parachutist scare, which had emerged when I was at El Adem and had since somewhat died down, now reared its ugly head again. It was reckoned that the enemy might take it into his head to deliver a paralysing airborne attack on the Allied LGs as a preliminary to a general assault on the troops that the aircraft using the airfields protected. Accordingly, we, in line with all other units round the Gambut LG, had to prepare our own all-round defence scheme and stand-to every morning from about half an hour before dawn until half an hour after, this being reckoned to be the dangerous hour.

It meant that we had to spend a cold and depressing hour in the half-light each day in full battle order and steel helmets, waiting for something we sincerely hoped wouldn't happen, before getting down to our normal work.

One morning during the last week in May, we really thought that such a show was about to begin. A fusillade of AA fire opened up on the far side of the LG and aircraft scrambled off in all directions. Then there were aircraft all over the place just beyond the escarpment where Eighth Army HQ lay, bombing and machine-gunning all ground targets in sight. We all stood-to and scanned the skies for the expected JU 52 parachute transport aircraft, but nothing hove in sight and after quite a lot of dog-fighting at almost ground level, as in the turmoil I had experienced at El Adem previously, the raiding aircraft streaked away at very high speed. Apart from a few vehicles set on fire, very little damage was done and eventually we were stood-down and retired to breakfast.

Just to make life difficult, 283 Bty had trouble with a jacking screw on one of their guns, involving something that required a welding and turning repair. The fault prevented the levelling being adjusted. I do not remember whether it was on a Mk I* or a Mk III gun, and, if the latter, it would seriously interfere with getting the gun into or out of action, whereas with the Mk I*, the gun could still be raised on to its wheels by the built-in davit-and-chain device I have mentioned previously. They sent it in to us to deal with urgently, a massive hunk of machined metal. Jakeman had it deposited on the ground beside the machinery lorries and it was now awaiting its turn on the big lathe. The day then followed its normal course...

About mid-afternoon, I motored over to visit Marshall – it was no good sending an NCO – to see if I could scrounge from him some parts with which we could complete the repair of a Bty motorcycle. From my own experience of Marshall, I was prepared for a long argument, for Marshall was quite likely to tell such a harrowing and tear-wringing story about the hard life his penurious and ill-equipped Regt was forcing him to lead that, at the end of it, one would almost be ready to let him have the whole motorcycle in sheer compassion.

I found 15 LAA Wksps throwing kits and stores into their lorries, and Marshall was crisp and to the point. Didn't I know the battle had started that morning and why wasn't I getting a bit more mobile instead of mending motorcycles? I knew nothing about this and silently cursed my own RHQ for leaving me in the dark on such a vital matter. Marshall was forthcoming with quite a lot of circumstantial detail: the balloon had gone up at dawn that morning; German armoured forces had come round the southern end of the British defensive line in considerable strength and might now be somewhere between Bir Hacheim and Sidi Resegh. And Sidi Resegh was only some twenty miles away – a nice hour's run for the supposed armoured forces! He himself had had no direct orders from his Regt, but his Adjutant had tipped him the wink to get his kit off the ground with all speed.

Abandoning all thought of motorcycle repairs under the shadow of this momentous information, I thundered off to my own RHQ, where I accosted the Adjutant, a pleasant, but, in my opinion, a somewhat ineffective young man. He admitted, under pressure, that German mobile forces were out and about somewhere in the hinterland behind Acroma and El Adem, when last heard of, and revealed that there was already a plan, in the event of an advance on Gambut, for all AA guns to form a "keep" round the LG, while all the "soft-skinned" units were to move some miles to the east to a rendezvous until the flap had died down. I cursed him for not letting me know that morning and sought to ascertain what it was proposed to do if there was a sudden flap. That, apparently, was dead easy. Everyone, like the Arabs in the poem, would silently steal away, but unlike the said

Arabs, wouldn't fold up their tents – just leaving them standing and all their kit on the ground in them. It seemed that they naïvely expected that all this kit would still be there undisturbed when they returned a day or two later. He was shaken when I asserted that it would be looted at once by our own troops, or the enemy, or both, and asked what my workshop was supposed to do, for to leave all our equipment and stores on the ground and exposed to wholesale pillage, except in the direst emergency, would render it inoperative as a workshop. And what was supposed to happen to any of the regimental vehicles that I had half-stripped down in the workshop?

In the end, he agreed that I should at once pack up to a scale comparable to two hours' notice to move and that he would, from then onwards, give me good warning in advance of any impending move and he gave me the map reference of the rendezvous to which all "soft-skinned" units would retire, 'just in case there is no opportunity to do it later.'

I lost no time in returning to the workshop, a bit frightened, I must admit. The old game was on again and I had to play it, not with the seasoned 2 LAA Wksps, with whom I knew where I was, but with this green and untried mob, and that without any adequate warning. Were I to have had three or even two more days to prepare, the essentials of my reorganisation would have been completed. Instead, we had not been vouchsafed even this small breathing space, and who knew that the enemy might not by now be approaching Sidi Resegh as suggested by the pessimistic Marshall? There was no time to be lost in getting as much of our stores and equipment on wheels before any definite instructions came through, since I felt I could not rely on the Adjutant to tell me as quickly as he promised. After all, I reckoned, a trifle more calmly, we had a lot to be thankful for, in that the flap hadn't come a week ago, when we would really have been in the soup.

In my estimation, it would take us four or five hours to pack up to the two-hour state of readiness. It was then after 5.30 p.m. and although it would be dark at about 8.00, there should be a bright moon and with that we could finish the job before turning in. We dared not pack down for the night unless we could move

289

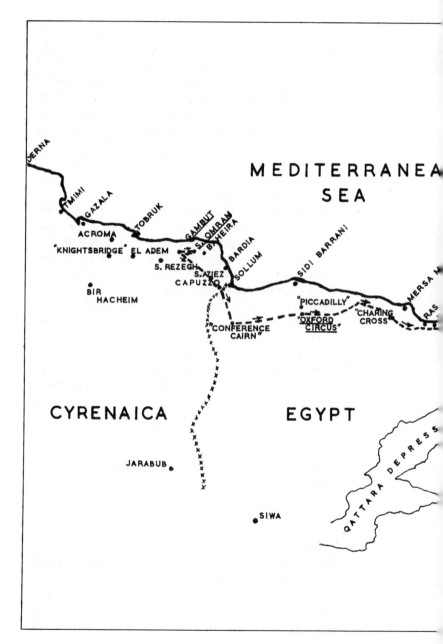

MEDITERRANEAN SEA

DERNA

TMIMI

GAZALA

ACROMA

TOBRUK

"KNIGHTSBRIDGE" EL ADEM

GAMBUT S. OMBAN BAHEIRA

S. REZEGH BARDIA

S. AZIEZ SOLLUM

CAPUZZO

BIR HACHEIM

SIDI BARRANI

MERSA M

RAS

"PICCADILLY" "CHARING CROSS"

"OXFORD CIRCUS"

"CONFERENCE CAIRN"

CYRENAICA EGYPT

JARABUB

SIWA

QATTARA DEPRESS

290

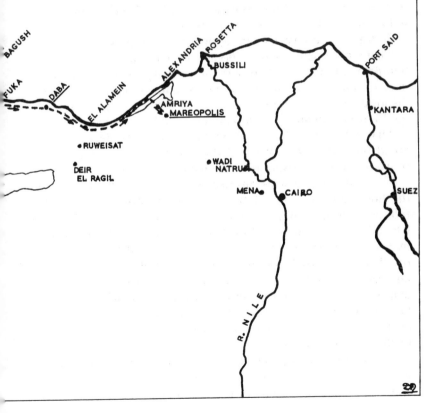

THE WESTERN DESERT ——
94 HAA WORKSHOPS - MAY 1942- OCT. 1942

ROUTE FOLLOWED -   – ◄ – –
WORKSHOP SITES   MAREOPOLIS

Scale

0   20   40   60   80   100   120   140 miles

BAGUSH

ROSETTA

FUKA

DABA

ALEXANDRIA

BUSSILI

PORT SAID

EL ALAMEIN

AMRIYA
MAREOPOLIS

KANTARA

RUWEISAT

WADI
NATRU

DEIR
EL RAGIL

MENA

CAIRO

SUEZ

R. NILE

out in the dark without delay. I called Ardis, Farbrother and the three Warrant Officers together as soon as I got back and we had a brief discussion on the urgency of the situation; we had all, I may say, a pretty clear idea of what needed to be done, but it was important not to start any sort of flap, which would slow us down. At that moment, the Workshop was just knocking off for the evening meal, so we divided them up into shifts, one of which went straight on to tea and the other was set to packing stores into our vehicles and rendering "runners" or at least "towers" of the few vehicles in the shops. They were then despatched to their tea and the first squad took over.

This second lot had just finished and were filing back to work, when the Adjutant rang through to say that the emergency plan was being put into operation forthwith. The guns were going into a "keep" on the LG and we were to leave immediately for the rendezvous and report to him there on arrival.

That would have been at about 6.30 p.m. Such was the speed with which RHQ complied with this order that some ten minutes later, when I phoned them up to clear some point about vehicle disposal, they had already gone and I could get no reply from the Signals exchange. They had presumably gone too.

That left me with the unpleasant choice of decisions: we could obey the letter of our orders, pile into our vehicles and move off at once, abandoning the balance – a very large balance – of our stores and work-in-progress behind on the ground, in the hope that they would still be there on our return – if we returned. Or we could continue packing up and move off when we had finished, thereby risking the possibility of being overrun by the enemy while doing it. I chose the second course; my fear of what Estlin would say was infinitely greater than the fear of an enemy raiding column. I would never hear the last of it, if I lost half my stores and equipment within a couple of weeks of taking over my new command. So we set to work, and the evening sunlight cast longer and longer shadows across the face of the escarpment behind us.

I gave orders to Horsfall, my batman, to put all my kit and his into the Humber – oddly enough, that was the only order that was completely obeyed that evening and we were the only ones that brought away all our complete kit – and went out to lend a hand to the lads in the general pack-up of the workshop and to steady them by my presence.

Two men were sent up to the top of the escarpment above us to observe the horizon and to give warning of any suspicious movements of vehicles to the west, and arrangements were made for their relief every half hour. They reported heavy lorry traffic moving in groups along the Trigh Capuzzo, about half a mile away, coming from the direction of El Adem or Sidi Resegh and heading off into the darkening east in dusty columns.

Ardis reported that, of the eight vehicles we had under repair in the shops, three were in such a dismantled state that each would take several hours to make them even towable, so I ordered they were to be immobilised as far as possible, by the removal of essential parts and the repair effort to be concentrated on bringing away the other five. The decision grieved me, but, in the circumstances it seemed justifiable.

Each man in turn was given five minutes to fall out and get his personal belongings packed into his allocated vehicle, and I regret to say that in many cases the efforts of the senior NCOs had to be wasted in rounding up members of the unit who were slipping away in the gathering dust and seeking to remove their fancy dugout furniture in preference to packing up the workshop. Gradually, the piles of stores and gear on the ground diminished and Pratt reported first this and then that vehicle ready to drive away.

Just as the light was fading, I went up to the lookouts on the escarpment, to see how things looked. I found them scared almost out of their wits and, although I tried to cheer them up, I don't think I did any good.

The stream of vehicles on the Trigh Capuzzo seemed to have dried up; only the occasional truck went bucketing along in a cloud of grey dust, as if all the devils of hell were behind it. On the LG, the gathering gloom and a slowly drifting haze of dust obscured the scene, but there was no indication that any of the RAF ground parties remained, although the guns were presumably in their A/tk positions. Away to the west, both on the

293

escarpment and below it, small flickers of flame sparkled, suggesting burning vehicles or small dumps of abandoned stores ablaze. And, right on the horizon, at Bu Amud, Sidi Resegh or El Adem, there seemed to be a great fire burning, colouring the clouds with irregular pulsations of rosy-pink light, with occasional bursts of white. Although nothing could be heard, I could distinctly feel, in the still air, the sharp, familiar pulse of gunfire. From their faces, I think the lookouts could feel it too.

It seemed to me that whatever was going on in that direction was at least 25 or 20 miles away, but it was disquieting evidence of enemy action far behind what we had come to regard, maybe misguidedly, as the front line. Telling the lookouts that I would send up their reliefs at once, I went down to the workshop and found some confusion, where a number of our men were clustering round a truck that had blundered into our lines. With difficulty, they were dispersed back to their jobs and Ardis brought the two occupants of the truck to me.

They professed to be members of an RASC company attached to an Indian infantry Bde and what security checks we could improvise on their pay-books, personal kit and vehicle supported this claim. They were very scared men; their story was that their unit had been overrun, that morning, somewhere south-west of El Adem by a large force of German tanks and in the dispersal they had got away to the vicinity of the forward base at Bu Amud, where in the afternoon, further enemy AFVs had turned up and there had been some confused fighting on the El Duda ridge with a British anti-tank unit. An officer in the latter had told them to get the hell out of there, as quickly as possible, and the Germans had shot them up as they left. They reckoned that the enemy was in great strength and was by now probably across the main Bardia–Tobruk road, cutting off Tobruk.

Their panic was spreading among their listeners and as there was nothing we could do for them, I got Ardis to evict them from the site as quickly as possible, but by now the damage was done. I will not say that the men actually panicked, but the level of discipline wasn't up to keeping them steadily at work and a lot of them, not excepting some senior NCOs, rather lost their

294

heads. Equipment was flung so hastily and thoughtlessly into the Italian trailer that one of the body sides collapsed and a lot of the contents spewed out on to the ground and had to be reloaded. Several of the "stationary" workshop or machinery lorries were found to be short of petrol and in the mêlée round the petrol store one of them ran over a tent and another motored into a slit trench. The AEC stores lorry refused to start and somebody backed the 30cwt recovery lorry up to give it a tow, but instead of using a tow rope, they tried to pull the heavy lorry away with the block and tackle on the jib, thereby bending the jib badly. By this time it was also just about dark and a horizon moon gave little useful light, so that people were stumbling around, looking for objects still on the ground, searching for vehicles on which to put them and colliding with each other on the way.

In the course of the next hour or so, several other vehicles blundered into our lines. They were Indian "B" echelon troops mainly, and they were all lost and very scared, an array of white teeth and rolling eyes in the half light, trying to get to some place of safety, because the Germans were coming. The Germans were coming! I had heard that one before; it had a familiar and unpleasant ring and the unit became more and more jumpy every time it was repeated.

One of the lookouts came down from the escarpment, to report that there were troops up there, digging in, and I went up in the darkness to find out what was going on. They were Indians, too, and they appeared to be digging weapon pits covering the approach along the escarpment. A British officer accosted me and wanted to know who I was and what the hell I was doing there, anyway. I managed to identify myself and explained my unit was down below just about to evacuate the site and he advised me "as a friend" to get out quick and take my unit with me. He didn't know what was going on, but his information was that the enemy, mainly Germans, were all over the place in the area Bu Amud – Sidi Resegh – El Adem – Acroma and no one knew whether the defensive "boxes" at El Adem and to the westwards had been overrun or just bypassed. The only forces he knew of between us and them were 4 Armd Bde in the desert slightly to the south-west.

On my return to the camp, ASM Jakeman reported that everything was about packed up except the tents and should he set about dropping them? That would have taken at least a quarter of an hour more, but as we definitely could now hear gunfire not so far off, I decided to leave the tents standing and get out while the going was good. There was no adequate way of determining whether we had indeed got everything possible into our vehicles and anyhow I doubted whether the majority of the unit could have been persuaded to stay any longer, even if there had been half a ton of gold to load up. I gave the order to pile into our transport and we bumped off unevenly in single file, leaving our derelict tents flapping in the moonlight.

It was now getting on for 10 o'clock and I found myself really praying that I would be able to get this rabble to the rendezvous in the dark, without anyone getting lost. I was aiming for a map reference on the Bardia side of Gambut some 15 miles away, below the lower escarpment and between that and the main road; one step down as it were. I had never been there by daylight, let alone in the dark, and all I could see from the map was that it was at the foot of the escarpment where the next track went down. From my experience of similar escarpments at Sidi Resegh and El Adem, it seemed likely that there would literally be no other way down before that one, so I told my driver to set the trip on his speedometer at zero and let me know when we had covered the right distance. I offered up a prayer that my reasoning was correct and we set off along a faintly defined track leading in about the right direction.

Marshall was long gone, but it looked as though he had packed up pretty thoroughly before going. He seemed to have set fire to the remainder of his petrol store, or something, before moving, and the flames lit up the crannies and chimneys of the upper escarpment as well as ourselves, making us feel outlined with unpleasant clarity. I was glad to get past and into the more nebulous obscurity of the moonlight. Behind us in the distance, someone was dropping flares and we could see the quick flower of bomb bursts and hear the hollow thumps of the explosions, some not so far away either, or so it seemed.

The flat land we were traversing towards the lip of the lower escarpment was waist high in dry camel-thorn and seamed with many cross-tracks which never appeared to follow the same course for more than fifty yards at a time, so I held to my self-chosen bearing, switching from track to track in the process and hoping to pick up the main track that instinct and experience told me should lie along the lip of the escarpment. Once we ran foul of a column of vehicles that converged on us, blundering down the centre of the "step". They were part of an RASC unit heading for Sidi Aziez and they were grateful for my relatively exact information as to where they had got to. They, too, said that there was hell's delight going on up forward, with the enemy on the loose almost unchallenged all over the place. As a parting shot they told me that the reason why they were up on the escarpment was because the Germans were busy ground-strafing the coast road with any aircraft they could muster and that it was most unhealthy.

After several miles, we struck a broader track running more or less east and west and I turned east along it, relieved that my intuitions were correct: this was undoubtedly along the top of the escarpment, for the sense of distance in the space to the north was most marked, even in the moonlight. Away in the distance, we could hear the sound of aircraft and the chatter of machine-gun fire. Presumably that would be the enemy strafing the road.

Some fourteen miles by my speedometer from our starting point, we came to a major cross-track which slipped over the edge of the escarpment into the darkness below. So far, so good. My prayers were being answered. We turned left and bumped slowly downhill.

An unpleasant sight met my eyes as we reached the foot of the hill and had time to look around. The coast road lay parallel to the escarpment about half a mile away. It was being strafed in four or five places by enemy aircraft; the position of each one of them, presumably light bombers, could clearly be pinpointed by two little jets of tracer diverging from an unseen moving source, spraying down and bouncing in tiny fountains of fire as they struck the hard ground beneath.

One of these aircraft passed us as we watched, about eight or nine hundred yards away. It was all I could do to prevent the majority of the unit leaping from their vehicles and hiding, ostrich-like, in the camel-thorn. According to my calculations, RHQ should not be very far off, so I handed command over to Ardis to get the vehicles reasonably dispersed and await my return while I went forward alone to find RHQ.

We had progressed only a few hundred yards, when I got one of the worst frights of my life. My driver had a fright as well, but I venture to claim that his was nothing like as bad as mine, for he was driving, whereas I was standing on the front seat with my head and shoulders projecting out of the open sliding roof and had a very close-up view of the incident. We were just breasting a slight rise, when I felt, rather than heard, an aircraft almost on top of us. My driver gave an involuntary swerve and ran over a large rock which caught on the underside of the chassis and brought us to a dead halt. For a couple of centuries, or so it seemed, we just teetered there, naked, alone in the brilliant moonlight, in the middle of the open desert, a staff car flying a blue flag and with an officer standing three-parts out of the sliding roof.

Maybe our sudden emergency stop was fortunate, for a great black shape stormed by, just in front of us, some couple of hundred feet up. It was a twin-engined bomber with a transparent nose that glittered in the moonlight, and we could see the flames shooting from its exhausts; two jets of tracer bullets swung in our direction as it passed, kicking up splinters of rock or ricochets which flipped past with the sound of plucked bowstrings or clattered on the car's bodywork.

Then it was gone and the darkness overhead swallowed it up. I lowered myself from my perch and cursed my white-faced driver for not watching the road ahead. In retrospect, his mistake probably had saved us through the car's sudden stop, but that did not occur to me at the time.

The search for RHQ proved ridiculously easy. We drove into a group of dispersed vehicles and we nearly went into a slit trench in which a man was sleeping. It happened to be the Captain and Quartermaster of 94 HAA Regt and he said that the rest of the whole so-and-so desert was at our disposal and that

298

we could leaguer down where we liked, as long as we kept out of his slit trench, before turning over and returning to sleep.

I brought the rest of the unit over and we dispersed on the fringe of the RHQ party. It must have been well after midnight, but we all dug slit trenches for ourselves before putting our bed-rolls in them to sleep the sleep of the exceedingly tired, little disturbed by the occasional marauding aircraft out on the strafe. I recall that I was awakened by the dawn and found my trench inhabited by assorted wandering and interested beetles of various sizes, but all with a sardonic expression.

Discussion with the "rump" of RHQ the following morning elicited nothing in the way of news. They had packed up and cleared out on the orders of Major Jones, the acting CO, in about ten minutes and had with them little more than their blankets and haversack kit. They were all of the firm impression that, as soon as the flap was over, they would return to their old site and find everything exactly as they had left it. My firmly expressed opinion that they would never see any of it again, as it would certainly be looted by one side or another, struck an uneasy chord and I was unpopular for making them even more depressed.

Major Jones and the Adjutant had retired into the airfield defensive area with the Btys and there was no news from them. Meanwhile we set about getting ourselves somewhat more organised and began repacking our stores and equipment in more accessible form for instant work. There was quite a lot of this to be done, since the "B" echelons of the Btys were near at hand and every one seemed to have broken something in the flap evacuation. Getting the unit to consider work after the stresses of the previous night was a hard job; tools had been lost or left behind; vital parts of vehicles had been forgotten; and the men themselves, with a few notable exceptions, had a dispirited "all is lost" attitude. I think they were a bit stunned by the loss of all the creature comforts they had been enjoying ever since their arrival in the Middle East, either at Beni Yussef, Ras Hawala, Matruh or Gambut, in the way of beds, tents, illicit camp furniture and the like. Their world was upside down and the spice had departed from their lives. They had had enough and wanted to go home. The "notable exceptions" were AQMS Harris (Instruments), SQMS Pratt (MT) and Cpl Brittain (Recovery). This nucleus set to work with a will to shake some form of life back into the unit and gradually things began to get moving.

By early afternoon, since no one at RHQ appeared to know what was going on and nothing seemed actually to be happening, I sent Ardis back to Gambut, with RHQ approval, to find out. He returned with the report that an anti-tank screen was emplaced round the LG area and no one was being let through. Things seemed to be quiet and the A/tk gunners thought that the flap must be dying down. He wasn't able to contact Major Jones or anyone from the 94th party that had remained behind, but no one else had any real news and there were no signs or sounds of the enemy.

Our stay at the rendezvous which, by reference to the map, we now discovered to be called Sidi Omran, lasted three days, during which time we worked in the broiling sun by day and slept in the deepest slit trenches we could dig at night, while enemy aircraft prowled around and took pot-shots at anything that took their fancy. They seemed to have that field to themselves, because the RAF was lying low, licking its wounds and getting reorganised.

Nevertheless, the spirit of the Workshops began to revive a bit when the men found it was quite possible to maintain life under the barbarous conditions now forced upon them and that their entry into a German prison camp wasn't as imminent as had previously been thought.

Then, suddenly, orders were issued to send back parties for any kit that had been left behind at Gambut, tents and personal belongings, etc., ready for a move – rumoured to be a rearward one – and morale fell to a new low. I sent Ardis and a working party, along with the main RHQ lot, to drop tents and bivvies and to collect all or any equipment which might be still on the ground there and forgotten in the hurried move.

Three hours later, and long before Ardis's return, counter-orders told us to return properly to our previous sites at Gambut. Apparently the flap was over and the enemy raiding parties had withdrawn; the RAF had decided that the LG at Gambut was safe to be used again. We all piled into our vehicles and straggled up the escarpment in better spirits. Somewhere on the way we must have passed Ardis and we arrived back in the twilight, to find not a stitch of tentage to sleep in. Ardis didn't rejoin us until the following morning and we spent an uncomfortable night.

Morning light revealed that only two of the vehicles we had left behind were still there. They had been so badly despoiled as to be written off and the third had just disappeared – presumably pinched. Worse was to come. 283 Bty came on the phone as soon as we were reconnected, to ask urgently after the state of completion of their jacking screw, the absence of which had gravely inconvenienced them when packing up during the flap. I stalled them while I investigated by saying it wasn't ready and I would put some pressure on.

I sent for Jakeman and he said he didn't know what the position was; the screw had been on the ground by the machinery lorries before the pack-up and he thought it had been put into the Italian trailer. He went to look and returned some time later to report that the screw was nowhere to be found on the site, in the trailer or in any other vehicle.

That shook me; I remembered the way things had been just chucked on to the Italian trailer and how the side had collapsed with the load. The screw must have fallen out then and must have been hastily thrown back on top of the other things. Somewhere along the bumpy tracks, it must have been shaken loose and was now on the side of our route, in the waist-high camel-thorn. There was nothing for it but retrace our route taken that night as best I could to see whether we could find it. I was worried that in the dark I had been switching from track to track so as to keep on the compass bearing I had set myself and I was by no means sure that I could repeat this. I collected a number of potential searchers and we set off. Surely we couldn't miss such a large hunk of metal, about three feet long and with a steel pad a foot in diameter on the end!

But our route had been some fifteen miles long and, try as we might, criss-crossing through the camel-thorn, we failed to find a trace of the wretched thing. Eventually, as darkness gathered, I

301

called the search off; we could retrace our steps again the following day, but I had no great hopes. The prospect of a Court of Enquiry – did they have such things in the forward area? – loomed over me. I would be held responsible as the OC of the unit for the shortcomings of my men.

It was the last straw. I called a parade of the entire Workshop and gave them a further harangue on the traditions of the RAOC Workshops, dwelling on how poorly their own behaviour during the past couple of days comported with that. As a result of their lack of discipline, a valuable piece of equipment had been lost, which rendered a whole gun unusable and there would be hell to pay for it. I was thoroughly ashamed of the unit's performance and they ought to be too. I was tired and I really let my hair down. Farbrother said afterwards it was masterly and he couldn't have bettered it himself; I had spoken for some fifteen minutes and didn't repeat myself once. For the remainder of that evening, no one dared to speak above a whisper and they avoided my eye.

Now the next thing was to report the loss to authority and take the can for it. 283 Bty still didn't know the wretched thing was lost and I reckoned I had better confess my misdemeanor to Estlin first, before the gunners got in on the act and demanded my head. 1 went over to Bde HQ first thing next morning and made a full confession to Estlin that my unit had lost an important part of one of the Bde's 3.7" guns.

He heard me out in silence. His first action thereafter was to get on the phone to Morton – 88 HAA Wksps was still at Baheira – and detail him to send the Rogers trailer (from the Tobruk Wksps) which was still with 12 AA Bde, together with our spare Matador, to 283 Bty at Gambut, complete with a competent recovery NCO. That team would remain with 283, available to move the gun until the missing part could be replaced. He then spoke to the Bde Major and sorted out the arrangements for onward transmission of the information through RA channels.

After that, he extracted from me exactly what had happened during the flap and commented that it seemed to have been a thorough shambles. Somewhat to my surprise, he didn't reprimand

302

me, contenting himself with remarking that every dog should be allowed one bite, adding rather as an afterthought that I had just had my bite and that I had better make sure that nothing of the sort happened again. From the way in which he spoke it seemed that he was fully aware of the situation I had been facing on taking over 94 and he went on to say that if my solution was to ask him to get some of my NCOs transferred to another unit as unsuitable, I had better have another think coming. If my NCOs were not up to their jobs, it wasn't fair on other units to transfer them; they should be the subject of an official adverse report, which, if sustained, would enable the Bde Commander to reduce them. 'To the ranks, if necessary!' he concluded, waving me out, in the sort of voice the Queen of Hearts might have used when saying 'Off with his head!'

I returned to the unit chastened, but relieved, and had another heart-to-heart talk with the NCOs, telling them that Estlin had his eye on the Workshop and emphasising the importance of not giving him any further cause for complaint. They retired, more than a little shaken.

We sat there at Gambut for another couple of weeks and in that time by superhuman efforts on the part of all ranks we got ourselves just about straight. Notwithstanding our renewed searches, however, we never found the missing jacking screw. Meanwhile, the war went on. We learned that the initial enemy thrusts had been beaten back, but there was now fierce fighting over the whole front line area from Gazala to Bir Hacheim. 292 Bty went back to El Adem to stiffen the defences as possible anti-tank artillery in addition to their normal role as AA, and 281 from 88 HAA Regt pushed off one night to do a similar job further up the Trigh Capuzzo at the track junction to Bir Hacheim, which had acquired the name of "Knightsbridge".

The battle now turned into a war of attrition. There were no further wild armoured penetration sweeps and, instead, the enemy began a "nibbling" offensive aimed in turn at individual "boxes" with suddenly concentrated local strength. One of these "boxes" with its whole garrison, an entire Bde Group, was overwhelmed and the enemy flowed in as far as Knightsbridge and spread out to assault Gazala and Acroma from the rear, not with armoured forces but with infantry. The area round Knights-bridge became known as "The Cauldron" and was the scene of massive armoured encounters, which swayed backwards and forwards for some days.

To our surprise, the Base Ordnance Depot at Abbassia now tardily produced a large quantity of the Persian sights and we had a mad rush to finish new sight bars for them. Since 281 Bty was somewhere very much in the front line and no one knew exactly where this front line was, the problem was how to get them to the Bty. The first attempt proved a failure; the consign-ment was entrusted to a bombardier from Bde HQ and he contrived to run into a party of Germans, who commandeered his truck and with it the sights, but instead of putting the crew in the bag, they were given a metaphorical kick up the backside and told they could walk back to their unit. The Germans were taking no prisoners. The party arrived back at El Adem, footsore but greatly relieved to be still free.

Then Estlin took over; he loaded another consignment of the sights and set off personally to deliver them. He successfully set 281 Bty up with them and either by intention or chance became marooned there throughout one of the tank battles in the Cauldron. He arrived at Bde HQ several days later, looking as cheerful as a cat that had discovered a saucer of cream and commenting that the sights were just the job. Several days later, he suddenly appeared wearing the ribbon of the Military Cross and no one knew what it was for. I asked Lewis and either he didn't know or he had no intention of telling me for he wasn't forthcoming. He suggested that I should ask the Major, but that wasn't a thing one liked to do. The guess in Workshop circles was that he had done something damned silly up at Knights-bridge, quite mad and Estlin-like, fully in keeping with his warlike spirit, and had been awarded an immediate decoration by the Corps Commander there. Alternatively, it was suggested that it was for defending Bde HQ single-handed from that air attack some weeks ago and shooting down an enemy aircraft. I never heard what it really was for.

The fighting round Knightsbridge and the Cauldron surged backwards and forwards, from time to time reaching as far as El

Adem, and 292 Bty were in and out of the El Adem "box" several times in the week. On one occasion, while putting in good work as medium artillery, they caused great alarm and despondency among the ranks of 90th Light Division, the motorised support force for 15 or 21 Panzer Division who believed themselves to be beyond 25-pdr range. Some counter-battery exchanges ensued with the Germans replying with their 88mms. I heard later that one of the latter's shots landed bang on the 2 LAA Wksps stores lorry in the "box" and exploded on the steel bins, sending the vehicle up in a sheet of flame as the fuel tank caught fire.

Then both 292 and 283 Btys were suddenly withdrawn to Gambut and we were put on an hour's notice to move, while the "B" echelons of the forward troops flowed back past us. We learned from them that the Free French had finally been ousted from their stronghold at Bir Hacheim, which had been the target of continuous attack since the battle had started and there were sudden widespread rumours that *something* had occurred "up there", some frightful disaster, far exceeding the loss of the Bir Hacheim position. Everyone looked uneasily at his neighbour and we were put on 15 minutes' notice. We were to learn later that our armoured forces had been totally defeated in a major tank battle and the enemy was now calling the shots.

After we had been packed up and on 15 minutes' notice for a couple of days, without anything happening, and were just learning how much (minor) repair work could be done with that notice, the lads were getting a bit browned off with the inaction, so I decided to do something to help ourselves. The Workshops had a Humber utility, belonging nominally to Farbrother, which he used for minor radio repairs as well as being his personal transport. It never seemed to be out of the repair bays itself and was a complete liability. It was, however, the apple of Farbrother's eye, but I had finally persuaded him that he must part with it by handing it in at the nearest Returned Vehicle Park and receiving a receipt which would enable him to draw a new vehicle in lieu. In the meantime, I allocated one of the Dodge 8cwts to tide him over and when the third day dawned without anything happening, we put the Humber on the recovery trailer,

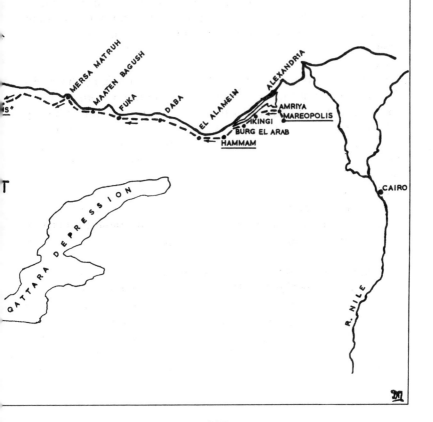

THE WESTERN DESERT ——
94 HAA WORKSHOPS - OCT 1942-JAN 1943

ROUTE FOLLOWED — — ⚊ — —
WORKSHOP SITES — MELAH EN NOGRA

Scale

0   20   40   60   80   100   120   140 miles

MERSA MATRUH
MAATEN BAGUSH
FUKA
DABA
EL ALAMEIN
ALEXANDRIA
AMRIYA
MAREOPOLIS
IKINGI
BURG EL ARAB
HAMMAM

CAIRO

QATTARA DEPRESSION

R. NILE

307

hooked that on the back of the Leyland recovery, gave the driver and his mate two days' rations and our blessing and packed them off to the RVP at Capuzzo.

About mid-afternoon, I received an obscure telephone message from 88 Wksps at Baheira, 40 miles away, to the effect that our Leyland had broken down outside their site and would we do something about it? I despatched Ardis and a party (also with full kit, etc) to see about it.

Some three hours later, I was summoned to a conference at RHQ. We were told briefly that the Army had been rather badly mauled and that the forward troops were falling back on to a line Tobruk–El Adem. This made the Gambut LG untenable for the RAF, who were withdrawing forthwith to Oxford Circus – miles back *in Egypt!* We were to set off at once – approximate route herewith – and be clear of Gambut by 7.00 p.m. No one knew what was happening up front, but it was a shaker. It sounded nasty.

I got back to the camp to find Farbrother organising the pack-up and, almost at the same time, Ardis returned from Baheira. The Leyland had seized a differential and was quite immovable; it wouldn't even tow. He had left the men camping for the night, oblivious of the flap and movement orders, although 88 would presumably tell them, and he had come back himself for instructions.

Something had to be done quickly so, for the Signals folk had already cut the telephone off, I set off across the LG to Bde HQ. I had an idea that Estlin could "fix" 88, who would otherwise refuse to do anything about the Leyland, and to tow it away, if necessary.

It was a grey afternoon and a cold wind was blowing dust across the LG, half obscuring the sun's dropping red ball. The LG seemed deserted, except for a few crashed and abandoned aircraft and the odd isolated RAF rear party throwing their few belongings into the backs of lorries. Here and there an empty tent flapped drearily in the wind and all around lay the litter of a hastily broken-up camp: petrol tins, fuel drums, wood, little pieces of furniture, broken motor vehicle parts and unidentifiable rubbish. Everywhere was deadly quiet; the only sound was the singing of the wind through the piles of fuel drums and the place was so strange and different that I had difficulty in finding my way to Bde HQ.

They were packing up feverishly, too, amid a welter of stinging dust as I delivered my message to Estlin. He said that 88 would most certainly bring the Leyland along – he would see to that – and we could take it off them at Oxford Circus.

Back at our site, I found we were all packed up – we were getting better at this – and, since the light was already fading, we moved out at once in a long winding column, up the escarpment, through the minefield at the top and on to the Trigh Capuzzo lying along the lip. I looked back from the top of the hill at my string of vehicles winding away towards the red sunset and I thought back to that similar occasion five months ago when I had moved out of Antelat; my feelings of foreboding increased. This seemed like a repeat of that retreat. I had seen it all before...

We spent the night on the deserted LG at Gasr el Arid and moved off at dawn down the Trigh Capuzzo. There was a great deal of traffic in both directions and we made slow progress, reaching Sidi Aziez, 20 miles from the Wire, about noon and struck out to the south-east towards Gap D in the Wire, where we were scheduled to go through. However, we came across another gap a bit north of Gap D, intending to push on to the desert railway and follow it to Mischeifa and then to Oxford Circus, but the presence of new minefields deterred me and, since we were short of petrol and water as a result of our hurried departure, I decided to cut north to Capuzzo to get some.

The road at Capuzzo was an unforgettable sight. Coming down from the far western horizon was a solid jam of vehicles, moving slowly forward and, after passing us, dividing into two streams to descend either the Sollum or Halfaya hills. Every kind of vehicle was there: light trucks, tank transporters and trailers, 3-tonners, big RASC 10-tonners, Army and RAF staff cars, all thrusting, shoving and creeping eastwards.

We stopped at the transit camp, where less than a month earlier I had spent the night on my way to leave. The staff had left the tents as they were and had departed for the east. As we asked for directions to the petrol dump, someone hailed us from a passing truck: 'You're going the wrong way, mate. Jerry's up there!'

At Capuzzo we managed to get some petrol, not enough, but some, filled our water tanks and bought as much drink from the NAAFI there as we had money for. This was rather a bad sign, since such things were normally strictly rationed, but they were not yet actually *giving* goods away as I had heard they did when there was a real flap.

Then we turned south on the Libyan side of the Wire down to Gap D, turned through and set off on the Hamra–Mischeifa track. All along the Wire were detachments of South African troops more or less in battle positions. They didn't seem to know what was going on or what they were there for. Since we were now at least sixty miles behind the Tobruk–El Adem line, Ardis and I didn't like the look of things, but kept the thought to ourselves.

About twenty miles on, we saw some of RHQ 2 LAA Regt encamped for the night. We pulled in beside them and celebrated my third "pip" with some of the drink I had bought at Capuzzo. They were apparently the "B" echelon of the RHQ and they supposed that Helby and the guns were still in the El Adem box. The Workshops were out of the box and coming down the coast road somewhere.

Next morning we moved on and shortly afterwards encountered RSM Bliss of 2 LAA looking for RHQ. He said the guns were out of the box, which had been abandoned; the Colonel was with them, bringing them back. He had also heard that the Army had no intention of holding Tobruk this time and indeed German infantry forces were already across the Bardia–Tobruk road in some strength near Bu Amud.

On we went and at Conference Cairn – a conspicuous landmark some twenty miles further – we came up with RHQ, who were sitting down waiting for 291 and 292 Btys to arrive from El Adem. There were large numbers of South African troops dispersed on the plain, just sitting in their vehicles. They said they were 1 (SA) Div and they told us that they were from Gazala, which had been abandoned a couple of days earlier, and

310

that the remains of 50 (Northumbrian) Div, also from Gazala, less most of one Bde who had been lost when the 150 Bde box was overrun by the Germans about two weeks earlier, was at Hamra some few miles off. 2 (SA) Div was supposed to be following, but this wasn't correct, we heard later; they had, (for some unknown reason) retired into Tobruk, where they had been surrounded and mopped up. 22 Guards Bde from El Adem were also squeezed into Tobruk, but had fought their way out and got away, although we didn't know all this at the time.

All this didn't sound cheerful news, since at that rate there seemed to be very little between us and the enemy except the thin line of South Africans manning the Wire, so we pressed on behind RHQ, reached the railway line and followed it to Oxford Circus. During this final twenty miles, disaster overtook us and five of our vehicles broke down; we were obliged to leave them to be called for later since we had no recovery lorry. However, we found RHQ on a stony slope just north of the LG and settled down near them. I sent out a fitters' party for our wayward trucks and before dark they were all in.

As yet there were no aircraft on the LG and we just sat waiting for them and taking stock of our wounds. The guns were also just sitting on the hard stony ground – not dug into pits – in case there was another sudden move. We were told that the RAF was still operating from Sidi Aziez on the other side of the Wire, but on the following day they, too, flew in. Libya had been abandoned except for our "forward patrols". With them came Bde HQ, who spread themselves out near us.

Estlin reported that our recovery lorry was with 88 Wksps at Sofafi, somewhat further back along the railway, and Morton was screaming for us to fetch it. Apparently they had towed it along from Baheira with the rear wheels on our recovery trailer and the front wheels on the ground. The Humber station wagon, which we had thought to evacuate to the safety of the RVP at Capuzzo, had been tipped off the trailer, to make room, and set on fire, a lonely pyre in the evening of the great retreat. On hearing this last, Farbrother was furious because there was now no receipt that would enable him to claim a replacement. Spooner dropped in to see me and told me that Capuzzo itself, when they passed through, had been a deserted city, with only the railway engineers seeking frantically to clear the sidings of wagons and locomotives. The Officers' Shop had been open to the mob and he had come away with a dozen pairs of suede "desert boots", one of which he presented to me, before distributing the rest.

I selected the 30cwt Morris, the only spare vehicle that might tow the Leyland, keeping my fingers crossed that there would be no flap in the next few hours, and sent it with a crew to bring in the old wreck on its trailer. They brought it in, a pitiable sight, nose down and with its rear wheels on the trailer. One of the rear differentials was completely solid, but we got the vehicle on the ground with difficulty, because 88 had lost the ramps, and set to work to remove the complete assembly so that the vehicle would drive after a fashion on one rear axle only or, if necessary, could be towed. Meanwhile, a 3-tonner from one of the Btys came in with a broken steering column, about which we could do nothing in our present condition, so it took its place, front end up on the trailer, instead of the Leyland. I might mention that since the ramps were lost, we had had to dig a hole in the stony ground to lower the rear end of the trailer sufficiently to manhandle the Leyland off and this new burden on.

By dark we had done whatever we could for the Btys with our restricted facilities and retired to bed in our clothes, expecting something to happen. And it did; in the small hours, a messenger came round to summon me and all unit commanders to a conference at RHQ. We gathered in their office tent, Major Jones, acting CO, the Adjutant, Bill Emslie, OC 291 Bty, the Signals officer, myself and the Regt's RASC officer. Major Sir Iain Macpherson-Grant of 292 Bty wasn't yet there. We were all clad in whatever we had hurriedly thrown on and were rubbing our eyes. After a few minutes Macpherson-Grant showed up tastefully attired in pale blue pyjamas under an ankle-length "Hebron coat", a roughly finished sheepskin garment as sold in the souks of Cairo. He apologised to Jones for being a bit late and explained that he had just been ensuring the guns were being put on their wheels. Jones asked him who gave him orders to do that and he replied no one, but he didn't suppose a conference would be called at this godless hour if it didn't mean a fast move off in some direction or other. Just Scottish second sight, maybe.

Major Jones said he had just had a signal from the Brigadier that the Germans had taken Tobruk the previous day and were pushing on eastwards with speed. At last light it was apparently assumed that either 90 or 164 Light (Motorised Infantry) Divs might be through the Wire and heading for Sidi Barrani. We were to move back to Daba at once.

There was a sudden hush. We all sat still, rather stunned; the bottom seemed to be falling out of our world. Tobruk, the invincible Tobruk, which we had held for so many months at such a cost, seemed to have fallen like a ripe plum. And Sidi Barrani was only some sixty miles to the north on the direct road to Matruh, whereas we had to cover the route to Daba over desert tracks. What had happened to the Army? The retreat seemed as unstoppable as the earlier one from Agedabia to Gazala.

Jones's orders were that all units should make their way to Daba independently, under their own arrangements, within the hour. That meant, to me, that I wouldn't have to hang around after the Btys, picking up their wrecks. They could tow their own. I had enough wrecks of my own and few spare tow-hooks anyway. I mentioned this to the two Bty Commanders and they agreed.

292 moved off at once, helped by Macpherson-Grant's second sight in getting them on their wheels early, followed by 291 and finally RHQ and the Signals Section; then we got going. The official Bde route was along the Trigh el Abd (The Slaves' Road), an ancient track running west to east some fifteen miles south of the Trigh Capuzzo, and finally deviating north towards the coast.

We were now in the clay-pan and soft gravel country and I assumed it would be like that all the way to Daba; my heavily loaded vehicles would perpetually be sinking in the soft stuff, so I turned a blind eye to Bde orders, meaning to use as much as I could of the good, hard track that I remembered running beside the water-pipeline instead. This would be easier going and it

313

seemed to offer the best hope of getting my doubtful vehicles away. We joined it at the cross-tracks just north of Oxford Circus.

The old Leyland was now in motorable condition after a fashion. We had stripped its rear seized-up differential out of its casing and disconnected the flexible shaft between the two diffs, so that it could now run, driven by the first axle instead of the pair, but it was unable to pull anything. None of the Leylands had a spare wheel and those on the recovery were a bit dicky. I bet Cpl Brittain that he would never reach Daba. He took me on in umbrage at the slur on his ability and I lost.

Some four miles along the pipeline from Oxford Circus, the Leyland's engine caught fire and, after we had extinguished the flames, it wouldn't start. We put it on tow behind one of the machinery lorries and went on. The track was a trifle stony and after fifteen miles more, one of the recovery's tyres blew out and caught fire. After surveying the damage, it was decided to put the four best remaining tyres on its front wheels and those of the intermediate axle. That left only one wheel on the remaining axle, so we took it off and chained the axle up to the chassis, the Leyland becoming a four-wheeler instead of a six-wheeler.

We had stopped near one of the pumping stations on the pipeline, while we were fixing the Leyland, and I walked over to it. Half a dozen dirty and tired-looking but incredibly cheery South African engineers were hoisting the pumping plant out of the bowels of the earth on an improvised sheerlegs and loading it into a lorry. They told me that all the pumps between here and Capuzzo were already out and they would be taking them out as far as Matruh. They didn't think that the enemy was yet through the Wire and certainly not as far as Sidi Barrani.

So on we staggered towards Matruh and in about another twenty miles our Italian 8-ton trailer burst two tyres. We had only one spare tyre, so we were forced to stop and mend the tube. Night overtook us then, when we had covered only about fifty miles from Oxford Circus in fifteen hours, and we camped there.

Next morning we started bright and early and followed the pipeline to the Barrani–Matruh road, only to find it packed solid with traffic coming down it in haste and considerable confusion, so we kept off the tarmac and pushed on towards Matruh in single file along a side track that no one seemed to want to use. I suppose they thought it was mined, but it didn't seem to be.

Just short of Matruh, near where the Siwa track forked, we came up to the old Italian minefield. The gap through it on the road made a bottleneck, and a seething mass of vehicles twenty wide by two miles long was being sorted into single file by two harassed Military Police. It was going to take hours to sort it out and why no German aircraft took it into their heads to strafe it was a mystery. To our right was the railway and a pushful subaltern went to recce the gap there through the minefield, returning to tell me that this seemed to be clear. We turned immediately towards it, followed by a host of other units, hoping to bypass the bottleneck.

We all went through the minefield area bumping along the sleepers and fanned out on to the desert as soon as we were through. I led my column past the vast Returned Vehicle Parks at Mohalfa, where the desert railway joined the Egyptian State Railway line. These were deserted and hundreds of broken-down vehicles were lying there with no means of getting them away. The railway engineers were concentrating on clearing the railway sidings of trucks and locomotives. From Mohalfa, we were directed across the desert to Sidi Haneish, south of Bagush and everywhere around one could see lines of dust as the Army retreated in seemingly endless columns. And everywhere also were parties of Egyptian civilians trying to thumb lifts. The Germans had advertised themselves as the "Protectors of Islam", but the locals didn't appear to believe that.

We spent our second night near Sidi Haneish and pushed on for Daba in the morning. The Bagush "box" and defences were another frightful bottleneck, and as we came round to the road beyond it was fairly empty so we bowled down to Daba in much quicker time, where we established ourselves among the sand dunes along the seashore. Here at last we handed the Leyland recovery to the Army RVP and got a proper receipt for it and authority to draw another vehicle, although where from was anyone's guess. A jubilant Cpl Brittain came up to me and collected the bet he had won. I reckon he deserved a Mention in Despatches for his sterling work and exemplary demonstration of selfless duty.

12

Daba when we reached it was in a turmoil. It was only about 100 miles from Alexandria and all through the desert war it had been as nearly a Base Area as it could be. All sorts of L of C troops had been living there for over two years and had fairly dug themselves in. The place was littered with Nissen huts, concrete-floored super-tents and wooden chalets, and it had the biggest and most well known NAAFI roadhouse-restaurant, "The Noah's Ark", on the road from Alex to Derna. Now the war had reached it instead of being anything up to 600 miles away in Libya and everyone was being uprooted and bundled out at top speed, to make room for the likes of us, traipsing sadly away down the road towards Alex. Their world, too, had had the bottom knocked out. The Daba LGs had been the far back base of Wellington bombers and these were also clearing out their accumulation of months to make room for the fighter squadrons coming back from the far west.

The main impression I gained, during the couple of sunny June days we were staging there, was one of almost peevish annoyance that the folk "up there" had let the enemy get this far, as the army of "dug-outs" and "bomb-proofers" packed up and left their comfortable homes and trekked back towards the Delta in the shimmer of heat haze and dust.

No one knew what was happening either. This was the normal state of affairs with which we had been living for several months. It was confidently asserted that the Germans were now in Sidi Barrani and Oxford Circus and were steadily advancing on Matruh. It was stated that we were intending to hold a

317

defensive line south along the Siwa road from Matruh, but nobody believed that.

Passing through Daba, going west, were brigades of tough New Zealand troops and a lot of very "pink and-white" British reinforcements. These latter stared with interest at our dirty clothes and sunburned bodies and our dust-caked vehicles festooned with sand-channels, hessian netting and dangling blackened petrol-tin brew cans. Some of these newcomers were even wearing pith helmets of the type we had worn when we first came out but had discarded long ago. The lads waved to them, asking whether they had left any beer behind in Alex, and promised to come back and help them when they had finished what was left. 'You want to watch out lads,' someone called, 'Jerry's up there and he bites!' He was echoing the words he had heard at Capuzzo a couple of days ago.

I set up the workshop about a couple of miles on the Matruh side of Daba and started work on vehicle repairs. Bde HQ had established themselves up the road at Sidi Haneish where the foremost fighter squadrons were temporarily. They had given us no sort of guidance as to how long we might expect to be at Daba and, since the Signals had not yet given us a line to them, I decided that I would have to go and visit Estlin to find out what I was supposed to be doing and for how long. Estlin was pleased to see me, saying, 'Oh that's where you are! I thought you'd get away all right. How mobile are you?' He then told me to bring the workshop up to Sidi Haneish tomorrow and gave me lunch in the Bde Mess, but before I left the order was cancelled and I was instructed to remain at Daba on two hours' notice and await further instructions. Just afterwards, the CO of 88 HAA Regt accosted me and asked if I knew where he could lay hands on a spare limber for a 3.7" since without it he would have to "abandon a gun". Presumably he had already tried Morton, who was now at Fuka, without result, and I was a last resort. I told him I had seen one on a BLR gun in the evacuation yards at Mohalfa only yesterday.

'That's no good,' he said. 'It's under shell-fire.'

Mohalfa was six miles beyond Matruh and thus only 40 miles from here at Sidi Haneish. It sounded ominous, too: "abandon a gun". That was a thing AA Regts just did not do, except in exceptional circumstances.

As I left, I saw an unforgettable sight, that of a group of red-tabbed Brigadiers sitting in a circle on the sand by the roadside amid a welter of unloaded office equipment. They were writing in notebooks on their knees while being harangued by an even more senior brass-hat standing with his back to me.

The following day Bde HQ and all the fighters moved back to Daba from Sidi Haneish. No one knew what was going on, but there were reports of fighting at Matruh. Rumour had it that a proper defensive line was being prepared at a place called El Alamein about forty miles from Alexandria, where the relatively impassable Qattara Depression approached the coast, making a narrow defensive line. What for? Oh, just as a precaution. No need to worry. We're holding the Matruh-Siwa line.

The next day, the news came through that Matruh had been evacuated after heavy fighting and it seemed doubtful if Bagush was going to be held. It was no longer called the Bagush "box". Boxes were out of favour these days.

88 Wksps were hurriedly whipped out of Fuka, halfway between Matruh and Daba, and were reported to heading for somewhere "behind Alamein". Other units followed and we were on to two hours' notice. The HAA guns deployed into their A/tk mode and lookouts were ordered to watch the country to the west and south. In the absence of any official news, it was being rumoured that the Germans were through the defences of Matruh "like butter" and were still coming, and transport of all sorts began streaming back down the road.

Then we heard that the fighter group was moving back to Mareopolis on the Cairo–Alexandria road and they flew off. Mareopolis was only some fifteen miles from Alex and my worry was about Phyl. No 3 General was at Bussilli, miles on the far side of Alex, and they would have to move out through the city. 94th HAA Regt was ordered to cover the LGs, while they were still being evacuated. We in 94 Wksps just sat in our vehicles, wondering if, once again, we had been forgotten, and watched the LAA guns draw off the LG and string themselves out in A/tk positions across the road, half concealed in the waist-high scrub at 100-yard intervals.

All through that hot late-June morning we just sat and brewed tea at intervals. Thirty miles away to the west we could just discern the blue line of the Fuka escarpment wavering in the heat haze. Somewhere between it and us we now knew were two armies, the pursued and the pursuing, but only very occasionally could we pick out the sound of distant gunfire. Every so often, we would start up our vehicle engines, just to see that they *would* still start.

Then we were suddenly told to despatch all heavy and slow vehicles back to a rendezvous at Mareopolis and I sent the majority of the Workshop off under the command of Farbrother and Jakeman, remaining behind myself with Ardis and a small party under SQMS Pratt. And still we waited through the scorching afternoon, while the dust clouds miles away to the west rose and shimmered and eddied, and the road traffic dwindled to a trickle and ceased. In front of us the LAA gun teams polished their clips of ammunition and positioned their gun tractors ready for a quick getaway.

Finally, at about 4.00 p.m. we were told to "get out" – and we got out in a couple of minutes. The Noah's Ark, the famous NAAFI roadhouse, was deserted as we passed it, abandoned with its wire-mesh doors and windows banging in the wind. In front of it stood an open staff car with a red-tabbed field officer and his two aides standing in it. I was sitting on the roof of our vehicle and gave the brass-hat a smashing salute as we passed. He returned it as a man might do in a dream, without looking at me, and resumed his hunched, arms-akimbo stance with his head bowed and his eyes gazing absently up the road, as the retreating army rumbled by. Then I saw a small Union Jack fluttering on the front wing of his car and I realised that the brass-hat could only have been the GOC in C, Middle East, General Auchinleck. Only the C in C was entitled to fly that flag. Although we didn't know it at that time, he had superseded General Ritchie and was now personally in command of the Eighth Army.

The road was a two-deep jam of slowly moving transport. All sorts of odd slow-moving vehicles were holding it up: caterpillar tractors from RE companies; wingless aircraft on trailers; and tank recovery vehicles; all lost and unitless and blindly making their way to some hoped-for safety in the east, where someone would know what was happening and would tell them what to do. Most of them had been on the road for days, but had now been overtaken by the faster-retreating army.

This was no good to us. Following the practice that had proved useful in the past few days, I struck off the road and went down the side of the rail line, mingling with a thin stream of frightened Egyptians going the same way, on foot, in carts and on donkeys. They were disorientated refugees seeking to escape a war which last week was being fought by the British in Central Libya and was suddenly on their very doorsteps. Those on foot tried to thumb lifts from the soldiers but only got covered in dust as the lorries went by. I felt sorry for the poor devils; this wasn't their war, but they were suffering for it. A couple of trains went by, Delta-bound; truly amazing sights, with natives clinging on to any projection that might support them. They were crouching on the tenders, perched dangerously on the buffers and couplings, lying on the carriage roofs, holding precariously to the steps and to the bracing structures below the coaches, a squirming mass of terrified humanity. So much for their belief in the "Protectors of Islam", I thought again.

By nightfall, we had become separated from the rest of the Regt, after travelling about forty miles, and at sunset we came upon companies of South African troops feverishly laying minefields and stringing barbed wire. They grudgingly let us through and told us to get the hell out of there, and we threaded our way past some mechanical excavators digging deep trenches or anti-tank ditches. All we wanted was to find somewhere where we could stop and brew up before it became too dark. About this time we passed a railway station and its name board caught my eye. It said "El Alamein"!

Heavens above! Was that the famed "Alamein Line"? A few strands of barbed wire and a half-completed ditch? I listened with misgiving to the sound of gunfire away to the west and didn't feel happy. I was wondering where Phyl was and what she was doing. I was appalled at the thought of her lonely hospital stuck out on the Delta beyond Alex, with only one line of retreat, forward *through* Alex. There was nothing I could do about that, though, and I fell to wondering whether we would next meet in Palestine or India or the Sudan, or, worse still, whether we would ever see one another again... It was all very depressing.

As we brewed up our tea, we heard the sound of aircraft, presumably German aircraft, and hurriedly extinguished all lights. It was deep purple twilight, but there were several of them, coming in pretty low, and the bombing started over to our left with vicious little flowers of flame and the thump, thump of explosions. Something went up in flames. 'They're bombing the road,' Ardis said.

Then, coming across at a diagonal angle, another line of bursts and another and another, zigzagging across the country just to our rear. The Germans were clearly having a go at the infant Alamein defence system to slow down its growth. Every now and then one of them spotted something on the ground and the aircraft would be pinpointed in the sky as the invisible source from which sprang two streams of tracer.

Then one of the Germans decided to have a go at the railway line and we dived under our vehicles hurriedly as the line of bomb bursts seemed to be advancing straight at us. The bombs fell with a steadily increasing scream which lasted for what seemed ages, like a train coming out of a tunnel, and then there was a roar that shook the very nuts and bolts of the vehicle above us and knocked down on top of us the accumulated dust of weeks, in the manner that I had experienced near Tobruk several weeks earlier.

After the end of that run, the workshop was moving again towards some safer place in less than a minute, tea forgotten. No one had been hurt, but it was reckoned that the neighbourhood of El Alamein was not the best place to stop. We finally leaguered several miles on and in the morning – 30 June, I think it was – we set off eastwards again. Our track led through several small Egyptian villages, the inhabitants of which were hastily packing up and getting out. The neighbourhood had recently been a considerably developed Base area, but they had now all moved out and the only signs left were the holes for the dug-in tents and wheel tracks.

At Burg el Arab, where I had had my first taste of the desert with 2 Light a year ago, the MPs slung us off our track and we were deviated on to the main road where our progress gradually slowed to a crawl. As far as the eye could see, the road ahead was a solid jam of vehicles, halting, moving a few yards and halting again. But not a German aircraft in sight.

About eight miles from Alexandria, the coast road which had been winding among the white sand dunes, groves of fig trees and clumps of date palms forked, the left fork going straight on to Alexandria and the right fork – the "Desert road to Cairo" – went downhill, crossed the two-mile wide Lake Mariout by a narrow causeway, climbed the bluffs on the south shore and proceeded through the villages of Amriya and Mareopolis to Cairo some 100 miles away. It took us four hours to cover the last ten miles; it was like a Bank Holiday jam rather than an army in retreat.

12 AA Bde had set up a report centre at Amriya a few miles south of the level crossing and we drew off to report at the RHQ rendezvous. The RAF had already settled like locusts on either side of the main road and were establishing roughly graded runways, about ten in all. The ground was flat hard-packed earth – like Antelat of evil memory – and here and there the locals had made an attempt to till the soil into irregular furrows. It was obvious that if we were to be here for more than a week or two the whole area would be cut up by wheel tracks and the dust would be hell. In fact we were there for four months and hell it was.

We set up shop in the most dust-free bit of virgin desert I could find and started work immediately to clear as much of the casualties of the journey as we could, for no one seemed to know whether or not we would be going further. I was the unhappy possessor of "Officer Only" instructions for implementation in the event of a further retreat down the Cairo road to Mena and then across the Nile to the Canal Area. We were all

323

dog-tired and dispirited; the bottom seemed to have fallen out of our world.

All the rest of that scorching day we slaved on, trying to make broken-down vehicles into "runners", or at least towable, and all the time, the packed Bank Holiday jam on the road moved, halted, moved and halted again in its crawl towards Cairo and the Canal. And what might have happened to Phyl I didn't like to think.

The following morning early, I set out for Alexandria, in the hope of scrounging a wheel or tyre for our recovery trailer still carrying the 3-tonner, which had burst a tyre on the latter part of the journey from Daba. We had no spare and I was doubtful of its ability to carry on. I suspected that the Base Ordnance Depot wouldn't be over particular about the proper Army Form required.

The traffic jam was still on but not so bad on the road into the city and I got to the BOD without much trouble. Alexandria presented a most impressive spectacle of unconcern. I think it was the July 1 or 2 (I forget which); anyhow, it was the day, I vas told later, that the enemy caught up with us at Alamein and Rommel said in his "Message to the Troops": 'Tonight you will sleep with the women of Alexandria'. Everything appeared to be going on absolutely normally; brightly polished cars filled the streets; crowds of well dressed men and women strolled along the pavements; the usual hordes of Egyptian pedlars tried to foist their wares on you; the cinemas were open and the cafés were doing a roaring trade. But there was not a single soldier to be seen and if one appeared, the civilians asked him: 'Where are you going? What is happening?' Everyone seemed to be waiting for something with one ear cocked and they were whispering amongst themselves. It was said afterwards that everyone probably had his or her German or Italian flag in the drawer, ready to produce it and wave. I could well believe it.

All vehicles in the retreat had been ordered to carry a grenade, or Mills bomb, with which to render the engine useless if we had to abandon the vehicle and I was no exception, although I had taken the precaution against accidents of taping the pin very carefully in position. As I arrived outside the Base Ordnance

Depot, I was surrounded by a motley crowd of street pedlars, but when I opened the door to put a foot on the pavement, the Mills bomb fell out among them and I have never seen a crowd disperse so quickly.

The BOD were unable to help me, for they were frantically crating their stores and sending them off to Palestine and were not in an issuing mood. However, the Base Ordnance Workshops just down the road were showing no signs of panic, though working like madmen. If or when it became necessary, they intended to blow the place up and until then there was much work to be done. I got my tyre and a complete spare wheel as well, and by telling a sad story I managed to get several sets of spanners and taps and dies to replace the tools lost in the Gambut flap. I also tried to ring up No 3 General Hospital on the military network, but there was no reply from the Signals exchange, so I sent Phyl a very illegal civilian telegram, which linked the name of the hospital with the name of the place. Remarkably, she received it, just as the nursing staff were waiting for the transport and were being evacuated by train to Kantara on the Canal and it put her mind at rest. She had had no news of me since the latest retreat had started.

As I was leaving the BOW, there was an alarm and everyone stood to with rifles and steel helmets. The Germans were attacking the Alamein defences and whispers were circulating that their armoured cars were through and heading down the road for Alex. I beat it back to Mareopolis in haste and was greatly relieved to find the unit still there and no sign of any flap.

Although we didn't know it, the Great Retreat which had begun at Agedabia in January was over. But, not knowing this, we spent an uncomfortable night in our boots. We were in the last ditch and this is not good sleeping quarters.

It was scant compensation to learn that we were now not RAOC, but REME. The Royal Electrical and Mechanical Engineers was a new workshop and engineering corps formed from the workshop facilities of the Royal Army Ordnance Corps, the Royal Engineers and the Royal Army Service Corps. No one had any of the new cap badges, but I was lucky enough

325

to buy three for myself and my two juniors at a shop in Cairo some time later, when we were withdrawn for a refit. At the moment, we had more important things to worry about....

For four days thereafter, we sat and watched an endless column of "soft" troops: Royal Engineers, Pioneer Corps, RASC and other ancillary forces and the like, heading off down the road to Cairo as the entire area was cleared of everything but fighting troops. We listened to the enemy guns somewhere to the west of us and wondered whether the Eighth Army was intending to hold them permanently at Alamein or whether it was just another rearguard delaying action, but on a grand scale, to cover the evacuation of the Whole Delta area.

Then Estlin pulled me out of 94 Wksps and attached me temporarily to Bde HQ "for special duties" and I joined him a few miles up the road at headquarters. What these special duties were, I never found out. I asked S/Sgt Lewis, Estlin's Chief Clerk and he just said that the Major never did anything without good reason and doubtless he would tell me himself in good time. Rebuffed, I sought information from ASM Spooner, who suggested that the Major was lonely and wanted someone to talk to.

This seemed a reasonable answer, for Estlin appeared to be much immersed in something at a higher level; Wray had been seconded elsewhere and Estlin was alone in the office, except for Spooner, Lewis and a couple of junior clerks. He set me to answering his telephone, even if he was in the office tent with me. A call would come in from somewhere and Lewis would say that the Major was engaged and put it through to me. I had to take the message and get all the appropriate facts and offer to ring back. Estlin would ask me what it had been about and I found myself acting as a filter of the information between him and the outside world. Then he would ask me what I proposed to do about it and I was obliged to rack my brains to produce a reasonable suggestion. Or he might discuss what had been requested, giving his own opinion, bringing out what I ought to have thought of, and an answer was agreed. Sometimes it even might be the thing that I had proposed myself.

He knew that I was personally familiar with the workshop officers on a different plane to himself and on generally good terms with them, and he would seek to know what I thought they would be able to do. And then he would instruct me to organise what had been decided and I was left to carry the can with the help of Lewis, who knew the Bde procedures and would take down dictation of the resulting orders from me, making sure that what I was saying was in accordance with Bde practice and would not conflict with what Estlin would have said.

It was most instructive and I believe that, apart from the benefit to me of an appreciation of how the Brigade worked, it relieved Estlin of much donkey work of administration. As a bonus, it introduced me to the other (RA) officers with whom the work had to tie in. After a few days, I found that I was effectively acting as the Bde OME, under Estlin's overall supervision. I was not on my own, for Lewis was there to advise me on the general practice of the Workshop organisation and of course Spooner could help with the practical side.

At this time, the Germans had arrived in front of the line at Alamein and were probing for an exploitable gap in the defences. The general opinion in the Mess was that they must have effectively run out of steam and were suffering the same problem as we had when at Antelat, of a very extended supply line from their base, whereas the Eighth Army was sitting, albeit uncomfortably, right on the doorstep of our own Base Area in the Delta, with no equivalent logistical problems. It was believed that the enemy was now overstretched and was ripe to be upset by an energetic push from our forces, and Estlin was charged with the problem of planning the workshop support for the AA defences of the RAF forward LGs when they advanced. This "push" had been allotted the code name of "Plop" and Estlin gave me the task of planning the movement of the Bde's AA Workshops when this move forward took place. I had personal experience of what was possible and also was personally known to the majority of the Workshop commanders.

It was all unfamiliar work but I found it fascinating. It made me realise how wrong my ideas of staff work were. The Bde was like a team, all working as friends and deferring to the senior members, but taking things less seriously than I had been as the OC of one of their Workshops. There were some things that one just didn't speak about, however.

Estlin introduced me to the Brigadier when I joined the Mess and he remembered me as the officer who sat on the towing vehicle, during the far-off days of the anti-tank practice at Gambut. He asked me if I was any relation to the new GOC of the Eighth Army. I hadn't heard of the recent appointment of General B. L. Montgomery to this post, and apparently General Auchinleck had been replaced as C in C Middle East by another new man, General Alexander.

There was one special social routine in the Mess that amused me. After dinner we all took our coffee into the tent that acted as an ante-room, to listen to the special Afrika Korps German radio programme broadcast from Greece or Crete at 9.00 p.m. It always started with Lalli Andersen (the German "Forces' Sweetheart") singing *Lili Marlene*. By time-honoured custom, it was the Brigadier's duty to fiddle the knobs on the set and if he happened to be a bit late coming out from dinner, there was consternation that we might miss our daily ration of *Lili Marlene*. But, I was told, he never missed it; there was a pregnant hush as we all sat round the set and the Brig walked over and tuned it to the appropriate wavelength, before the dulcet tomes of Fräulein Andersen filled the tent. I believe that she became the "Forces' Sweetheart" of the Eighth Army, too, and it adopted *Lili Marlene* as its signature tune. It would have surprised the Germans how much we appreciated their programme.

But back to the conduct of the war. My old friends 1 LAA Wksps were loosely responsible to 12 AA Bde, and when Bentley went sick and was evacuated to Base Hospital, it fell to Estlin to find a replacement, even though 1 LAA Wksps was attached to 7 Armd Div and not in 12 AA Bde. Estlin looked through his private and highly confidential records of officers which he kept strictly under lock and key and asked me what I thought of Ardis. I gave him a good report, and he said it confirmed his own assessment; he was proposing to transfer him to 1 LAA Wksps and recommend him for promotion to Captain. I pointed out that this would leave me a bit short at 94 and he made an odd remark that he didn't think I would suffer, and it might not concern me anyhow – he sounded as if he had something up his sleeve for me, but didn't enlarge on the subject. So off went Ardis to the LAA Regt supporting 7 Armd Div and I heard later that he took to the Division as a duck to water. They took him under their wing and he never looked back.

After a few days, the German attacks at Alamein seemed to falter and we suddenly received the signal "Plop". I was much involved with the movement orders for the assorted Workshops under command and had to liaise with the RA planners to make sure that the Regts were still going to the same places as originally planned. It was all most exciting and we got the Workshops on the move satisfactorily.

All went well for a couple of days and then the enemy resistance stiffened, the push came to a stop and the dust settled. I don't think the RAF actually moved at all and the AA was repositioned just a bit forward of their start lines. Then the Germans again began "nibbling" at the Eighth Army's defences and General Montgomery decided that no further "pushes" on our part were to be made. He also said that we would not be retreating again and when asked what would happen if the Germans broke through and reached Cairo, he was reported to have said they would come up against the massive forces of GHQ MEF and would be overwhelmed by sheer weight of numbers.

All this meant that the planning previously associated with Exercise "Plop" was run down if not actually cancelled and Estlin had a good look at his activities and decided that he had no immediate further need for my services. Accordingly, he thanked me for my assistance and returned me to my unit.

94 Wksps was still in the same place and I felt the loss of Ardis, more particularly when a couple of weeks later, Farbrother went into hospital with a poisoned knee and I was left as the sole officer in the unit to deal with three men's work. The next four

months had a damnable sameness about them. As I had expected, the vast hardened mud and earth plain turned to dust through constantly being cut up by the wheels of aircraft and motor vehicles. The RAF had a simple solution to the problem. Whenever the dust got so bad as to interfere with flying, they graded a new LG somewhere else and moved a few hundred yards. They had priority; we were not so fortunate and were forced to stay where we were in ankle-deep dust which felt like walking on soft snow. The slightest breeze raised it in rolling, billowing clouds. We breathed dust, we ate dust; it penetrated our tentage, our beds and even our packed luggage; it got into our hair and covered our faces in yellow masks as we sweated under the blazing sun on the open, shadeless plain.

In fact it was beastly and I think it brought home to the lads what they had been missing hitherto. They buckled down and got on with the work in a manner that was quite different from the lackadaisical take-it-or-leave-it attitude I had first been aware of in Gambut. They were realising that the war was only going to be won by solid hard work and they put their backs into it.

When they saw the manner in which the RAF were forced to operate, they were aware that there was something even worse than repairing vehicles and guns. The LGs at Mareopolis were used by both fighters and light bombers and 1 believe that the RAF was responsible for stopping the enemy where he was. Flights of eighteen Boston or Baltimore bombers went out every twenty minutes, complete with fighter cover, and on returning in clouds of dust, the ground crews fell on them and readied them for another sortie. I didn't hitherto have much time for the ground crews but I took my hat off to them now. They slaved every hour of the day and night and were an example to us all, amid much worse conditions than ourselves: dust, heat and the continual shattering noise of aircraft engines that drowned speech.

So it went on, week in, week out, and news trickled through of two or three minor successes on the ground at the front as well. The retreat *had* stopped.

I learned that No 3 General Hospital was back in the

Alexandria area again and I decided that I must see Phyl. Alexandria was out of normal bounds to troops – otherwise the place would have been full of them, skiving from the desert – but I had developed some symptoms of toothache and, armed with a certificate from the MO, I got Horsfall, my batman driver, to drive me into the the Dental Centre in the city. Afterwards, we motored out on the Rosetta road to No 3, where, to my great disappointment, they told me that it was Phyl's afternoon off and she had hitched a lift into Alex.

Greatly disgruntled, I returned and in desperation got Horsfall to drive slowly round a circuit of the main shopping areas. Eventually, he suddenly asked: 'Is the young lady you're looking for, the one in the photograph on your table? Well, I think that's her over there!' And lo and behold, there was Phyl walking down the pavement ten yards away.

I jumped out of the car, fell into step beside her and said something foolish like: 'Turned out nice again, hasn't it?', or 'Do you think it will rain this weekend?'

For a moment, I honestly thought she was going to faint! Then, I wondered if she were going to cast decorum to the winds, throw her arms round my neck and kiss me, then and there in the middle of Alexandria! This was quite out of the question; officers just do not embrace on the public streets of a foreign (or any other) city. Then she recovered and wanted to know where I was stationed and what had happened to me since we had last seen each other. I gave Horsfall some money and instructed him to go to the main NAAFI for an hour or two while we strolled off to a café for several cups of coffee, and talked and talked. Apparently, the Hospital had been evacuated to Kantara on the Canal, bound for Palestine, but, while waiting for further movement orders, the flap had collapsed and they had been returned to Bussilli. We both went back to our respective units much refreshed and in much better spirits than we had enjoyed for several months.

After that, malign fate stepped in. Phyl's Hospital was being moved elsewhere – I think to Syria – and she managed to get herself transferred to a unit in Cairo, rather than move with them, since I was unlikely to go to Syria. It was an abortive attempt; after about a week, she was re-posted to No 12 General Hospital in Palestine, and there was no chance of changing that!

I went back to the dust and heat of the Mareopolis LGs, getting more and more fed up with running the entire unit without any assistance.

Eventually, a replacement for Ardis was posted to us, a Lt Reg Phillips, a chubby, prematurely balding, round-faced gnome of a man, looking like a younger edition of the actor Alasdair Sim. I took to him on sight. He was a good officer and quite unflappable. We had a common interest outside the Army in that we both had been Ulster Austin 750cc enthusiasts in peace time. He had been No 4 in the official Austin team at Donington Park in 1939, but had never actually raced in earnest. Air-raids didn't sees to worry him. I recall one occasion when he was writing letters in our Mess tent and, when a German bomber began dropping a stick near us, he just looked up and said, 'They don't normally do this on a Tuesday, do they?' He then returned to his writing. I also got, on temporary attachment, a radio repair officer to hold the fort until Farbrother came out of hospital, a gangling youth by the name of Tuck, nicknamed "Friar" for obvious reasons.

In mid-August, the Workshop was withdrawn by Estlin for a ten-day partial refit at the Abbassia Base Workshops in Cairo. I cannot say that I enjoyed the break; it was too hot and humid after the desert and, although we were billeted in buildings, it was much too super-civilised and far from the war for my liking. I had last been in Cairo almost a year previously and felt like Rip Van Winkle.

One good thing came out of it, however. The officer in charge of Artillery Development was a Major Macpherson, a very approachable Australian. I sought him out and we swapped stories on the problems of keeping the 3.7s on the road. He was already aware of the "barrel bounce" I had encountered in service and he told me it was caused by wear engendered on the elevating pinion at one point due to excessive barrel "bounce" when in the travelling position, because of inadequate support. He had a design for overcoming the shortcomings of the UK design, which he showed me. It consisted of a massive A-frame of welded angle iron attached to the rear axle assembly, with a semi-cylindrical bed to support the barrel about two-thirds along its length when in the towing position and folding back when in the firing mode. I said it was just what 94th's Batteries needed instead of the puerile little brass turn-screw assembly support fitted as standard. He presented me with a set of working drawings and suggested I made sets for 94th's guns. It was going to be issued as an official modification sometime, anyway, and there was no reason why I shouldn't start right away on our guns. In due course, the "Macpherson struts" became a standard modification and were adopted throughout the Middle East.

On the way back to Mareopolis, I came across a very odd-looking but obviously useful little vehicle being driven by an American up the road to Alexandria. He pulled in at the Halfway House and I questioned the driver as to what it was. Apparently it was the US Army's replacement for a motorcycle, a 4×4 "quarter-ton" open runabout made by Willis-Overland, as a sort of counter to the German People's Car which I had first seen at Mechili last autumn. Two large US manufacturers – Ford and Willis-Overland – were producing them in vast quantities, as the Willis type MB and the Ford type GP. The driver said it was the best thing since sliced bread; it could go anywhere and could carry men over bumpy ground at phenomenal speeds. Its only flaw, he admitted, was the width of its rather narrow tyres; it could have done with fatter ones to avoid getting bogged down in the worst of the terrain. Since the version made by Ford was in much greater production, the Model GP was the one most likely to be encountered and the GP came to be affectionately known as the "Jeep".

We arrived back at Mareopolis to find that Estlin had been promoted and moved elsewhere – no one knew exactly where – and there was a vacancy for a Bde EME. Rumours were rife as to who in the Bde would be promoted to fill his place. It was naturally assumed that it had to be one of the present workshop commanders, since no outsider would be able to understand the complexity of the job at this crucial time. Greatly to my surprise, I seemed to be the favourite in the betting, on the grounds that I was the longest-serving OC Workshops still in the Bde and that I had been with the Bde throughout the previous campaign. A subsidiary reason was that I must have been Estlin's choice, my attachment to Bde HQ having been a ploy to acclimatise me to the job and to allow Estlin, who knew of his imminent move, to study my ability at close quarters. I confronted Lewis about this rumour and he insisted he knew nothing about it; it would be for the Brig to make some move in this direction. However, the rumour became so pronounced as we awaited the result that even I myself became expectant.

Then a newly promoted Major Walker arrived from the Delta where he had been an OC of a Searchlight Wksp on the Canal. He was a rather fussy and opinionated character, who evidently had been the next in line on the GHQ MEF lists for a Major's appointment. Nobody seemed to think much of him, partly, rather unfairly, because he wasn't Estlin, but also on account of his lack of experience of desert warfare and partly, perhaps mainly, because he refused to learn from his more desert-blooded subordinates. He immediately got under my skin and that of Morton, both of whom had served through the recent campaign, and we both put in to GHQ MEF for transfers to another AA Bde, seeing there was no chance of promotion in this one. I think he must have heard of this somehow, for he seemed to take a dislike to us.

Nothing came of our applications and there was nothing we could do but soldier on as best we could. Lewis commiserated with me when I came to report to Walker, hinting, as far as an NCO could, that the Major had a lot to learn, and he hoped we could help him in that direction. I gained the impression that perhaps Estlin might have put my name forward and GHQ MEF turned it down for the reason I have mentioned. I never knew the whole story.

Anyhow, here we were back at the Mareopolis LGs in time for the "last gasp" assaults by the Afrika Korps against an intentionally weak point in the defences. They broke through down the famous "Barrel Track" with the way open invitingly to Cairo, but they realised that the British forces were massed on either side and got cold feet; they didn't quite enter the trap.

When they hesitated, they became the target of massed artillery bombardment from both flanks, not to mention continuous air strafes, and they began to withdraw. The withdrawal quickened and finally become dangerously near a rout. The tanks of the 15th and 21st Panzer Divs went up in smoke on the uplands of Deir el Ragil and Alam Halfa. The flap was over and they didn't try again. For the first time in the desert a major German attack had been repulsed.

There wasn't much enemy air activity and what there was was mainly at night. They would sail over and drop flares and then let go showers of "Butterfly Bombs", horrid little anti-personnel things that jumped about like firecrackers, if disturbed, spitting a hail of steel balls in all directions.

On one occasion, soon after I returned from the refit, I called in at the Bde EME's office and found Spooner, Lewis and the two clerks sitting on the sand behind a pile of sandbags. Walker had gone out somewhere. I asked them what on earth they were doing and they pointed to a small object about twenty yards away sitting half-buried in the earth. It was a butterfly bomb which had failed to explode on hitting the ground.

Spooner explained that they had all attempted to detonate the wretched thing by creeping up, placing a live Mills bomb beside it and then retiring at speed to the safety of the sandbag breastwork. He thought it was probably a dud, but added, 'You can have a try, Sir, if you like. You might have better luck,' and he offered me a Mills bomb with the pin still in.

It was a dare, and I couldn't back out. I took the bomb from him, pulled out the pin and tiptoed to the little half-submerged device, clutching the release lever in my little hot hand. I laid it gently beside the intruder and, releasing the lever, legged it back to the sandbags at a phenomenal speed, to throw myself flat, just as the Mills went off, scattering fragments and sand through the air above me. Spooner and Levis complimented me on my speed and pointed out that the butterfly had still not gone off. I told them to ask Major Walker to oblige as soon as he returned from wherever he was, and returned to my unit, feeling I had been a fool to play with a Mills. We should have tried a rifle or revolver bullet or something like that.

In September, a new Division came up the road, to the sound of the pipes, wearing Scots bonnets and almost flaunting their HD flashes on their arms. It was a badge that we were to get used to, for they painted it over everything they passed. They were the reconstituted 51st (Highland) Division which had been captured almost complete in 1940 at St Valéry whilst with the BEF.

They had a pronounced chip on the shoulder, and one either liked them or one didn't. The Australians did and reckoned they were good cobbers, but the majority of old desert hands were a bit doubtful, taking it amiss that the Scots seemed to believe that they had been sent out here to finish things off and were ready to do so.

At the beginning of October, my resistance to desert conditions suddenly collapsed. Hitherto, I had rejoiced in the belief that the local complaints were for others, not me. But now, suddenly, my cuts wouldn't heal, I developed impetigo on my face and as soon as that was healed, my right foot began to fester and swell. Nothing the MO did produced any relief and finally I was packed off to hospital in Alexandria with a temperature of 103 degrees F and a foot like a blue football, feeling very sorry for myself.

13

The ambulance took me to No 4 General Hospital on the east side of the harbour at Alexandria and I was put into a ward that seemed to specialise in acute cases. I was treated with one of the new "sulfa" drugs which made me feel rotten but my foot began to clear up. Then they threw me out and I was taken by ambulance to No 8 Gen Hosp at the western end of Alex, where they found my foot so much improved that they started treating me just for athlete's foot.

By this time, I was able to walk and started hinting that it was time for me to be discharged. However, the hospitals in Alex were now being cleared for the reception of wounded from the imminent big battle, and the whole ward was carried off to the main station and loaded into a hospital train. My fellow sufferers were most anxious to find out where we were going, so, since I said I was able to walk, they deputed me to go and find out. The person most likely to know seemed to be the engine driver, who happened to be British and, although he was probably surprised to be accosted by a patient wearing slippers and a dressing gown, he helpfully told me that the train was bound for El Margha in the eastern desert, beyond Qassassin, where we would be offloaded at No 27 Gen Hosp. On arrival back in my coach, I told my friends and was just slipping into my bunk, when the Sister arrived and gave me a thorough ticking off for leaving my bed without permission. She refused to believe my protests that I was now recovered; my sheet didn't say so.

At No 27 I was seen on arrival by a doctor, who wanted to know why on earth I was still on the sick list, implying that I

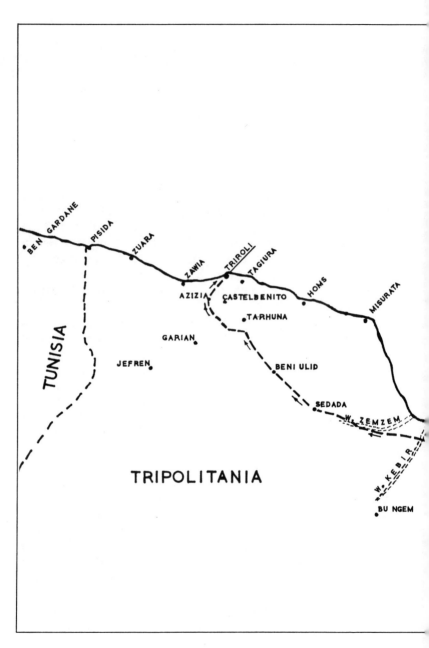

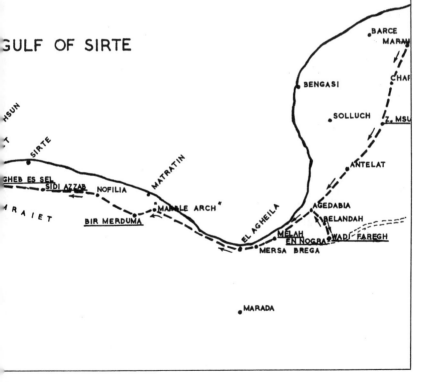

THE WESTERN DESERT ——

94 HAA WORKSHOPS - OCT 1942-JAN 1943

ROUTE FOLLOWED - – ← –
WORKSHOP SITES - MELAH EN NOGRA

Scale

0   20   40   60   80   100   120   140 miles

MEDITERRANEAN   SEA

GULF OF SIRTE

BARCE
MARAW

CHAR

BENGASI

SOLLUCH   Z. MSU

HSUN

SIRTE

MATRATIN

ANTELAT

GHEB ES SEL

SIDI AZZAB   NOFILIA

RAIET

MARBLE ARCH

BIR MERDUMA

EL AGHEILA   AGEDABIA

BELANDAH

MELAH
EN NOGRA   WADI FAREGH

MERSA BREGA

MARADA

must be malingering, but on finding I was not, he decided to discharge me to the REME Base Depot at Qassassin, with a recommendation for a two weeks' sick leave. I persuaded the Orderly Room that I would benefit most by spending the leave in Palestine, rather than some desert camp, received my discharge papers, picked up a ticket and caught the night train to Tel Aviv, after sending a letter to RHQ 94th, to the effect that I would be returning to the Base Depot at 6.15 a.m. on such and such a date and "please meet, if you want me back".

On arrival in Tel Aviv, I booked in to a hotel, hitched a lift out to Sarafand and presented myself at the reception desk asking for Sister Ball. She immediately took me to the Matron and applied for a week's leave, introducing me as her fiancé who had just come back from the retreat after being wounded in the desert and had now been discharged from hospital for sick leave.

Her Matron was a sympathetic soul and gave her the leave almost on the spot, so we set off for Haifa, where we stayed in a hotel overlooking the harbour, just doing nothing except lazing around and occasionally having meals at an open-air restaurant on the top of Mount Carmel. One day, we took a taxi to Acre and hitched a lift in a truck going to Tyre. Tyre was in another Command and our passes didn't take us further than the Lebanese border at Ras el Nakhoura, so we had to come back.

My leave went almost too quickly. On the last day, I caught the afternoon train from Haifa, and sadly dropped Phyl off at Lydda (for Sarafand). She didn't like the prospects of my future movements at all, but – bless her! – resolutely talked about something else all the way. I then travelled on through the night to Qassassin and the REME Base Depot, arriving at the prescribed time, to find my Humber parked outside a tent containing Farbrother wrapped in a sleeping bag. After awakening him, we proceeded to the BD office and I managed to get myself signed off their books. I think they were quite relieved that they didn't have to go through all the palaver of posting me somewhere. As soon as this was complete, we left for the "Front" at a reasonable speed.

The Workshop, Farbrother told me, had moved when the battle began to the LGs at El Kanabish, near Hammam, some twenty miles further up and about the same distance behind El Alamein. The lads seemed quite pleased to see me back and I took up the reins without trouble. We were positioned on a hillside overlooking the Hammam valley and were only very lightly deployed. We were living, cooking and eating very nearly in the open and expected orders to move hourly, although we didn't get these for several days.

It was apparent that things were definitely "up and doing" at the Front and everyone and everything around seemed to be crushed up as far forward as it could conceivably go. The empty wastes, which a few weeks ago had been merely the sites of the "B" echelons of the fighting troops, were now covered with parked aircraft, ordnance dumps, reinforcement camps, vast RASC echelons of loaded transport sitting "on wheels", and parks of tank transporters. Everything seemed to be of the most temporary nature and everybody was living very rough in makeshift bivouacs or under groundsheets and cooking in mess tins over petrol fires. Away to the west, the steady rumble of artillery fire rose and fell like a swarm of angry bees and by night we could see a continuous ripple of light as the guns pounded the enemy positions. The dust churned up by the long columns of transport heading forward along this or that track swirled over the bystanders as they sat in the sun and sweated, waiting for the breakthrough, and by night the heavy autumn dews soaked clothing and ran down the outside of our bivouacs.

No one knew or was able to guess when the move forward might be, so eventually I decided to motor back into Alexandria and drop my trunk off at Thos. Cook's depository so that I could do the campaign really "light" this time. We arrived in Alex at about 9.00 a.m. and everything seemed normal, in that the population did not actually stone us, but regarded all troops with their normal cold, aloof, "it's none of our business" look.

While in the city, a sort of ripple seemed to run through the streets and in ten minutes the attitude of the mob changed from one of casual and slightly veiled hostility to one of beaming friendliness. I managed to get a newspaper and read the headlines: "Great Eighth Army Breakthrough. Germans in Full Retreat".

My return journey out of Alex was a memorable one. We were sandwiched in the middle of a column of reinforcements of Australians heading for Sidi Abdel Rahman, a dust-covered Humber staff car with its desert impedimenta on the roof and the Eighth Army shield on the number plate. The fickle populace lined the pavements and cheered us as I had never experienced it before. As each vehicle came by, they cheered, waved and raised hands making the Churchillian "V" sign at us, and ran beside the column shaking hands with the Australians in the trucks. Small boys deluged us with flowers and everyone seemed quite off their heads in demonstrating their joy, relief and loyalty to the victorious British.

Back at Hammam, the Workshop was already packed up and preparing to move. The columns in the valley thinned out and stole away in the wake of the advancing Army, leaving the plain empty and dead, littered with rubbish and rusty petrol tins.

In the evening, we too were off, down on to the coast road in the wake of the Regt, column after column of rolling dust clouds in the setting sun. We had no idea where the enemy was, but my orders suggested that we were bound for Oxford Circus with the RAF – about 400 miles in the first hop. This was very different from the aborted "Operation Plop"; an advance with a vengeance!

We spent the night about twenty miles from Hammam in the "B" echelon area behind the former Alamein Line, which was now deserted except for the occasional Field Dressing Station. That night, it came on to rain and simply pelted down for about a couple of hours. I began to wonder if this was going to be another Antelat and hinder us getting away on our travels.

The following morning we were up and away at first light, since we were some way behind the Regt and wished to make up some of the distance. We did not know where they were, nor really where we were going. All the instructions I had been given were that there were Bde Report Centres at Daba, Bagush and "probably" Oxford Circus, which was a bit vague and covered several hundred miles.

To start with, the war situation was itself more than a little vague. All we knew was that the enemy had broken off the battle and was withdrawing rapidly; isolated pockets of resistance along the coast, particularly at Sidi Abdel Rahman had been or were being liquidated. No one we spoke to on the road knew where the fighting now was, although there were rumours that it might be as far on as Matruh and the mention of Oxford Circus as our possible destination sounded promising. Why, we might even drive the enemy beyond the Wire! No one at that stage realised how completely he had been defeated.

In a few short miles we came to the Alamein Line, which lay principally on a rocky ridge extending inland from the salt marsh on the shore into the dusty distance of camel-thorn to the south. As we drew near to the famous "Line", we first encountered extensive minefields edged by single strands of barbed wire; then zigzag wire entanglements; and then a dirty, dreary waste of tins, corrugated iron sheets and rotting camouflage netting. It all reminded me of the approaches to Tobruk. I could see very few "fortifications", although my unpractised eye didn't know what to look for. The road itself was bad and the tarmac was considerably damaged and with occasional long grooves which I put down as the ricochets of unexploded shells. Apart from a few smashed and burnt-out British tanks and other vehicles, there was little to indicate that there had been a big battle here in the past week or two.

Two small noticeboards by the side of the road stick in my mind. The first said: "The Germans are on the other side of this ridge". The second said: "If going further, please take one", and from hooks below this wording hung several small wooden crosses about six inches high.

As we crossed the top of the ridge, the outlook changed; behind us was the famous Alamein Line, relatively undamaged, but ahead the terrain seemed to have been hit by a massive typhoon and for the next ten or twenty miles, as far as the eye could see on either side of the road it was littered with indescribable wreckage: German and Italian tanks, turretless or trackless and burnt-out, with their guns pointing helplessly to the sky; vehicles, burnt-out, blown to pieces, on their sides or upside down and riddled with holes; wrecked field guns surrounded by mountains of shell cases; and all around were smaller items of military hardware: abandoned machine-guns, rifles, webbing equipment, bayonets and ammunition, all scattered in the sand. There were also rags, blankets and bits of clothing clinging to barbed wire, itself scattered like a ball of knitting wool, unwound and cast aside. The very sandhills seemed to have been stamped flat by some giant heel. And the place smelt; of burnt diesel fuel, cordite and death.

The road was now crowded with assorted vehicles in a slowly moving traffic jam, extending for miles but, due to the recent rainstorms, the desert on either side had become a treacherous waste of clay with a hard crust on to which only the very foolhardy tried to drive. The verges were, in any case, littered with large numbers of German and Italian lorries, including shoals of captured transport, now embellished with large black crosses. All were pointing west and although some of them were battle-damaged, a lot of them were either just bogged down in the mud or completely intact, having apparently run out of fuel and been abandoned. Most of these latter had had the wheels removed. I learned later that this was a German tactic of immobilisation, the wheels being thrown away a few miles further on.

They presented a depressing backdrop to the road; most had their bonnets open and their canvas canopies flapping in the stiff breeze, and each one was surrounded by a litter of its former load, now scattered and looted. The verges looked unsafe and no one seemed inclined to pull off to let anyone pass, since there was a mess of discarded "live" ammunition and lots of the horrid little Italian "red devil" hand grenades lying everywhere.

Along the sides of the road, we now encountered groups of potential prisoners of war, twenty to fifty strong, mainly Italians, all looking fed up, fagged out, dirty, unshaven, wet and covered with mud. They stood around or sat huddled on the rubbish, guarded perhaps only by a solitary British OR with a rifle, and making no attempt to escape. A couple of unguarded groups, in fact, tried to surrender to us as we passed but got no change from us. I heard later that when the retreat began, the Germans had taken the transport from five or six Italian Divisions in order to ensure their own escape and had left them to walk or surrender. Later, we came to advanced temporary POW cages, bare squares of barbed wire in the mud and dripping camel-thorn, into which were herded a seething mass of grey-clad Italians and from which the red-caps were bundling them like sheep into big captured Fiats and Lancias. These crackled off down the road we had just come up, often with their own drivers at the wheel, in convoys of a dozen or so. Some of the vehicles had guards but mostly not. Not that they looked like trying to escape; they were too weary and depressed and they were going at last to Egypt, which had been their promised goal for a couple of years, where they would be fed and allowed to sleep and not deluged with rain or high explosive. They were leaderless sheep and the advancing columns watched them go without any emotion except a sort of pity, mixed with slight contempt.

Soon after midday, we reached Daba and pulled in to the car-park of the once-famous "Noah's Ark" NAAFI roadhouse. It had been razed to the ground, together with the big depots and camps of six months ago. From there, we made for Fuka and encountered a gigantic traffic jam at the point where the road climbed in a couple of zigzags up the escarpment. At its foot a slight trough was flooded for about 300 yards. A safe passageway had been marked in this with barrels by the Military Police and they were letting the traffic through at thirty-yard intervals.

I had an idea of deviating to the south here and following the railway to bypass the block, but it proved a complete failure. The ground was too soft and our heavy machinery lorries bogged down at once. We spent a couple of hours digging them out and then, to cap it all, my Humber car broke its offside steering track arm at the brake back-plate and had to be a

345

suspended tow behind our 3-ton Dodge recovery lorry, which replaced the hitherto standard Leyland. I transferred my "flag" and kit to Farbrother's Ford Utility (Radio Testing) – Farbrother had now managed to get one of the new Jeeps for himself – and, since it was nearly dark, we packed down for the night on the driest spot we could find and brewed up tea and bully beef stew, to warm us. My stock with the lads went up considerably. They had been expecting that I would press on relentlessly until dark. Such was the reputation I seemed to have gained!

On the wireless that night there was an announcement that there had been large scale landings in North Africa and we felt that the end of the war must be getting nearer. "They'll finish the war in Africa, before we get anywhere near there" was the general opinion. Phillips, Farbrother and I had a stiff drink and turned in to sleep in our vehicles rather more cheerfully, regardless of our wet blankets.

Once again, we were up and about before the pale light in the east was enough to read by and we trundled through the bottleneck and up on to the Fuka plateau without difficulty. Then we brewed up one of the most welcome breakfasts I can remember, whilst a watery sun rose and looked in bleakly for a few minutes before taking cover behind a bank of mist, leaving us to the biting wind.

The road between Fuka and Bagush lay across a waste of stone, scrub and dust, now mud, with occasional views of the sea to the right. Notwithstanding our early start, we were soon crawling along in the usual mobile traffic jam, with no hope of overtaking on account of the muddy verges. Not that we wanted to, because every patch of apparently hard ground seemed to be strewn with recent mine casualties among the older ground-strafed German wrecks.

We now began to pass quite a number of undamaged German vehicles that had been abandoned on running out of fuel. At one point, too, there was a string of Italian tanks on the verge, quite untouched, which also must have just run out of fuel. By contrast, any German tanks we passed – and they were very few – were badly shot-up. At Bagush, I scouted on and found the 12 AA Bde Report Centre, which proved to be an officer and a

346

sergeant sitting on upturned petrol tins at the Sidi Haneish end of the former Bagush box. I was told that the guns had passed through earlier that morning and that we were to make for Oxford Circus without further orders. If there was no one there, we were to go on with all speed to Sidi Aziez, on the Libyan side of the Wire and report there. They didn't know much about the war situation, but it was apparent that the enemy was retreating westwards rather more quickly than we could follow.

That was at about 1.00 p.m. and the congestion was so great that four hours later we had got only as far as Ras Hawala – twenty miles – and, rather than fool around Matruh in the dark, I decided to pack it in, choose a suitable spot, have a sea bathe, a good brew-up and an early night. The lads being wholeheartedly supportive, we settled among the sandhills near my old 2 Light Wksps site.

The following morning we were up good and early and bowled merrily into Matruh. The weather was improving, sunny and warmer, and we seemed to be running out of the water-logged area. Matruh was in complete chaos, an advanced enemy base that had been abandoned overnight, a maze of tents just left standing, dumps and vehicle parks, very little damaged. One of the vehicles there was a Humber staff car, and we had a short halt while a party of fitters removed the essential parts of the front suspension and track rods and put them in the boot of my car to be fitted as soon as we stopped for the necessary time.

The road uphill on the far side of the town was a litter of hastily abandoned Base Workshops among which an armoured formation was reforming with crowds of tank transporters. But still the traffic was surging westwards and showing no sign of drawing off the road. Morale was definitely at a peak and the folk that we spoke to were talking of "Bengasi next stop".

I had decided that the easiest route to Oxford Circus from Matruh was to retrace the way we had come on our retreat in June, up the Barrani road to about Km 70 and then cut left and follow the water pipeline out in the desert. The big railhead vehicle evacuation centre at Charing Cross looked exactly as it had when we had passed it in June; as bit rustier, perhaps, but otherwise untouched by the Germans.

By the time we turned off the Barrani road, we were making steady progress and when we deviated left no one followed us; this made me wonder why, for, when we were alone, we batted along without incident at a good speed over quite reasonable going on the old tracks which the enemy had seemingly little used. The pipeline had been well and truly wrecked during the retreat; blown up every hundred yards or so, but the railway had been left virtually intact. I suppose the Germans had had hopes of using it themselves, but never did.

As we drew near Oxford Circus we saw that the LGs were in use and RHQ was easily identified. They told us to deploy on almost exactly the same spot we had occupied in June, and we were immediately faced with as many repairs as we could tackle without opening up and unpacking more than was absolutely necessary, for the stop was apparently to be of a very temporary nature. Everyone was working in the open, and even eating standing up and sleeping in vehicles rather than in bivvies or tents. The guns were in action positions on the bare ground without being dug in to pits or protected by sandbag walls. I was told that we were not likely to be more than one day at Oxford Circus and that we were really bound for Gambut, because the RAF considered Oxford Circus was too far from the possible action and were ready to move on as soon as somewhere suitable and nearer the enemy could be found.

By nightfall we had patched up most of the Regt's transport, including our own, into reasonable running order and we packed in, ready to start off at first light. The following morning we set out to follow the Btys westward along tracks that more or less covered the same route that we had used on the retreat. Gambut in one day was a bit too hopeful and we spent the night somewhere near Gap D in the Wire that we had come through some months before.

At first light, our party pressed on through the Wire and motored north along it to join the Trigh Capuzzo near the old Transit Camp at Capuzzo then turn off it to reach our previous site below the escarpment at Gambut, which was even more dusty and messed up than before. We had made a full circle.

348

"The 94th Workshops' Return to Gambut". It sounded like the title of a Scottish pipe march. Well, not so inappropriate, perhaps. After all, the 94th was a Scottish TA Regt...

We were a short time in Gambut, during which Major Walker caught us up and began to exert his authority. While we had been at Mareopolis and Hammam, he had been a new boy to the Bde, but now he obviously felt it was time to organise the Workshops as he believed they ought to be organised. There were four such units in 12 AA Bde now staging in the neighbourhood – 88 and 94 Heavy and 15 and, I think, 27 Light – and he called us all together and propounded his Great Idea.

This was that all the Workshop Sections in 12 AA Bde were to be grouped, under his personal control, in a single locality – he had decided that a site at Bu Amud between Gambut and Tobruk would be most suitable – and would remain there for upwards of a week operating as a combined repair unit for the Bde as a whole while the Regiments would send back their equipment to it. This composite pool of talent and equipment would be able to deal with everything that was sent back according to which was the lightest loaded Workshop at the time.

This was a sort of static Base Workshop and in fact it followed the precedent that Estlin had established at Ras Hawala with 2 Light and the South Africans. Walker reckoned it was just the cat's pyjamas and it seemed to derive from his previous experience on the Canal. It was basically a good idea, but it had one massive flaw: The war had gone mobile and the Regts would be following the RAF and could be up to two hundred miles ahead in no time. I pointed this out, supported by Morton of 88, to be told that Walker had received the Brigadier's blessing and that was that. I should remember that he was in technical control of the Workshops in the Bde.

Almost as soon as I got back to our site, I received a summons from Major Jones, still acting CO of the Regt, to come to RHQ and receive orders for the next morning's move with the RAF, who were setting off for Gazala, or even Martuba, in Central Libya. When Jones came round to instructing me to

349

follow up the Btys more closely than had been possible during the frantic rush after the breakout from Alamein, he was greatly taken aback to learn of my orders from Walker. What then happened then, I am not sure, but I think Jones went straight to the Brigadier, insisting that his workshop should move with and provide the immediate service for 94th's Btys and that he had full confidence in me to do just this. I suspect that the CO of 88 may also have done the same thing, but Jones got in first. Anyhow, the Brig had a word with Walker and the Great Idea was stillborn. Walker got round to believing that I had "protested to the Brigadier over his head" and it was a black mark against me, so S/Sgt Lewis told me privately. Not that we – or at least Morton and I – cared; we had had just about enough of Walker by that time.

At first light the following morning, we pulled out of Gambut and made off westwards along the main coast road. This was "new ground" for most of the lads, for Gambut had been the farthest west that they had come before. I was now unexpectedly in possession of a Scammell six-wheeled heavy recovery lorry which Walker had attached to my unit the previous day as part of his grand composite workshop/recovery scheme, and in the subsequent excitement he had forgotten to tell me to send it back. It came complete with driver and mate, who were all for the move because they wanted to see more of the war and because I had somehow acquired the reputation of getting into the thick of things. I was glad to take it with us, because we were five 3-tonners and a recovery lorry short on our War Establishment anyhow, and the Scammell was streets better than anything we had had so far, even the Dodge which replaced the ill-fated Leyland. It was almost as good as a Matador, and had a really massive jib and crane. It eventually reached Tunis with one or other of the Bde's Wksps.

The main coast road was very much as I had last seen it, only a bit more chewed up. There were a few more smashed vehicles, lying upside down by the road beside the more rusted ranks of the casualties abandoned in the two previous advances and retreats, and there were a few more bullet pocks in the crumbling plaster walls of the Gambut roadhouse, but generally

350

things seemed pretty peaceful. We were out of the battle area and beyond even the enemy base area which had been the target of so much of our air attack.

The day was warm and sunny and we bowled along in rear of the regiment. Reg Phillips had organised a recovery section consisting of our three breakdown vehicles – 30cwt Morris, 3-ton Dodge and the Scammell – travelling as sweepers at the rear of our column, with secondary instructions to bring along any abandoned British vehicles which looked as if they might be made into runners and so ease our critical transport deficiencies. My experiences in the previous campaign warned me against acquiring any ex-enemy vehicles, since road patrols were forcibly dispossessing units of unauthorised German and Italian transport.

Most of the traffic still streaming west was being directed by the Red-Caps on to the "Tobruk Bypass" to El Adem and Acroma, but 94 HAA Regt, for some reason, was allowed through Tobruk itself and we were pleased at this, since we all wanted to see the place. It looked just dead, with a few more wrecks in the harbour and a lot more rubble on the ridge above. At the T-junction at the foot of the hill a gigantic ration dump was being guarded by troops, but further on was a waste of empty blue-green camouflaged tents, about three thousand of them, abandoned and flapping emptily and wetly in the light wind. Tobruk had been turned by the Germans into a big hospital, convalescent and reinforcement centre several hundred miles behind the original fighting, which had been abandoned in some great hurry as though the Germans were never coming back. There was a finality about the sight that depressed me.

As we turned left on the Derna road, some groups of coloured men dressed in ragged travesties of South African and Italian uniforms cheered and waved; they were thin and dirty, but immensely cheerful – all white eyes and teeth. They said they were Cape Coloureds and Hottentots from 2 South African Div who had been taken prisoner in June. They had been used as labour gangs, and when the Italians had fled a couple of days before they had just walked out of their POW cages and were now hanging around hoping that somebody would know what to

351

do with them. We gave them a few packets of Army biscuits and they cheered us again.

About a mile out on the Derna road, we passed a derelict 3.7" gun at the roadside, a bit burned at the towing end, but no sign of the towing vehicle. It was probably one of those captured in Tobruk in June – most of them had been thoroughly and effectively wrecked before the surrender – or it could even have been one from 261 Bty's missing troop at Antelat. The Germans had obviously been trying to take it away, but the towing vehicle must have been shot up from the air. Just beyond it were two of the deadest mules I had ever seen. They too must have been killed several days before by an aircraft anti-personnel bomb that had spewed out their guts over the verge. They were a mass of flies and stank to high heaven.

All the way from Tobruk, the 94th column seemed to be the only unit in Libya. The rest of the main body of the Army was going round by El Adem to Acroma and we would meet them where the main road joined the *Achsenstrasse* some miles on. The occupying and administrative units were miles behind us.

The air of peace was emphasised by groups of Arabs and their flocks which had been swept over and left behind by the recent advances and retreats of the occupying Germans. They were now placidly plodding through the young grass and green budding camel-thorn brought on by the recent rain. Each man was carrying a bulging sack and they would stop at each wrecked lorry and grub about among the German stick grenades and the Italian little "red devils" strewn profusely around. They must have been suffering casualties fairly heavily but no one seemed to be worrying about that. Indeed, we were witnesses to one accident; a camel trod on a big German Tellermine and just disappeared in a cloud of smoke and dust, then large pieces of camel splattered down from the sky.

One other little incident sticks in my memory. Coming suddenly round a bend in the road, we surprised two Arabs hurriedly doing something with a spade a short distance from the road. On seeing us, they turned and fled into the wadis, casting guilty glances behind them to see if they were being followed. One was carrying a German entrenching tool and the other a pair of good, new German knee-boots. They had presumably been burying the body of their previous owner.

We wound our way onwards through the big wadis to the west of Tobruk, over bridges that no one had thought fit to blow up and past innumerable clusters of tents, or huts made of wooden ration boxes nailed together. The crudely painted unit signs pointed to where this or that unit had lived for five months and had made itself comfortable. Eventually, we reached the foot of the Gazala escarpment, just as it began to rain.

The Regt collected here and detached one Bty to provide cover for the RAF on the LGs, for, in view of the rapidity of the enemy withdrawal, Gazala was already considered too far from the action. Pending further orders, we deployed in a fine, chilling drizzle on the northern side of the Gazala plateau, where it fell away towards the sand dunes on the edge of the sea. However, we were so busy that we hadn't much time to think about such things and on the following morning the weather brightened and the rain stopped. Even the sun made a few brief appearances and the sodden ground dried up slightly.

Our expected move didn't come that day, although the Bty that was still on its wheels pulled out and trundled off up the road with the RAF advance parties to be ready to occupy the Martuba LGs by that evening. Martuba lay in the centre of the Cyrenaica "bulge" to the north of Mechili, which latter the RAF had decided was a non-runner after the dusty debâcle of the previous autumn. This new site was 85 miles on up the road in the high moorland behind Derna and had been the place where the Stukas had been based for the attacks on Tobruk in past years. Rumour was growing that the enemy was going to be driven right out of Cyrenaica and was intending to take cover in the marshlands at El Agheila. No one was contemplating any advance beyond that, for it was assumed that the First Army, recently landed in Algeria, would drive the Germans out of Tunisia long before we could get there ourselves, and would advance to take Tripoli.

The following morning opened bright and sunny and we pulled out on to the road behind the rest of the Regt in a fast-moving column of other transport going the same way. I had no directions other than to look for a Regimental Report Centre 15 miles beyond where we turned off for Martuba from the Derna road, but, since that was about as much "directions" as we ever got these days, it didn't worry me. Phillips with his three recovery vehicles brought up our rear with its usual roving commission and we soon lost them.

As I remembered, the road from the foot of Gazala hill ran for about a couple of miles on a sort of causeway across areas of salt marsh and then on the farther side rose slightly into the foothills of the Jebel Akhdar range that filled the Cyrenaica "bulge". The enemy had made quite a good job of making our passage as awkward as possible by blowing up the culverts, causing bottlenecks that slowed up the traffic. These were the first real demolitions we had encountered. The REs had made deviations round each water-filled hole with temporary layers of forty-gallon drums, covered with brushwood and mud and secured with stakes and a bit of faith. I would be glad to get into the foothills, but about three-quarters of the way across the column in front of us stopped and so did we.

There was a solid stream of halted traffic for two miles in front of us and some six miles to our rear; a lovely target should the Germans care to send aircraft to do some damage. However, it was warm and sunny and the countryside was all green after the recent rains. I dismounted and, strolling ahead, asked the OC of the next convoy in front – an American Field Ambulance – if he knew what the hold-up was. He said he believed that the enemy was strafing the road ahead and the sun seemed immediately to go in. What a target, if they found us – quite unable to leave the causeway!

'Say,' said the American, 'what do we do if he comes here? Lie down in that shit?' indicating the reeds and slime on either side.

We heard three or four heavy thumps ahead and a ragged spatter of small-arms fire and then, before we could speak, three large, black, twin-engined aircraft sailed out of the woolly clouds in front, bearing down on us in a shallow dive. There was nothing for it. The American dived into the reeds, as if touching down in one of his football games and I shamefully took cover under the nearest vehicle – his ambulance – beneath the shelter of the Red Cross.

However, for some reason, no bombs were dropped; why I just don't know, because it seemed a magnificent target. Perhaps the bomb-aimers found they were slightly off-line or something, but their rear gunners sprayed a few bursts in our neighbourhood, regardless of the large red crosses on the ambulance roofs. One of the nastiest sounds I can remember was the thin bird-like noise the ricochets made as they skated off over the mud flats. The local wading birds took off in their dozens and left for somewhere less dangerous.

Everybody got to their feet and said: "Phe-ew!" as they watched the enemy disappearing down the road, and some 40mm LAA guns, which had had time to get into action, opened up at them, sending up lazy skeins of tracer that made them sheer off and climb into the low clouds. Just at the far end of the causeway, one of them dropped a small stick of bombs before disappearing and I saw the columns of mud and smoke shoot up. Then the column ahead of us began to move again towards the hills, where a lot of rolling brown smoke and yellow fingers of flame indicated that something had been hit. The Americans waved us to overtake; they were still stationary and were trying to turn one of the ambulances round to send back down the road to where evidently there had been casualties. Also, a couple went axle-deep in the mud and we had to pull them out.

Such was the disorganisation this caused that, by the time I, at the head of the column, reached a flat open stretch of open scrub country beyond the causeway the workshop was strung out for several hundred yards and I drew off to let them catch up and concentrate. Then we heard the sound of aircraft again and our air-sentry pointed and shouted. Through a gap in the clouds, we could see the three aircraft coming in again in a wide circle from seaward with the evident intention of having another go at the causeway.

Everyone snatched up his rifle, including me, and cascaded out of his vehicle. I was glad to see the AA Bren team of Armourer S/Sgt Skiggs slam a magazine on to the gun, which was pole-mounted on the office lorry, always ready for action. I heard Skiggs shout to the riflemen to set their sights at some range and not to shoot until he said so. This disciplined reaction was all a great improvement on the chaos of the previous May, but I didn't stay to consider that or to take any credit for it; the Germans were said to have a habit of shooting up staff cars, so, stuffing a few extra clips of .303 ammunition into my pocket, I legged it to the shelter of the only tree on the flat. Here I found myself beside AQMS Harris, who was already loading clips into the magazine of his own rifle. He suggested I set my rearsight at 500 yards and I did so, realising that Harris, as an old regular soldier, would know what to do. He was credited with probably being capable of telling you what "lead" to allow when shooting with a longbow at a crossing target of armoured knights. A useful man to have beside one in these circumstances.

The aircraft never came within rifle shot after all, but converged on the causeway and let the unfortunate ambulance column have all they had. Great spouts of mud and water went up all round and the Germans sailed off into the clouds with their rear gunners pumping bursts into the rolling dirty smoke.

We streamed back to our vehicles and sought to get moving again. Some were still missing down the road but the heavy Leyland machinery lorries, each towing an equally heavy trailer, were all there, steadily sinking axle-deep in the soft ground. Cursing the absence of Phillips and all the recovery teams, we set to to tow them out with what we had. It was the hardest and filthiest three-quarters of an hour I could remember enduring, for all the heavily loaded Leylands had to be unhitched from their trailers and towed out backwards separately in a wide three-hundred-yard sweep on to the harder ground before rehitching. Eventually, covered in mud from the spinning wheels, I got them all in a ragged line and prepared to lead off into the traffic stream.

Most of our strays had turned up while all this was going on and, ignoring all shouts of "Stay on the so-and-so road you so-and-sos!" by all concerned, they drove straight on to the soft stuff and had to be towed back on to the hard ground. There was no sign of Phillips, but Farbrother suddenly skated up in his

Jeep, almost unrecognisable in a covering of mud on everything except his moon-like spectacles, hopping mad and almost inarticulate. He and his Radio Repair party had been strafed, but were all unhurt.

'No damage?' I asked.

He almost howled at me: 'The bastards have knocked the carburettor off my Ford!' This was the Radio Testing Ford Utility that I have mentioned before. It now had a 20mm hole in the bonnet and the carburettor and part of the inlet manifold had completely vanished. It came in on tow behind one of our 15cwts and the driver of the latter, in a sort of mental blackout and deaf to the thunderous and blasphemous shouts of all the spectators, drove straight into the mud, which now resembled a ploughed field. Both vehicles began to submerge.

By now we had everything else back on the harder standing by the road and it was time to go; we were holding up the traffic, so I called out to Farbrother to keep back the Chevrolet stores lorry – the 3-ton Chevrolets were the only four-wheel drive vehicles we had – ready to tow out anyone else who made a mess of it, and drew out on to the road.

I had gone little more than the first two corners in the road, when my heart, almost before my ears, heard a heavy *thump!* Looking back I saw, over the shoulder of the hill, a dirty brown column of dust rise and turn over at the top like a giant Prince of Wales's feather. I remembered the fate of the camel earlier that day and there was no mistaking where this was.

Feeling rather sick, I shouted to Harris, the nearest senior NCO, to take the column on for a mile or so and then stop on the verge at 100-yard intervals. Horsefall turned my Humber and we hurtled back down the road. My worst fears were well founded. The Chevrolet was nosed into the ground like a horse on its knees, its frame bent in an extraordinary way just behind the cab. Its offside wheel had disappeared; its bonnet was standing in strips straight up in the air and its windscreen was starred and shedding pieces of glass. Eyewitnesses said later that, as the mine went off, the whole vehicle reared right up on its back wheels and then came down on its nose with an almighty slam.

357

They had just got the driver and his mate out. S/Sgt Skiggs was the passenger and he had been peppered over the head and neck with metal fragments and small stones, but he was conscious and except for the shock and blood everywhere, he didn't seem seriously hurt. Jakeman was coping with him; tying a field dressing over his face and eyes. His driver, "Good" Evans – his silly nickname came back to me as he was extracted and laid down by his mates – had of course been right over the mine when it went off, and probably owed his life to the sandbags that I had insisted all vehicles must have on the floor to guard against just such a happening. The memory of the truck that had run over a mine, back in my 2nd Light days was enough to make me insist on this. The crew there had bled to death. Evans was badly concussed and half his right boot was gone; what remained of his foot was not a pleasant sight. His little toe was seemingly hanging on a thread.

All the lads were standing round looking uncertainly at the blood, so I had to do something. I had heard of people having to cut a boot off, but I had never expected to have to do it. Army boots are very tough and Evans was moaning and just regaining consciousness. Telling someone to rip out a field dressing from his battledress trousers, I took a proffered clasp knife and gently slit the boot away and then the sock, binding the dressing in place.

Now we had two casualties and I ran out on to the road, my hands still covered in blood, to flag down another American Field Service ambulance that was just passing. The driver must have seen what had happened, for he held up the traffic immediately and turned back. He and his mate took over and Skiggs and Evans were gently carried on board. We gave the driver their details and bundled their small kit in and the ambulance left at once, turning eastwards against the oncoming traffic, not ten minutes from the moment of the accident. Those American ambulance volunteers were good lads; I think they were Quakers.

We turned back to our stores lorry. I was told that it had just towed out the 15cwt and had gone back for the Ford Utility.

358

They were just motoring out again when it went up. I don't know whether this was an isolated booby trap, or if there had been more on this open area, for the mud beside it was criss-crossed by wheel tracks. We had just been lucky not to run over any more, and unlucky to run over this one.

Leaving a small party behind to wait for Phillips and to tell him how to tread when winding in the two bogged-down vehicles and to bring the stores lorry back somehow, we went on, shaken and silent. By tacit consent, it was decided not to have a lunch stop, because no one felt like drawing off the road again, and for other reasons. I set our course for Martuba. We were climbing steadily, but not steeply, up all the way on to moorlands not dissimilar to Dartmoor, for these outer foothills of the Jebel Akhdar were covered with a heather-like shrub, among sickly-looking birch trees, and the upper slopes cul-minated in tor-like outcrops of grey and yellow lichen-covered rocks. Everywhere there was bright green moss and pools of brownish water and the heavy, peaty soil was completely waterlogged.

At the Matuba fork, where we turned left, the road straight on had a newly-painted board which said: "Road blown at Derna hill. No way through. Mines". Our road ran along the top of a bleak and barren tableland and then plunged down a narrow glen on a muddy macadam side-road that had seen better days. The RAF ground staff units were setting up along-side this track and there was a big well, which we were very glad to see, since we were getting short of water. Here we picked up a guide from the Regt who had been sent to meet us and he led us to the left on an atrocious track on to the escarpment where the LGs lay, to find RHQ sitting above a sea of mud on a bright and breezy headland. Here we set up our workshop and here, several hours later, Phillips found us. He was towing a number of vehicles that he had picked up on the way, including Farbrother's Ford utility and our damaged stores 3-tonner on the back of the Scammell as a front-sus-pended tow. We were together again.

Phillips reported that he had had quite a close-up view of the earlier bombing of the causeway. He and his gang had stopped at the Gazala end to strip a burnt-out Matador for spares and they were wakened to the proximity of three large and hostile aircraft by a hopelessly concertinaed RASC unit letting off vast amounts of small-arms fire right at their doorstep.

'There was I,' he said later, 'with several tens of thousands of pounds worth of recovery vehicles belonging to someone else. We just cast ourselves in frantic dives under the vehicles and started praying.' They were deluged by a wave of mud, stones, dirty water, explosive fuses and bits of shrapnel.

They had one casualty; the unit's senior electrician, Craftsman "Taffy" Williams from Llanfair P.G., etc. near Menai Bridge in Anglesey took a fragment of hot steel in his buttock and was roughly bandaged and disposed of to another of the American Field Service ambulances. He was going to be missed in the unit for his irrepressible cheerfulness. He was short, "as broad as he was tall", and was reported to have said as he lay prone while someone applied a field dressing to his bottom, 'There's pity, too. If I had been standing up, it would have gone over my head, boy!'

Another member of the recovery gang, one Driver Smith, was nearly another casualty. A 20mm aircraft shell struck deep into the mud just beside his prostrate body, before exploding and he received a massive bruise on the thigh but no lasting damage. He was lucky to be able to come back to the workshop to tell his mates the tale.

Before dark, we had to take cover from a storm of fine driving mountain rain that lasted all night and we scrambled into bivouacs uncomfortably pitched on wet and stony ground. It had been a bad day; three casualties and a lorry written off, but we were all tired and slept the sleep of the exhausted. However, first, I had to write letters to each of the three wounded and hope that these would reach them in whatever hospital to which they were sent.

Weeks later we received a copy of the Army Part II Orders which deal with the movements of personnel and the like. Among the mundane notices such as "LEAVE – Pte Snoggins, Base Workshop Abbassia: granted seven days leave in Palestine with higher meal service element", came this notification:

360

WOUNDED IN ACTION – 94 HAA Wksps.
Armourer S/Sgt Skiggs
Craftsman Williams
Driver Evans.

I hoped they and their families would see this, but I never heard.

14

The airfield at Martuba was scarcely a place I would have chosen and after a day or two the RAF came to the same decision, but there was nowhere else to go. The Germans were still in Bengasi and this put Benina and Msus out of play, so they had to make the best of it.

The LGs were sited on a slightly concave plateau, which seemed to collect all the water from the recent rains like a saucer, and the admin units lived up on the harder rim or in the gullies leading down to the surrounding plain. "Digging in" was impossible.

The actual landing area was very muddy and the RAF had difficulty in getting the aircraft airborne sometimes. The situation had been made worse by someone on arrival driving a lorry column across the strip and this put nearly half the field out of commission with deep ruts. In order to prevent such a thing happening again, the RAF positioned a couple of machine-guns on the edge of the LG, opening fire on any intruder. "Careless driving" stopped very rapidly! I was told that the Germans had not been using Martuba recently and had only reverted to the place because the peacetime airfield at Derna had become even more waterlogged and was quite unusable. Fortunately, after our arrival, the weather changed for the better and we had no more driving rain. The place began to dry up.

As a result of the casualty of the stores 3-tonner, our mobility problem was parlous; we just could not carry our stores. I reported our problem to Walker as soon as he arrived in the area and put in for a replacement. He had nothing to offer, but he remembered that we had his Scammell and said we could keep it until there was something else to replace it. Big deal! The Scammell's carrying capacity was almost nil. We would have to do something about it ourselves. I asked Lewis where the Bde OFP was so that I could draw a carburettor and inlet manifold for Farbrother's Ford utility, and he told me sadly that it was still at Hammam, near Mareopolis, and was being sent for. Shades of Estlin!

It became necessary to consider what was called unofficially "The Desert OFP", namely the wreckage strewn about that might come in useful. This name had been originated by Estlin when asked for simple stores he hadn't got. I recalled an occasion several months previously, before the retreat from Gambut, when a newcomer to the Bde – the OC of 27 Light Wksps, I think it was – had complained about his lack of nuts and bolts for some modification he was supposed to do. Estlin had asked him if he had any fitters and if those fitters knew how to handle spanners. 'Yes? Then, laddie, send them out to take the necessary things from all those damaged Italian vehicles out there. Good as any OFP in the desert. And don't come bothering me.' The young man never dared to complain to Estlin again.

There were no repairable 3-tonner wrecks anywhere near Martuba, search as we might, so we looked for abandoned Italian trailers. The Italian Army, as I have mentioned before, went in for massive 10-ton trailers which they towed behind six- or eight-ton lorries and on retreats these tended to get abandoned in profusion if they broke down. They could be had by anyone with something able to tow them away. We brought in two, one of them the most splendid trailer I had ever seen, which was carrying a broken-down small Italian tank when discovered. We had no use for the tank and somehow my scrounging party managed to ditch it and brought the trailer in empty. Then, with much expenditure of blood, sweat and tears, we slacked off the bolts holding the undamaged body of our stores lorry to the wrecked chassis and winched, jacked and prised the complete body – bins, stores, canopy and all – on to the trailer, where it sat very snugly, and bolted it down. We found by experiment that this "stores trailer" could be towed by one of the Leyland machinery lorries, provided the ground was hard enough. With its canvas canopy it looked exactly like a gigantic "Cape cart" and Storeman Powell had his leg pulled as "Kruger" for a considerable period. Just to tidy up, we stripped all the usable parts from the wrecked chassis and engine for possible spares, so that the remains were hardly worth taking away.

All this eased our minds a bit and made us fairly mobile again, since we had welded up a special A-frame whereby the Ford utility could be towed, with its steering locked, by another vehicle, until we found or otherwise obtained some parts that would fit and make it driveable again.

Martuba was the first occasion on which we encountered a new enemy tactic – that of strewing anti-personnel and teller-mines liberally over the usable areas which they abandoned. We hadn't come across this ploy until now, since in their initial retreat the Germans hadn't had time to do anything but skedaddle as quickly as possible, but in these more rearward areas there had been time to make things uncomfortable for us. The RAF had cleared the surface of the actual LG (they hoped), but elsewhere a vehicle had only to drive off the track to run over a mine of some sort. We had an uncomfortable few days walking with extreme delicacy, like Agag in the Old Testament, down wheeltracks carrying winch ropes with which to pull the wrecks back out of the danger area.

After we had been at Martuba for a few days, Spooner, who was still with Walker at Bde HQ, tipped me the wink that there were a lot of cylinders of gas on the Derna LG and he believed that some of them might be oxygen and acetylene. Owing to the OFP fiasco, we were chronically short of welding gas, so I decided to pay a visit and investigate secretly, because Derna was out of bounds to the likes of us. I took our welder and a couple of handy lads in a 15cwt truck with driver and we headed off down the deserted road towards Derna.

Derna airfield was an unforgettable sight; it lay on the brink of an escarpment overlooking the town of that name far below, in country pleasant in the summer – but as it was now mid-winter it was not, definitely not. The LG lay on one side of our road; a grey-green expanse of hardening mud where the recent floods were now drying out. On the other side lay the airfield buildings and hangars, roofless and smoke-blackened, rising gauntly from the ooze. Inside them was a jumble of wreckage, and their courtyards were piled with brand new Daimler Benz aircraft engines in crates with the seals still on.

The LG was an abandoned waste of water, covered, literally covered, with aircraft, axle deep in the water and slime. One or two were nose-down or at odd angles where they had crashed on landing, but the vast majority seemed quite undamaged and had apparently been abandoned by the retiring enemy, simply because they couldn't be flown off. Some RE mine-detecting parties were paddling round in gumboots with detectors and a few wading birds were sculling around on the waters, but otherwise there was not a sign of life and no movement except the flapping of torn aircraft fabric. I asked the REs if there were any mines in the main courtyard and they said no, but just to be quite sure I had the truck reversed in so that if it did run over one it would be the rear wheel that would take it and there would be no human casualty. Some helpful individual revealed this to my driver (who was blissfully ignorant of the reason) and he nearly had a fit.

Inside the building, the front was piled high with wrecked aircraft parts, but beyond, to our delight, there were a couple of hundred cylinders of assorted gases – oxygen, acetylene (only a very few), hydrogen, carbon dioxide and compressed air – all abandoned. We took on board as many oxygen and acetylene cylinders as we could find or carry and left.

On the way back we were held up by a halted troop of LAA guns coming up out of Derna, who were pulling one of their 15cwts back clear of the road where it had unwittingly run over a mine, and while they were doing this, a German aircraft came over and dropped a few bombs. It was the wrong time and place for us to be; the whole troop went into action in less time than I would have thought possible and the intruder sheered off rapidly, spraying the area with machine gun bullets. We took to our heels into the scrub and when we got back to our truck, we left for "home" in the workshop without more ado.

About 21 November, we learned that the Germans were

365

pulling out rapidly from the Bengasi area and beyond and the RAF, greatly daring, decided that anything was better than Martuba and sent off an advance party to open up the LG at our old stamping ground at Msus. One of the 94th Btys went with them and three days later all the rest of the Regt, including ourselves, packed up thankfully and followed.

It was reckoned that the journey to Msus would take two or possibly three days. The battery with the advance party had reported by wireless, with a certain amount of feeling, that the normal route, due south to Mechili and then west along the "F" track, was almost impassable, so the proposed route was westwards inland towards Barce and then south into the desert at a place called Maraua, sone ninety miles away. This was new country even to me; we headed for Charruba and the route by which we had retreated with 2 Light in the early days of the flight from Antelat. So off we went at the tail of the Regimental column over a winding moorland road between Dartmoor-like stony outcrops, green heather-like scrub and stony pools of rainwater. I remember it was a clear blue-and-white day like an English spring with a strong breeze; the rains seemed to have blown away.

We made good progress, notwithstanding our heavily laden Italian trailers, and the way that the retreating Germans had blown up a number of strategically awkward culverts. This forced us to make tedious detours along hastily constructed tracks and we got mixed up with the large amount of other traffic bound for Bengasi. Boards alongside these tracks warned "travellers" that the verges should be treated with caution, since it could not be guaranteed that they were not mined. No one tried to pull off.

In the afternoon, we came to the Derna–Barce main road which was wider and in reasonable condition, so that we could make better progress up hill and down dale on the tarmac. We had now left the bare, bleak moorland country and entered into tree-clad hill country with clumps of rhododendrons beside the road. This was the "Colonial" country of the Italian occupation of Cyrenaica and dotted around in the valleys and on the hill slopes were the little white box-like farms of the settlers. Here and there, we saw the tapering carillon tower of a church amid dark-green cypress trees.

All the little farms were identical: a pair of gateless pillars at the roadside, bearing the words *"Ente Colonnisazzione Libia"* and the number, say 1023, of the farm, from which a neat track led up to the flat-topped, four-roomed bungalow standing in the middle of a well tended smallholding. There was no sign of any human life; all the inhabitants had cleared out to Barce or Bengasi when the retreat passed over them, and the only signs of their previous existence was an unhitched tumbril in the yard and, perhaps, a forgotten cow munching hay from the rick in the byre. The identical little farms lay glinting in the sunlight silent and empty, with smokeless chimneys and open doors, a burnt-out tank among the lilies of the front garden and ravens flapping and bouncing on the porch steps.

I felt sorry for the little farmers, overtaken by a war not of their making, and forced to leave all that they had created to the marauding Arabs who would surely arrive shortly, taking over that dead world.

Dusk found us amid a small hamlet centred around a white stone pillar from which a clear gush of water fell from a gargoyle spout into a stone cistern and tinkled away down the valley. The pillar was crowned with representation of the Roman *fasces* and announced briefly: *"De Martino. Anno XV. Duce"*.

We pulled off on to the broad well kept sward of the "village green" in the middle of the hamlet, which we could see had not been disturbed by mine-laying, and packed down for the night, surrounded by the silent empty windows of the hamlet. We were watched by a couple of Arab children, some goats, a pi-dog or two and the ever-wheeling kites.

After seeing the unit settled for the night and given their evening meal, Phillips and I strolled over and glanced into one or two of the houses, without venturing inside. The doors and windows of most of them were open, anyhow. Looking in through the windows, we could see that they had very little furniture and they seemed to have been used as billets by some Italian unit. The rooms were in a filthy state. Opened and discarded boxes of small arms ammunition littered the floors suggesting a sudden withdrawal. Some ceilings were black with soot from campfires on the stone floors and the little tiled bathrooms had been casually used as latrines. The walls in most were daubed with the same slogans I had seen in Sidi Barrani a year ago: *"VV il Duce"* and *"Vinceremo"* as if nothing had happened since to change their minds, although I remembered the soldiers, after Alamein, that had tried to surrender to us or to anyone who would take them in and feed them. In one room, the walls had been crudely decorated in charcoal with highly pornographic drawings. I wondered what the owners would say when, or if, they returned. It saddened me to think that Italian soldiers had so misused the property of their own nationals like this. In the doorway of one of the houses, an abandoned child's toy pram lay on its side, containing a little girl's rag doll. Phillips said it made him feel sick. It did me, too.

On the following morning, we pushed on. The road began to run out of the fertile country into Martuba-like moorland again as we came to Maraua, a hamlet of a couple of white cottages, overshadowed by a squat, massive fort on the hill above. It made one think of *Beau Geste*; there were hundreds of such forts scattered about the Libyan littoral, reminders of the days a decade or so ago back when they were used for garrisons to enforce the "civilisation" being imposed on the native and rebellious Senoussi tribesmen by the colonising Italians. Here we turned off the metalled Barce road and struck out over the moors on a track going south in the direction of Charruba. During that day the terrain gradually changed from the green-grey moorland to the familiar rock and scrub desert, and just before evening we were back in the packed gravel and clay-pans of central Cyrenaica.

We camped for the night by the ruined fort at Charruba, the scene of my troubles during the early retreat in January, when I had three of my Leylands towing guns for 261 Bty. Near our site were half a dozen burnt-out Mack 10-ton lorries, fire-reddened and full of rusty petrol drums. They hadn't been there when I was retreating, so I assumed they had become casualties during those dark days soon afterwards, when, so rumour whispered, whole supply columns of RASC lorries – out of touch with the progress of the fighting – had driven straight into the arms of the advancing Germans and just disappeared.

Msus, when we got there, looked very much as it had a year previously; it had obviously never been used by the enemy. The tide of battle had just flowed over it and left it behind untouched. I deployed the Workshop in a wadi I knew of and which I had always coveted during my previous stay and we were almost overwhelmed with work at once, mainly on the guns. The continuous battering over bad terrain at speeds they were never designed for was taking its toll and we were fighting a losing battle to keep the Regt's guns "on the road". It was the old story repeating itself as the campaign wore on: every time the Regt moved, the pace of the advance was just too fast for the equipment and we would stop, one day here, two days there. During these halts the Workshop would labour like the damned to make them just capable of moving again at short notice, by welding, riveting, turning up parts on the lathe, patching and improvising. Then we would move on for another 150 miles or so and the process would have to be repeated.

It was all very trying and I was obliged to apply an immense amount of tact with Major Jones and the Bty Commanders in seeking to persuade them that operational requirements must surely permit of slightly lower speeds. But the Germans were retreating at such a speed that such pleas were of little use. We had reached Msus in the afternoon of 27 November and it was officially announced that we should have three clear days there, since the Germans were known to have evacuated Bengasi a few days before and the RAF had nowhere further to go until they could use Belandah (of evil memory) when the enemy had retired beyond Mersa Brega on the coast road and couldn't suddenly turn and bite. Accordingly, I decided that a quick sortie into Bengasi might result in some useful pickings in the way of expendable stores. It would be a two-day trip and I set off with a 3-tonner and a couple of useful lads, to have a look.

369

The sortie was most successful, but several pictures remained in my memory afterwards. Our route lay through Solluch, a little white Italian colonial town on the edge of the desert near Beda Fomm where Wavell's Western Desert Force had surprised and destroyed the whole Italian army under General Bergonzoli, retreating towards Tripolitania in 1940. Solluch lay deserted among shady palm trees, empty except for a few dirty Senoussi and a goat or two. Its fine spacious buildings were shell-pocked and the railway station (of the narrow-gauge Solluch–Bengasi railway) was a tangled mass of girders, rubble and twisted, burnt-out rolling stock.

The town was almost surrounded by barbed wire and, inside this, their guns pointing outwards, were a score of British tanks, all disabled and rusting. I never found out what had happened there during those wild January days ten months before, but the place had a "last stand" look about it.

Bengasi was pretty badly chipped; the harbour was a mass of sunken wreckage, over which a pall of smoke brooded from a ship that had been fired by the retreating enemy almost a week before. The dockside was a welter of gaunt ruins, twisted steelwork and rubble and the buildings around were bomb-damaged and spattered with splinter-pocks.

It looked a ghost town, but, surprisingly, it wasn't. By day some pioneer troops worked to get the harbour facilities into action; but, as evening came, a few white-faced, undernourished civilians – the first we had seen since leaving the Delta – crept out of the woodwork and gathered in little groups, whispering uneasily. I learned later they were Jews who had somehow escaped death during the German occupation.

We scooped up quite a lot of tinned food left behind by the Germans together with large quantities of packets of *dauerbrot*, which was a close-textured brown cake-like substance pre-served in waterproof wrappings and apparently was a sort of "iron ration". There were also a few gas cylinders, mainly oxygen, but a few acetylene, in the ruined waterside ware-houses.

As we left Bengasi down the long straight asphalt road to the south-west, sprinkled with the usual harvest of wrecked German civilian-type lorries, we came upon a signpost which said: "Tripoli. 1400km". It sounded a long way. Something like 800 miles. We had come that distance already from the Delta and our equipment was getting tired.

Back at Msus that afternoon, I found the Regiment already preparing to move on westwards and the Workshop packed up and ready to leave at first light. I was encouraged by the way my subordinates had coped without my presence. Msus LG was already deserted except for a few RAF rear parties burning refuse. It appeared that the Germans were already back on their old El Agheila position in a series of defended areas in the salt marshes and sand, stretching from Mersa Brega on the coast, ten miles in front of El Agheila, to Marada, about forty miles south.

The RAF had decided to go down to Belandah on the high ground south of Agedabia and to El Hasieat in the Wadi Faregh further to the south of Belandah. 94th was bound for El Hasieat. The Wadi Faregh had the reputation of being composed of bottomless shifting sands. This didn't bode well for our heavily-loaded machinery lorries and our Italian trailers.

So, off we went the following morning under a clear blue sky on the well known track to Antelat, past the place where I had been machine-gunned on my first retreat, past Antelat fort and on into new, even for me, uncharted country.

The country to the south-west of Antelat was similar to that around Msus, but stony and rock-covered, for we were now heading for the coast again and out of the gravel lands. Our journey was much hampered by having to share the track with 51 (Highland) Div who were going the same way. We had seen them last on their move up to Alamein in September and they didn't seem to have altered their methods much. They still painted their HD signs over everything they passed and still halted for meal stops right in the middle of the track.

Agedabia, which we reached in mid-afternoon, was a pleasant-looking semi-Arab village of white walls amid green palm trees astride the coast road. It was very little knocked about and was in the possession of an RE detachment who were operating a water point from an enormous well. The surrounding area was seamed with trenches and liberally festooned with strands of barbed wire, marking charted minefields. The Germans had apparently been proposing to make a strong point of the village, but had decided to leave in a hurry before this could come about.

At this point, we turned off to the left for El Hasieat, which lay out in the desert, some forty riles south-west of Agedabia. We bypassed the LGs at Belandah, where the Pursuit Group of the US Air Force were setting up shop. This was a new one on us, although we were to see a lot more of them in the near future. That was evidently why the RAF was not using Belandah and had been obliged to establish the Forward Fighter LG at El Hasieat. And so we arrived at the Wadi Faregh...

El Hasieat lay about 40 miles to the south of Agedabia and was somewhere in the Wadi Faregh, of which I had heard terrible tales of impassable sands; not the place to arrive at without reconnaissance in daylight, so we camped for the night near Agedabia, but well outside the mined area.

This Wadi Faregh was a shallow canyon about 50 miles long in the flat coastal plain, which wound its way in a generally north-west/south-east direction and petered out rather indecisively at each end. We learned that the floor was very soft sand in places and the country on the south-west side got softer and sandier still, almost impassable, in fact. At El Hasieat, the wadi was almost half a mile across and some 150 feet deep. The LG was actually inside the wadi on a broad shelf about fifty feet below ground level and the RAF loathed it from the start, bitterly regretting the GHQ decision that had handed over Belandah, which they had reconnoitred previously, to the Americans. It appeared there were odd thermal air currents which played hell with the landing of the high-speed fighters and it required the nicest of judgements to come down without running slam into the cliff face above, or overshooting down on to the wadi floor below. I guessed our stay was likely to be a short one.

We picked the only hard spot in the whole valley and sat down in it quickly, possession being nine points of the law. Work was plentiful, especially as one of the radar sets had broken its frame and the platform of one of the guns was starting to show ominous cracks. Any spare time we had left was spent in winching people out of the soft sand.

It was at Hasieat that Farbrother finally completed his own Grand Design. Almost single-handed and amid great scepticism from all concerned, he fitted his jeep with fat 900×13 wheels and tyres from a wrecked staff car, which he had spotted and picked up some time before. The experiment was surprisingly successful; with these massive low-pressure tyres the jeep proved virtually unditchable and would negotiate steep dunes of fine sand without turning a hair. Farbrother was simply unbearable for days and we were all keeping our eyes open for further wheels, to convert other people's jeeps. I reported this useful modification to Walker, but he declined to pass it on, on the grounds that we were unnecessarily subjecting the steering of the vehicle to stresses for which it had not been designed. However, he omitted to order us to revert to the original narrow wheels and so Farbrother continued to sail about the Btys with his nose in the air.

Our stay at El Hasieat lasted a week, while the RAF took counsel with Higher Authority about where they could relocate the LG. By this time the Germans had withdrawn completely into the El Agheila position, with Mersa Brega as a sort of forward post, and the fluid battle had become static for the first time since El Alamein. The two armies now faced each other on fixed lines separated by defences of minefields and barbed wire. Preparations were obviously afoot to assault the notorious Agheila Line before the momentum of the advance was lost and which, although momentarily checked, was very far from being expended.

At about this time, we realised that the seemingly impossible was becoming very possible and everyone was talking confidently and openly of Tripoli and even throwing the Germans out of Africa for good and all. The First Army in Tunisia had become bogged down without capturing even Tunis and it was the general opinion that the Eighth would have to capture Tripoli and bail them out. "Exercises in England", it was universally asserted, were no preparation for real war, although the poor blighters would learn by experience in time.

Meanwhile, it had been decided that the RAF would set up the forward fighter LG at Melah en Nogra near the main coast road and only a paltry fifteen miles from the German-held Mersa Brega. The RAF must be feeling unusually brave and sure of themselves, we thought.

As we were preparing to leave El Hasieat, we were engulfed by a huge armoured and motorised force, mainly New Zealanders, who flowed around and through us at great speed and with much dust. All day they came down the Agedabia track in endless columns, passed across the wadi and disappeared on the other side in the direction of Marada to the south. Something big seemed to be brewing.

To reach Nogra, we had to retrace our steps up the Agedabia track and then down the road towards the forward area. I found, to my horror, that the guns in front of us were not travelling on the tarmac, but had been routed on to a parallel grader-made track on the soft stuff and were making very heavy weather of it. I thought it best not to enquire why and, since we had three massive Italian trailers which were difficult enough to tow even on hard surfaces, we turned on to the road and bowled off happily to the rendezvous. This we reached several hours in front of the sweating Regiment. The road was being reserved for something else, which had not turned up when we arrived, and we got away with the deviation from Regimental orders.

This main road ran through undulating country bordered with a sandy soil, in which the winter rains had produced a pleasant greenness, with grass stubble and little red and blue flowers. The road ran on, straight as a die across numerous sandy ridges, uphill and down dale, now in cuttings and now on embankments. It was a wonderful piece of engineering, presumably pre-war Italian, since it was periodically served by the familiar white-walled roadhouses, now damaged and smoke-blackened, each bearing the sign "*Strada Littoreana Libica*". The Red-Caps warned us not to enter, since most of them were pretty heavily booby-trapped, and we left them well alone.

Nogra LG proved to be a small flat space in the middle of the sandy wastes to the south of the road. We found a harder spot for the workshop in a sort of valley and opened up, watching the fast fighters just managing to get airborne and somehow managing to land without running into the sand. RHQ and the Signals settled in the next sand valley, separated from us by a massive 50-foot high ridge of sand covered with flowers, and the gun-sites were in almost inaccessible positions on the sand ridges, from which, they said, all they could see was the distant Mediterranean.

Soon after our arrival, the Germans sent over a reconnaissance aircraft, but it received such a hot reception from the Btys' AA fire that we had no more trouble of that sort from the enemy. They seemed either to be short of aircraft at the moment, or were needing them for some other purpose.

We were over a week at Nogra and we were glad of the respite, for there was work in plenty to keep us busy virtually from dawn to dusk. The frame of the radar set had now broken in half and we were reduced to strapping it up by welding on bumper bars off wrecked lorries as stiffeners. Added to this, the faulty frame of the 3.7" gun I have mentioned had buckled so badly that it was in danger of collapsing on to the ground when moved – all nine tons of it – without warning and in the middle of the desert! There was nothing for it but to have a go at repairing it on site, although it was really a Base Wksp job. We got the Bty fitters to strip the whole front end and we jacked it up and welded on innumerable pieces of steel in appropriate places, until it looked rather like a Christmas tree, but it was now safely mobile again.

This consumed a vast quantity of welding gas and, when Walker came to see what I was doing, he impressed on me the utmost importance of keeping the Regt on the road, but regretted he was unable to release to me any further gas than my meagre ration from the OFP – which had now caught us up – as it would depreciate his reserve. He would order up further stocks from Tobruk, or somewhere. In short, he offered all assistance except actual help and left us to it. One couldn't blame him, for he was right out of his depth, but I felt the lack of Estlin's authority; he would have got us the gas somehow.

By now, the Regt's vehicle engines were beginning to show signs of getting "tired" and, in these sandy and dusty terrains, when that happened, it was only a short step to complete failure. Again Walker was unable to help; he had no spare engines in the OFP and promised to send an urgent indent to the nearest Base OFP, probably in Bengasi, or possibly even Tobruk, for urgent replacements. Again, we had to do something ourselves and were reduced to recovering engines from damaged or blown-up vehicles in the desert, stripping them down on the bench and, if not badly worn, reconditioning them a bit and slamming them into the Regt's lorries. This "make do and mend" worked surprisingly well and our reputation with the Btys rose accordingly.

While we were at Nogra, we received, at last, the replacement 3-tonner for the stores lorry we had lost on the mine on our way to Martuba. We shifted all our stores into it and breathed once more, for it had arrived complete with bins; this meant that we could now dispense with one of our massive Italian trailers which were pulling the guts out of the vehicles that were towing them. Major Walker heard about this and requested we should transfer it to Bde HQ for use by the OFP to carry the additional stores he now realised he needed. I cannot say the one he got was our best, but we warned Spooner and Lewis about its faults and Spooner reckoned he could cope. In the light of its subsequent unhappy performance, I feel he must have regretted its acquisition.

We had, in the time since the catastrophe on the road to Martuba, been doing something ourselves to allay our perennial shortage of transport. With memories of the manner in which the Military Police had come down heavily on us and impounded our captured German vehicles in the earlier advance, I had decided to "capture" only British vehicles this time. By the time we reached Nogra, we had three additions to our vehicle strength, which for as long as I was with 94th were known by the descriptions of "The German Ford", "The LRDG Jeep" and "Congo Maisie". They all proved useful in different ways, although only the German Ford was a load-carrier, being a standard British 3-tonner which had been captured by the enemy

376

and, when found abandoned in a ditch near De Martino, had newly painted Luftwaffe markings and an aircraft cannon shot through the radiator, evidently the reason for its abandonment. Even the wheels were in position, quite contrary to the normal practice by the retreating Germans.

Phillips and I went back to look at it that night, and we found it almost complete, lacking only a few minor oddments missing from the engine. We had it towed in and pulled it along with us through Msus, Hasieat and finally Nogra. Here we found time to do something about it, which involved putting in a new radiator, replacing the missing minor engine components and, of course painting out the Luftwaffe markings. It wasn't a frightfully brilliant acquisition, but it motored, so we dumped in one of the "recovered-from-the-desert" engines and subsequently fitted a new one. Since our replacement stores 3-tonner had come already equipped with bins, we now transferred the bins from our late lamented mine casualty and threw away the 3-tonner body now in our "Cape Cart" trailer, thereby making space for coal for the blacksmith's forge. (Our official allowance, as decided presumably by the UK scale, was a paltry two hundred-weights, but the middle of the desert was a bit far from replacement suppliers and experience dictated that we should always carry at least a ton.)

We felt easier in mind, since we could now send a lorry of specially selected stores with any advance party, as became the standard drill when moving.

The "LRDG Jeep" came into our hands at Hasieat. At the time the armoured column passed through us, a harassed LRDG (Long Range Desert Group) officer came into the Workshop, towing a jeep, and begged us to take it off his hands, saying it had an engine that didn't work on account of a broken big-end and a duff clutch. Since he was about to engage in a trip of some 300–400 miles behind the enemy lines, he just dared not be burdened with a dud vehicle. So we said we would deal with it and he rushed off without even asking for a signature.

On examination, we found that the clutch was merely out of adjustment and the engine failure was due to a broken valve and not a big-end. It all seemed too good to be true, so we adjusted the clutch, turned up a new valve out of a piece of half-shaft and hardened by the blacksmith and – presto! – we had acquired a second jeep. We removed the give-away special LRDG fitments – heavy machine-gun mounting and spare petrol-and water-can brackets – and took it into use. We were not entitled to a second jeep on our War Establishment, but, if questioned, we could assert and demonstrate that we were still several assorted vehicles short and anyway we could find a good use for the jeep.

"Congo Maisie" – heaven knows how it acquired that nickname! – was a Morris four-wheel-drive former anti-tank portee designed in the early days of the war to carry the 2-pdr pea-shooter gun. I had come up against one previously at Ras Hawala, when Estlin had had ideas of mounting a 20mm Breda on it as mobile AA convoy protection. It was useless to carry the 6-pdr that replaced the original gun, let alone the 17-pdr that was now the standard, and they had been converted to carry two 180-gallon water tanks instead. Maisie was one of these; she had belonged to the RAF and just before their departure from Nogra the engine had suddenly and irretrievably died, rendering her useless to them. The RAF might, of course, have towed her back to Agedabia and handed her in to the Returned Vehicle Park, but with the RAF's lofty contempt for the finer points of accounting, they decided that it would be too difficult and proceeded to abandon her complete in the desert, after removing the water tanks. As an afterthought, since we were friends of theirs, they told us where they had left her, "just in case we might want to strip it for spares", so we pulled her in. We were delighted to find that she was in excellent condition and discovered on examination that the fault was merely a sheared camshaft-drive key, which had let the valve timing slip. This was rectified only half an hour before we left Nogra and L/Cpl Fowles, the fitter who had worked on the job and was rapidly regarding her as his ewe lamb, then drove her into Tripolitania without any bodywork, until he could fit a standard 15cwt truck body. Later still, we found that Maisie, with her big engine, high power-to-weight ratio, 4 massive tyres and four-wheel drive, would go anywhere even on sand and could tow the heaviest 3-tonner through soft stuff without turning the proverbial hair.

One day we came near to losing Farbrother. He had gone out in his jeep in search of something – probably bumper bars to repair his ailing radar set – and motored westwards down the road deep in his own thoughts. He subsequently was rudely awakened by the sound of several loud thumps and the sight of dirty clouds of dust rising from the desert just to his right; the desert seemed unnaturally empty, too, and then he came to a kilometre stone reading "Mersa Brega 3". Now fully awake, he turned and fled back to safety.

Then, suddenly, came the almost unbelievable news. The New Zealand force we had seen heading for Marada had crossed the marshes between the German strong points and was racing in strength to cut the road near "Marble Arch" some 150 miles to the rear of El Agheila. Faced with this threat to their communications, the Germans were hastily withdrawing from the Agheila position without a shot being fired and were beating it westwards at high speed. There was some confused fighting somewhere beyond Marble Arch where the New Zealanders, now established astride the road, attempted to cut the whole Afrika Korps off, but the Germans broke through by sheer weight of numbers and began falling back on Sirte, some 100 miles further still. The Highland Division, which had been all set for the main frontal assault on El Agheila, piled into its transport and moved up the road in pursuit, painting HD signs as they went.

Official handouts on the progress of the war informed us that the enemy was expected to pull right back to the next defensible position on the line of the Wadi Kebir, a big valley running inland from the coast for fifty miles and situated 100 miles or so to the west of Sirte. The situation resembled the one in the "bulge" of Cyrenaica, namely that the Agheila–Marada position was equivalent to that at Gazala and once the Agheila–Marada marshes had been penetrated, there was no suitable defensive position until you came to this Wadi Kebir.

Furthermore, although it seemed that our forward elements were going to keep in touch with the enemy, there was to be a bit of a lull before the next proper assault was made. Reserves had to be built up and the Agheila defences needed reversing to face the other way. It was a case of "once bit, twice shy". The Eighth Army obviously wasn't going to be caught out again and there must be no mistake this time. The final assault on Tripoli would not take place until some time in January.

Meanwhile, the RAF was hopelessly out of touch at Nogra and was preparing to move up into the Marble Arch area forthwith. The chosen site was the ex-enemy LG at Bir Merduma some 15 miles inland from the coast. On 18 December, there was a sudden flap and 12 AA Bde decided to send an advance party of one Bty as AA defence for the RAF advance party, who were intending to make the site ready for the main body of the Fighter wing, since the Germans had adopted the policy of ploughing, or otherwise messing up the runways before leaving and it would take a couple of days to grade them into a usable condition. This type of "scorched earth" action was a new departure on the part of the enemy, for it seemed to indicate that he did not expect to use these LGs again, which was encouraging.

I forget whether it was 291 or 292 Bty that went forward in a hell of a hurry, with an advance nucleus of RHQ, and I was ordered to send a small Workshop party of about ten strong, to do simple repairs and, more important, any recovery work. Phillips was to command this detachment and he chose a selection of tradesmen with hand tools and three vehicles and the 30cwt recovery lorry, while I retained the 3-ton Dodge and the Scammell. At the last minute, L/Cpl Fowles, chosen as a Fitter (MT) by Phillips, asked permission to add Maisie to the party, pointing out her superlative performance as an additional recovery vehicle. It was just as well he did, for Phillips was taking the "German Ford", now re-naturalised as British, to carry the advance spares and tools. The wretched thing decided to get temperamental and misfired, so that to keep up with the column it had to be towed by Congo Maisie from Mersa Brega all the way to Merduma.

Phillips had instructions from me to recce a decent site for the main Workshop party, who would be following them very shortly. Some three days later, the rest of us moved out as well. We staged the night at El Agheila and headed for Merduma the following day, passing from Cyrenaica into Tripolitania and into real unknown, "enemy", country.

The road on from Nogra was a continuation of the coast road from Agedabia: straight up hill and down dale across transverse ridges, until we arrived at Mersa Brega. There, the terrain changed abruptly, opening out into a broad open slope which rose in front of us and commanded the whole area. On the top of this rise had been the forward German position, and we entered a network of minefields, barbed wire entanglements and abandoned gun positions. There were no indications of any fighting around there.

Beyond the Mersa Brega ridge, the ground sloped down again, ending pinkly in the light of the setting sun in the famous salt marshes. The El Agheila position proper stood on another transverse ridge of rocky land with an old Italian fort looming at the seaward end and below it the road passed by on a rib of harder ground which stretched westwards for about ten miles with a width varying between one and three miles. On either side of this ridge lay the marshes, wild, dreary and treacherous expanses of low sand dunes covered with rippling grasses and gleaming salt flats which, when the north wind blew high tides on to the beaches, became vast shallow lagoons of seeping sea water, a few inches deep, to dry in the sun into gleaming white salt. Except in the most exceptional circumstances, it was impossible to drive across them.

The only way through was the causeway along which the road ran and this had been filled almost solid with mines by the retreating enemy, which the REs were busy clearing.

We staged for the night near the entrance to the causeway, where the REs said it was safe to do so, and brewed up with the Agheila fort brooding above us on its bluff. I remember it as a glorious moonlit night and surprisingly peaceful.

The next day we were up early and pushed on towards the intriguingly named Marble Arch. The Germans had made quite a thorough job of blowing up the causeway road every few hundred yards and we crawled along over detours of hastily laid tracks of wire mesh, skirting huge craters in the road filled with scum-coated water which bubbled obscenely in the sun. Large skull-and-crossbones notices warned us of the dangers of straying from the tracks that were bordered with white tapes on the edges of otherwise unmarked minefields. Large numbers of mine clearance parties were already at work and every now and then a great gout of mud, water and smoke would go up with an unmistakeable "thump", spattering everything around with slime.

The terrain on the farther side, when we reached it, was flatter, stonier and much less green, criss-crossed by numerous small wadis and gullies heading northwards towards the sea. Here again, the Germans had industriously blown up the culverts over most of the gullies and we wallowed through more hastily devised deviations.

About noon, we reached the fabulous "Marble Arch". It appeared on our Italian-based maps as "*Arco dei Fileni*" and I had long wondered exactly why the spot had been allotted this nickname by the British as long ago as 1941. It was now apparent.

Whilst still some ten miles away, we could see a slender white column rising out of the desert ahead and the road ran as straight as a die towards it. As we drew nearer, we could see that it wasn't a single pillar, but two massive concrete structures leaning towards one another and joined together at the apex, possibly 300 feet above the road, which ran through it at ground level. At its confluence was a panel of human figures in bas-relief and some daring RAF climbers had been "improving" these with silver paint. One well formed damsel in her birthday suit, for example, now appeared to be chastely clad in gleaming bra and panties; others had RAF roundels in appropriate places!

I was told, although I cannot vouch for it, that the arch was erected in commemoration of the completion of the great road from Sollum to Tripoli. It was a typically flamboyant Fascist bit of self-aggrandisement which must have been extremely costly and difficult to build.

Some RAF were setting up shop in the former enemy fighter LGs close by the Arch. The LG was heavily surrounded by wire, as protection against ... what? – raiding Arabs, or, perhaps, the depredations of the SAS? Piles of wrecked aircraft testified to the accuracy of our own bombers.

At Marble Arch, we turned off into the desert, over a small rocky ridge that rapidly shut off the Arch from view, and a few miles on was the LG at Bir Merduma. I was struck by the similarity of the terrain with that of the Western Desert in Egypt. Here we were, 1000 miles on our way to Tripoli, and one might, after closing one's eyes for a moment, imagine that one was just south of Sidi Barrani on the track to Oxford Circus, Bir Enba, or Sofafi in those strange far-off days of mid-1941 when the desert was a big uncharted place, through which men moved with a compass uneasily in hand. It was the same infinite, grey-green and slightly undulating sea of stone and scrub, through which distant vehicles moved amid a column of dust rising in the still air.

The Bir Merduma LG was sited in a shallow bowl in the folds of the desert and was one of those places that made one wonder why the original surveyor had decided to put it just *there* and not in any of the exactly similar spots all about. The RAF were getting rapidly into action around the landing strips and I found Phillips established on a piece of clean, hard desert on the slopes, well to the south of the LG. He told me that, according to all reports, the LG had been heavily mined, but it was now reported to be "clean" for 50 yards round as well, and beyond a 500-yard radius it was virgin desert and "safe".

We were to be at Merduma until just before the New Year. Everything was pretty quiet and even the RAF were almost non-operational, because the Germans had apparently abandoned Sirte and were now retiring so rapidly as to be nearly out of Spitfire range. This was considered to be a good thing, because it ensured that the Christmas festivities would not be interfered with.

With vivid memories of the fiasco of the previous Christmas at Msus in 1941, I had decided that we must do much better this time and we had amassed over a considerable period quite a stock of good things, including seven quart bottles of beer per man, which presented quite a noticeable additional load in our cookhouse stores.

By common consent of the entire occupants of the LG, it was unofficially agreed that Christmas Day 1942 should be a complete holiday and, as far as we were concerned, it was an unmitigated success. We started with a late reveille, after which came a 9 o'clock breakfast, a morning football match against a team from the RAF, an enormous Christmas dinner of roast pork and currant pudding, served in traditional style to the men by the officers and senior NCOs, and continued through an afternoon and evening of increasing somnolence, good fellowship, community singing and alcoholic satiety. All Officers' Messes in the Regt kept open house and everybody did a complete tour of them all. Goodwill and peace toward men, even Germans, reigned noisily supreme far into the night and we resumed work the next day feeling that it had been a Good Thing and that we could face some more of the war, albeit with somewhat sore heads. The RAF, being somewhat better organised with alcoholic supplies than we were, treated Boxing Day as another holiday. They were, anyhow, probably incapable of flying aircraft operationally until 27 December, but the war seemed to go on the same, notwithstanding. Fortunately, the enemy made no attempt to involve us in it. Maybe they were also celebrating. We hoped so and wished them luck.

Christmas was also marked by the permanent acquisition of the Scammell recovery lorry, which Walker had borrowed from some unsuspecting unit back at Gambut. They had found that he still had it and asked for it back, but he came to some satisfactory but dishonest and Estlin-like agreement about "operational necessity" with the High-Ups at Army HQ and they let us keep it *sine die*. The rightful owners, losing heart, plaintively asked if at least they could have the driver and his mate back and they were returned much to their own disgust. The Scammell was taken on to the Bde strength and handed over for maintenance to 94 Wksps.

Bir Merduma means "Well of Bitter Waters", but, search as we might, we couldn't find a trace of a well there, much less any water, bitter or otherwise. This meant we had to send back as far as Agedabia for water. By now, we had two small 100-gallon water trailers, a 100-gallon tank which lived in the cookhouse 3-tonner and a bigger 180-gallon tank we had picked up in the desert, and had mounted on a trailer made out of the back end of a cut-down lorry chassis. It needed considerable ingenuity to keep all available tanks always full ready for a move and this meant sending the bigger trailer back the long distance to Agedabia as frequently as we dared. The trouble was that, being a trailer, it needed a vehicle to tow it and that meant detaching one of our limited stock of load carriers at a moment when we might have to move at short notice. We discussed the possibility of putting the tank back on Congo Maisie but we could never find the opportunity to do this.

About this time, two events took place that were of interest for me personally. The first was the departure of ASM Spooner from Bde HQ. He had been Estlin's man; I don't think he had been happy after the Great Man left and after several months he left on a posting to something more in his line. He joined 51 HAA Wksps at Bengasi in another AA Bde that was following us up steadily doing port AA defence. I was sorry to see him go.

The other event was the reuniting with 94 Regt of 261 HAA Bty, (of the Antelat disaster and once good friends of mine) who had been reformed and re-equipped. They were now only 60 miles down the road at a place called Ras el Aali. In order to relieve the congestion on the Agheila–Sirte road, stores were being off-loaded from lighters at any point on the intervening coastline which had sufficient anchorage for them and since Ras el Aali boasted a small stone jetty, it had become a "vulnerable point" needing AA protection almost overnight. They were now so much nearer 12 AA Bde than their parent Bde in Bengasi that it seemed sensible to make the transfer.

Whilst glad to remake my contacts with 261, I was concerned to receive orders from Major Jones to provide a small section to look after the newcomers. Since we had already agreed to provide an adequate advance section whenever we moved at short notice as well as keeping the main workshop working full time, this savoured of trying to split a prime number, but, by a certain amount of reorganisation, I was able to pack off a S/Sgt and about eight assorted tradesmen with hand tools and a couple of lorries, in the hope that 261 would not require any complicated repair work. I pointed out to Major Jones that, if there were any more calls like this, we would be in danger of becoming so fragmented and dispersed that none of the sections would be of much good. You cannot subdivide a skilled turner or welder, for example. Also this perpetual rebuilding of the Workshop organisation to suit such local circumstances ought to be avoided, since it interfered with the team spirit which I was succeeding in building up and thus in the long run it adversely affected production. I am glad to say that he took my point.

Just before the end of the month, the RAF awakened and decided to make another bound forward to a pinpoint on the map called Sidi Azzab, about 40 miles south-east of Sirte. Off went the CO, an advance party of 291 Bty and Phillips and his merry men. The main party of 94 HAA Regt moved out of the Bir Merduma LG on the morning of 30 December and we took up station to the rear of 292 Bty. The LG was not going to be reoccupied and soon the bowl would be covered with drifting dust that would obliterate all traces of our temporary residence there.

We proposed to stop for the night somewhere near Nofilia, where one of the old Italian forts was marked on the map, half-way to our destination at Sidi Azzab, involving a trip of about 50 miles for the day's run. I was glad of this, because due to the loss of the transport taken by Phillips's advance party and that with 261 Bty, we had been obliged to overload the Italian trailers with the stores that would have been carried by the absent lorries, and these monsters took a mean bit of towing and were very slow.

As we pushed on westwards, the character of the country changed appreciably, becoming more broken and hilly. It was wild and seemed deserted and, except for a party of Military Police putting up signs marking this track as, I think, the "Y" Track for some following formation, we saw no one throughout the day.

Nofilia proved to be a small green hollow among the rocky

outcrops, which contained little more than a couple of white Italian Colonial buildings and was dominated by the fort on a bluff above. A big well in the centre of the green sward had been converted into a water point and a long string of unit water trucks was rapidly churning the wet turf into mud.

We passed through and bivouacked with the rest of our column on the higher ground beyond. The desert here, far from being deserted, fairly hummed with life, for an armoured formation was in the process of refitting and re-equipping. All around us were workshops, tank delivery squadrons, transporter companies and the like, dispersed in the hollows of the hills and dales, whereas for miles around, all one could see was small black dots on the skyline and pillars of dust as squadrons of tanks milled about on test, or in training exercises.

We saw 1943 in under a brilliant moon, which dimmed even the enormous desert stars. 94th, being the City of Edinburgh HAA Regt RA (TA), was in origin a Scottish formation, if now somewhat watered down with Sassenachs, and as such was not likely to ignore the traditions of Hogmanay. The celebrations were considerably more restrained than they might otherwise have been due to lack of much of the necessary spirit, Christmas having made a bigger hole in the stocks of this "ammunition" than had been expected, but a good time was had by all. Farbrother and I, coming back from a round of the bivouac groups, discovered a forgotten half bottle of rum in the back of my Humber and we proceeded to have a subsidiary party with the Padre and the Doc, who happened to be "lost" in our lines at that moment. It was a cold and almost frosty night and very warming our rum proved to be, but the enjoyment was slightly marred by the Regt's RASC officers firing Very lights into our camp. However a few rounds of counter-battery work with our signal pistol, using German signal cartridges (which broke into six flares, each terminating with a loud bang), soon put a stop to that and we went peaceably to our camp beds under the stars. Away to the northwards on the coast, bursts of tracer and Very lights were going up in erratic confusion and we reckoned that either a first class air raid was in progress, or, much more likely, the Highland Division was celebrating Hogmanay.

The following day, just after we started, we encountered a large armoured formation, possibly a Regiment with tracked ancillaries, which crossed our path and we had to stop to let them go by. I wasn't able to count them, but they were massed in line of columns, something like ten columns abreast and each column about fifteen deep, all clanking along in close formation at some five miles an hour amid clouds of dust. They looked frighteningly impressive, but who they were or what they were doing there, I never learned. It was the first time I had seen such a phalanx of tanks in battle array.

After crossing a series of large, steep-sided wadis, we arrived at Sidi Azzab, which was situated on a virtually limitless plain, covered with little black pebbles like that at Gilwakh, on which tufts of dispirited-looking grass were trying to survive, and bounded by nothing in particular. There were, apparently, two LGs in use by the RAF, Sidi Azzab 1 and Sidi Azzab 2 (sometimes known as Chel) about three miles apart, and it was a matter of conjecture as to which was the dustiest. Our site was on Sidi Azzab 2 and it remains in my memory as the only place where I saw the dust moving steadily in the opposite direction to the prevailing breeze.

Needless to say, we were inundated with work as soon as we stopped. Several of the older guns were showing signs of packing up on the base of the mounting, where a traversing lock was supposed to prevent them from slewing in rotation while on the move. On the worst case the lock socket had fractured down in the bowels of the platform and the gun had swung violently round, when on the move, thereby tearing its minuscule securing stays bodily out of the platform, so that the gun had nearly overturned. Major Jones had had greater confidence in our powers to rectify this damage than we ourselves had; he was "sure that REME could fix it", but I was obliged to point out that it was a job that would normally be one for a Base Wksp, and that it had been occasioned by the Bty (292) moving at much more than its scheduled speed, arriving at the rendezvous some three hours early, so that they had had to sit down and wait for the rest of us. More in sorrow than in anger, when I pointed this out to Major Macpherson-Grant, the Bty Commander, he said sadly that he had had a specific order from Jones to make the best speed he could and that it was REME's job to mend things. Macpherson-Grant and I were good friends and he begged me to do our best for him, but relations between REME and RHQ were somewhat cool for the next few days.

Meanwhile, we had "to do something about it". The job was, strictly speaking, far beyond our capacity and the gun should have been returned to Base Wksps, but the latter were a thousand miles away and so it devolved on us. To get at the base ring, the entire gun and mounting, six tons weight, needed to be lifted off the platform. At Base Wksps this would easily have been effected with an overhead crane, but, not being so lavishly equipped, we were obliged to strip the entire gun and mounting, component by component, until the weight was within the capacity of our Scammell. We thanked God for it and its three-ton jib, otherwise we would never have done it. As it was, it took us nine days, with our fingers crossed that we wouldn't have to move, and we just made it, by the mercy of heaven, before the Regt received orders to move on. Though I say it myself, it was a classy job when we had finished and, by taking progressive notes, we devised a drill whereby we could do it with another gun in far less time on some subsequent occasion.

While the gun was reduced to its component parts, we organised classes of officers and senior NCOs from the Btys and gave them object lessons on the awful things that were happening to the "innards" of their guns. There is something about a jagged lump of sheared steel produced from the innermost recesses of the mounting of a gun that impresses far more than six academic hours of cautionary lectures. We also impounded all the Bty artificers to help us, so that, by working with us, they could appreciate exactly how much work they were causing REME. It seemed to impress them and they went back sadder and wiser, if exhausted, men.

I wished we had been able to equip all the guns with the Macpherson struts, but only 261 Bty had been provided with them. We devised special systems of lashing and use of Spanish windlasses, so that with the increased care by the gunners the

389

guns managed to survive the frightful strains of the next three weeks' wanderings.

Sidi Azzab was a foul hole, catching every wind that blew, and every time the wind rose over a gentle breeze, the dust would blow up in stinging, whirling streams. One day, we had a full-blown gale which flung before it clouds of icy, blinding grit for several hours on end and during which the Officers' tent collapsed, scattering our possessions across the hissing, rustling desert.

After something over a week, the RAF had had enough and off went the advance party together with 291 Bty to find a "better 'ole" at a map reference called Negheb es Sel just on the hither side of the Wadi Tamet, quite a distance further towards the enemy. The Germans had made some attempt to hold the Army's advance on the Wadi Tamet, but had been encouraged to retire by the unexpected appearance of the New Zealand Division, which had swiftly slipped round their exposed southern flank, and the enemy had retreated some thirty miles to hold the parallel and more formidable barrier of the Wadi Kebir which was much more defensible. Our fighter aircraft would be well within striking distance of the enemy at Negheb and it seemed likely that they would respond to our presence; our Intelligence reported that the Germans had recently brought over a quantity of the very latest version of their ME 109s to assist the defence of Tripoli.

The landing strip at Negheb, which was being bulldozed out of virgin desert, was found not yet to be ready for squadron service, on account of the quantities of small, flinty stones that would play havoc with the aircraft tyres, and involved all hands being turned out to pick them up manually until the place was judged safe. As a result, the main party didn't move from Sidi Azzab for several days. I heard an amusing anecdote about the visit of the CRE (Landing Grounds), a recent arrival in the Middle East, to the site, where everyone there from RAF ground staff and the AA defences were picking up these stones. On his tour of inspection, this choleric old gentleman came across two of the pickers sitting on a wheelbarrow, clad only in shorts, socks and boots, smoking a cigarette. He started in with a

colossal rocket and a soul-stirring harangue on the noble traditions and high ambitions of the Royal Engineers, finishing
up by saying that they were a disgrace to this fine Corps by
publicly slacking on the job. The two miscreants listened
attentively.

'What is your unit?' demanded the CRE finally, to receive
the totally unexpected reply, '239 Wing RAF and 291 Bty
RA.' The Senior Officer retired worsted in great embarrassment.

Phillips's advance party had been stocked with stores for
about two days only and, as it seemed likely that we would be
further delayed for longer than a couple of days, I decided to
make a quick trip forward to see what the situation at Negheb
was. Negheb was about 70 or 80 miles away at the far end of the
Hamraiet (an extensive plain of dead level or slightly undulating
gravel and pebble desert on a rock bed, intersected here and
there by deep wadis).

It was one of the dullest runs I had had to make, along a dead
straight track which had been used just sufficiently to render it
rather worse than the desert on either side. All around were units
and formations resting, refitting and re-equipping for the final
assault on Tripoli. It made me think of a big spring being wound
up. In fact, there was nothing between the LG at Negheb and the
Germans on the other side of the Wadi Kebir, if they wanted to
make a sortie; all our armour and the best part of the rest was on
the Hamraiet to the rear.

We arrived at Negheb just at lunch time and found 291 Bty
with some difficulty, because everyone seemed to be living in a
state of dispersion comparable with that of mid-1941. I learned
later that there were three LGs at Negheb, but only one was in
operation and the American Pursuit Group was using it, and to
reach 291's two gun-sites, it was necessary to skirt the American
lines.

Every fifty yards or so, or so it seemed, we passed a massive
seven-foot long .50 calibre machine-gun on an AA mounting,
watched over by an equally massive steel-helmeted GI, sitting
on an upturned petrol tin and pensively chewing gum. The
atmosphere suggested that everybody was just waiting for the
accident to happen.

391

Phillips met me as I drew up outside Bty HQ.

'Lunch is just up,' he said. 'Come right in and bring your steel helmet.'

I was welcomed by Majors Jones of RHQ and Bill Emslie of 291 Bty. I noticed that several steel helmets were hanging on the tent pole. Jones explained that the enemy had suddenly chosen to become much more uppity than usual and was in the habit of sending over a bunch of the latest ME 109s every few hours with the object of preventing, or at least delaying, the completion of the other LGs. Apparently things became very wild and most dangerous whenever that happened; hence the ready availability of the steel helmets. In this morning's shoot-ups two or three men in 291 Bty had been wounded.

'I wouldn't mind the shoot-ups so much,' said Emslie, plaintively. 'It's the American Civil War that gets me down.'

I asked what that was and, in reply, Phillips clapped his hands in the air as though summoning an Egyptian waiter. 'Air raid for the gentleman,' he ordered.

Almost simultaneously, the air raid signal gun went off and the warning shell burst low over the centre of the LG.

'All done by kindness,' said Phillips, reaching for his steel helmet. We all did the same and drifted out to have a look. All was peaceful, a pleasant midwinter's day with a blue sky and bright sun.

Then, suddenly, out of nowhere, it seemed, there were aircraft all over the place; one moment there was nothing to be seen and the next there were Messerschmitts, a dozen of them, plunging down out of the sun. Almost at ground level, they came sweeping across the LG, weaving and rolling, with every gun they had raking the ground in front. As they appeared, anything on the ground that would shoot opened up on them. For just a moment, we could distinguish the heavy crack of the 3.7s and the lighter "ker-bunk, ker-bunk" of the 40mms and then their noise was swallowed up in a mighty chorus of machine-gun fire, like a hailstorm beating on a tin roof, the sound rising and falling like waves on a beach, deafening and deadening in its intensity. In a second, the air was full of flying bullets, 5 percent German and 95 percent American, and we lay prudently flat on

392

the ground, endeavouring to make ourselves as inconspicuous as possible.

When an American fires a machine-gun, he fires a machine-gun; any thought other than keeping the trigger pressed and his sights on the target is excluded from his mind. Not for him are such fussy conventions as "safety angle" and "dead zones". Single-mindedly, he ignores them as ideas devised to prevent him bringing down the enemy. Only when his ammunition belt is exhausted, is his concentration interrupted.

The ME 109s were hedge-hopping and therefore the LG at ground level was swept with a swathe of half-inch bullets at an almost horizontal trajectory. We could hear them going by just above us like the crack of a thin whip and knocking splinters off the rocks behind us which mewed through the air like plaintive kittens.

This attack took about 45 seconds and then the 109s skated away, brushing the camel-thorn with their fuselages, and the firing withered and died away. As far as one could see, little damage was done.

Bill Emslie rose to his feet and dusted himself down. 'That,' he explained, 'is the American Civil War,' as we went back to our lunch.

I asked Phillips how he had managed to predict the attack so correctly. 'Just influence,' was his offhand reply.

My last memory of Negheb was that, as I drove past, of a massive GI, jaws working a steady rotary movement, sitting behind his .50 machine-gun and staring hopefully at the sky.

Back at the unit, I found them tentatively packing up. Something was about to happen and 261 Bty was being moved in a hurry from Ras el Aali to join us. They had orders to stay on their wheels and not deploy into gun-pits on arrival. Then, vast columns of vehicles flowed past, several Divisions on the move at once, all coming from the rear areas and heading south and west. The whole desert was alive with them; as far as we could see, there were moving columns of lorries, guns and armour, spread out over a frontage of a couple of miles, each column in a cloud of eddying dust and swarming like ants up hill and down dale. Most of them seemed to be New Zealanders, we noticed. It reminded me of the troop movement we had encountered at El Hasieat, when the left hook had driven the Germans out of El Agheila.

A couple of days later, we moved to Negheb and we were told not to unpack anything more than necessary. 261 Bty would come in shortly and sit down next to us. We learned that 94th was going to Tripoli with the New Zealand Division as "Divisional HAA", something that had never been tried before.

15

We were concentrated at Negheb for about two and a half days; days quiet and uneventful, albeit very work-filled, and the Messerschmitt shoot-ups which had welcomed me on my trial visit a few days before were not repeated. It appeared that we were waiting for receipt of our movement instructions from the New Zealand Division under whose command we expected to be moving.

Our period of suspense was notable for the acquisition of another 3-tonner, a former LRDG Chevrolet, which Phillips had spotted bogged down on the floor of the Wadi Tamet and apparently abandoned. It had the name "Rotomahana" painted in big black letters across the bonnet – presumably by the LRDG – and it was relatively undamaged, except for an aircraft cannon shell through the radiator; obviously that had determined its abandonment. That was something which we could easily rectify, once we had got it up out of the wadi. This wasn't so easy; it took us the best part of a day and a half to get the thing out and most of the following night to make the radiator repairs. It then motored like a lamb to Tripoli without further attention. It had lost its floorboards in the cab, but this could be got round without difficulty. We painted our own Regimental badges on it forthwith and it proved a welcome addition to our vehicle strength.

It was easy to see why the enemy had decided to attempt to hold a defensive line on the Wadi Tamet. The terrain around here had hitherto been level for miles with a surface of scrub-sprinkled, hard-packed, stony gravel, and we had been expecting to find the normal dry watercourse for which the Arabic word "wadi" had customarily been used in the western desert, from small gullies upwards. This Wadi Tamet was a shock, for it resembled a cross between a rift valley and something that had happened with extreme violence on the moon. The flat gravel-land just came to the edge of this wadi and then fell down abruptly in almost perpendicular cliffs and screes to the valley floor. Some half a mile away were corresponding cliffs and from then on the gravel plain continued as though nothing had happened. The valley floor was filled with fifty-foot high hummocks of pure sand, across which the wind rushed and whirled plumes of sand around pillars of jagged rock rising to the level of the plain outside. The only way across was by following side wadis that penetrated down into it like the tributaries of an orthodox river. There were only one or two hard tracks across the soft floor. A horrid place and a formidable obstacle which the Germans had abandoned almost without a fight when the New Zealanders had turned their flank and they had retired to the even more menacing Wadi Kebir a bit farther to the rear.

After breakfast on 13 January, Major Jones called a conference and told us that we would be moving across the Wadi Tamet that afternoon, to join up with the New Zealand Division, who, with 7 Armoured Div were doing an operation like the one that had been intended for "Benforce", driving straight across the deserts and mountains of central Tripolitania to cut the enemy off west of Tripoli. Concurrently, 51 (Highland) Div and an armoured brigade or so would make a fighting "right hook" assault up the coast road through Misurata and Homs. The Army Commander's intention was to be in Tripoli in ten days. (In actual fact, it took eleven days.) 94 HAA Regt was to accompany the NZ Div as far as Tripoli, acting as HAA protection on the way and then remain as temporary port defence as soon as it was captured.

261 Bty joined us from Ras el Aali during the morning and with them came our detachment that had been servicing them. The latter had a problem: their Dodge 8cwt had broken its front axle and was undriveable. Since we had neither the time nor the necessary parts to effect a repair, the only thing we could do was

to sling it up as a front-suspended tow behind the Morris recovery lorry and in that manner it went all the way to Tripoli.

Jones, now officially with the rank of Acting Lt Col, would have liked us to provide a small section to go with each of the three Btys and we had a lengthy discussion on whether this could be managed. Finally he agreed it wasn't possible and we reverted to the well tried scheme of Phillips and his detachment going with the forward Bty and the rest of the workshops, including the section that had come up with 261 Bty, following with the Regt's "B" Echelon. In point of fact, this scheme did not work as we had intended, since a Bty was deployed with each of the NZ Bdes and the procedure turned out to be for the Bdes to leapfrog one another, so the other two Btys had to rely on their own Bty fitters rather than calling on REME. However, this worked reasonably well, since the Btys had swapped their best transport into the forward groups, leaving their "doubtfuls" with their own "B" Echelons, near us, and so we had our work cut out just to keep them going.

My Workshop was duly lined up on parade and the situation explained to them. They took a good view of the idea that they were likely to be the first AA REME unit into Tripoli and even my sober warning that for the next fortnight or so they were going to be more overworked and subjected to greater hardships than ever before failed to dampen their spirits.

That afternoon, we moved over individually to regroup as a Regt at a rendezvous on the western side of the Wadi Tamet, before joining the NZ Div on the following day. It was quite a memorable occasion, because it was the first time that the complete Regt had been in operation in the same place since disembarking in August 1941. It was a cold, windy and thoroughly unpleasant afternoon, with visibility down to about a hundred yards and the wind roaring down the Wadi Tamet with the sound of an express train.

All the Army seemed to be packing up and moving west down into the wadi and along the hard tracks below, muffled to the eyebrows to escape the cutting wind-driven dust and grit. We had to fit into a gap in the columns, and toiled across the wadi floor and up the far side, where we fell in to the rear of a

NZ Army Service Corps Company behind whom we were expecting to move onwards the following day. Our "Trip to Tripoli" had started; we were off!

In this manner, we travelled a few miles westwards. The country ceased to be flat and became more and more rolling as we progressed; stone, rock scrub and gravel. Finally, we arrived at the lip of a giant bowl in the hills, probably ten miles across, and here we halted.

Across the floor of the bowl and in the side wadis of the surrounding slopes, lay hundreds of vehicles of all sorts: tanks, lorries and guns, scattered at 100-yard intervals over the country; all silent and alert, although seemingly sleeping in the warm afternoon sun. Through field glasses, one could pick out each individual tank or lorry crew brewing up. The place looked like an ant-run, frozen into immobility. As the afternoon wore on, they gradually packed up and faded away so unobtrusively that one never seemed to see them go, but progressively there were just fewer and fewer of them still in view. Sometime during the afternoon, our Btys went with them and we were left behind in the pale winter sunset.

Tripoli lies at the apex of a slight northward hump on the Tripolitanian coast. This coast is rocky and inhospitable, like most of the southern shores of the Mediterranean and shelves off to the west into the wastes of sand dune and salt marsh of the Tunisian border. Eastwards, the rocky coast continues through Homs to Misurata, where it takes a dog-leg south to Buerat el Hsun, at the "mouth" of the Wadi Kebir, then it goes eastwards again towards Sirte. The stretch between Homs and Misurata is flatter and harbours the familiar region of marsh, salt lakes and desolation, so that the main coast road lies back from the sea by a number of miles. And across the area south of Homs lies a tangle of mountains, reckoned by the enemy to be virtually impassable, except by a secondary road from Tripoli towards the Hamraiet, which ran through a gap in the hills at Tarhuna, some forty miles from Tripoli. Here, so air reconnaissance and the intelligence coming back from the LRDG and similar forward groups said, the Germans had concentrated some defence, to avoid being outflanked. South of these mountains,

398

we were to learn, the terrain was a land of hill and valley, a maze of rock and ravine, small wadis and clay-pans, gravel plains and crags; uninhabited even by the Arabs, because the Arab is not such a fool as to try to live there. It eventually merged with the level gravel plains of the Hamraiet in the east and to the south it faded away into the sands of the Sahara Desert.

It was across this uninviting wilderness that 30 Corps (2 NZ Div and 7 Armd Div) proposed to advance to support the main assault that the Eighth Army was intending to launch on the strong enemy defences on the Wadi Kebir and its second line on the Wadi Zemzem, some miles to the rear.

We did not know what the Army Commander's battle plan was; we only knew what did happen and this happened so smoothly that it must have been his intention all along: the classic "left hook" into the desert bypassing the defences that had proved so successful at El Alamein and subsequently at El Agheila.

Somewhere near Buerat, three large wadis converged on the coast from the hinterland. Their "mouths" at the sea end were relatively close together, but they radiated outwards like the spokes of a wheel, the Wadi Tamet running almost due south, the Wadi Kebir south west and the Wadi Zemzem slightly north of west. Each was a formidable natural obstacle and an obvious line of resistance and the bitter fighting of the previous few weeks had in turn forced the Germans out of the Wadis Tamet and Kebir, so that they were now holding a much less satisfactory line on the Wadi Zemzem with its right flank on the mountains and the heavily defended Tarhuna Gap.

30 Corps moved out on the morning of, I think, 15 January, making contact with 15 Panzer Div and pushing them back behind the line of the Wadi Zemzem, and then heading north west towards the Tarhuna road in the direction of Sedada, while 51 (Highland) Div and an Armd Bde attacked on the coastal sector.

So much for what I knew of the broader picture. My recollections of the following few days are a bit confused. Some views stand out in my mind, as vignettes without any background, and

I have no idea where on earth along the route they came. Since my Workshop was following in column sandwiched between units of the NZ "B" Echelon and I was not directly responsible for any navigation, I have only the sketchiest memory of where we were going and what the terrain was like. It took us three days of unsparing driving to reach Sedada, some 80 miles from our start line and it was a period of frantic conformity with the NZ desert convoy discipline, which varied from columns of three abreast to sometimes ten abreast, when the going was suitable. We halted for short stops whenever the Convoy Commander found it necessary to enable the stragglers (usually 94 HAA Wksps, I fear) to catch up and we leaguered down for the night far later than I would have liked. They were very good at it, far better than we, having been at this sort of thing, they told me, since going to Greece in early 1941.

I fear we, with our heavy vehicles and dreadfully un-desertworthy Italian trailers, must have been an absolute pain in the neck to them, but they came cheerfully round in the evening to see how we were coping and I never heard the slightest complaint. I was glad to offer some help with our recovery lorries, whenever any of their vehicles became really ditched in soft sand or in some unseen small wadi, but basically I am sure we were a liability rather than an asset.

Twenty-five miles a day average for a motorised column does not sound very much, but the "going" was generally atrocious. We faced steep climbs over stony hills and patches of soft sandy ground in the valleys. Added to which, our passage, or at least that of our forward troops, was not unopposed, for we had frequent stops for several hours while, I was told by those in wireless communication with higher command, pockets of enemy resistance were being encountered and had to be cleared out before the column could proceed. We frequently heard gunfire ahead, but any aircraft we saw flying over were friendly.

We were awakened every morning by a bugle call sounding Reveille in the unit immediately behind us and it behoved us to swallow an expeditious breakfast, because the column would move off in less than an hour. Word was passed back when the Column Commander decided it was appropriate to make a midday halt, no matter in what circumstances and on what surface it found us. We became good at such unscheduled halts in producing a quick brew of tea to be passed round in large cans, while we provided each vehicle every evening with a set of dry rations for the next day's journey. All this worked quite well.

Somewhere along the way, I recall looking down from some ridge and seeing a rugged mountain on the other side of a broad circular plain below, across which our parallel columns were crawling like files of disciplined ants. Somewhere else, there was a gigantic wooden tripod bearing a massive counter-weighted cross-arm, from the end of which a rope descended into a hole in the ground paved around with stone slabs; presumably it was an abandoned, or dry, well, for there were no signs of any human traffic on the surrounding ground.

On 18 January, we arrived at Sedada on a darkening winter's afternoon. Sedada lay on a wide plateau with one of the old Italian forts near the edge of what appeared to be a downward dip in the track. At this point, some obstacle in front was causing a hold-up and the vehicles ahead of us seemed to be forming into a single line as they approached this limit of visibility and then disappeared from sight. Suspecting what the reason was, I signalled to my Workshop column to draw off the track and wait while I drove forward in my Humber, to see the situation for myself. It was as I had supposed; the track just tipped over the edge of a sizeable escarpment and clawed its way down some-thing like the great hill at Gazala, cut into the side of the escarpment on one hand and with a nasty drop on the farther (unprotected) side. Below me in the distance, the columns were just visible, continuing in the murk.

As I got back in the fading light, I said to the OC of the NZ party just behind us, 'I'm not taking my lot down that hill in the dark. I'm staying here until we can see what we are doing. If you're going on just bypass us.' He nodded and waved his vehicles to follow him towards the edge, while I instructed 94th to draw off and leaguer on the flat well away from the track. 'We're staying the night here.' It was a popular decision; I heard a cheer of 'Good old Monty!' as they drew off.

401

SQMS Pratt, who was in charge of the recovery section at the rear, came up to me as soon as we were settling down in the dusk and reported that one of our 3-tonners and crew was missing. They had somehow tagged on to the NZ column and had gone down the hill with them. There was always someone who would do this! I remembered the stores lorry from the Bde Stores Section that had gone astray at Antelat. I wasn't worried unduly; they would find out soon enough that they had gone wrong, but would be unable to return up the hill against the still-descending throng and would have to wait for us to come down in the morning. They would have to rough it out, too, because they were missing the hot meal that we set about brewing up and would have to make do with the remains of that day's vehicle rations (if they had any left, of course) until we picked them up the following morning.

Before long, the NZ parties also drew off by the side of the track, they too having apparently decided that the hill was too dangerous to attempt it in the dark.

We were now on our own, having lost our allotted place in the columns, but that did not seem to matter much, because all the traffic was going our way anyhow. We had breakfast in our own time the next morning, 19 January, slotted in between the following units, by mutual agreement with the local OCs and got down the hill somehow, more by good luck than by good driving. Half a mile on, the crew of the missing lorry flagged us down and appealed for the day's rations. I gave the NCO in charge a proper wigging for not concentrating on convoy discipline and told them to go to the cookhouse truck and see what could be done about rations.

In the afternoon of the following day, we stuck a metalled road running roughly north and south and the NZ columns among which we were now moving turned north on it, following signposts reading "Beni Ulid", "Castle Benito" and "Tripoli". Apparently, the road south headed for Fezzan and Murzuk, oases far down in the desert.

Beni Ulid, when we came to it, was quite a surprise. We had been motoring through sand, rock and stone desert for several days, without seeing as much as a blade of grass, or anything greener than dead camel-thorn, and suddenly we were passing through a neat little settlement of white houses in the Italian Colonial style round a sort of village green, with palm trees bordering the roadside. There were no inhabitants visible, however, but at least the place had not been looted by the local Arabs.

On the further side of the village, the road wound down another hill to a broad plain below. At least this hill had a more reasonable gradient than the one at Sedada and did not cause us any bother. This road obviously went through the Tarhuna Gap on its way to Tripoli and sounds of gunfire ahead suggested that passage through the gap was still being disputed by the enemy; it did not surprise me, therefore, to receive orders to halt and disperse out across the level plain. The opportunity was also taken to do some re-forming of the order of march to correct the gaps that had appeared and restore the proper convoy formation.

All that day, we waited for something to happen and eventually towards sunset we got moving again. We turned left off the decent road and headed out west on a narrow stony track which wound among the foothills and was wide enough only for a single vehicle at a time, with the foothills looming on our right. A few miles on, the column leaguered down for the night, somewhat earlier than usual, and the New Zealanders told me cheerfully that the track ahead was really "crook" and something only to be tackled in daylight. So the evening of 21 January found us out in the open looking up at the mountains and listening to bursts of gunfire away to our right. Our New Zealand colleagues in the convoy, who were in better touch with the outside world, told us that the gunfire came from the Army's speculative assault on the Tarhuna position and that the Germans were still vigorously resisting the probing actions of our forward troops, but were believed to be pulling out.

Then, just as dusk fell, orders came through for the advance to be continued and we all packed up again and moved off in single file in the fading light. All one could do was to follow the dim tail lights of the vehicle ahead in the manner I had already endured on our ill-starred initial advance into Libya with 2 Light at the start of the previous campaign. However, this time the

403

pace was one that my heavy vehicles could cope with; it was a much more professional job, with frequent stops to ensure that we were all keeping together, not like the mad dash adopted by McKeown.

I have no idea what the surface over which we were travelling was like; whenever there was one of these stops, I alighted and examined the terrain, which seemed to be flat plates of stone forming a sort of uneven patchwork quilt of rock with clumps of camel-thorn in the cracks. And all the time the continuous flashes of artillery fire on the horizon to our right outlined the shapes of the mountains.

Dawn found us, weary in body and mentally exhausted, out on a wide upland plateau which sloped downhill on all sides. Here we encountered one of 94's HAA Btys deployed for action stations on the surface, for the stony ground did not permit the digging of the normal gun pits. The Troop Leader advised me that RHQ was stationed a quarter of a mile forward if I wanted to report and it would be sensible to spread out as much as possible. Apparently, there had been a couple of German air raids already that morning and the bombs exploded on the stony surface giving rise to unpleasant horizontal showers of rock splinters.

I passed this warning on to Pratt, when he came to report that all the Workshop had reached this spot, and motored off to look for RHQ, where I reported to Lt Col Jones. He told me that the latest news was that 7 Armd Div had forced the Tarhuna Gap during the night and the enemy was now apparently fighting a dogged rearguard action to cover its retreat towards Tripoli and was being harassed on its left flank by forward echelons of 51 Div coming up fast on the coast road. It sounded promising and I returned to the unit to issue instructions that they must be ready to move at fifteen minutes' notice.

The complete "B" Echelons of 7 Armd Div and the NZ Div all around us hung on to the stony forward face of the mountain ridge for the rest of the day, just awaiting orders for some move. These came suddenly (it was the night of 23/24 January my diary told me) and there ensued a frantic downhill scramble in the dark, following some sort of invisible track. We finished up on a wide plain in the lower foothills, where we leaguered for the rest of the night, all units very much mixed up with each other in the dark and thankfully brewing up cans of tea. It seemed that the New Zealanders on either side of us thought that some unexpected move by the Germans was taking place somewhere ahead, but our informants did not expect any further advance until daylight and they were stopping there until they could see where they were. We were completely out of touch with RHQ and had received no instructions from them since noon, so we did the same, brewed up and went to bed in our boots.

We were awakened at dawn by bugles sounding Reveille all round us, and the NZ transport companies to front and rear began hurriedly packing up for a move. Their officers told me that it was believed that the Germans were pulling out of Tripoli and heading back westwards along the road through Sabratha and Zuara in the direction of the Tunisian border; 7 Armd Div was believed to be in contact with them, but not in sufficient strength to interfere with their withdrawal. I was to learn later that advanced elements of 7 Armd Div collided with the main body of the Afrika Korps on the tracks out of Tripoli between Azizia and Zawia and were brushed aside in some confused fighting. 11 Hussars, the Reconnaissance Regt of 7 Armd Div, brushed past the German rear guard and, to their great satisfaction, entered the port before their rivals from the Highland Div arrived to claim the honour of having liberated Tripoli.

But to return to our own saga: after a couple of hours motoring over the stony tracks, we encountered a formidable natural obstacle; a stretch of pure soft sand, some two hundred yards wide, across our track. The NZ Companies in front of us had made very heavy weather of it with their 4-wheel-drive 3-ton Fords and Chevrolets and had reached what appeared to be a decent metalled road heading towards Tripoli, leaving the ploughed-up surface for us to deal with.

It was the worst sort of terrain that we could have wished to encounter so late in the campaign, with our overloaded lorries and the wretched Italian trailers that bogged down almost to the axles at once. I sent Pratt with the three vehicles of our recovery section, to the farther side of the sand bar, ready to use their winches and haul across anything that got stuck, which most of our vehicles promptly did.

Our slow progress through the sand vas obviously holding up the entire advance on Tripoli; the NZ Companies behind us were piling up as if behind a dam. There was no doubt about it; I must let them through. Signalling Pratt on the other side of the sand to let no more of our vehicles through, I stopped any more of them from starting to cross and waved the next NZ unit to bypass us.

As soon as it was realised that they had a clear run, we were almost inundated by the impatient mob. Taking a bit of a run at it, down the slope, they charged across like lemmings, trusting on momentum thus available to carry them to the far side. They made it amid clouds of churned-up sand into which each vehicle disappeared, and on reappearing was shepherded by the Divisional Military Police into tidy columns and "shooed" off up the road. They left behind a hollow track, scoured down almost to bedrock, between two walls of thrown-up sand, hard enough for most of our vehicles to get through without even a run at it, as soon as there was a lull in the flow. Only the stores lorry and the Italian trailers needed assistance from the recovery team.

By the time we were all on terra firma and formed up ready to proceed, further waves of NZ support troops came charging through. Some, I noticed, were driving straight across the road, heading north-westwards towards the sea, going hell-for-leather in the dust, while a lesser number stuck to the road and evidently were proceeding in the direction of Tripoli, some thirty miles away. This would seem to be the moment to forget our temporary attachment to the NZ Division. I recalled Col Jones's comment that 94th was intended for early defence of Tripoli port and that was where we should be going too. RHQ had been ahead of us in the columns and would by now have "peeled off" the NZ column and would be heading for Tripoli. Lacking any orders to the contrary, we should do the same.

It was now late in the afternoon, so we pulled off the road to check that all our transport was capable of making the rest of the journey after the rough treatment of the past week and to make

406

any adjustments necessary. This seemed the moment to give the lads a break, serve a hot meal and start betimes the following morning. For once, we could have a reasonable night's sleep.

And so it turned out. The remainder of our journey was almost ridiculously easy; just pleasant motoring in convoy along a good tarmac road, with the kilometre stones recording the steadily decreasing distance from Tripoli. I have little memory of the trip; there were few signs of the hasty German evacuation and we bowled along steadily amid increasing greenery, flanked by tall date palms at the roadside. Just on the edge of the city, we came to a Military Police reporting post. Our name was on their list and one of the Red-caps spoke on the phone to someone – we waited while an officer from RHQ arrived and guided us to a site on the outskirts which had been allocated to us for our workshop.

We breathed a sigh of relief. We had got there... The great trek that had started at Mareopolis, fifteen hundred miles away in Egypt, was over.

PART THREE

TRIPOLI AND AFTER

Onward Fifteen Army Group
Marching as to war.
With the AMGOT spearhead
Going on before.

We are not divided,
Fifty thousand strong
Fifty thousand brigadiers
Simply can't be wrong.
Onward into battle
Banishing our fears.
On to win the fight for freedom –
Freedom of Algiers.
Onward ... etc

Nearly out of caviare,
Of our greens bereft.
ENSA has departed.
EFI have left.
Tighten up your belts, lads.
Rough it with a smile.
While there's bumf, there's hope, lads,
So start another file.
Onward . . . etc

(ANON)
(Verses of Battle Hymn of
HQ First Army)

16

The site allotted to us for our workshop area was a bit of a culture shock. It brought home to me the difference between the conditions to which I had been accustomed as the OC of a mobile unit, over two years' service in the desert, and those necessary in a static workshop in port defence. We had now no say in where we would operate; it had been decided for us by Authority, based on some statistic, I suppose – our unit vehicle strength, possibly.

What we were given had been the showroom and some sort of distribution store room for motor vehicles, and consisted of a large, roofed warehouse with a fair-sized yard to the rear. At the front was a small two-roomed office area, which I earmarked for the officers' living and sleeping quarters, and I then set the unit to dig latrines in the furthest corner of the yard and clean the place up a bit. The yard itself was adequate to hold all our non-specialist vehicles, with some spare space for "work in progress". The machinery lorries could come into the main building, operating together as a group, and one end of the roofed space was taken up with a screened-off area for the other ranks' living quarters; the cookhouse trailer was outside in the yard. The senior NCOs preferred to erect a tent, which they had acquired from heaven knows where, in a secluded corner of the yard, giving them a measure of appropriate privacy.

I left Farbrother and the senior NCOs to get on with all this, before any work came in from the Btys, and took the opportunity to seek out RHQ and report. I found them ensconced in considerable comfort in the former palace of the Italian Governor of Tripoli, General Graziani, up on the bluff overlooking the eastern end of the harbour. The stained glass windows and marble flooring contrasted with the basic and unattractive accommodation that was my lot.

They hung on there for several weeks, until an Allied Military Governor arrived to run the port, one Brigadier Lush, who promptly took a fancy to the place and evicted them in order to use it as his own HQ. I cannot say that I was sorry at this turn of fate. It savoured of poetic justice.

Tripoli was situated on the southern side of a large harbour, protected from the vagaries of the Mediterranean winds by a long mole or breakwater. This extended from the western end of the harbour, where the old walled Arab (or Turkish) town lay, and ran parallel to the coastline, towards another breakwater, the Karamanli Mole, which projected towards it at right angles, leaving a narrow gap for entrance to the harbour. A broad, tree-lined esplanade, or *lungomare*, ran along the waterfront and disappeared at its western end into the old city, which was a warren of narrow alleys and out of bounds to the troops. Most of this became familiar to me during my stay in Tripoli and wasn't obvious in my first quick scan of the place.

My first task, on returning to the workshop was to ascertain how mobile we might be, should there be another swift move, and I was appalled by the damage sustained by a great deal of our transport and which cried out for immediate attention. I was in a conference with Phillips, Jakeman and Pratt when the flood of work started to come in from the Btys, and we had to allocate priorities and send some of them back to await their turn. As if that wasn't enough, before the end of the day, some junior staff captain from the QMG department of Rear HQ Eighth Army breezed in and gave orders for my workshop to take part in a massive manufacturing exercise, making towing bars to enable the Army to evacuate all its BLR vehicles in the RVPs that were still towable back to some Advanced Base Wksp at Bengasi (nearly 700 miles away).

He explained it to me: all that was required was two lengths of half-inch diameter steel rod bent to form eyes and welded at either end of a six-foot length of I-section girder. Hundreds of such solid tow-bars were needed and every one of the workshops now in Tripoli was press-ganged to manufacture them. The scheme apparently was to make up trains of six, ten, or twenty vehicles in series, each with its steering locked, to be towed by a Matador, or similar heavy vehicle all the way down from Tripoli to the Adv Base Wksp, wherever it was. Since the main coast road was pretty straight and without significant adverse gradients, at least as far as Bengasi, 700 miles away, it sounded as though the scheme ought to work. Oncoming columns, I was told, needed to take cover from the whiplash of each wavering "snake" of driverless, towed vehicles careering down at a high speed.

We had to scrounge the necessary materials ourselves to do the job and after a bit of searching we found vast quantities of the lightweight rails in the stores of the disused Tripoli–Solluch Railway. We hadn't any welding gas to waste on such a massive task, so we were forced to use the generator on our 15cwt truck on hand control, because the governor wasn't capable of coping with the sudden heavy currents. ASM Jakeman found out the drill necessary by experiment but, instead of passing this simple task on to one of his subordinates, he remained sitting over the throttle of the gen-set for the next couple of days, instead of dealing with his normal work, which annoyed me more than somewhat. As a WO I, I felt he ought to have known better.

Meanwhile, Phillips, assisted by Pratt, was obliged to cope with all the incoming MT repairs of the Btys as well as our own transport. Somehow, we managed to make inroads into the latter and our output of tow-bars for the Army was a bit better than nominal. I had a bit of a tussle with the young Staff Captain, who complained about our poor performance, and it was necessary to point out that his work wasn't the only thing we had on our plate and we were doing the best for him that we could. He retired hurt, murmuring threats about telling his DAQMG, but I never heard anything further about it.

On 3 February 1943, Tripoli was visited by the British Prime Minister, Winston Churchill, and everybody had the day off to line the streets and cheer. Nominally, his visit was to congratulate and review the Eighth Army, but, although he made a speech to that effect, the review turned out to be only of the 51

413

(Highland) Division, which was quartered in the city. I must admit they put on a most impressive show of swinging kilts and pipe-clayed spats; half the troops and all the pipe bands were in their kilts, which must have been hastily transported in bulk from the Delta, if they hadn't been carried in their regimental vehicles all through the advance. I think Churchill might have been (wrongly) advised that the capture of Tripoli had been solely a Scottish affair; the New Zealanders and 7 Armd Div, who were in contact with the enemy and living rough under canvas in the olive groves outside the city, were mildly scathing at the honour "usurped" by the "Highway Decorators". Anyhow, the Great Man held another review on the following day of these other formations, before leaving by air for a conference elsewhere, in Morocco, I think.

One day, soon afterwards, the Army Commander took it into his head to make a visit to the REME workshops in Tripoli. He had expressed a wish to meet the OCs of the AA Wksps and was taken to the site occupied by 9 HAA Regt Wksps, a unit recently arrived by road from Bengasi and in pristine condition in men, vehicles and equipment. The other Officers Commanding Workshops were lined up to meet the Great Man and were introduced by the Bde EME. He shook hands with us and said a few words to each. I recall him as a little man with sharp features and very blue eyes. On hearing my name, he said it was a familiar one and wanted to know whether I came from Northern Ireland. He congratulated us on the work we were doing to keep the guns in action. Then we dispersed to our (less spick-and-span) units and got on with our proper work.

We in 94th had the (unofficial) task of straightening out damaged jeeps belonging to my old friends 261 Bty. Their new OC, Major the Honorable Douglas Watson, son and heir to some lord, was a popular officer and a good friend of mine, but quite mad. His lads had discovered a wooden oval banked cycle-racing track on the outstirts of Tripoli and "Horrible Doug", as he was popularly known to his gunners, swiftly spotted the possibility of using the banked circuit as a "testing" ground for jeeps. Two abreast could run at any one time and "testing"

414

rapidly degenerated into jeep racing – the "straightening" to which I have referred became increasingly necessary. Eventually, this came to the ears of Authority, much to Doug's disgust, and the sport was banned.

Two items stick out in my memory, while in Tripoli. The first was a comment by Col Gerald Taylor, the ADME of 7 Armd Div, whom I met when visiting another unit with Phillips. Taylor had just returned from a (literally) flying visit to his opposite number in First Army HQ at Algiers. His reception had been a bit of shaker, he said.

'All the troops at HQ were in beautifully laundered and pressed battledress, with green-blancoed webbing. And,' his voice dropped to a horrified whisper, *'everyone was wearing his gas mask, at the ready, on his chest!'* No one had had a gas mask in the Eighth Army as far as I could remember, although the canvas case was a useful receptacle for rations or shaving kit.

The other item I remember was the discovery of the motor-racing circuit at Mellaha, to the south-east of Tripoli and, naturally, I decided to drive round it in my Humber car. Mellaha had last been used for the Tripoli Grand Prix in 1940, I think, and was still properly surfaced with the warning signs of corners and the pits and grandstands still in position; all very shabby and disused-looking. The Humber wasn't very well suited as a racing car, but I got it up to speed and was travelling at nearly 65mph on its fat tyres when a string of camels elected to stroll across my path. Somehow, I managed to drift round them on the sandy tarmac surface, but it shortened my life. I drove home in a chastened spirit and contented myself with workshop administration from then on.

As soon as the Army had found its way about in Tripoli, steps were taken to reopen the defunct brewery in the city so as to produce the drink to which they were accustomed for the thirsty soldiery. The latter had already discovered another source of alcoholic refreshment available in these early days. Large quantities of a local dark-red wine similar to Chianti were found in vast tanks and this was broached and quaffed by the simple soldiery by the pint as though it was the same strength as beer, which it certainly wasn't. This wine – locally christened "plonk" – was rough and pretty strong, and had disastrous effects. As a result, regimental orderly rooms were clogged with unsophisticated and sore-headed ORs, scooped up from their alcoholic slumbers in the gutters by the Military Police, on charges of "drunk and disorderly".

Not long after this, I left 94 Wksps. A posting order "with immediate effect" arrived on my desk, cross transferring me to command 51 HAA Wksp, which had recently turned up in Tripoli, and the OC of 51 to take over 94. I pondered what I should do, for I didn't want to leave 94. Had Estlin still been with us, I would have tried to have the order reversed, but I felt I was not *persona grata* with Walker. It occurred to me that this wouldn't have done any good anyway. I had been in the Western Desert, unrelieved, for nearly two years, so perhaps someone at GHQ in his wisdom had looked at my records, and had decided that it was time to move me into something static, before I became "sand-happy".

Now that defence of the port of Tripoli was being taken over by another Brigade up from Bengasi, the opportunity was there. Whatever the reason, I would have to grin and bear it. Anyhow, Phyl would be pleased. She had never been happy about my being, like Uriah the Hittite, "in the forefront of the battle". The OC of 51 HAA Wksp – I forget his name – was a stocky, no-nonsense character of about the same seniority as myself. He and I conferred about our respective personnel before he moved over and I gave him a good report of my erstwhile command.

51st had come up the coast road from Bengasi and their transport was much less battered and war-weary than 94th's – the OC said he would have to do something about the latter's roadworthiness. He reckoned his Humber car was in much better condition than mine, so we organised a swap. I called a muster of 94th to bid them goodbye and to introduce the new OC, and transferred my kit to the commandeered top-storey flat that he had been occupying as a mess. His two junior officers were Lts Mahoney and White. Mahoney was an AEME, a commissioned ex-WO I, and White, the Radio Repair Officer,

416

was another graduate press-ganged straight out of university in the same manner as Farbrother, but he was quieter and more studious. I thought we could all get along together; they both seemed competent types. Mahoney, in particular, was knowledgeable about the Army's ways and his experience would be valuable to me.

Their WO I was, of course, none other than ASM Spooner, formerly of 2 LAA Wksps and 12 AA Bde HQ under Estlin who had escaped from the shadow of Major Walker some months ago. He greeted me enthusiastically as an old friend. I would have no trouble with him. He introduced me to all members of the Sgts' Mess and I think he must have spread it around with the ORs that I was a reasonable chap to work with and had the experience of two mobile campaigns under my belt, for the lads accepted me without looking back on their old OC with regret.

My new unit was also busily engaged in manufacturing the tow-bars, but since their other commitments were minimal, they were getting on with it like the proverbial house on fire under Spooner's excellent organisation.

94th moved on and the balance of the port AA defences came up from the Bengasi area. 12 AA Bde also moved on and were replaced by the AA Bde that had the duty of defending the forward ports of supply. Tripoli now housed, in addition to 51st Heavy, 9th Heavy and two LAA regts, with their Workshops. I was visited by the Bde EME of the new Bde, whom I found to be a Major Cowper. Tony Cowper had been a fellow student in the 2nd AA OME's course in Stoke-on-Trent and Bury in the summer of 1940 and we were both glad to see one another. Tony had spent the intervening years in the ME in the Delta and thus had been available for promotion in the manner that Walker had got his Crown.

Tripoli had had a quiet time since its abandonment by the Germans and there was considerable pressure to improve its coastal defences, both against a sea invasion and against aerial attack. Tony got raked into these preparations by the DDME, Eighth Army, and sought my assistance in finding more artillery of both sorts.

My first job was to survey what the Italian maps showed as a coastal defence battery on a tiny island to the west of the old town. Cowper decided to accompany me on this occasion and we set out to find a rowing boat to get to the place. As it happened, there were several suitable boats on the shore opposite, but when approached, their Italian owners just shrugged their shoulders when we asked where the oars were. The *Tedeschi* (Germans) had pinched them all before retreating from Tripoli. Tony was inclined to believe them and was considering approaching the Navy for help, but I routed out a team of willing thugs from the Workshop as rowers and we manufactured ad hoc oars from handspikes then and there on the beach, which just fitted the rowlocks, and took to the water. I was one of the rowers and Cowper, who had been in his school rowing eight and knew something about it, took the tiller and told us what to do. The unskilled team propelled the selected boat swiftly across the intervening couple of hundred yards and Cowper was landed dryshod for his inspection. The battery's guns, as far as I remember, were undamaged and in proper firing order and as a result of that afternoon's work, four guns of about six-inch calibre were handed over to the Navy, to stiffen their port defence.

Next, we heard that there was a 90mm Italian HALA (high angle/low angle) gun mounted on a giant lorry chassis somewhere in the Army RVP, and Spooner and I went to inspect it. I had some difficulty in gaining entry – RVPs were notoriously difficult with visitors, whom they assumed just wanted to cannibalise some truck for spares, but I was allowed to inspect the gun and found it apparently complete, while Spooner examined the vehicle, a big Lancia of the type that the Poles had had in Tobruk and which Dean had managed to start.

This gave us the idea. Spooner got talking to the NCO who was accompanying us (just to see we didn't pinch anything), and told him the gun was needed to stiffen up the AA defences of the port. We finally bet him that, if we could start the engine and could drive the gun away, we could have it. The NCO took up the wager, thinking that he was on to a good thing, and was greatly surprised when, after priming the diesel pump, Spooner and I set to to wind up the massive flywheel and engage the clutch. The engine fired and we drove the monstrosity out of the RVP, in triumph.

I reported this to Cowper and he decided that it couldn't be handed over to the RA until it had been tested, so we motored it to a flat stretch of land overlooking the sea. I believe it was the playing field of the Tripoli Girls' High School. He rustled up some gunners and got permission to fire up to ten rounds out to sea. The gunners were a trifle chary of this unknown weapon and were most careful to supervise the positioning of the massive legs which supported the chassis, to make sure the vehicle didn't move on recoil. They then had a wonderful time destroying a rock that stood up from the sea about 1000 yards out. I don't know what happened to this weapon, but Cowper submitted a report and the Army RVPs were scoured for similar models.

The Germans were now awake to the news that we were opening up Tripoli as a major supply port for the Army and we had an increasing number of air raids to contend with. It was decided that, although two HAA Regts seemed about enough to deal with them, the deficiency of LAA weapons was crucial and the place had to be combed for ex-enemy AA guns to make up the required strength. The city's stores and dumps were examined with a fine-toothed comb, before Spooner's gang unearthed a number of abandoned Italian 37mm AA guns which had been rendered useless before being left, by the simple method of firing a round with another round reversed in the end of the barrel. This had the result of blowing the barrel to pieces, while leaving the mounting undamaged. We looked everywhere for replacement barrel assemblies but without success, until one of Spooner's search teams broke into the Tripoli Naval Museum and found there a number of, not 37mm pieces, but the equivalent version of the 20mm weapon. No 20mm mountings, however.

Spooner had the whole lot brought back to the workshop and, after a lot of measurement and head scratching, we found that the 20mms could be modified to fit on the slides of the larger 37mm units. The snag was that the balancing springs for the 37mm piece were much too powerful for the little 20mm replacements and, without the counterweight of the 37mm barrel, our composite gun was horribly breech-heavy and unusable. Spooner pointed out that we needed some extra weight at the muzzle end to compensate for the loss of the heavier barrel, and dug up – I think from the railway yards – several massive round-headed bolts, some two inches in dia-meter and six feet long. When their threaded ends were inserted into some holes in the mounting and secured by locknuts, the balance was quite reasonable, although the appearance of the tiny 20mm barrel sticking out between the two giant bolts looked like the proboscis of an insect between two knobbly-headed antennae. We showed it to the Bde IG and the OC of one of the LAA Btys and they were delighted with its manoeuv-rability, but reckoned that the big bolt heads of the antennae were dangerously close together, just beyond the end of the barrel. In fact, the gap was only 25mm. Italian 20mm ammuni-tion was notoriously unreliable and, it was pointed out, if the already live round were to touch the bolt head, it would explode just in front of the gun-layer's face. They thanked us for our efforts but turned the modification down on that account only. So, back to the drawing board.

It was our blacksmith who suggested a solution. He believed that with a large enough fire, he could bend these massive bolts apart and we tried it. The gun now looked even more like an insect, but the gap between the two bolt heads was now over a foot and the balance, when corrected by altering the bolt length, by slacking off the locking nuts and re-locking them when it was just right, was all that a gunner could wish. The IG now passed our hybrid for use by the RA and we constructed a total of twelve, the number being limited by the number of 20mm pieces we had found.

Six of these were sited at the base of the Karamanli Mole and six under the wall of the old town at the other end of the harbour, and the gun crews laid out lines of fire so as to cover the entire harbour, without shooting at each other. The odd appearance of the new weapons excited much speculation among the uninitiated troops, so we spread the rumour around for the benefit of any German spies that they were the Army's new secret weapon. The "horns" on either side of the barrel were there to activate a magnetic fuse as the round left the barrel and thus home in on the metal of the target aircraft. It was a good story and I was told that this explanation got into print in *Parade*, the Forces' local picture magazine, but I never saw the article.

A couple of days after our guns were commissioned, the enemy mounted a really massive air raid, hitting several ships in the harbour. We went out on to the roof of our officers' quarters, from which we could see the skeins of tiny shot from our new toys converging on the low-flying aircraft. One of these, coming in low to the attack, passed just over our heads as we stood on the roof and we decided it would be safer to go down to the *lungomare* and observe our little guns at closer quarters.

Mahoney, White and I piled into my Humber and I drove down to the gun-site by the Karamanli Mole. In a lull in the raid, the gunners told us they were charmed with their new toys, which behaved just as they were supposed to do. I then headed off down the *lungomare* towards the other half-battery under the walls of the old town.

I was halfway along, when a burning ship alongside the mole at the far side of the harbour and just opposite us, blew up before our very eyes. I was told afterwards that it was carrying a large quantity of ammunition. I had the driver's side window open and, out of the corner of my eye, I had a ringside view of what occurred. My memory is quite clear; I had somehow assumed that an explosion of this nature would be instantaneous, but it all seemed to happen in a sort of slow motion, like those clever nature films of flowers opening. It must have gone on for several seconds, for, during the worst of it, the car travelled fifty yards along the harbour frontage. First, a brilliant star of white light appeared amidships, then it turned to a deep red and expanded with dramatic slowness into a surging column of pulsating crimson flame, which rose in a leisurely manner, unfurling itself in the darkened sky in a sort of glowing mushroom of billowing, red-tinted smoke, which lit up the entire harbour. The ship just seemed to vanish in a welter of foam and fire, and large chunks of it began to rain down from

421

the sky into the harbour, kicking up enormous spouts of water. Then a massive wave washed over the *lungomare*, just in front of us.

The odd thing about it all was that I was never aware of any sound, notwithstanding my open window, nor do I remember feeling any pulse of air pressure after the explosion, but the trees further along the harbour front seemed to bend over as if hit by a mighty gale, shedding leaves and branches.

When we skidded to rest by the other half-battery of 20mms by the old town wall, the gunners were much shaken and told us to get the hell out of their lines of fire. We motored back to the workshop over leaves and small branches torn from the trees, to find the workshop's massive gates had been blown from their hinges and were lying flat on the ground in the gateway.

Spooner had started some men clearing up and he came out to greet us, asking where we had been. When I told him we had been right on the *lungomare* when the ship went up, he just looked at me oddly and said, 'You were very lucky, Sir.'

In retrospect, I think he was right. I don't know about lucky, but certainly I had been very foolish...

17

While all this was going on, the battle was getting further and further away from us. The Eighth Army was penetrating into Tunisia, with fighting at Medenine, the Mareth Line and the Wadi Akarit in the Gabes Gap between the sea and the salt lake of the Shott el Fejaj. We heard of these actions. but one must consult the history books for details. I wasn't involved.

The First Army and the US Fifth Army were making heavy weather of their advance across the Algerian mountains towards Tunisia and it began to look as though the Eighth Army might reach Tunis before the First; the situation that had resulted in the capture of Tripoli seemed about to be repeated.

One thing that sticks in my mind about this advance was the report of an American thrust to the south in an attempt to encircle the retreating enemy in Tunisia. This got as far as Kasserine and Gafsa, inland from Sfax, where they came, as innocent lambs to the slaughter, up against a battle-hardened Panzer Div and were badly mauled. The Eighth Army was obliged to detach a force to retrieve the situation and get them out of their self-imposed hole. The expressed opinion in Tripoli was that the GIs must think that superior firepower was everything, and that they would only learn by hard experience that some knowledge of warfare against a battle-hardened enemy was necessary.

The port of Sfax was captured on 15 April 1943 and it was decided that it must be used as the Eighth Army's forward supply base for the final assault on Tunis; the Germans were retreating rapidly northwards through Sousse to their next defensive line in the mountains at Enfidaville, covering Tunis and Bizerta. 51 HAA Regt was ordered to proceed at once to protect the port of Sfax against aerial attack, and we went mobile again.

Sfax was 305 miles into Tunisia from Tripoli and it took us two days steady motoring up the road to get there. I was pleasantly surprised to find that my new unit was much more businesslike in its approach to packing up and moving. The move took us a bit over two days, with the first night's stop at Wadi Senem, just short of the Tunisian frontier and the second outside Gabes. We reached Sfax about midday on the third day, after passing the battlefields of Medenine and the Mareth Line and the Wadi Akarit in the Gabes Gap. A surprise to me was at El Djem, where we passed a magnificent ruined Roman amphitheatre, about which I had never so far heard, and which appeared to contain a whole village of the local Berbers. I would have liked to stop and view this antiquity at close quarters, but our programme dictated otherwise and we pressed on. Gabes itself, which hadn't been defended by the enemy, seemed to be little damaged by any fighting. At Sfax, by contrast, the town had been flattened by the US Air Force when the port was still in enemy hands. I was told later that their target had been the actual port installations, which were only a couple of hundred yards away, and, although the Americans were stated to have been satisfied that all had been "taken out" by their high-level "precision bombing", this was (according to local Eighth Army sources, who were a bit biased by the recent debâcle at Kasserine) just another American balls-up. I believe the damage was minimal and the port could be taken into use immediately.

RHQ suggested that suitable accommodation could be found for the Workshops at a former French Army barracks, an abandoned set of buildings rather like concrete Nissen huts, which were cool in the summer heat. One of these had been extensively decorated internally by a nameless but skilful artist, who had painted some lewd and highly erotic frescos on them. By common consent, this hut was placed out of bounds and its doorway boarded up.

While we were in Sfax, I received a letter from Phyl, who had heard of my posting to 51 HAA Wksps and had wrongly assumed that, since 51 was engaged on port defence, I had now finished my "wanderings" and had become stationary in Tripoli. She had, therefore, and without consulting me, applied for a transfer to No 48 General Hospital, now stationed in the port. She had recently arrived there, only to find that I, to her great chagrin, had already gone up towards the "Front" again and was "somewhere in Tunisia".

Sad, but anyhow she was now nearer than the Delta and, when some Regimental requirement called for someone to travel back to Tripoli I volunteered for the job. I reached Tripoli (305 miles) in a single day, taking turns at the wheel with my batman-driver and dropped in at No 48 as soon as my official business was over. Phyl was greatly astonished to see me; it was the first time we had met since that snatched hour in Alexandria, when I was at Mareopolis and the Axis forces were at the city gates.

Alas, we had only half a day and, since I had to return to Sfax the next morning, we decided that this chasing one another around the Middle East wasn't any good. Moreover, it wasn't doing either of our morales any good, so we mutually agreed that we ought to initiate the procedures for marriage forthwith, while we were together for once. Accordingly, Phyl sought interviews with her Matron and Colonel, to introduce me and allow them to question me as to our (or more correctly my) intentions. We had, anyhow, agreed not to try to start a family until the war was over. All went well and I was approved; we could get married as soon as the paperwork was through and, of course, whenever the exigencies of the Service permitted. I think we had innocently assumed that the ceremony would take place in Tripoli, and the necessary paperwork was initiated before I left for Sfax.

But it wasn't as easy as all that. Not long after I was back with the unit, the war took another turn and we appeared to be about to move on to Sousse, some fifty or so miles nearer the front, under the shadow of the mountains where the enemy was about to make his final stand before Tunis at Enfidaville. After consulting RHQ, I motored on up the coastal road, to spy out the land and seek a suitable site for the Workshop.

It was a cold, grey and windswept afternoon on a dusty plain, brooded over by the Enfidaville range, and the afternoon was getting on as we turned to go back to Sfax. A lot of motor traffic was crawling out of the dust clouds across my front, coming up from somewhere to the west. As I watched them, it suddenly came home to me that the vehicles had a familiar look. It was 94 HAA Wksps, still with their couple of overloaded Italian trailers, grinding along in the dust and heading northwards to the battle front. I stood up in my Humber and waved; someone waved back, but they were too far off to determine whether they had really seen and recognised me.

That was the last I saw of the old crowd: dirty, battered and still slogging along in the dust. I watched until they were out of sight in the dust and the darkening late afternoon murk and then we drove back to Sfax.

51 HAA didn't move to Sousse, after all. The war in Africa was just fizzling out; there was some brisk fighting at Enfidaville, the Eighth Army broke through and their flank forces joined up with the British First Army and the Americans – now operating as 15 Army Group under General Eisenhower – and the remnants of the German–Italian force retreated into the Cape Bon peninsula. The first troops into Tunis, to our great delight, were the armoured cars of 7 Armd Div's recce regt, the 11th Hussars, from the Eighth Army, just beating those of the Derbyshire Yeomanry, their opposite numbers in the First Army, and the combined forces swept on to harass the demoralised and retreating enemy. There was no escape by sea and their commander made a point of seeking out and surrendering to Gen Montgomery, rather than to Gen Eisenhower.

It was all over. Africa had been cleared of the Axis forces and the talk was now of an invasion of Europe across the Mediterranean.

Talk was now of return to the Delta for re-equipping, ready for the invasion, and we packed up and hit the road for Tripoli. We were billeted outside the town, as we waited to be called forward by units, in case the enemy took it into his head to mount another air raid on the harbour, while we and our

426

transport were awaiting loading on to the ships. I had a couple of evenings, during which I managed to get into Tripoli and see Phyl; she too was far from happy about the ruin of our plans, but bore up philosophically. Our farewell on the second evening was a bit subdued; we were wondering when, where and indeed if, we would meet again until the war was over.

It so happened that all our transport was allocated to a ship that was loading with its own derricks and not any dockside crane. Spooner, who I deputed to liaise with the loading, stressed that the weights of our larger vehicles, which we had stuffed with stores to the limit, bore no relation to what the "book" weights for the type said. The ship's crew ignored him and promptly sought to lift the first of our machinery lorries with what they deemed in their innocence to be the proper derrick for the "book" weight. The lorry remained on the quay, attached to a bent derrick. This made us highly unpopular. I was called over the coals about the damage, but I confirmed that we had given them proper weights which they had ignored, and nothing more was said, although they took some note of what they were told from then on.

The Regt's personnel travelled in the hired transport *Yoma* and the trip to Alexandria took about four days, with a destroyer escort. On disembarkation, we were told, greatly to our disgust, to remove the much-prized Eighth Army flashes from our sleeves and from our vehicle plates, since there must be secrecy about our unit formation in case the enemy's spies got wind of the build-up of forces for the coming invasion. In the meantime, we would be GHQ MEF troops and our vehicle badge would be the derided white camel on a black ground, the mark of all the Delta "Chairborne Forces" that we had so despised. We were then crammed into waiting lorries and carted off to a staging camp at Amriya on the far side of Lake Mariout and, when reunited with our transport, we drove to a transit camp at Qassassin in the desert to the east of Cairo and on the road to Ismailia and the Canal. Here, under the lee of Base Ordnance Depots and the Base Workshops, we were set to re-equip.

We had a couple of weeks of hard work and then one night I

suffered a violent internal pain low down in my back and had to report sick. The Regt's MO bundled me off to No 6 Gen Hospital at Tahag, just round the corner, where I was kept in a day, for observation, and they diagnosed a stone in my kidney, possibly the result of short water rations over a long period. They wheeled me in to an operating theatre, stuffed a probe up into me to dislodge the cause of the trouble, after which I was downgraded medically from Category "A" to "B". Under Category "B" I would not be able to remain with 51 HAA Wksps, since the Regt was under notice to proceed on active service – believed widely to be the invasion of Italy or Sicily – and only Category "A" personnel were eligible for that. I would have to be moved to some more static workshop where such active service would be unlikely.

So, in a great hurry, I was cross-posted with my former colleague Captain Purcell, from whom I had taken over 94th under similar circumstances, when he was evacuated to the Delta a year before. He was now in command of 2 HAA Wksps, situated at Port Fouad, on the eastern bank of the Suez Canal, opposite to Port Said. This was the second time I had taken over a unit from him in some hurry, but this time it was I that was the victim. He, apparently, had fully recovered from his own medical problem and we commiserated and congratulated one another respectively. Purcell's two junior officers were both pretty experienced lieutenants; his 2 i/c was Harry Gray, but I cannot remember the name of the Radio Maintenance Officer. I said goodbye to 51, whom I had hardly had time to get to know properly, and I think the only one of them who was really sorry to see me go was Spooner. The rest took it on the chin as just one of those things.

About this time, the authority for my marriage came through. It took the form of a sort of Special Licence, valid within a particular period of time and specifying (on the assumption that it was to be in the Canal Zone) the English Church of the Holy Trinity in Port Said, in the "Parish" of Moascar, as the venue. A copy was evidently sent to Phyl, for I got a letter from her saying that she had put in for compassionate leave and would be arriving by the next hospital ship to depart from Tripoli. I started

428

making provisional arrangements; the Regimental Padre recommended a Services Club as the best place for the "wedding breakfast" and Harry Gray cheerfully agreed to act as my best man, as long as I didn't want to wear Khaki Drill Service Dress, which I had but he hadn't. It all seemed fixed at last.

Then malign fate took a hand. Unexpectedly, 2 HAA Regt also received orders to prepare for active service overseas, presumably the invasion of southern Europe. The wheels whirred round in GHQ ME and it was spotted that I was not eligible to go as the OC of 2 HAA Wksps on medical grounds. Somebody did some quick thinking and I was cross-posted to the equivalent Wksps of 93 HAA (City of Chester) Regt RA TA, with effect forthwith, in exchange for its OC, Captain A. Parkinson. 93rd had just arrived in the ME and were situated at Kubri, just outside Suez, where they were being equipped. And, even now, Phyl might already be on her hospital ship bound for Port Said or Alex, in the innocent belief that I was ready to marry her at Port Said!

Cursing my luck, I drove headlong down to Suez and reported to the CO of 93rd, where I explained my personal problem to him. He was a charming man, with whom I subsequently got on very well, and he heard me out sympathetically, saying something that has remained in my memory ever since: *'Marriage is an institution of which I wholeheartedly approve.'* And he continued, 'As soon as your fiancée arrives, take a week's leave and get the knot tied.'

While I was in Suez, Harry Gray telephoned me to announce that Phyl had turned up in Port Fouad that very afternoon and was devastated to find that I had been posted away yet again. She was now fixed up in a hotel in Port Said, awaiting developments. I asked Harry to make my peace with her and tell her that the wedding was still definitely on, as planned, and not to worry; I was coming back to Port Fouad at once. So, after a few words with a slightly bewildered Parkinson, I drove the hundred-odd miles back up the Canal in record time, crossed over to Port Said by the ferry and turned up at Phyl's hotel.

She was not quite certain whether to laugh or cry, but things were soon smoothed over and we had dinner together. She announced that she needed to do some shopping in the town, since she had "nothing suitable to wear" and could I arrange the ceremony for the next day but one, July 26, if I could be trusted still to be there in two days' time. I left her to it and returned to Port Fouad, to find Harry Gray entertaining Parkinson, who meanwhile had come up to take over his new command and was a trifle put out to find that I was not there to receive him. I gathered that his views were that, if this was the way they worked in the Middle East, it must be a rum place. He mellowed later and entered into the spirit of the occasion.

The Great Day dawned. All participants: myself; the best man (Harry Gray); the Regimental Padre (who had hoped to conduct the service, before the Chaplain General, MEF, appointed his own nominee, and was mollified on being invited by me to give the bride away instead); and the Lt Radio Maintenance (who didn't intend to be left out), all dressed ourselves in well ironed bush jackets and slacks, caught the ferry over to Port Said and met the officiating Padre at the door of the church. In due course, Phyl arrived, supported by none other than Megan Lloyd Hughes, still in her white uniform, who had turned up at the last minute from Syria or somewhere especially to act as an unexpected but very welcome bridesmaid, greatly to Phyl's relief and delight, and a couple of the ladies from the Services Club to which we were going to repair afterwards. I am ashamed to say that I can remember nothing of the service and surfaced only when we arrived afterwards at the Services Club, with my newly acquired wife on my arm. She admitted later that she didn't remember much of what went on either.

At the reception we all made speeches. I did; Harry did; the "bride's father" did; the officiating Padre did (he commented that it was nice to be able to keep his hand in – weddings were few and far between in his all-male flock). Then we all kissed the bride and her bridesmaid and, after I had surreptitiously paid for my own wedding breakfast – the "bride's father" declining to be financially involved – we were packed into someone's jeep and put on the train to Cairo, amid much cheering and, greatly to our annoyance and embarrassment, the public throwing of confetti over us on the platform.

430

Cairo had three railway stations. We arrived at Cairo East, the terminus for the line to Suez and took a taxi to Shepheard's Hotel – this was the old hotel, later to be burnt down in the riots – where we signed our names. I remember Phyl started to write "Ball", but crossed it out, to the amusement of the reception clerk who, with a knowing leer, had us conducted to a splendid suite of rooms. It must have been the honeymoon suite. Were we as obvious as all that?

I had only one week's leave, but Phyl had two. We spent most of my week just sitting in the shade on the raised terrace overlooking the street, consuming iced drinks and watching the world go by.

When we had to go back to the Canal, I fixed Phyl up in a reasonable hotel in downtown Suez and got a sleeping-out pass from the CO, so that we were able to enjoy a further week together. She said that my return "home" after a nine to six shift at work, made her feel properly married at last. Then it was all over; she had to report back to some hospital in Cairo for onward return to Tripoli. But, against all the buffets of Fate, we had done it! We could face the future with equanimity from now on.

18

After seeing Phyl off on her journey back to Tripoli, I returned to my Workshop and got down to some pleasurable planning to bring it up to the state of efficiency that I wished it to have.

First, I met my two junior Officers, who were fresh out from the UK: Lt Ron Harris, my 2 i/c, and Lt Reg Holdsworth, the Radio Maintenance Officer. Both were keen to learn from one who had been through the Desert Campaigns in 1941/2 and 42/3. They were good lads. Harris took me to meet the senior NCOs and I was content with their bearing and potential capabilities. To my surprise, one of them, Sgt Axcell, had been an apprentice with me at English Electric in 1938 and we had been in the same digs.

Next, I called a muster of the entire workshop and gave them a short pep talk, to which they listened attentively, stressing the importance of mobility. This had been proved essential, both in the Western Desert Force and, later, in the Eighth Army. It was the goal that I would aim at and encourage them to attain. I recall, now, that I was wearing my ribbon of the newly-issued Africa Star on my shirt, to which I had sewn a figure 8, carved by my own hands from a piece of scrap silver, and this added to the importance of my words.

In answer to my 'Any questions?' someone piped up and asked whether it was proper for the workshops to take part in the Regt's guard rosters, like personnel from the Btys. Surely REME had more useful work than gunners, who had nothing to do, he implied. I replied that this was something I was not aware of and would investigate. Apparently Parkinson hadn't raised any objection, and it had become something that RHQ had taken

432

for granted. I gently took it up with the Adjutant, who admitted he had no backing for the practice, so I explained that maybe this had been customary in the UK, but it wasn't the practice in the ME. It could mean that, when we went operational, some of my most needed tradesmen could be off workshop duty for part of the following day, when their particular skills might be urgently wanted for repairs to the Regt's equipment. He had a word with the Colonel and the order was rescinded. My stock went up immediately as soon as this was known.

The unit's ASM seemed a keen type and a good disciplinarian, and, unlike ASM Jakeman, he had reached his present rank through merit, although not a regular soldier. He was keen to keep the unit at "top readiness".

Next, Harris took me on a quick round of the Btys and introduced me to the Bty Commanders. We had a short discussion with each on the problems they were likely to encounter when in a mobile role in the ME. I asked them whether their newly-issued 3.7s had the Macpherson struts fitted. None of the ones that I saw had and the BCs hadn't heard of them. They were still working through the sheets and sheets of modifications that were issued with their new guns and had not yet come to these. I stressed the value of the struts, and suggested that I take the Quartermaster to Abbassia, to talk with Major Macpherson, where he could see what they looked like and could put in indents for them. My workshop could fit them, when they arrived.

We went to Abbassia in Parkinson's Dodge 8cwt and I realised at once what I had been unaware of in Little Audrey. We were virtually shaken to bits and we decided that Harris should do a round of the Bty Captains, and obtain a list of all the vehicle types in the Regt, so that the Wksps could get ready a stock of spare springs and lengths of the necessary spring steel to make new leaves.

One of our first priorities was to stiffen up the springs of our two Dodge 8cwts, so that they were less battering on the posterior. 93rd had a good blacksmith and he joined enthusiastically in this work, now that there was no guard duty. We also had a little Ford 8cwt, in lieu of a motorcycle, and we rebuilt its springs too. It was a nice, clean little vehicle and I appropriated it for my own use, fitting a folding bed transversely across the front end of the body, and added a 12 volt reading lamp and fold-up desk, so that I could sleep and work in it, if necessary. In fact, I actually did sleep in it for a couple of nights, just to test its suitability, to the great interest of the lads, who heard about it and approved.

We had nearly a full scale of our War Establishment's hand tools and equipment, so I set the two Lieutenants and the ASM to work out an agreed loading schedule for each of our vehicles and detail the crews to each. One thing more was needed; like all the other units in 93rd, we were using a tent for our office. I had a fundamental dislike for tents; they took time to erect and dismantle and that wasted valuable minutes. I discussed their needs with my Sgt Clerk and his fellows and we set our carpenter and welder to fit out one of our 30cwt vehicles with fixed wooden desk surfaces and filing cabinets. I think, doubtless with my example before them, the clerical party also worked in a couple of collapsible beds for themselves.

All this took about a month, and when all was presentable, I suggested to the Colonel that he might like to come and inspect the Workshop. He did so and expressed much interest in what we had done; he commented to me afterwards that things seemed to be satisfactory after my efforts to this end.

By August, the fitting out of the Regt was complete and we were ordered up to Alexandria as port defence. In the Big War, we heard that the Eighth Army had taken part in the successful invasion of Sicily and were now poised to cross over into the Italian mainland.

So once again I led a convoy up the Desert Road from Cairo. Alex was much emptier of troops than heretofore; we had accommodation in some sort of barracks, where we could spread ourselves and use a large yard for our Workshop. The war seemed very far away. The lads, however, were becoming very conscious of their merit, as a result, I hoped, of my "applied psychology" and were standing tall and in danger of needing bigger hats. We now had our own unit canteen, a football team and a hockey team, in which last I played several

434

games. In fact, they walked with a swagger and, when someone suggested that a unit photograph would attract considerable support, I engaged a local photographer. Shots were taken of the assembled complete unit and another of the Officers and NCOs.

One morning in early September, I had a message from Reg Holdsworth, who was inspecting one of his radar sets at a bay to the west of the Port; he said that something was happening that he thought I would be interested in seeing. Intrigued, I drove out and joined him on a bluff looking down at the sea. The bay was filled with grey warships of all sizes, and more were coming in as we watched. It took me some minutes, before I realised, with a bit of a shock, that that were all flying the Italian flag. We had heard the previous day that Mussolini had been overthrown and that Italy had surrendered to the Allies. This must be the whole Italian Fleet that had refused to surrender and, rather than be seized by the Germans, was seeking asylum in Alexandria. Something really big was happening in the war!

All this made me think that 93rd might soon be going on active service and I immediately sought another Medical Examination to get myself regraded, if possible, back to Category "A". I would then be able to remain with my new command that I had done so much to inspire with enthusiasm. The Colonel and the Regt's MO backed me in my appeal against the previous medical decision. As a result, I went before a Medical Board in Alexandria, which, after studying my documents in detail, decided to put me back into Category A (fit for General Service), much to my satisfaction. Their findings were sent back to Medical and REME Records in Cairo and I believed that I was now in the clear.

While near the bright lights of the City, I visited a high-class ladies' lingerie shop and purchased a set of petticoat and matching pants for Phyl. I was unable to tell the "Madam" in charge, in my schoolboy French exactly the size I wanted, so she cheerfully lined up half a dozen girls of differing sizes from her staff and, amid much giggling, I chose the one nearest to Phyl's size. My stock went up in Tripoli when the parcel arrived and Phyl wanted to know how I had managed to remember her measurements so accurately.

435

She told me in a letter that her ward had been visited by the King (George VI) and he had spoken to her. He had stopped at the bed by which she had been standing as the Royal procession came through, accompanied by the Matron, the Colonel, and various other red-tabbed worthies. Noticing the heavily-bandaged character in her bed, His Majesty asked what his injuries were, but before she could reply, the Colonel chipped in firmly: 'Battle Casualty, Sir!' and she was saved the embarrassment of answering. Actually the man had fallen off his motorcycle! The incident appeared in the British Movietone News account of the visit, which was seen in Folkestone by Phyl's parents. They went to the cinema manager afterwards and he had a couple of the appropriate frames cut out and given to them. I still have this record of *The King and I*.

In early September, my family gave me the name of the LAA Bty in which my cousin Garth was serving, known to be in the ME. I found out where they were, called in on the Bty Commander and told him I would welcome a few words with my cousin. L/Bdr Montgomery, G.R.G. was found with a gang, peeling potatoes behind the cookhouse and we had ten minutes of family chatter. He had no time for the war and had no wish for any sort of promotion. Two of his close friends were now Sgts, but he was quite happy as he was.

There was now great activity around the Eastern Mediterranean with landings on the Aegean islands of Cos and Leros, and in October, 93rd was withdrawn from Alexandria and sent to a transit camp at El Shatt opposite Suez at the southern end of the Canal. Here, I was foolish enough to report a small "tummy upset" to our MO and he misguidedly sent me off to the local Hospital, where I was X-rayed front, back and sideways in an attempt to convince the medics that I had a recurrence of my previous renal calculus. I was discharged with the statement that the X-rays had just possibly detected something that might just conceivably have been a minuscule stone, and they would call me back in about three weeks for a further check. However, I could return to duty in my present Medical Category. I realised afterwards, from the wording, that they believed I was still in Category B and had not received the result of my regrading by the Alexandria Medical Board some weeks earlier.

However, in the Big War, something was obviously starting up and we were awaiting a very hush-hush move up through Palestine into Syria; the operation had the code-name "Pugilist" but that was all we were allowed to know.

Just as this was about to happen, I received two conflicting orders from different departments in GHQ, one saying that I should move with 93rd (someone had obviously noted my medical history) and another, by the same "post", from the Hospital authorities, instructing me to report there forthwith "for further tests". I showed them to my Colonel and he told me to disregard the second one and stay with the unit. He sent a signal to GHQ with his decision.

Early in November 1943, the Regt moved out of El Shatt and bumped along over appalling tracks on the eastern side of the Canal, going north. By dark, we were somewhere on the far edge of the Sinai desert and struck a road going into Palestine. We stayed overnight at a place called Asluj on the southern border. After seeing the lads fed and settled down, I retired to my little truck and slept very well, content that I was on active service again.

On the following day, we learned that our destination was "probably" Aleppo (all very secret and hush-hush); our column moved into the hills of Palestine, finally encamping on the flat land below Nablus. We were under orders to conceal who and what we were and we covered our vehicles with camouflage netting. We lay all that day in the stony fields and at dusk began moving north through Palestine, passing the Sea of Galilee and climbing the winding road up out of Palestine and into Syria, where we stayed for the rest of the night, again under wraps, at a little Arab village called Merj Ayoun.

It wasn't until I got there that I found that Harris, who had been bringing up our rear with the Recovery Section, was missing. He turned up, dog-tired, just before dawn, having had to do recovery work on one of 93rd's guns that had overturned on a steep hairpin bend and had to be winched back on to the road. It was fortunate that we had a really heavy recovery lorry, this time, a Mack six-wheeler with a powerful jib and winch, for the gun was nearly upside down in a hollow. It had to be taken back down to Haifa and handed in at the Base Depot there, so that a replacement could be issued. After getting the gun back on to its wheels and seeing it start off safely down the hill with its Matador and crew, Harris returned to the fold and joined us. He had done a good job and it was recognised as such by the Colonel.

That day was spent under camouflage in Merj Ayoun, sleeping and carrying out our vehicle maintenance, before moving on again at dusk up the Bekaa valley between the Lebanon and Anti-Lebanon mountains. When we reached the main Beirut to Damascus road, we turned northwards and, in the starlight, I spotted pillars rising from the ruins of ancient Baalbek, about which I had read. Once again, I would dearly have liked to stop and view these famous ruins, had time and the exigencies of the service permitted, which they didn't.

The main road northwards led through Homs and Hama and I was getting very tired, not really having had much sleep since leaving Asluj, due to duties with the unit. My driver and I were taking turns at the wheel of my 8cwt and, while I was driving between Homs and the next village, my eyes almost out on stalks, I was convinced that I was overtaking a pair of elephants, ambling ahead. I have no idea whether they were there or whether it was my imagination, for they seemed to stroll off into the darkness on the verge, before I had to do anything about them. My driver was, anyhow, asleep in the passenger's seat, so I said nothing, but it had me perplexed for some time. Was it likely that elephants were loose, unattended, in Syria?

Somewhere on the approaches to Aleppo, someone flagged my column down in the dark, and I was called forward to a meeting with the Colonel, who had gone on ahead the day before. I found the RHQ cluster at the top of a hill, looking down on Aleppo. I remember the sight most vividly. The plain below was a mass of lights; shaded street lamps of the modern city in the foreground and, beyond that, the entire plain was covered with little twinkling lights, presumably from small domestic lamps. In the middle of the latter was a great black hole, where there was complete absence of light of any sort. I found later that that marked the position of the mighty citadel which dominated the city on its rock, reminiscent of Edinburgh and its castle.

Aleppo, we found the next day, lay in the foothills of the snowcapped Taurus mountains, which formed a barrier to the north and it was vastly different from the parts of the Middle East which we had just left. The climate was cooler, or at least less hot, and the air was clear and bracing in a wind that seemed to blow straight from the steppes of Central Asia. The main road out to the east had a signpost to Deir ez Zoar, which my map showed me as situated on the River Euphrates! The people were much paler-skinned, too, and I was reminded of pictures I had seen of the men of Afghanistan, proud, tall, hook-nosed, shaggy-haired and with large knives in their belts; they were dressed in ragged sheepskins and turbans, quite unlike the Egyptians we had left behind. The women were tall and graceful and carried themselves well.

I felt we had arrived on the very edge of a different culture and that they and their kind stretched away far into the east. My main impression was one of colour. In particular, on one of my forays around our site, I passed a small tumbling stream in a green wooded valley, where a group of women were standing hip-deep in the water, washing great skeins of bright royal blue and scarlet wool.

That first afternoon, the Colonel called a conference of Unit Commanders at RHQ, about a mile from us. My Ford 8cwt was undergoing its daily maintenance, so I decided to use the Mack recovery, which was not otherwise required, to get to the meeting; I hadn't so far had the opportunity of testing it out. Its high seating gave us a magnificent overview of the countryside and the road ahead. Its power-assisted steering enabled me to back it easily in between the cars of the Bty Commanders, where it stood out like the Queen Mary among a mooring of small yachts. This caused much amusement among my peers; there was no doubt as to whose it was.

At the Conference, I learned more as to where our future lay.

439

The Regt was going into Turkey, which at that moment was an unhappy neutral under the lee of the German-dominated Balkans. In order to conceal our intentions until we were established in Turkey, we were going to take a leaf out of the enemy's book and infiltrate into the country in civilian garb. Our guns and lorries would have to travel by train under tarpaulins on low-loading flat cars and all concerned were issued with dimensions of the Turkish Railways' loading gauge, because the line passed through tunnels in the Taurus Mountains.

At the meeting, we were told that there were some of the flat cars in the sidings of the Aleppo railway yards and I asked the three Bty Captains to meet me there as soon as possible with a gun and a Matador, so that we could see whether they could be made to pass the loading gauge in practice, as distinct from on paper.

The train of low-loaders had been backed up to an end-loading ramp, when I reached the yards with my ASM and above it was one of those suspended swinging hoops of iron to represent the clearance required in the tunnel. In a nearby grass-grown siding, was a string of dirty Pullman coaches with boards indicating that they had been part of the "Taurus Express". I suppose they had been becalmed there since 1939...

It became quite clear, as we towed a gun up the ramp on to the flat car, that it, at least, could be made to pass physically under the loading frame, with a few odd projecting items removed, but although its width was satisfactory, the Matador's height was too great. We had some discussion on possible solutions, and the gunners were becoming gloomily acclimatised to the idea of cutting the whole cab and canopy off, so as to convert the vehicle to an open one – an alternative they viewed with great disfavour on account of the climate – when (though I say it myself) I had a brilliant idea. The canopy was the main problem. It was supported by a number of hooped channel sections and I proposed that these hoops could be sawn through at the lower end and a small tongue of steel welded on the inside of each channel and projecting from it. This tongue would fit into the lower (fixed) remainder of the canopy hoop and be bolted there during normal travel, but by removing these bolts,

440

the whole canopy could be lowered bodily into the vehicle, which would now be within the loading gauge. Furthermore, if necessary, the cab could be flame-cut to the same level and similarly located with steel tongues. All this could easily be fixed in the Workshops and the dismantling and re-assembly could be carried out by the Matador's own crew in a matter of minutes.

The proposal was put up to the Colonel for his approval and we commenced a rush programme of sawing, welding, drilling and bolting without delay. My stock in the Regt rose accordingly.

I never saw the end of all this work, for I received a preremptory signal to report back 'forthwith' to the Hospital in the Delta for a medical check. Once again, the Colonel tried to keep me with him, but, this time, GHQ was adamant and he had to acquiesce.

I was put on a decrepit Wellington bomber, which was leaving Aleppo that very morning, to start on my 900 mile journey back to the hospital. The other passengers had obviously just come out of Turkey, for they were almost identically clad in "sports jackets, Army Mark I (civilian)" and grey flannel trousers. Who they were, I never found out, for throughout the flight, they didn't say a word, even among themselves, and sat silently side by side along the bomb-racks. I decided to stand with my head in the perspex astrodome, where, at least, I could see something. What I did see as we taxied off didn't cheer me; the port engine was leaking oil in a quick dribble and I wondered if I was even going to reach the Delta.

We flew at a fairly low altitude and it was a bumpy ride, through the clouds, with the wings flexing to a phenomenal degree with each bump. However, they didn't come off and, when we left the aircraft at Lydda, the port engine was still leaking oil in the same quick dribble. I suppose it had been spraying the countryside of Syria and Palestine with oil for the whole flight.

I reported to the Movements Office on the LG and showed my papers, asking how I was supposed to get to the Delta. The Sgt took my details, gave me a pass to get a bed in the transit area if necessary and undertook to let me know when – or if –

441

something going my way could be found to take me. It didn't sound very promising, so, since I had no Palestinian money even to get a drink, I sat in the sun and watched the Spitfires taking off and landing. The thing to do, I decided, must be to take up the undercarriage the moment the aircraft was a few feet above ground, for I saw it done almost every time. If the engine had faltered, the propellor would have ploughed into the runway and there would be one less Spitfire operational, but it never happened.

Early that afternoon, the Sergeant was as good as his word, for I heard myself being paged over the tannoy and found I had a seat on a four-engined US Transport Command C54 "Skymaster" leaving for Ismailia almost at once. Slinging my kit in, I found the contrast between it and the Wellington was almost unbelievable. Most of the fuselage was a cargo compartment, but forward of that were some twenty padded seats occupied by only six other passengers. A gum-chewing attendant guessed we could do with something to eat and produced plates of sandwiches for each of us, even before we took off. Once we were in the air, the Captain drifted back and asked was there any place we would like to see on the way. Someone said he would like to see the Dead Sea and the Captain just said "You're welcome", so we set out east, in the opposite direction from our route to Ismailia. This route involved climbing up over the Palestine plateau and then dropping in a steep dive down to the Dead Sea, where we flew slowly at what seemed like a couple of hundred feet above its surface, before the pilot gunned his engines and we climbed back over the lip of the hills, some six thousand feet above us. (The hills were 4000 ft above sea level, while the Dead Sea was 2000 ft below it.)

We then turned westwards and flew smartly to our proper destination, landing at Ismailia just before sundown. As we were getting out, the Captain said with a grin: "Guess you can now tell your folks you've been a couple of thousand feet below the sea in an airplane and see what they make of it!'

I hitched a lift in a lorry to 63 General Hospital at Helmieh near Cairo and reported to the medics there in accordance with their wretched order.

442

I was in hospital – a most unwilling patient – for a week or more, during which time they put me through the whole old routine of X-rays and, finally, a senior doctor broke the sad news – sad to them, I mean – that they couldn't find anything wrong with me and, therefore, that there would be no change in my medical category. They were still talking as though they believed I was Category B, which I wasn't.

I would be discharged to the REME Base Depot as soon as the paperwork was completed. Big deal! I had been rooted out of my unit and might have to revert to my War Substantive rank of Lieutenant, if I couldn't return to 93rd. Accordingly, since Helmieh was quite near Cairo, I caught the "Metro" into the city. This Metro was what a Naval Officer who was in Helmieh with me called "a seagoing tram". It ran at speed on a sort of railway track for the first ten miles or so, using a pantograph on the overhead wire and, at the city boundary, changed over to an ordinary pulley collector and wound its way clangingly through the streets.

At GHQ, I found the department that dealt with postings of REME officers up to the rank of captain. In passing, I learned that the DAAG (REME) was the man I needed to see – postings of majors and above were the province of the Military Secretary's Department. Here I poured out my story to him and asked to be returned to 93 HAA Wksps.

The DAAG was sympathetic, but was unable to send me back to 93rd, because they had had to do something in a hurry on account of the urgency and importance of "Pugilist". Harris had been promoted to captain in my place and a subaltern had been sent to fill his vacancy. All that couldn't be untied – Sorry, old man!

'But what about me?' I asked. How could I avoid being forced to take down my third pip through no fault of my own? The DAAG looked through all his papers and told me there was no vacancy, or likelihood of one, for a captain in any of the AA Wksps still in the Middle East. He was sorry, but that was that. Was the command of an AA Wksp what I really wanted, or would I be interested in doing some staff work?

Because there might be openings in some planning exercises he knew of.

I decided to take the plunge; I had already come to the conclusion that AA Wksps were a dead end for me and I ought to get out of it into something else with more prospects, so I said I would be interested. He told me to go back to the hospital and he would let me know what he could turn up in a couple of days.

He was as good as his word and sure enough a movement order came through for me a couple of days later to report to ADME HQ Force 686 at an address in Cairo, quoting an authority: Ref so-and-so. It sounded interesting and I committed myself to a line of employment in which I remained involved for the rest of the war.

HQ Force 686 was established on the third floor of a building in a tree-lined suburban road overlooking the River Nile. All occupants were supposed to have passes, so since I had not, a military doorman conducted me up to the office of the ADME, Lt Col Humphries. He had a short chat with me to find out what I was like and what my previous history was and then handed me over to a Major Sherman, who was his deputy, working in a separate office with another captain, who I later learned was the specialist in radar and radio maintenance; I cannot remember the latter's name. Major Sherman wasn't then in REME, although he was in the process of being transferred. At that moment he was still wearing the beret and badges of the Royal Tank Regt.

Sherman introduced me to the Brigadier heading Force 686 and his GSO1. The Brig turned out to be none other than my erstwhile CO, the former Lt Col Helby, of 2 LAA Regt, and the GSO1 was Major Claud Phillimore, the one-time Adjutant of the same Regt. Both had a welcoming word with me and I somehow felt that they must have picked my name out of some list they had been offered to choose from, as someone they knew. I also gained the impression that, although there were four REME officers in the HQ, these two were the only RA ones so far in it.

I was provided with a desk and chair and Sherman outlined the work that was expected. Although there were maps of Spain

444

and Morocco on the wall, apparently they were purely for disinformation of the enemy's spies, who were believed to be rife in the city. The real project on which we were engaged was the invasion of Turkey in which my friends of 93 HAA Regt in Operation Pugilist were playing a part.

At this point in my account, perhaps I should mention that Pugilist was only one of a series of operations going forward, each with a separate code name. They seemed to be parts of an overall plan, which I never fully learned because it wasn't politic to know too much of things in which one wasn't directly involved. In addition to Pugilist, there appeared to be Accolade and the series called the Hardihoods. There were certainly Hardihoods 1 to 5 and possibly more, but maybe they were successive stages of the same plan. However, they were all concerned with bringing Turkey into the war on the Allied side. I now think that the landings on Cos and Leros might have been parts of this master plan, which had been put into operation too early and went wrong.

Pugilist and the units of some other plan were intended to provide AA cover over the Dardanelles narrows and in several places on the Aegean coast of Turkey: Aydin, Izmir and Çanakkale, covering the inshore passage between the Turkish coast and the Greek islands – which were all in Axis hands – up to and including the Dardanelles itself. There was a rumour that all this was to provide sufficient air defence to enable the Italian fleet to pass through the straits into the Black Sea, in support of the Russians, but I never saw or heard anything official about that.

Meanwhile, since we had nothing else yet to do, Major Sherman set us to familiarise ourselves with the hinterland of Asia Minor and construct distance tables for the road communications between the coastal battery sites. Every time anyone arrived, particularly if it was an Egyptian, our map was hurriedly shoved into a drawer and we moved coloured pins about on the map of southern Spain.

Under Sherman's tutelage, we descended into bad habits. The HQ had a long lunch break and we returned to the office at about 4.00 p.m., when it was becoming cooler. About 6.00 p.m.

(half-time), we sent out for glasses of Cyprus brandy and ginger ale with ice and this carried us through until knocking-off time at about 8.00 p.m.

I cannot say that we did any real forward planning work, for nothing seemed to be happening in the eastern Mediterranean, apart from the Cos and Leros operations, which were meeting very strong opposition and the troops were eventually withdrawn after suffering considerable casualties. Claud Phillimore told me that the landing force on one of the islands included one of the LAA Btys that I had known well in the desert – I forget which, but it might have been 274 (NH). Claud said they had had a lot of casualties, about half its strength, which was depressing, for I had had a lot of friends there. 93 HAA Regt presumably were still in Aleppo, although what they were doing there wasn't clear.

Once, Helby and Phillimore instructed me to work out a plan of REME assistance for HAA sites in places as far apart as Aydin on the south coast, Izmir opposite Cos and at Çanakkale on the Dardanelles, all operating simultaneously. Phillimore read the riot act to me, when I expressed the view that what could be done by splitting one HAA Wksp would be almost negligible, telling me that it was an order and not for me to question it. I think he was worried about something, for, when I detailed in a report the men that could be apportioned for such a split and what they could do with hand tools only, he said nothing more about it. My personal belief was that we were trying to cover too great an area with only one HAA Regt Wksps, but it was accepted that this might have to be faced. There just didn't seem to be enough troops to go round in the area.

I heard various bits of information, mainly from Phillimore, about some of my old friends. 12 AA Bde had been in the thick of things in Sicily and were now somewhere on the mainland of Italy. The Bde was now commanded by the former Lt Col Wheeler of 27 LAA Regt, replacing Calvert Jones, who had been posted elsewhere, believed to be the Far East. I remembered Wheeler; he was a TA man, a hard-working gunner with grey hair and a bristling moustache, nicknamed "Flash Alf" by

446

his troops. He was famous, when in the desert, for his decrepit staff car, known locally as "Leaping Lena" and also notorious for a little foible, one that didn't endear him to the troops: his interest in the many Roman ruins in Libya, for which he insisted on providing guards from his Bty, in case they might suffer damage. It wasn't until after I left the desert that I learned he was the well known archaeologist, Mortimer Wheeler in pre-war life, whom I remembered excavating the site of Verulamium at St Albans.

All this time I was accommodated, at the Army's expense, in civilian "digs" run by a Greek couple. They provided me with a breakfast and an evening meal; this left me to find something to eat at midday in the city. As it was now getting cooler, I spent a lot of the long lunch break in walking round the streets of Cairo and sometimes going for a swim in the baths at the Gezira Sporting Club.

Time hung heavy on my hands and once, while when my walk took me out near the Nile, I happened upon a POW cage surrounded by barbed wire, containing some German prisoners. I don't know what they were doing in Cairo, but they were very much on their military dignity and strutted about as though they didn't care a hoot about being looked at. I felt a little sorry for them being put on show like that to be gawped at by a lot of scruffy Egyptians.

Back at the office, our so-called planning petered out and it became apparent that there was some hold-up which was causing the Turkish authorities to think again about letting in a lot of British troops disguised as tourists. Eventually we heard that the cause was the action by the Germans who had politely dissuaded the Turks by moving two armoured divisions in Bulgaria to just short of the frontier at Edirne (Adrianople).

The troops assembling at Aleppo dispersed and HQ Force 686 received orders to disband. Col Humphries asked me did I want to continue in staff work, or did I want something else? I told him there was nothing for me outside in the Middle East and staff work appealed to me. Could he help me to find something else in that line? He thought that he could put my name forward for a course at the Middle East Junior Staff

School at Sarafand. It wasn't something that I could have applied for; certain vacancies were allocated to Commands, Armies, HQs and the like and there was usually a vacancy or two allotted to the EME Directorate at GHQ. The object of the ten-week course was to instil into appropriate junior officers such knowledge as might be necessary for an efficient staff officer. It was generally accepted as placing the candidate's foot firmly on the bottom rung of the ladder to further advancement.

He must have been satisfied with my work, for apparently there was only one vacancy for a REME officer from the whole Middle East. I have no idea what he said, and that was an encouraging thought. In no time at all, I was summoned to an interview with the DME MidEast himself, Major General Tope, who chatted for a short while, I suppose to sum me up, and then asked me why I wanted to do staff work. I said I liked it and wished to gather knowledge that might improve my future usefulness to the Corps. I somehow got the impression he thought that I was hoping to stay in the Army after the war. Once again, I must have given a good impression and was considered suitable, for I was selected for the REME vacancy and posted to the 9th Course at the Middle East Junior Staff School, with effect from 4 March 1944. This was quite a feather in my cap, for there were only three such staff schools in the British Army: Camberley, Quetta and Sarafand. On graduating, you had the distinction of the letters j.s.c. after your name in your military records.

The school was situated in a former hotel on a hill overlooking the little "town" of Sarafand and surrounded by orange groves all ablaze with ripe fruit, the famous Jaffa oranges. The sixty or so male "students" (a few majors but the rest captains) were accommodated in airy concrete Nissen-type huts in the grounds, partitioned so that each officer had a single room, simply but adequately furnished with bed, wardrobe, table, desk light and chair, etc; also a telephone to the main switchboard. Some ten female ATS officer "students" (ATS, not FANYs) of rank equivalent to captain and on a different course, were housed in the main building, which also contained the quarters of the Commandant and his wife, the mess room and ante-room

448

and various lecture theatres. The instructors, called Directors of Studies (DSs), were billeted elsewhere in the neighbourhood. Specially vetted local Arabs came in to clean the rooms and do general duties. A tennis court and a squash court were within the grounds for the use of the students.

On arrival, late on Saturday afternoon, we were allocated to our rooms and interviewed by the Chief Instructor. I learned there was another REME officer on the course (from North Africa) and the other students came from North Africa, the ME, Italy, East Africa and the Persia/Iraq Command. Only a few had had some staff experience and the Chief Instructor told me that I appeared to have seen more active service (two years solid campaigning in the desert) than almost anyone else on the course.

Sunday was a day of rest, to acclimatise ourselves and meet our fellow students. I was able to have a most enjoyable afternoon's tennis, the first for four years, before the main work began on Monday.

Our hours of work, we were told, were to be PT 0645–0715 each morning; then breakfast; two sessions 0830–1100 and 1130–1300 with a short coffee break in between; lunch; then 1400–1600; and occasionally, if we got behind in our programme, 1700–1900 before dinner. Later in the course we were to spend time outside on special exercises.

At 1100, the parched multitude scrambled to be served coffee through a hatch and for which we were truly thankful. (Later in the course, we produced a Course Magazine and I recall one of my friends contributing a short poem, *pace* Lewis Carroll, which began: ''Twas levens and the drouthy coves did clush and stample at the hatch...')

We were divided into groups of ten and different DSs took us for various subjects, including:

- Staff duties (the standard way to write military reports and orders, the standard abbreviations to use, etc);
- The organisation and composition of Armies, Army Corps, Brigade Groups and Divisions and the ranks of officers involved;

449

- Operation orders and the information they must contain;
- Army accounting methods and the use of Army Forms;
- Military law; Court Martial procedures;
- Military support of the Civil Power in civil disobedience uprisings;
- The use of radio sets and the correct procedures for speaking on them (this took place out of doors in the grounds).

Each period took the form of a lecture, during which we took copious notes, and then a question and answer session in which the DS resolved (?) any misunderstandings. There was some free time in the evening after dinner, to be used to write up our notes in proper form as course work, to be inspected later.

Sometimes, just as we were breathing a sigh of relief, an additional lecture was announced at dinner to take place from 2030 until, say, 2230 or even 2300, before we could retire to bed.

The single squash court was bookable in quarter-hour sessions, either before breakfast or after the afternoon lecture period, before dinner. One of my fellow students and I used to play a game or two to loosen up before PT, since at that time we had the place to ourselves; it was fully booked just before dinner.

Dinner was quite a formal affair, at which we were expected to attend in clean and correct battledress, later khaki drill (with ties), because the Commandant and his wife were present. Afterwards, we queued at the hatch again for cups of coffee and could relax in wicker chairs and chat. We had no opportunity for any rough games to let off steam, for the Commandant and his wife (and his dog) came to sit with us by the open French window in the anteroom.

The dog was actually a fat, old and overfed bull terrier bitch, which lay like a slobbering slug by Mrs Commandant's feet and growled, or groaned, if anyone came near. It was universally disliked by the students. One evening, while we were milling round the hatch drawing our coffees, it was noticed that one of the cups had a crack round its base and the finder, on lifting it from its saucer loosed its hot contents all over the coffee tray.

This appealed to our baser instincts and the defective cup was replaced in position, to catch out the next unfortunate, not in on the secret, to lift it. The game went on for quite a while, until one of our number, Major Donald Caughey, NZEF, politely asked Mrs Commandant if she would like another cup of coffee and his offer was accepted. Only at the last moment, those in the know realised that it was the faulty cup he was filling. For some unknown reason, the base stuck on when he carried it across the room, as we watched in silent horror, and then it came off loosing its hot contents all over the somnolent dog. It gave a scandalised yelp, took to the woods through the open French window, with an agility we never thought it possessed, and disappeared for the rest of the evening.

The Commandant exonerated Don Caughey, on learning that the cup must have been faulty, and his wife's dress wasn't soiled, so we heard no more about it. Later that evening, however, in someone's quarters, an *ad hoc* committee produced a citation and awarded Don Caughey a bar to his Africa Star "for outstanding courage in the face of the enemy, resulting in the latter's being driven from a previously entrenched position with heavy losses".

Our Sundays were free, but we were not permitted to leave the school compound. The tennis court was much in demand and so were the women officers, who could pick and choose who should partner them in mixed doubles. The rest of us queued round the squash court area, or retired to our huts for a well earned Sunday nap.

On Saturday, we received instruction in motorcycle riding from a hard-bitten RASC Sgt over a sort of "mountain course" in the grounds behind the school. It seemed that all officers up to the rank of Lt Col were expected to be able to ride a motorcycle. Colonels, Brigadiers and above were expected to ride pillion, which sounded much more dangerous. Some six slightly battered 500cc side-valve Nortons were available and it was announced, as a carrot, that successful students would be allowed to use one of them on Saturday afternoons to go down to Lydda for shopping, haircuts and so on. My course was very short; I had done a couple of laps (it wasn't very difficult) and was watching my colleagues overbalancing and falling off, when the instructor came up and said, 'You've done this before, haven't you, Sir? You're passed. You can now dismiss!'

Later in the course, things got more complicated. We were provided with maps of some area, such as southern Bulgaria, and were told to work up an operation order detailing the steps by which we (individually) would set about the capture of the town of Plovdiv (formerly Philipopolis), for example. Another time we had a lecture by the GOC of the King of Transjordan's Arab Legion bodyguard on the problems of peacekeeping in the Middle East. General Glubb Pasha turned up in person; he had succeeded Peake Pasha, the founder of the Legion, some years before.

In lighter vein, we had to devise an order of battle for an Armd Div. I recall the relish with which we detailed the Short Range Shepheard's Group as the Recce Regt, and Armoured regiments called the Gezira Lancers and Groppi's Horse (Groppi's was a well known ice cream parlour in Cairo). I forget the rest. Another time we had to draw up a G1098 (War Equipment Table) for a Heavenly Host. This produced "rockets, most imperial" and like flights of imagination.

All this sort of thing had to be submitted in our best writing on paper for our DSs, and we had to read our effusions out in the next session and answer questions about them from our fellows. It was all very thought-provoking and we had to burn much midnight oil individually in our rooms to get them done before the following day.

Not everything was done on paper. On two occasions, the entire class was carted off in trucks to peculiar places in the neighbourhood and we had to devise some plan of operation "on the ground", as it were. One was up in the hills on the road to Jerusalem, where we had to decide how to overcome an enemy holding the road at a particular spot; the other involved a contested river crossing at one of the few permanent rivers in Palestine, the R. Yarkon, a muddy, reed-fringed stream near Tel Aviv. In both cases, someone was picked on to produce a plan, the rest of us were invited to criticise and all our contributions were noted down by our DS.

452

At the end of our last week, the climax came. The entire course was involved in a mammoth tactical exercise in which we were cast as the Corps and Divisional staff of an attacking force entering Palestine from the north against enemy defences. Each one of us in turn was allocated an appointment (GSO1, Commander RASC, etc) and had to fight the battle from first principles laid down by the DS. Every so often, the appointments were suddenly switched and a new participant had to carry on the war, cold as it were, and make the best he could of the situation. All this was done by telephone, using the correct procedures. Every so often some of us were allowed to relax and retire to our rooms, hoping for a quick nap, to be rudely awakened to take over some entirely different role.

I remember I started off playing the DDME of the forward Division and was engaged in recovery under fire of a number of wrecked vehicles and men which had strayed too far beyond the front line, when I received a signal that the GSO1 had been severely wounded and I had to take his place! As the new GSO1, I nursed the conduct of the battle a bit further without committing any actual catastrophe for an hour or so, before my relief arrived and I could "stand down" and retire to my room. This frantic action went on for some 48 hours and, when our forward troops had "reached" Beersheba, the enemy "surrendered". This occurred at about noon on the second day and the somewhat bleary-eyed contestants tumbled out to the front of the school to greet an enemy envoy (a DS wearing a German helmet and riding a donkey), seeking an armistice. Our Arab staff looked on, somewhat bewildered, as everyone cheered. Then we repaired to the hatch in the ante-room for a fifth or sixth cup of much-needed coffee, swapping tales of valour or calamities endured during the past 48 hours.

That was the end of the course. The Commandant had been down to GHQ ME during the week, taking our dossiers with him, to decide where each of us would be posted. On his return we were each summoned to an interview with him and he made known our fate. He had the individual reports from our DSs in front of him and he commented briefly on our performance. I cannot remember exactly what he said to me, but he had no adverse comment; in fact he said I had an enquiring mind and appeared to have benefited from the studies.

I was much relieved to hear that I was posted to HQ Allied Armies in Italy (AAI) "for employment in a 'Q' capacity" and to report to some transit camp in the Delta for onward transmission, after a week's leave. That suited me. I wanted to get out of the Middle East and I had been receiving guarded letters from Phyl in Tripoli for some weeks now hinting that she was waiting to move to the CMF (Central Mediterranean Force) as well. Maybe we could meet up somewhere there!

19

Two of us decided to stick together for the first part of our seven days' leave. I had been posted to the CMF; my friend was going to Paiforce (the Persia/Iraq Command), which no longer looked likely to be threatened after the German defeat at Stalingrad, and would go there without returning to Cairo. So, as a final fling, we thought that we would explore the Lebanon, which neither of us had visited before, staying in Beirut for three days and then split up at Sarafand, whence my colleague would strike east to Persia and I would have a leisurely hitchhike down to the Delta and play it by ear once there, before reporting to a specified transit camp on 21 May.

We hitchhiked from Sarafand in two stages, changing vehicles at Haifa, where we had a simple lunch, and then some kind driver took us on to Beirut, passing Tyre and Sidon on the way. From the old frontier at Ras el Naqura, from which Phyl and I had viewed the "Promised Land", it was all new territory, but our movement papers enabled us to cross and we reached Beirut in time to get a room at a reasonable hotel and have an evening meal.

Beirut was completely untouched by the war; it had been a French Mandate and all the surroundings were French-built and French-owned. We spent the first two days sunning ourselves on the seashore, or gently ambling round the pleasant city. For our last day, we decided to hitch over to Damascus, a place that I felt it would be a shame to miss, and very glad I was to have been there.

Once again, we hitched a lift, this time in a staff car, which stopped at our chalked sign "Damascus?". Rather to our embarrassment, the occupant was a brigadier, but he was charming

455

and gave us a running commentary about the route we were following. The road climbed from Beirut through the forests and up over the bare moorland between the peaks of the Lebanon Mountains, which were still snow-covered in May on their northern slopes. It then dropped down into the central valley, still some 3000 feet above sea level, and then climbed over the bare, dusty slopes of the Anti-Lebanon range.

Damascus lay in a fertile valley though which tumbled streams of clear, blue-green snow-water. I suppose two of them were the Abana and Pharpar, "the Rivers of Damascus", whose waters Naaman the Syrian suggested would do him more good than the muddy Jordan to cure his leprosy. I wouldn't have blamed him, having seen both.

While looking for some sort of souvenir in Damascus, I had a very pleasant and instructive surprise. I was in the silver market and was much taken by a half dozen little filigree coffee spoons, but the price to which I managed to beat down the bearded merchant was still above the amount in my Middle East banking account in Barclays D.C. and O. in Cairo. I sadly shook my head and the vendor, still hoping to conclude a deal, asked if I had a British banking account and chequebook. I had and he suggested I write a cheque for the sum on that, waving aside how he would get the money from this. I asked him whether he was worried that I would be unable to honour a UK cheque and he said, 'I trust your word. A British officer would never let me down' or words to that effect. So he wrapped up the spoons, gave them to me and we had a cup of coffee. Months later, after I had returned to the UK, the cheque was presented.

On the way back to the Delta, I dropped in at the Staff School in Sarafand to collect any mail for me and I was surprised and delighted to find a letter from Phyl. She said, guardedly, that she was going abroad; but definitely implying that her destination was indeed Italy, where she hoped that we could meet again before long.

On arrival in Cairo, I spent quite a lot of the remaining couple of days' leave at the EME Directorate, impressing on the folk there that I would welcome a return to a more active life in the

CMF. I hoped that they could pass this on to their opposite numbers at HQ Allied Armies in Italy.

About a score from the course were destined to sail to the CMF together and we were accommodated in what was described as the Officers' transit hotel, awaiting onward routing. This "transit hotel" was a grandiose name for a requisitioned and almost completely unfurnished apartment block, somewhere in the back streets of Cairo, where we lived rough for several days. We slept on our own camp kit and blankets and we ate, by arrangement, at the nearby Officers' Club. I was expecting a long wait, but things went very quickly and we were soon transferred to Port Said and put on a small ex-Polish liner, the *Batory*, carrying as passengers a large draft of Indian Army Service Corps personnel going to Italy as reinforcements, as well as ourselves. As soon as all were on board, the ship proceeded out of the Canal, and as we passed I was just able to see in the distance the church where I had been married ten months before and also the site where 2 HAA Wksps had been.

As a result of the victory in Tunisia and the subsequent relief of Malta, the Mediterranean was much less dangerous than previously and our trip was uninterrupted by any sort of enemy action. The sea was fairly calm and our draft was challenged to games of volleyball by the officers of the IASC. Most of us, like myself, had never played before and we soon found that our opponents were experienced, so that initially we were trounced and came back for our revenge. I never felt so exhausted as at the end of that trip, but we eventually managed to salvage some of our pride and won a game or two.

We landed at Taranto and were put into a sort of transit camp for several days. Taranto was a bit of a dump. The harbour was still cluttered with sunken shipping, including some warships, after various Allied air raids, and the population seemed to be listless and looked underfed, particularly the children. All the Fascist embellishments had been removed and nothing had been put in their place. It looked and felt like a ghost town; my first impression of mainland Italy was that the place was decrepit and the people seemed mentally and morally defeated.

457

And nothing worked… The electric light frequently failed; the plumbing was just a joke, with leaking taps in the broken basins and sewage systems that were almost non-existent; and the windows were boarded over where the panes were broken.

Such was my first impression of Italy; a people defeated and rudderless. The bottom had fallen out of their stable Fascist world.

We were a couple of days in Taranto and then, one morning, we were bundled on to a train going north-west through the mountains. I was glad to be out of the place. Our destination proved to be another transit camp in the hills at the back of Naples, near a village called Paolisi. There, to my intense delight, I learned that No 48 Gen Hospital was staging under canvas at a neighbouring village, Cancello, about ten miles away.

After asking at my camp whether I was likely to get sudden orders to move somewhere else, I sought permission to visit my wife at Cancello. The Camp Commandant expressed surprise and told me to get going and make the most of my day. I think his words were, 'You lucky bastard! Take as much time as you want.' I found a truck that would take me part of the way and walked the remaining three miles, presenting myself at the guard tent at the hospital, asking for Sister Montgomery.

Phyl was doing nothing – the hospital was waiting to go to Rome, as soon as it was clear to do so, and her Matron allowed her two days leave, under the "special circumstances". Nice old body! The first day, Phyl organised some sandwiches and we went walking in the wooded hills behind her camp to a small ruined castle overlooking a sort of ravine, where we just sat and enjoyed the rural scenery. *Cancello* apparently was the Italian for a gate and the small castle guarded the pass through the hills. It was a wonderful reunion and we wandered back after dusk; I then set out to walk the ten miles back to Paolisi, with a light heart.

The following day, one of Phyl's friends was organising a trip to Pompeii and I was kindly added to the party. We had a pleasant tour round as much of the ruins as were visible; they

458

had been thoughtfully re-covered with rubble during the fighting after the Allied landing at Salerno, "in case they got damaged". After that, we went on towards the coast near Positano and sat in the sun until it was time to return to camp. We were both surprised how dirty the sands were; they were covered with fine black pumice dust from the recent eruption of Vesuvius and the sea had a black oily film that made it look most uninviting. We found a YWCA hostel in a beautiful situation overlooking the sea at Positano and they agreed they could have us there together, if or when we could get leave.

We had another couple of days like this and then the idyll ended; there had been another hard-fought, but successful, landing at Anzio south of Rome which was evacuated by the Germans on 4 June 1944, and the hospital was packing up, ready to move there. They went silently one night and I was left kicking my heels at Paolisi.

However, shortly afterwards, I received a posting to Q (AE) Branch at HQ AAI in Caserta, some twelve miles up-country from Naples. Q (AE) was the department that dealt with Army equipment, with the supply of vehicles and other controlled warlike stores. On reporting, I was to find, much to my disgust, that it seemed to be a sort of glorified Ordnance branch of HQ and I was required, as Staff Captain Q (AE) (Statistics) to keep records of such transactions. It was work that could have been done by a staff sgt, RAOC, or a junior commander in the ATS. So much for my field experience as an EME and my ten weeks' expensive training at the Staff School!

It seemed clear to me that the EME Directorate at HQ didn't know what to do with me, and after a week I sought an interview with the ADME, Lt Col Guy Crittall (Director in peacetime of Crittall's Windows) – a First Army man – asking to be transferred to some more active role. He expressed surprise, saying that my present job was a good one and had encouraging prospects for promotion, but he would see what he could do; apparently all such posts were already filled (I believe, with First Army men) and he said there was no vacancy going.

I should explain that at this time the personnel operating in

Italy were in three categories: First Army men, Eighth Army men, and folk straight out from the UK, pale-skinned and with white knees, nicknamed *Ingleses*. The two Armies were intensely proud of their backgrounds and both tended to look down on the Ingleses as lesser mortals. I once heard someone say of someone, 'He wasn't an Eighth Army man; he wasn't even a First Army man; he was an Inglese.' No prizes for guessing the affiliation of the speaker. It took several months for the disparate streams to coalesce and realise that they were all fighting on the same side. All of them, for some reason, tended to look down on the Americans at first, particularly the First Army men, who had soldiered alongside them in North Africa. I heard it said that Gen Eisenhower had decisive ideas as to how to wage a war; they were those of the last (US) general to whom he had spoken. This was a bit unkind, since "Ike" was particularly keen on stamping out inter-service dissensions.

I make this digression, because I found myself at quite a disadvantage at HQ AAI. I didn't seem to think the same way as those that had come here from North Africa or the UK, who were in the majority and I began to doubt whether my course at the MEJSC was getting me anywhere in Italy. They didn't seem to want a Staff School trained officer with new ideas busting into their cosy little circles. HQ AAI was basically "First Army" and some of the staff seemed to have a slight inferiority complex about Eighth Army veterans "on their patch" and felt that I was some sort of interloper demanding special treatment.

Crittall, however, as I have said, was sympathetic and promised to keep an eye open for an appointment that might more suitably utilise my background and experience. So I went back to my statistics and lived in hope.

HQ AAI was housed in the former Royal Palace of Caserta, a vast and complex building, reminiscent of Versailles, erected by the King of the Two Sicilies in the late eighteenth century before the state was overrun by Napoleon. It had four courtyards and numerous enormous interconnecting rooms served by endless corridors; the upper floors were reached by gigantic curving marble staircases.

The frontage of the Palace was set incongruously right up

against a dusty country road, but at the back a magnificent water garden rose up the lower slopes of a hill, with lakes descending in steps, starting at the upper end in a baroque fountain at the edge of the woods, from which a stream gushed down to feed the pools.

The surrounding countryside was attractive and inviting for walks, but it had been fought over during the Allied advance from Naples only a couple of months earlier and one was advised not to stray onto the verges, on account of the danger of booby traps. I set out one Sunday to walk along the road as far as Capua and the River Volturno, a twenty-mile round trip, just to see if I could do it. It took me the whole day, eating my sandwiches at Capua and looking over the river, which had been the site of a contested crossing, and comparing it with the exercise we had done in Palestine. I must say I was pleased to complete the walk and find I could indeed do it.

There was some excitement on hearing the news about the landings in Normandy and it looked as if the campaign in Italy might become a bit of a backwater. I heard from Phyl that she had just reached the Eternal City and was wondering if I might be coming that way soon.

About that time, a posting came through for me. I had been angling for the post of adjutant to the C REME of a Division and had been given the nod that one was just becoming vacant. However, someone with such experience turned up at the last moment and I was offered the job of "Captain REME" on the staff of No 1 District. Crittall suggested that it might have further possibilities and recommended me to take it, so I did, to get out of HQ AAI.

HQ No 1 District didn't yet exist and was being created to provide administration in the L of C area just behind the Front. The REME side consisted of a DDME, Col R. A. Holt; a DADME, another Major Walker, and a Staff Officer (REME), myself, the Chiefs outnumbering the Indians by two to one.

Holt was an experienced officer, who knew what he wanted and saw to it that his subordinates put their shoulders to the wheel. I am not sure what his past history was (which Army), but I fancy he was a regular soldier and I liked him and could

461

get on with him as I had done with Estlin. Walker was certainly a First Army man; a bit colourless, but he had no chip on his shoulder about my antecedents. The HQ was commanded by a colonel and had two majors, one as DAAG for personnel and one, Major Frampton, of whom I was to see quite a lot, as DAQMG. All this was in addition to the REME faction.

The HQ was being formed at Afragola in the hinterland behind Naples and, after we had been there for some seven days under canvas, we moved up through Capua and along the main road towards Rome. This took us past the sites of several battles, including the famous ruined hilltop monastery of Cassino, which towered above us amid what looked, from a distance, like lots of matchsticks, stuck vertically all over the slopes. On closer inspection, these turned out to be the stems of trees which had been destroyed in the aerial bombardments over a couple of weeks, before the site was captured by the Poles, who had climbed up the ridge behind and driven the Germans out with the bayonet.

About fifty miles from Rome, we turned off into the hills at a little hilltop town called Frosinone, and threaded our way up wooded valleys to Fiuggi, where we halted and went into billets. Fiuggi, more correctly Fiuggi Fonte, was a little spa, where, in more prosperous days the infirm came to drink the waters. I don't know what the waters were expected to cure, but they must have been powerfully diuretic, for there were more public lavatories to the square mile than I could have believed possible. These were labelled *Signore* and *Signori* – Ladies and Gentlemen. I think it was Major Frampton who told me that the mnemonic to decide which to use was "I am a Gentleman; 'E isn't". I found myself in a very comfortable building, with a room to myself furnished with a bed with spring mattress, wardrobe, table and chair and wash basin, but no water; the retreating Germans had blown up the waterworks. Occasionally there was electric light.

The surrounding country in the early summer was seemingly untouched by war, with 4000-ft mountains all round, and picturesque little hilltop villages. Having little to do – we were just staging at Fiuggi – I set out to take an eight-mile daily walk to keep myself in a reasonable state of fitness and to explore the countryside, which reminded me of Shropshire. During these walks, I encountered many local Italians, whom I found friendly and from whom I was able to pick up quite a bit of the language, or at least some useful words. My billet had a small swimming pool attached and I got into the habit of taking an evening swim after returning from these walks.

Maybe this could have been the source of some bug I picked up that laid me low with a high temperature and resulted in the MO sending me off in Col Holt's car into Rome with a note addressed to some hospital, describing my symptoms. Our road took me past the village of Valmontone, where a complete German Armd Div had been cut off by the Anzio force and had "formed square" and shot it out until they ran out of ammunition. The place looked a complete mess.

On arrival in Rome, my driver located the hospital and thankfully deposited me in the reception area, where an RAMC clerk took my rank, name and number for admission. When he came to "next of kin", there was obviously some problem, for he suddenly said, 'This is the wrong hospital. I don't think you can come in here.' I said wearily, 'All right. Send me to the correct one,' and he departed, I thought to telephone to some other one in Rome. He was gone quite a long time and, when he returned, I was told that they would take me in, after all.

After I had been put into a bed, I remembered to ask which hospital this was and they said No 48! Phyl told me later that the snag was that there was an Army rule that wives should never, repeat never, be involved in nursing their injured husbands. The delay had been because she had been Sister in charge of this very Officers' Medical Ward and it had been necessary to move her out in some hurry. She had been moved to the post of "Home Sister", in charge of the Sisters' Mess – a post that rotated among the staff and was not very popular.

I didn't know this at the time; I was only glad to be received for treatment, for I was feeling pretty rotten. The sisters in the ward were very kind and considerate and I somehow felt I was getting special treatment. Apparently they had been told who I was; "Little Mrs Monty's husband, you know..."

Phyl wasn't allowed to visit me until I was off the "danger

463

list", for it was diagnosed that I had somehow contracted paratyphoid fever and consequently had to be kept under close supervision for the first few days. However, I survived and the MO said that I was lucky that it wasn't a more severe case. It appeared that paratyphoid fever was a highly notifiable disease and he plotted my movements over the past few weeks, in the hope that the source of this potentially unpleasant affliction could be traced. I don't know if they found it.

Eventually, I was moved from isolation into the general Officers' Medical Ward and Phyl used to come and see me and sit at my bedside for a couple of hours each afternoon. She would bring her knitting (very domestic) and we would do crossword puzzles. This made me the object of much envy among my fellow patients, whose wives or girlfriends were back in the UK and they hadn't seen them for months, or even years.

Once, when I was much better, Phyl brought me grapes, which were immediately eaten by my fellow-sufferers. They reckoned that having a wife to come and smooth my brow daily was bad enough, but a wife *and grapes* was really too much. Phyl was much in demand among them as a Sister who wasn't busy and could actually find the time to *talk* to them.

In all, I was in hospital for eight weeks. My temperature dropped to normal after four days, but I was then subjected to a weekly series of pathological tests to make sure that my paratyphoid had finally been eradicated. During this time, I was allowed out of bed and dressed; apart from not being able to leave the hospital confines, I was allowed to lead a normal life and I was permitted to have tea with Phyl in the Sisters' Mess three afternoons a week. It was quite domestic! Finally, when the time came to discharge me, the hospital treated me as a special case and authorised a highly irregular arrangement whereby I remained undischarged on their books, but was allowed to "sleep out" for a week. Phyl got leave and we spent the time at the YWCA – yes the YWCA – Club (the former Eliseo Hotel) in Rome. This worthy establishment, although primarily catering for the female forces, accepted genuine married couples as well. We had a lovely pair of rooms with private bathroom and were treated in the kindest manner.

Generally speaking, we took things pretty easily, rising late and dallying round during the day, getting to know one another for the first time as husband and wife in civilian surroundings. One evening, we went to the Royal Opera House in Rome and saw a performance of some opera, which didn't greatly impress us, and also the ballet *Coppelia* which was delightful.

One day, we happened to be in the streets when there was a military parade. I had been aware that the Allies had decided that some small contingents called *Gruppi di Combattimenti* of Italians, each about six or seven hundred strong, should be formed, to guard the rear areas; there were five *Gruppi* in all: the *Friuli*, the *Cremona*, the *Mantova*, the *Verona* and the *Legnano*, all cities in the Po Valley. Three of these *Gruppi* were equipped by the Americans and two by the British. This was a parade of the *Friuli Gruppo*, newly equipped in British Army battledress and webbing, but with Italian headgear and rank badges.

The watching crowds lining the street went nearly mad with excitement and joy, throwing flowers into the road in front of the troops, and rushing up to embrace individual marchers. It was a far cry from the defeated attitude of the population of Taranto. The sight of their boys marching again had raised morale to fever pitch. (I learned later that discipline in the *Gruppi* was almost non-existent. They took unofficial leave to visit their families when it suited them; they paid scant attention to their duties or to orders, and they were in the habit of selling their boots in order to buy wine.)

The YWCA was organising local tours and we went on two of these: Ancient (Roman) Rome, and to St Peter's and the Vatican. This last included a Papal Audience to members of the Armed Forces, in which His Exalted Nibs waved his hands over the assembled gathering and blessed us. It was a bit wasted on me, but it was quite an experience to see the Swiss Guards in their mediaeval finery and the Sistine Chapel. Otherwise, St Peter's didn't impress me. It was all too much like a museum with more sleek and well favoured priests than seemed necessary.

At the end of our week, we returned to the hospital and in due course I was discharged and collected by my unit. No 1 District was still at Fiuggi, but preparing to move on northwards. Our destination was Perugia, a university city and the administrative centre for the region of Umbria, where I was to remain until the spring of 1945.

20

When we first saw it, Perugia stood out over the upper Tiber valley, undamaged by the tides of war, rising like a citadel on massive walls, the lower strata of which were Etruscan and overlaid by Roman and mediaeval additions. In the centre was a small square with an elaborate (leaking and dry) fountain in the middle, the work, I learned, of the architect who was responsible for the famous (leaning) tower at Pisa. Facing each other across this square were the Duomo (Cathedral) and the Palazzo of the Priori (the City Council). This latter had been taken over by the local branch of AMG – the Allied Military Government (of Occupied Territories), formerly AMGOT, but the abbreviation had been imposed because AMGOT was said to be a dirty word in somebody's language – which dealt with the administrative problems of the civilians. No 1 District dealt only with the military equivalents and the two were supposed to work in harness. Sometimes they even did just that!

On arrival, the HQ's first objective was to find somewhere for its Mess and offices, also for billets. For help in this, we had to approach the AMG in the Palazzo. It was Major Frampton's problem as DAQMG, but his staff was merely a couple of Italian liaison officers who worked as interpreters. I have referred before to the preponderance of Chiefs over Indians in the HQ, so my boss, Col Holt, having no other work for me until we had an office, temporarily attached me to Frampton to assist him.

Frampton left me and one of his two Italian liaison officers in the reception area of the AMG Palazzo, while he went with the

467

other to put his case for requisitioning some buildings for the HQ's use. The large room was a positive Babel, with Italians all shouting for attention at a few harassed British or American officers who were sitting at desks just trying to sort out the problems being put to then. Close by us was a vociferous middle-aged woman, who seemed to be screaming her head off on being denied something she was demanding. I asked the Italian LO with me, what on earth was the cause of her frenzy. He grinned sheepishly and said the lady was asserting she was not an Italian, but an Etruscan and, since the Etruscans had never made peace with Rome, she was entitled to special treatment as an ally and not a defeated enemy. The British AMG officer stood his ground and she was still verbally belabouring him when Frampton returned.

He had managed to acquire the offer of two properties, one for the sleeping accommodation of majors and captains, but not for Lt Cols and the Colonel, and the other the whole ground floor in the residence of some Countess, which we could take over furnished for our Officers' Mess and Ante-room.

We went to inspect the "junior" officers' quarters first; these were the two top floors in a house built straight up from the city wall and commanding extensive views down the Tiber valley. They were unfurnished, but we all had camp beds, so that wasn't a problem. There was also a bathroom, but no water. Frampton gave me a list of the prospective occupants and said I could sort it out who had what later, after we had dealt with the proposed Mess; he said, with a grin, that, in allocating the officers to the rooms, there was no reason why I shouldn't look after myself properly. Charity began at home and he recalled the old saying that my grandfather had often been wont to use, namely that "the carver was either a rogue or a fool"; and he assumed that I wasn't intending to be a fool!

Frampton then departed to look at other properties for offices and for the senior officers. He took me to the house selected as our Officers' Mess and, after asking whether I had any command of French, left me there, taking the Italian LO with him. The Countess spoke some French, he assured me, before leaving me to it.

468

The lady was waiting for me in the hallway of the apartment, rather like a female spider expecting the arrival of her dinner. She was in her sixties and was accompanied by a limp and pallid young man, I supposed as protection of her chastity, for I couldn't make out whether he was her lawyer, son, some relative or perhaps her *cicisbeo*. At any rate he took no part in the subsequent proceedings and merely spoke when the wretched woman demanded some answer from him. At the start, she professed only to speak Italian and not to understand English (or French), but I gathered that she was most unwilling to allow me to inspect the rooms and seemed dead against letting any of her valuable possessions be desecrated by falling into the hands of the Allied Armies.

It was an uphill struggle, but I eventually got it across to her in my schoolboy French that the Allied Military Government had given me authority to requisition it all and then she feigned tears and, in French as bad as mine, but with an Italian accent to make it more difficult, came out with some sob story about her husband and how she was responsible to him for its safety – wasn't she, Giovanni? This to the young man, who gave her tearful and sombre support. I couldn't make out whether the husband was dead, or a POW or had just hopped it north with the Fascisti and was now in German territory. For a long time, we argued in broken French and finally she put her handkerchief away and pointed to a piece of decrepit and worm-eaten furniture that had been the apple of her husband's eye and which she held in sacred trust to his memory. If we had it, it would be a desecration of the most disgraceful... *Effroyant*... I couldn't see it being much use in an Officers' Mess on account of its condition, so I said she could keep that particular relic, but insisted she must accept that all the remainder would have to stay in the flat.

I think that by now she was getting a bit tired, or reckoned that honour had been vindicated, for she agreed rather loftily, threw the keys at me and retired with her lawyer/son/relative/ boyfriend in high dudgeon. I retired, too, to report to Frampton that the flat was ours, furnished. He commended me for my work – I think he must have heard about the Countess, for he asked jocularly if there would be need for a working party to mop up any spilt blood. I advised him to put one of his men into the place quickly, before she got in some heavy gang to clear more furnishings out.

Frampton had acquired accommodation for his other needs and we went back to the camped HQ party; we all packed up and moved in. I had a couple of protests from two majors who found themselves sharing a bedroom, whereas I, a mere Captain, had a smaller room to myself, but it all blew over and peace was restored. Later on in the autumn, the Mess was found to be bitterly cold, Perugia being on a hilltop and exposed to every wind that blew, and the REs were called in to construct a fireplace in the outer wall and pipe the smoke up to roof level outside. It made the place a bit warmer with a roaring fire of logs, but I never heard what the Countess said, when she saw evidence of this "*desecration effroyant*" rise above her windows on the upper floor.

As soon as he had an office, Holt called me in and I was deputed to visit each of the REME Wksps in our area to report on their effectiveness and find out what their needs were. Since No 1 District extended from Arezzo and Ancona in the north down to Spoleto and Terni in the south, this meant a lot of motoring over mountain roads and I soon found that the HQ motor pool was useless for my work, as the vehicles always seemed to be booked by other, more senior, officers for what they regarded as more important duties. I reported my difficulties to Holt, and he pulled strings and requisitioned a small Lancia saloon, which I could drive myself, although I always, or almost always anyway, took a driver with me. Holt also authorised me to sign the work tickets for my journeys, so that I was independent of the HQ bureaucracy.

My tour of inspection of the REME establishments enabled me to meet and become friends with several workshop commanders who were of use to me in later months. Due to the continuing shortage of skilled artisans, most of the workshops were being diluted with reinforcements of unemployed Italian personnel. A lot of these were ex-Italian Army and were very good workers when under proper discipline. I was told by one of

470

my new friends, operating at Fabriano, on the road to Ancona, that the first thing that his new recruits did on arrival was to construct a pasta-making machine and organise their own food from basic rations.

Most of my work so far had been as a sort of mobile aide-de-camp to Holt, feeding back to him the things he wanted to know and enabling him to visit the REME sites, properly briefed, or to put pressure on Authority as required, if there were things they needed. All this was fascinating; I was doing something I liked doing and I had considerable freedom to wander about the Italian countryside in my own right. I never found out exactly what Major Walker's duties were, but he didn't interfere with mine.

The HQ soon settled down to a dull, routine existence and only some of the highlights remain in my memory. One was the great bathhouse improvement. As I have mentioned earlier, there was initially no water in our billets, but Frampton came to some arrangement with an odd and rather scruffy hotel which had an enormous array of baths in the basement, right down in the Etruscan strata and, when provided with the necessary fuel, the hotel produced for us unlimited hot water.

While the reasonable autumn weather lasted, we played hockey in our spare time. The HQ had some hockey sticks in its sports equipment, so a group of us found a flattish field where we could play. The game caught on and we were able to stage several matches of mixed hockey between teams including some of the half dozen ATS in the HQ. The bathing arrangements provided a splendid end to a hard-fought game. I have no idea what the girls did, but they didn't join us!

I had become friendly with the major in charge of the Army Postal Services, the DADPS. I cannot remember his name, for he was always called "Postie". It was now common knowledge in the Mess that my wife was a Nursing Sister in Rome and when I told him that her father had been a Counter Supervisor in the main Post Office in Folkestone, that made me a member of the gang "at one remove", so to speak. Major "Postie" was in touch with all sorts of local activities, some legitimate and some not. It was he who unearthed a small backstreet character in the city who still had a stock of pre-war silk stockings at not-too-unreasonable prices, and I bought a dozen pairs for Phyl, which made her the envy of the Sisters' Mess.

Another time he discovered an angora rabbit farm that sold knitted garments on the site made from the soft rabbit wool by the local women and, with my personal transport, we visited the place. I bought Phyl a pale blue twinset, which put my stock even higher at No 48.

Someone else found some unemployed musicians in the town and they were willing to come and play for us in the evenings for a good dinner. There was a string quartet that was really outstanding; in particular an attractive young woman violinist, whose rendering of Gounod's *Ave Maria* was highly acclaimed. We never found out her background, because her voice and command of English didn't match her appearance, but I had a feeling that she had been a member of some elite pre-war orchestra. Some of the younger members of the HQ decided to ask her to play some modern jazz – *Where's that Tiger? (Dove Tigre)* for example – but she couldn't be brought to oblige.

About this time, the Italians, I remember, were increasingly encouraged to run their own affairs and one of the things they did was to restore the power to a little light railway – another of those so-called "sea-going trams" that ran alongside the road from Foligno to Gualdo Tadino, near Fabriano. When the volts were switched on to the overhead wire, no one remembered to tell the occupying forces and on one of the first occasions the line was in service, a British Command Vehicle with its long aerial fully extended used a level-crossing and the antenna shorted the overhead, bringing out the system and giving the off-duty Signals occupants, who were listening to the Light Programme and doing no harm to anybody, a considerable shock, in all senses of the word.

At this time, HQ AAI had changed its name to Allied Force HQ (AFHQ) and was still in occupation of Caserta Palace. It had under command two Allied Armies: the (British) Eighth Army on the Adriatic front and the Fifth (US) Army on the western side of the Appenines. In between them on the crest of

472

the mountains was the independently minded Polish Corps, who were nominally under the Eighth Army and usually at odds with the Fifth. Their positions were right on the crest of the Appenines, looking down on the rich city of Bologna and they were said to be positively salivating at the thought of the good things that would result when the war re-started.

The Eighth Army was commanded by General Oliver Leese, who had succeeded Montgomery, when the latter had gone back to the UK to command the invasion forces that had recently landed in NW France, and the Fifth Army was under General Mark Clark. I am not sure whether the Allied field forces were still called 15 Army Group, but the new overall commander was General Harold Alexander. The chain of command was confused by the succession to Eisenhower, who had also returned for the Invasion, of a US General MacNarney, whose grandiose title was Commanding General, European Theatre of Operations US Army (ETOUSA) and appeared to have a powerful say in what the US forces did or had. Where he came in to the picture, I never really found out, but he didn't interfere with No 1 District's part in the war, since he never moved out of the so-called comfort of Naples.

Some time in July, the Americans and Free French had effected an almost unopposed landing in the south of France and were now driving north. To provide this force, the troops had to be supplied from the Fifth Army, which now ground to a halt, much to the disgust of the British, who viewed the rapid advance of the Russians through the Balkans with concern. It was being said that the hope of liberating Vienna before the Russians got there was being jeopardised by the US belief that France was the major prize and that "Good Old Uncle Joe Stalin" could safely be left to drive the Axis forces from Austria, Hungary and Yugoslavia unaided, as they were already doing in Poland.

With the advent of winter, various other activities came to a halt too, including our hockey, because several weeks of almost continuous rain proved too much for the field drainage systems all across central Italy which had been so damaged or neglected in the fighting over the past year that the surface water just

473

didn't drain away. The valleys consequently became almost impassable morasses. Four-wheel-drive vehicles were essential and our little Lancia was restricted to the main roads on the higher ground.

Then, the rains ceased and the sun came out, but it became bitterly cold, with the higher peaks a picturesque background covered in white against a blue sky. Foreseeing trouble, the HQ decided to establish a plan for keeping certain through supply routes open and I was sent out to survey what might be done to provide REME assistance at three sites. These were the hills on the road from Perugia to Ancona near Fabriano in the north-east; the pass on the main road from Rome at Spoleto in the south; and the hill at Radicofani on the road from Orvieto to Siena in the west. It was agreed that meetings would be convened with the REs and Provost companies at each of these three sites to produce a joint plan for action when the snow really began at lower levels.

I started at the Fabriano site, in conjunction with the REME Wksp in the vicinity. The main road climbed over some high moorland very much exposed to the elements and it was obvious that there was no suitable place where the recovery vehicles could be parked, and certainly no place for the crews. The Red-caps had found a small hut near the top and proposed to put a couple of luckless men there, with telephone communication down to the village at the foot of the hill, and it was suggested my lot and the snow-clearing RE detachment should be found billets somewhere down there. The ideal place proved to be the village bakery, where there was an enormous barn into which the baker was willing to let us put the REME recovery lorries and the RE snow-clearance vehicles; both crews could sleep in a room over the big oven, which was seldom allowed to go out. My REME colleague reckoned that was just the job and affirmed that his men would be better off there than in his workshop. He would have no shortage of volunteers. We fixed things with the Signals to have a telephone cable to the Pro post at the summit.

So far, so good. The following day I went down to have a look at the hill at Spoleto. Spoleto was a hilltop town on a ridge

474

surmounted by a castle. Later the road was taken through it in a tunnel, but in 1944 it zigzagged up and down over the ridge. It would have been a horrid spot to drive over, if there was frozen snow.

The town itself was a maze of mediaeval cobbled alleys and since the main road on its climb over the spur was close to it, there was no problem about accommodation for the REME and RE vehicles and their crews in the town itself and again we arranged with the local Signals folk to run a telephone cable to the Red-caps' post in the castle.

On the third day, Major Walker decided he needed the little Lancia for a trip of his own and I was allotted an Austin pick-up from the HQ motor pool with driver. About halfway to Radicofani, in the middle of nowhere, the wretched machine broke down and it was then that the driver found that the vehicle had no tools. He hadn't thought to check before starting out and, since he was one of those country boys whose ears were held apart solely by solid skull, I had to see what I could do to trace the fault and then seek to rectify it. This took most of the rest of the morning and half the afternoon, because it proved to be an obscure electrical fault. By trial and error, I managed eventually to find it and the engine would start and run after a fashion. All this time, not a single vehicle passed us and, since I was now much too late for my appointment, I returned to Perugia and got on to the phone to see what had happened in my absence. Fortunately the other parties had agreed something reasonably sensible and I left it at that, putting in a stinker of a report to the HQ motor pool for letting a vehicle out without tools.

Hockey being "out" in this winter weather, I used any spare time I had to explore the city, which seemed to have changed very little since the days of the Baglioni in the Middle Ages. I found it possible to walk the full way round the walls and looked at the massive (Roman?) aqueduct on the northern side. This was quite enough to replace the exercise which had previously been provided by my hockey. Then the first snow enveloped the city and we were confined, shivering, to our quarters.

The short spell of really cold weather didn't last long and I

475

was due for leave. Holt recommended I should take it before the battle resumed, so I put in for ten days and went to Rome to meet up with Phyl, who had been on night duty and was due for five days' subsequent leave at about the same time.

I hitched a lift to Rome with my colleague from Fabriano, and Phyl and I fixed ourselves up at the YWCA in Rome for a second time. On this occasion, however, the stay was a bit of a catastrophe, for after a couple of days, I became really unwell with a high temperature and feelings of sickness and exhaustion. We stuck it out for two more days and then Phyl decided that I seemed to have "got something" and carted me off to No 48. They said "What, you again?" and admitted me. The doctors diagnosed it as possibly a touch of jaundice and put me to bed in the same Officers' Medical Ward where, as before, I was visited by my wife daily for the rest of her own leave and then occasionally thereafter when she was back at work. I do not remember much about my stay, except that one of my fellow patients was the one and only Lt Col V. Peniakoff ("Popski" of Popski's Private Army, the PPA). This was one of the small semi-independent forces that had sprung up in the CMF and which dealt with behind-the-lines skullduggery and sabotage.

I was discharged after a couple of weeks, because the doctors failed to pick on anything better than "slight jaundice" and I returned to Perugia, where Major Walker, who had not been told of my incarceration, was a bit shirty and put me to work again. The next thing I was to hear was that Phyl had, once again, applied for a transfer to some hospital nearer to me and had been transferred, almost at a moment's notice, to No 104 Gen Hosp in Rome, where she had been put over the Detention Ward, much to her disgust, because her patients were mainly murderers and rapists. No 104 had been sent out directly from the UK after the invasion of Italy and were therefore "Ingleses". Phyl reported to me in her letter that the staff were bemoaning their hard lot of having to live *actually under canvas* – in tents, forsooth! – for three whole months near Algiers, while waiting to come to Rome. The poor dears, Phyl said, not very sympathetically, they should have been in the Middle East!

After my return from leave, I got restless. A further addition had been made to the REME "chiefs" – a Lt Col, who didn't seem to have anything to do. I gathered that he was a protégé of Brig Broadhurst, the DME CMF at AFHQ and the whole reorganisation had the result of reducing me to the job of telephone-answering office boy. There didn't appear to be any opening for advancement in HQ No 1 District, so I approached Col Holt for a possible posting to some more active life. He said he would see what he could do and wrote a very supportive letter to AFHQ, which he showed me, recommending a change to some post where my experience and qualifications would be better employed than at 1 District. So that was that for a few months and the weather began to look more springlike.

I had one last fling which was more in my line. One day, Major Frampton had an appointment in Ancona, the port on the Adriatic, and Holt thought it would be sensible for someone to accompany him to report on the Eighth Army Returned Vehicle Park they had abandoned at Iesi on the outskirts of Ancona, which rested, apparently forgotten in No 1 District territory and being derelict on our hands, was open to all sorts of pilfering. Since the Army declined to provide even a very nominal guard on it, it was therefore just becoming a rusting dump. Frampton was only too pleased to take me, for we had a good relationship, and we went in his car up over the mountains at Fabriano, coming down to Iesi, where I took notes on the situation at the virtually forgotten RVP, before we pushed on into Ancona. There, as it so happened, his meeting was with some pretty senior officers from Eighth Army – a brigadier and a couple of full colonels – and, when the meeting came to "Any Other Business" – I stuck my neck out and waded in about the disgrace that the RAOC at Army was allowing to exist at Iesi. They heard me out in grave silence and said they would pass my strictures on to the appropriate authority. I thought no more of this, but much later I heard that the high-ranking party had taken my complaints up with the DOS at Army and steps were taken to clear the dump, while the contents were still usable. I met one of the colonels on the ship when we were going home and he recognised me, introducing me to his colleagues as 'the young man who arranged, single-handed, for the clearance of an

477

Eighth Army dump, and he was only a Captain, too!' and it was treated as a bit of a joke.

Ancona was a bit of a dump itself, having been badly damaged during the fighting, and the Adriatic Sea was dirty and unattractive, so we stayed for the night a bit up the coast in the fields near Senigallia, where, my memory reminded me, Cesare Borgia had executed his dissident captains. We returned to Perugia the following day.

Then news came that Phyl's hospital had been moved up to Assisi, just twelve miles away and precisely six days later I was posted back to Caserta! We had one afternoon and evening and two further evenings together, which wasn't much after so many months of separation. My posting, however, was apparently to fill an imminent vacancy and promised promotion at long last, so we both took it on the chin and hoped for something better before long.

21

Although I was told that I was being posted to AFHQ, I was moved first to the X(iv) list, which I learned was a sort of "siding" where officers might be held without drop in rank, pending, in this case, absorption into AFHQ. I reported on 13 March 1945, in my present rank of Temporary Captain. I had been told unofficially that I had been selected as the replacement for Major G. Camamile, the DAAG responsible for the postings of REME officers up to and including the rank of captain. Geoff Camamile, the present holder of the appointment, was, I learned, going to the Far East, having been asked for by Brig Gerald Taylor, whom I had met in Tripoli as DDME Eighth Army, and was now DME South East Asia Command (SEAC).

Camamile explained the set-up to me. The DAAG (Deputy Assistant Adjutant General), was responsible for the overall operation of the department and had under him a staff captain, who kept records of all REME Officers in the CMF up to and including the rank of captain. Promotions beyond that lay in the province of the Military Secretary's Department, who would eventually re-post me from the X(iv) List to G-1 (Br) as his replacement. All very complicated.

Thus, for the next month, I remained a captain, working alongside the Staff Captain, John Bollard, familiarising myself with the job. John was a First Army man, recently promoted to his present rank, and he was obviously fully aware of my service history, for he treated me from the first with some respect. He appeared to be very knowledgeable about the ways in which the department worked, being the keeper of the filing system. I

479

found that every REME officer in the CMF had a file – a complete "dossier" of his performance and history – and, if he was below the rank of major, his file was kept in the department. I tentatively asked whether I had one, and, if so, could I be permitted to see it? – John said "yes" and "no". There had been a file, but it was now empty, the contents having been extracted and passed up to the Military & Secretary's office. I found him a very pleasant young man and good company; we got on well together. There was no friction between us, for he was much junior to me in the Army List and would not have been considered for the DAAG post anyway.

The appointment that I was being groomed to fill had the abstruse designation of DAAG G-1 (Br) A9. AFHQ was organised on the American staff set-up: G-1 was part of the Adjutant General's staff and contained equivalent British and US departments, each subdivided into sections dealing with different arms of the Services. A9 dealt with REME and I remember A10 was the corresponding section covering RAOC. The whole set-up differed very considerably from what we had been taught at the Staff School, but since our activities didn't overlap or conflict with the US equivalent, all was reasonably straightforward.

Camamile was much occupied with the preparations for his move to another theatre of war, so he left the details of my indoctrination to Bollard. As I remembered it, from my previous short residence as part of HQ AAI, the Palace of Caserta where AFHQ operated was built as a hollow square, divided into four quadrants, with two storeys and an attic high up in the roof, and with a corridor running round the middle of each of the four sides ("wings"), with large rooms opening off either side of it, looking inwards and outwards respectively. In the middle of each side or "wing", a massive staircase gave access from the central courtyard. Finding one's way around this rabbit warren was a bit of a nightmare at first, and Bollard took me in tow for a tour of the Palace, which didn't provide me with much enlightenment, but I gathered some general idea as to where the G-1 (A9) office was and the best way to find it from outside.

To the rear of the building, I remembered a series of steps led up a steep slope to a ridge and on each step was an oblong lake, the whole forming a sort of water garden, fed successively by a stream gushing from a lichen-covered fountain in the hill at the top.

The officers had their Messes and sleeping quarters in roomy US tents, better than the EPIP marquees that had been the norm in the ME. They had wooden flooring and were erected in the grounds to the rear of the Palace, the British and US staffs having separate "camps", each "camp" having its own shower tent. Thus segregated, we didn't have much opportunity to mix socially with our transatlantic opposite numbers. It was the custom for everyone to keep to his own "camp". There were two classes of these; one for captains and below, in which I was initially allocated a place, and another for field officers – majors and lt colonels. Full colonels and above lived and messed elsewhere further up the hinterland on the rising ground, beyond the water garden area. General Alexander, with his personal staff, had a villa in the trees at the top of the rise and General MacNarney lived in Naples, only occasionally being seen at Caserta.

The first thing I had to do was to get an AFHQ pass, which was issued to me by the Camp Commandant, and also AFHQ flashes to be stitched to each arm, just below shoulder level. Whereas the British Army flashes generally had some nodding acquaintance with heraldry – the Jerboa of 7 Armd Div, the Cheshire Cat of 93 HAA Regt, the Camel of GHQ MEF forces, the Fern of the NZEF, and so on – US flashes were much simpler and cruder, being generally rather garishly coloured geometrical patterns and letters. AFHQ's was circular, with the capital letters AF in white in the centre of a blue field, with thin red and white peripheral edges to the blue circle.

After a few weeks, Camamile departed for home leave, prior to moving to SEAC, and I received my promotion notice from the Deputy Military Secretary and put my crown up. At last, I had attained the field rank which I had sought after for so long, ever since that time that Major Estlin had attached me so

481

inexplicably to 12 AA Bde HQ back at Amriya in 1942, and had been expecting with diminishing hope ever since. Due to the fact that I seemed to have been forgotten in the farthest reaches of the Western Desert, most of my contemporaries had now passed me in promotion; Tony Cowper, with whom I had been on the same AA OME's Course in 1940, was a case in point. Although the promotion was on the "A" side, rather than "Q", I was satisfied at having "got there", and since I reckoned that I had only another six months overseas service to complete before I became due for repatriation, I accepted it with gratitude for small mercies.

I had calculated that Phyl was due for home at the same time as myself and we agreed to keep in touch on developments. She, of course, knew what was in the wind for me, when I was whisked away so suddenly from Perugia, and it served to console her somewhat for being abandoned at Assisi, once again after having caught up with me for less than a week.

On writing home to tell them about my promotion, I was greatly surprised to find that they were expecting it, although I had told no one but Phyl, and that in strict confidence. It appeared that the faithless wench had passed the news on, also in the strictest confidence, to her mother, which was the next best thing to shouting it from the rooftops, for the good lady had spoken, again in confidence, to my family, who knew nothing about it from me!

Every time a new draft of REME officers arrived in the CMF from the UK, almost invariably in Naples now that the Mediterranean was no longer under constant threat from Axis submarines or aircraft, either Bollard or Camamile used to go down to the transit centre to talk to them, collect their completed CV forms and generally sum them up. On the first occasion after the departure of Camamile for SEAC, Bollard suggested that I might well wish to accompany him, to see how the system worked, and I accepted willingly.

Camamile had a fixed routine, he explained. Each member of the draft would be presented with a blank questionnaire, in which he was invited to fill in the details and dates of his previous service and then, when they had all done this, they were called in one at a time and Bollard would run through their CVs and ask questions too about their experience. He suggested that I should sit with him and listen to what was said. It sounded reasonable.

Bollard took me with him on two occasions and I saw how he managed things. The procedure was the same on each occasion. We set off in the bright spring sunlight down the coast road from Naples towards Pompeii, passing Vesuvius, smoking slightly, on our left, and turned off into the trees to the transit holding camp near Castellamare. Here, the half dozen new arrivals were assembled in a large tent, and Bollard and I sat down behind a blanket-covered table at one end. The blank questionnaires were distributed by a corporal.

Bollard stood and addressed them: 'Good morning, and welcome to Italy. My name is John Bollard and this,' indicating me, 'is Major Montgomery, the DAAG who will be responsible for placing you as soon as possible. If you will now retire and put down your particulars on these forms, we will call you in, in alphabetical order, and discuss your prospects.' The corporal shepherded them out.

The new arrivals were lieutenants, all pink and white in new KD shirts and shorts, and with white knees. Most seemed somewhat nervous and anxious to make a good impression. John ran through their CVs and asked a few pertinent questions, making brief notes as they answered. Although they spoke to him, I felt their eyes were on me, as the arbiter of their fate. I had taken some care with my appearance and they must have been wondering what to say to impress this sunburnt and silent major in spotless and well ironed KD, sun-bleached shirt, Africa Star adorned with the silver figure "8" and brown suede shoes.

After finishing his questions, John passed the completed questionnaire and his brief notes across to me and I nodded. I shook hands with each candidate as he turned to go, thanking him for his cooperation and wishing him well before he almost tiptoed out.

On our return to the office, we had a closer look at the forms and John opened files for them and added them to his card index. Then we turned up the list of "vacancies" that had been reported in CMF establishments and did a bit of juggling with the names to decide who might be most suitable for which vacancy. It made me feel that it was a bit like playing God, but we found a niche for them all and John initiated the paperwork to place them on the X(iv) List. The next step was to approach the CO of the unit with the vacancy and offer him the possible name, with a note on the experience of the candidate. If he was acceptable, John prepared a proper posting order for me to sign.

Much of my time, when I took over, involved working out the "Age and Service Group" for each of the REME officers in the CMF, enabling the staff to plan his future movement, i.e. how long he might be available in the CMF; when he was due to be repatriated for long service overseas; whether he was available for posting to the Far East; and finally the date of his ultimate release from the Army. There was a simple formula to be applied, which balanced a figure for the man's age against another figure for his months of overseas service. I had calculated that my age at April 1945 (30) combined with my 61 months overseas (March 1941 to April 1945), produced an Age and Service Group Number of 50, which meant that at present rate of turnover I might be eligible for home posting by September and release from the Forces in mid-1946. Phyl was the same age, and had come out on the same ship, so she would be due to be repatriated at the same time, which was reassuring.

Going back to the UK in this manner was given the code-name of "Python" and it was forecast that anyone with an A and S number below 40 would be available for SEAC. There were two other lists to be prepared, those of officers due for home leave in addition to their eligibility for Python (LIAP) and those taking it locally in lieu of Python (LILOP).

Soon after I took over, a complete AA Wksp Coy arrived from the UK as a draft: some ten officers, commanded by a major, and a hundred or so ORs. I went down to the Transit Camp and found that the OC was someone who had been on the same 2nd

AA OME's Course as myself in 1940 at Stoke and Bury. I could hardly tell him that his lot would probably be split up and used piecemeal to fill vacancies in the CMF, since he was hoping to lead them into service as a unit. I warned him, however, that AA had become rather a "Cinderella" activity over here, since the Allies had established such an air of superiority that the role hitherto filled by AA Regts in the CMF was now provided by aircraft alone. All this had had a knock-on effect on the need for AA Wksps. This had been going on in the Mediterranean even before the Axis had been driven out of Africa, when, owing to the shortage of UK-trained gunners, HAA Regts had undergone a process of "Africanisation" – horrid word – with transfers of unskilled men from southern African units, such as Basutos. Here, in the CMF, LAA Regts had been converted to Infantry; in particular my cousin Garth's, which had been fighting on the Adriatic Front, and in which he had been wounded in the knee and invalided home. I didn't think the Major quite believed me and I told him that his own position was subject matter of another department and suggested that he might care to sit in on the interview of his men.

I was already aware that REME officers coming out to the CMF direct from the UK had little idea about what they were coming to. Moreover, they spoke a different language, as well as having a sort of tunnel vision. Their world had been dominated by the V1s, the flying bombs, which they called "Doodlebugs". This was a trifle confusing, since in the CMF we already had our own "Doodlebug" to worry about; it was a small remotely controlled tracked vehicle, known to the Germans as their "Goliath" Tank – a misnomer if ever there was one – which, stuffed with explosives, could creep under the wire and be exploded in some inconvenient place in our lines.

Anyhow, one of these young Inglese lieutenants was proudly expounding at length his great experience in the arcane practice of laying what he called "Diver Strips". To hear him, one might have thought he was God's great gift to the CMF in the use of Diver Strips. He was in full song, when I felt moved to raise a hand: 'Hang on a moment. Let me get myself clear. What *is* a Diver Strip?' He stopped and just looked at me for a couple of seconds, as though I had asked, 'Who is Winston Churchill?' before stumbling into a confused definition of the thing. I am still not clear exactly what a Diver Strip was, but it appeared to be some sort of portable device swiftly erected by REME to provide a base which enabled a mobile 3.7" HAA gun to take on flying bombs.

It would seem that now, with the Second Front properly underway, the papers in the UK were looking on the troops in Italy as a sort of sideshow. I recall the annoyance with which the ill-judged article in some UK tabloid newspaper was received in the CMF, after the landings in Normandy. The fatuous journalist had made reference to "those troops in Italy, safely ensconced by the sunny Mediterranean Sea, who are dodging the hardships our boys are encountering in Europe". Almost immediately, a song arose, proclaiming: "We are the D-Day Dodgers. What earthly use are we?" sung to the tune of the First War ditty *We are Fred Karno's Army*, and with unprintable descriptions of the Press who lurked in safety in London. It was sung with scorn to any visiting VIPs.

By contrast, the US Fifth Army wasn't anything like a forgotten army in the US media. Our American friends tended to be plagued with hosts of visiting members of Congress, joining the "gravy train" to see for themselves the wonders of Naples, Italy, but, of course, officially to check how the money they had voted to maintain their forces overseas was being expended.

One of them, Congresswoman Mrs Claire Booth Luce, was less than impressed, and on returning home commented acidly on the inability of the GIs to conduct their warfare properly, unless they had a Mobile Bath Unit, or some such creature comfort, immediately at hand to which they could retire as soon as they got dirty.

Mrs Luce's diatribe was immediately condemned in the US Forces' local paper *The Stars and Stripes* under the banner headline: "Arsenic and old Luce"! I was told that their VIPs were advised to be more circumspect in future.

The Australians had suffered the same thing, and had had the idea, a little earlier, of "taking the mickey" out of the Germans.

486

The entire Australian Imperial Force of two divisions and ancillary troops had been withdrawn from the front after El Alamein and had been concentrated in Syria, some forty thousand hardbitten veterans, where they had marched past their GOC, General Morshed, *en route* for embarkation for the Far East, to drive the Japanese out of Papua/New Guinea.

A German broadcaster had been heard thoughtlessly to refer to the departing AIF as "those Australian robbers, who have left the ME for a soft option in the Pacific", and the lads concerned started to march to a catchy tune, singing verses of very non-drawing room content that had a refrain: "With Ali Baba Morshed and his Forty Thousand Thieves". This replaced the hitherto popular *Waltzing Matilda* and *We're off to see the Wizard, the wonderful Wizard of Oz* for some time.

It wasn't all work and no play at AFHQ. John and I often went walking in the hills behind the palace; there were several paths up the slope containing the stepped water garden which led out into the open country. Sometimes we were joined by the Staff Captain from G-1 (Br) A10, who was a pal of John's. He was looking forward to being one of the first to be released from AFHQ, on account of his A and S group being heavily loaded by his age, which was 40.

Our walks took us through several small moorland hamlets that had been missed by the war and we passed the time of day in our faulty Italian with the occupants. Every one seemed quite pleased to meet us and we didn't encounter any animosity.

One day, when we were right up on the ridge, we were caught by a violent rainstorm and took shelter in the doorway of a small cottage. No sooner had we got under cover, than the door was opened and we were invited within by the old crone who lived there. The place was very sparsely furnished, just a board table, a couple of stools and a single chair, which the woman, who must have been nearly eighty years of age, was occupying. Seeing our uniforms, she proudly pointed to photographs on the wall of a couple of sturdy young men in military uniform looking very stern and noble. They must have been her grandsons, for they were only in their early twenties.

John got talking in his broken Italian and she told him that

487

they were corporals; one was in *Egitto* (presumably as a POW) and the other was in the *Cremona Gruppo*. By then, she had realised that we were officers and pressed us to be seated, but, noticing that we were all on first name terms, although with different rank badges on our shoulders, she asked in sign language what they meant. She accepted that Bollard and his mate were Captains and asked why I had crowns instead of stars. On learning that I was a Major, she was horrified and hurriedly stood up, insisting that I should have her chair. Apparently, it wasn't right that she should remain seated when a *Maggiore* was standing! I couldn't make her understand that I deferred to her sex and age, but we finished up by all standing until the rain stopped and we could leave. As a sort of "thank-you" present, I produced a packet of ration cigarettes I had saved for John, and gave them to her. I didn't smoke, and I don't suppose she did either, but she was overwhelmed by my largesse. Cigarettes were valuable as currency and I have no doubt that she was able to use my gift as that.

After we had got to know each other better, John revealed to me that he had a highly unofficial, personal vehicle, an old "Army" Austin pick-up with a canvas rear canopy, that had been in so-called "private" hands for some time. He had acquired it from someone who had been leaving the area a while back, and for which he was managing to get petrol out of the US Army dumps – the Americans were much more open-minded about such things and asked no questions. Anyhow, they seemed to have almost unlimited personal jeeps themselves! I decided to turn a blind eye to all this; I think Camamile had done so, too, so I was in good company.

The weather was really hot and we found the little vehicle very useful for driving down to some beach on Sunday after-noons for a dip in the sea. The best beach, I was told, was near Gaeta, a bit further up the coast from Naples and we went there several times. When Phyl and I had met at Cancello several months back and we had been taken to Positano on the other side of Naples, the sea had been covered with pumice dust from the recent eruption of Vesuvius, but that had disappeared and the water here was crystal clear.

* * *

Caserta had a cinema, run by the (US) Camp Commandant's department, that catered for all ranks, officers and "enlisted men" alike. Some very good and recent (Hollywood) films were shown most evenings and we went several times. These were almost the only occasions on which we mixed with the US officers, with whom we got on well. The British ORs saw much more of their opposite numbers, mainly in the several bars in Caserta township outside the Palace, which both sides frequented. The only complaint I heard was that the GIs always seemed to have more money than the British and that was a constant source of minor irritation.

The friction boiled over one evening, when a full house was treated to a film called *Objective Burma*, starring Errol Flynn, in which the actor at the head of a platoon of US Rangers defeated the Japanese Army and liberated Burma, receiving a decoration from the hands of US General "Vinegar Joe" Stilwell.

I was mildly amused that the producer had felt it necessary to distort history to such a degree for the American public. It was thoroughly tactless to put it on in front of members of the British Army. As the evening progressed, the dialogue was hardly audible above the torrent of whistles and catcalls from the outraged "Limeys" and fights broke out in the cheaper seats. My friend and I left fairly smartly, before the US Provost Marshal and his posse appeared, for we knew that the White Helmets had no mercy and officers were as likely to be clubbed as ORs of either Army. The troubles developed into a full-scale riot, as the partisan audience dispersed out into the open, and much blood was spilled by the contestants and by the MPs. The film was taken off and another, less inflammatory, was substituted the next night.

Another – free – entertainment, put on later in the summer, was that of marching bands in the courtyard. It started as an American effort, whereby the military bands of various units vied with one another in complicated march and countermarch routines on different days. Some of these were quite good, but were all basically pretty similar, with the mace-bearer jigging up

489

and down in front. The shows were watched from crowded windows overlooking the yard and the GIs were cheered by their supporters.

British audiences were mildly interested, but not demonstrative, until, one day, the Band of the Royal Marines, Mediterranean Fleet, decided to take the floor. The US spectators gazed, open-mouthed, as the "Limeys in white sunhats" performed in faultlessly dressed lines, back and forth for about half an hour. The climax came when the mace was tossed up over a string of telephone lines strung across the yard at some considerable height and nonchalantly caught again on its way down, without any interruption in step, or in the music. The idea caught on; not to be outdone by the British, several of the GI mace-bearers tried to emulate the feat and the idea was dropped after a lot of maces clattered resoundingly to the cobblestones. The British contingent hooted each time this happened and were said to have explained that this was an inbred skill, the result of training and practice dating back centuries before the War of Independence. Tradition took time to perfect, you know...

Meanwhile, the war proceeded. As spring wore on, the Axis forces were tipped out of their strongholds in the northern Appenines and bitter fighting erupted into the Po valley. Some of this took place on the approaches to Bologna. I was told that, at the last moment, the boundary between the Eighth and the Fifth Armies was realigned, putting that city into the American sector. It caused no end of annoyance in the Polish Corps, which had been clinging by its eyebrows to the heights overlooking it all the winter, and they took action. The story went that, six hours before the main push was due to start, the Poles quietly descended from their eyrie, put the Axis defenders – mainly Fascist Italian troops – to flight and turned round to present the advancing Fifth Army GI spearhead with unexpected resistance. The latter were nonplussed at these Central Europeans who were not "Krauts" but were behaving in a most unfriendly manner, professed not to speak American and didn't seem to realise that they shouldn't be there anyhow. The event was officially hushed up, but it circulated rapidly as "How the Poles defended Bologna against the Americans". It was a good story and I don't know if it was true, but it was greatly appreciated in the Eighth Army.

On reaching the flat land, the two Armies diverged. The Eighth Army went east to link up with the Yugoslav partisans, in the hope of pushing on to Vienna before the Russians got there, and the Fifth went north to cut the Germans off from their supply routes through the Brenner Pass. It was said that their retreat left the Fascist Italian forces with little option but to surrender. Mussolini was apprehended in Milan by a band of the Partigiani and summarily executed. His body and that of his mistress, Claretta Petacci, who shared his fate, were hung by the feet on meat-hooks in the main square in Milan, but her executioners had the decency to tie her skirt up round her legs. Anyone who wished to put a bullet into the Duce's body or stick a knife into him was given free rein. Many brave Italians crept out of the woodwork and took advantage of the offer before the Allies arrived.

It was quite obvious by now that the war in Europe was sliding to a close. The British and Canadians were overrunning the plains of Hanover and the main US thrusts were cutting deep into southern Germany. And the resistance in Italy was on its last legs.

One day at the beginning of May, John Bollard, his opposite number from A10 and I went walking up the back of the water garden, intending to gain the hill ridge, but we lost the track we had hoped to follow and were confronted by a group of Red-caps with drawn pistols, who demanded to know who we were and what the hell we were doing there, anyway. It took quite a time to satisfy them that we were just innocent walkers and eventually we were put on our rightful path and told to get smartly out of there and not try to come there again.

The following day, the official bulletin said that Field Marshal Kesselring commanding the Axis forces in Italy had surrendered to General Alexander. It occurred to us that our near-arrest had been occasioned because the German Field

491

Marshal and his staff were in Alexander's villa to sign surrender documents!

After a couple of days, on 5 May 1945, a rumour swept like wildfire round Caserta Palace that the war in Europe was over and the American staffs went wild. Files and papers were jubilantly chucked out of all windows overlooking the court-yards, through which one had to struggle knee-deep in what looked like snow. The British were not accustomed to this "ticker-tape" method of celebration and didn't join in. After loftily watching the boys "having fun" and making fools of themselves, there was quiet amusement when it was broadcast over the tannoy that the war wasn't yet over and the work of the Palace must continue until it really was. I cannot believe that AFHQ's US forces were able to salvage much of what they had thrown out of their windows.

This false alarm had been caused by the news that Armistices had been signed between the Allies and the German command-ers in Germany, but those in far-off sectors like Norway would not have been informed until the following day, 6 June 1945.

One might have thought that people wouldn't have had the energy to celebrate twice in two days, but you would be wrong. They had. The news broke late on in the afternoon of 6 June, and at first no one believed it. Then confirmation came through on the tannoy and the whole Palace shook with the cheers. Everyone downed tools, or rather pens, and flowed out into the gardens to shake everyone else's hands and discuss the situ-ation. Dinner that night was a very rowdy affair and bottles of wine appeared at our tables. The Mess staff eventually turned us out at dusk into the open air, singing anything that we could think of, and most of the officers foregathered with their American counterparts; a great deal of whisky was produced from behind the filing cabinets and Anglo-American camarad-erie reigned. John Bollard was carried off by his fellow Mess mates and I didn't see him until I was coming back into the courtyard much later bearing a bottle of hooch. The hall on the ground floor was in a state of a near orgy and as I struggled towards the big staircase to our office, I cannoned into him and invited him to come up to the office and have yet another celebratory drink. We stopped at the foot of the marble flight to admire the lions that acted as finial stair posts, because some wit had tastefully adorned them with red-banded SD caps and stuffed lemons into their open jaws.

I remember watching an incredibly confused indoor rugby scrum that was in furious progress between two sides from different staff departments, but was brought back to my wandering senses by a ringing shout of "Tally Ho!", which re-echoed through the hall – I was nearly mown down by a red-tabbed colonel sliding at great speed down the polished marble banisters and crashing head-first to the floor over one of the lions at the bottom. He was hotly pursued by a brigadier who was waving his hat in one hand and slapping his thigh with his swagger stick in the other, shouting "Gone away!" as he whizzed round the bend at the half-landing and miraculously leapt off over the prostrate colonel, amid thunderous cheers from the rugby teams which had stopped in mid-scrum to watch.

John produced some glasses and, in no time, various other neighbours on the same floor gatecrashed in, starting with the DAAG A10, and we sang *Lili Marlene* and other songs until the bottle was finished, before staggering off to our beds. A good time was had by all, but then a war didn't finish every day...

22

The Morning of 7 June dawned gloomily over AFHQ, as the staff struggled with an almighty hangover and the realisation that, although the war in Europe might be over, the HQ was still responsible for the well-being of two Armies and numerous ancillary activities. Life must go on, even if peace had broken out.

It was obvious to us in A9 that there would be an immense pressure for the "boys", not to mention the "girls", to be brought home as soon as possible. Glumly, we got out our lists of long-service overseas officers and looked at them with distaste. We had to be ready for some rush repatriations.

And none too soon. The silly season was about to engulf us. Two incidents during the next couple of months stick in my memory. The first had a nuisance value. Apparently, an announcement had been made by some minister in the House of Commons to the effect that all those who had been overseas for four years would be repatriated forthwith! Big deal! The wretched politician made no mention as to how this was going to be effected with the British Army dispersed over half the globe, in Italy, in the Middle East and in SEAC. No thought seemed to have been given either to the amount or availability of the necessary shipping that this would entail, bearing in mind that millions of US troops would be clamouring to go home too, or to what would happen to the returning multitudes on arrival in the UK, with nothing to do.

We still had numbers of folk with overseas service of more than four and a half years on our books, who should be given priority (I myself had some four and a quarter years) before we

494

could get round to the four-year men. The situation in MidEast and SEAC would very likely be the same. Saints preserve us from incompetent and bone-headed ministers who just shot off their mouths in the hope of impressing their electorates!

I recorded with the appropriate authorities that I was due as soon as possible – that now looked like being late July 1945 – which allowed me just enough service in my present rank to become Temporary Major, so that, whatever happened, I couldn't be reduced to Substantive Lieutenant, only to War Substantive Captain.

And, of course, my wife, Mrs P. E. Montgomery, QAIMNS (R), at present with No 5 British General Hospital in Pesaro, had the same overseas service, having come out on the same troopship. Could she be returned, please, at least in the same convoy, if not in the same ship?

It was all documented and tidied up. I began to look forward to our return to the UK. My actual release in the UK looked like being about March 1946, according to the formula. John Bollard, who had more experience of the way the High-ups worked, wished me luck with all this and hoped that either Phyl or I wouldn't be shipped to Iceland in error.

And from the sublime to the ridiculous ... One day there was a phone call from the Military Secretary's office. One of the beautiful young men in that department was asking for me personally. The ensuing conversation is engraved, like Calais, on my heart.

He had noticed from my documents that I had been in Force 686 in MidEast – Had I met a Lt Col A. D. Humphries while there?

Yes, he had been my ADME for three months. Why?

Well ... The DAMS paused, as though getting to the difficult bit. Did I know him well? Well, personally ...

Pretty well. Why?

A long pause. It appeared that Lt Col Humphries had just been chosen for an appointment with the rank of full Colonel ...

Good for him! What had that to do with me?

Another pause. Apparently Humphries was swanning round his new command already, dressed as a full Colonel, rank badges, red gorget patches and all, and – tone of horror – *his promotion order hadn't even yet been issued!*

I could guess what was coming. Well, chum, you'd better get the order issued right away and make an honest man of him, hadn't you?

Ah, but this took time. You can't rush things like that! Extensive pause – we were wondering if, since you know the man personally, and we don't, you could possibly talk to him privately and ask him to wait for our order, before putting up his rank...

What? Me tell a full Colonel to take down his rank badges? You must be joking! Sorry, old boy. It's your problem – nothing to do with me. Do your own dirty work.

The DAMS retired hurt, murmuring that I wasn't being very helpful.

I never heard whether Donald Humphries was shot at dawn for jumping the gun, or if the MS belatedly covered him and themselves with some sort of order. It was just one of those things that arose in the confusion of the immediate post-war activity.

Something else was occupying my mind at the time: I was due for a week's leave and was in telephone contact with Phyl to ensure that our leaves coincided. We had decided to spend it on Ischia, where the CMF had established an officers' holiday centre, and I boldly booked places for us. The two islands off Naples – Capri and Ischia – had more or less been requisitioned by AFHQ for this purpose. The Americans had, of course "bagged" Capri, but Ischia, being less well known, was well recommended by the British as possibly the more attractive of the two.

I had been worrying that something would crop up at the last minute to prevent Phyl coming, but it didn't. Everything worked perfectly. She came down from Pesaro, partly by train and partly in a friend's staff car, arriving at noon on 4 June, in time for the afternoon ferry to Ischia.

The holiday hostel was all we could have wished. On arrival, all male officers removed their badges of rank, so no one knew who was who. The folk we messed with might have been lieutenants or brigadiers and it didn't seem to matter; we all were on holiday. The ladies were allowed to dress as civilians; this posed problems for Phyl, but she turned up a white tennis shirt and shorts. For the best part of our leave we did practically nothing, rising late and, after an *al fresco* breakfast, walking down to a little secluded beach where an enterprising local had erected a shelter at which he served the most magnificent omelettes and cool white wines. We spent most of the day there, sunbathing and taking to the sea whenever we wished to cool off. At the hostel, we fed like fighting cocks on unlimited eggs, fruit, fresh fish and vegetables and more wine. In the evenings we sat in the garden looking out over the Bay of Naples and everyone was most friendly and companionable.

One day we went in a small sailing boat owned by an old man, who took us round the island and had a tendency to relinquish the tiller to me, to produce a guitar and sing for us, in Italian, excerpts from grand opera. His voice was terrible, but it made our day.

We were there five whole restful days and came back by the morning ferry on the sixth. That left us two days in Naples, where we treated ourselves to a performance of *Pagliacci* at the Opera House. At the end of our leave, I borrowed Bollard's little pick-up and drove Phyl to Rome, had tea at the YWCA and put her on the train back to Pesaro.

At the beginning of July, I received my Calling Forward Notice, saying that "Under Authority 02E/PR/24/955 dated June 1945, the undermentioned officer is being returned to the UK on long service grounds. He will report to ... etc, etc". A replacement for me was named and arrived to learn about the job. Once again, John Bollard was obliged to do most of the indoctrination. He wasn't due for repatriation for some time yet.

There was an awful near-catastrophe at the last minute. On getting my movement orders, I rang Phyl and found she knew nothing about any move on her part. Then, it just so happened that a paper that had nothing to do with me was misdirected into my In-tray. I skimmed through it to see if there was anything I ought to read and was horrified to see that Sister (Mrs) P. E.

497

Montgomery, No 5 General Hospital, was being deleted from the list of Python 24!

Being in AFHQ was an advantage. I got on to the Chief Principal Matron somewhere else in the Palace and brought the whole sad case to her immediate personal attention. She was very gracious and said that she would see to it that Phyl's name was put back on the list forthwith. Phyl was, of course, only a name to her staff and there had been no link with mine. Phyl called me that evening to tell me that she had been called up for Python 24 and was trying to arrange transport to Naples. I sat back with a sigh of relief, brushing the perspiration from my brow. In the words of the Duke of Wellington, it had been a close-run thing. And if I hadn't been at AFHQ, it wouldn't have happened!

I was now in almost daily touch with Phyl in Pesaro and she told me that the problem was still how to get down to Naples in time for the ship. Eventually, she was put on an ambulance coming my way and arrived on the eve of our departure day, with a hastily packed suitcase, dirty, tired and furious at the way the needs of women were ignored in this male-dominated country. Apparently, she had had to prevail on the ambulance driver that she had need of some privacy, and he stopped outside a churchyard, where she was forced to duck down behind a tombstone to spend a penny.

On the following day, I handed over my job to my relief and reported to Movements at the docks. I found that Python 24 wasn't a convoy, but the White Star liner *Georgic*, which had been bombed and burned-out in the UK earlier in the war, but was now reconditioned and equipped as a temporary troopship. Since the end of the war, convoys were no longer needed and the *Georgic* was intended to travel solo in fast time.

If we had been expecting to have a cabin to ourselves, we were speedily disillusioned. I was in a former first-class twin-bedded cabin now converted to take four, together with three lt cols, while poor Phyl was on a lower deck in a dormitory with sixteen women.

The ship was so crowded that it wasn't possible to feed all the "passengers" at one time, so they were obliged to run meals in two shifts. We agreed we would opt for the first shift, which meant that we could finish and grab a couple of the limited number of deckchairs as the occupants vacated them to go in for the second shift. We were obliged to make sure that we didn't leave them temporarily afterwards, otherwise they would have been snapped up by others, and we stuck daily to our seats, effectively for the entire voyage. Some of the passengers formed bridge schools and in like manner monopolised the small tables in the overcrowded lounge. With memories of our voyage out in 1941 still in our minds, we missed the freedom to stroll round the decks. There was no manner of ship's entertainment either; the *Georgic* was just an overcrowded bus intended to get us back to the UK in the shortest possible time.

From Naples, we sailed first to Algiers, where even more "bodies" were crammed on board, making one feel that the ship must be in danger of bursting at the seams, or turning turtle. From Algiers, the *Georgic* lumbered off to Gibraltar, where we stopped for a day, for some reason I didn't understand; merely to record our passage, I supposed, for, fortunately we did not take on any further passengers, before turning north up the coast of Portugal into the Bay of Biscay.

The next time land was sighted was several days later on our starboard beam. The crew said this was the coast of Anglesey and that we should enter Liverpool Bay the following day. That evening, there was much discussion among our peers about whether or not the Customs would charge duty on the various bottles of spirits that everyone seemed to be bringing in their hand luggage. No decision was reached, since no one had done this trip before, but there was some general feeling that, if the bottle had been opened and partly drunk, it could be admitted free of Import Duty. Accordingly, everybody set about ensuring that there would be no problems on this score. Both Phyl and I had a single bottle of whisky apiece for our respective fathers and we decided to keep them intact and chance the Customs, but on that last night the lounge became an orgy to ensure the proper "liquidation of assets".

The following morning, I found myself, to my annoyance, detailed as Field Officer of the Day, responsible to the OC

Troops for controlling the discipline of the troops as we neared port. My main duty was to keep the milling hundreds below decks to prevent them charging from side to side in their excitement and thus upsetting the steering. I found myself lord of all I surveyed, communing with the ship's crew and the pilot, and getting a fine view of the entrance to the River Mersey and familiar hump of Bidston Hill on the Wirral side and the spires of the Liver Building upriver on the other.

The ship drew up alongside the pierhead just short of the Liver Building and the restrictions on movement of the "passengers" was lifted. It wouldn't have been possible to enforce them, anyhow.

Several gangways were lowered and the troops stormed off waving to relatives and friends beyond the barrier on the quayside. My duties as Field Officer of the Day should have been for a whole twenty-four hours, but I now reported to the OC Troops, to sign off. I had been overseas for four and a quarter years, I told him, and I was now going ashore – Sir! I saluted and left his office. He made no attempt to dissuade me.

As a result of this bit of extra duty, the gangways were now solid with disembarking troops and Phyl and I were forced to wait until the crowd on the quayside cleared a bit. We picked up our suitcases and descended to the pierhead, wondering what happened next, and there we were accosted by a Warrant Officer Class I of Military Police, the first I remembered seeing since that time on the outskirts of Tobruk in 1942. He came to a halt with a crash of boots in front of us and gave me a smashing salute. I disengaged my arm from Phyl, put down my suitcase and returned it as best I could.

'You don't particularly want to join in with that shower, Sir?' he enquired, indicating the long queue at the entrance to the Customs Hall. I shook my head and he continued, 'What is your destination, Sir?'

We said we were both hoping to get a train to Euston and he called up a couple of underlings in a parade-ground voice that must have been heard in Birkenhead and ordered them to take our bags to the Euston train that was drawn up in a nearby siding. 'And see that they get decent seats!' Somewhat bemused,

I thanked him and he gave me another copybook salute. 'A pleasure, Sir! Welcome home!'

So we didn't have to declare our bottles of whisky at all and got two comfortable first-class seats as well, without any trouble.

My parents were waiting to meet the train at Euston on the arrival platform (they had somehow found out the arrival time of the special that had met the *Georgic*) and they welcomed Phyl with open arms. We had decided that we would spend the first week of our disembarkation leave with our respective parents and then I would come down to Folkestone the following week to meet Phyl's. We all accompanied her across London to Charing Cross station and saw her, by now somewhat confused and emotional, on to the train to Folkestone, after telephoning Mr and Mrs Ball of its time of arrival. Thus for the last time, we went our several ways.

About a week into my leave, there was a news flash that "an Atomic Bomb" – whatever that was – had been dropped by the Americans on a Japanese city whose name I had never hitherto heard – Hiroshima – with tremendous casualties. A couple of days later, another similar bomb was dropped on Nagasaki and the Japanese surrendered. The war in the East was over, too.

I found myself posted to HQ No 1 AA Group in Knightsbridge, just to the west of Harrods, and Phyl was attached to some hospital in Kent. The Group was being closed down and I found that I had very little to do. I think that the War Office had a job to find some place for me in my present rank until my time for release became due. I have very little recollection of the place, nor my nominal duties, except that one of the officers in the HQ was the Sports Officer, a Captain Jack Peterson, whose name I remembered as a heavyweight boxer in pre-war days. I did, however, attend a concert in the adjacent Albert Hall given by the Glasgow Orpheus Singers under the late Hugh Robertson.

England was a disappointment to me. It may have been because I was wearing a row of medal ribbons and had come back from overseas, but I found that the population seemed to have a chip on its shoulders about something. Everyone I met

501

was eager to tell me what a terrible time they had had in the UK while I had been abroad, what with the night bombing earlier in the war and, more lately, the V1 and V2 attacks. "You missed all that, while you were away!" Also, something else I had missed was the short commons due to the rationing schemes. It seemed to my informants that I must have been living in clover, with as much food as I could have wished. They should have been with me at Msus and Antelat in Christmas 1941! I sympathised with them for the hardships they had endured, but what got under my skin was the creeping discourtesy in the shops. If I asked for the simplest of things, I was met with downright rudeness in the reply of 'You can't have it. Don't you know that there's been a war on?'

Then, about Christmas time I was transferred from 1 AA group to HQ AA Command. At least, the Admin HQ and Mess was at Carpender's Park near Bushey, while the main HQ was at Bentley Priory, where the RAF HQ was situated. Carpender's Park was another dying organisation, living in the greatness of the past, and I found my job was to organise the rundown of the overmanned REME units in AA command as quickly as possible.

To cope with this, I obtained details of all REME officers in the Command, finding that they were massively diluted with ATS, and did some calculations as to how to slim down the various workshop units. My suggestions were hotly refuted by the COs and speedily my name became mud. The whole matter developed into a farce; I asked each Wksp Coy to provide a list of names of officers they would be willing to transfer to other units so as to come down to new and slimmer establishments. I might have guessed. The names I received were the scrapings they had wanted to get rid of for months and which no other unit would accept. The situation was complicated by a special workshop at Walton on the Naze, which was developing guided missiles and which on no account must be touched.

My work was nominally under the jurisdiction of another repatriated officer, a friendly Lt Col, back from the Middle East, who was also serving out his time here and I finally appealed to him for guidance. He agreed with me that the UK establishment was a complete shower and that all I could do would be to publish my list and let the unit COs fight it out among themselves as to who gave which men or women to whom. The main point was to keep my own nose clean! I took his advice and, by the time of my release from the Army, the Wksp COs were still engaged in a sort of trench warfare.

The staff at HQ were little better. With the end of the war, they had little to do, except indulge in petty bickering. In particular, a certain Lt Col RA had a grudge against a Lt Norman Demuth, who I understood was quite a noted musician and composer in his own right, and who was producing satirical little ditties about senior ranks which he sang to his own accompaniment at the piano in the Ante-room after dinner. I liked Demuth, who didn't care what the authorities thought of him, since he was shortly due for release, but I was sharing a room with the Lt Col, so I had to tread carefully.

By this time the Mess at Carpender's Park was shut down and we all moved into another big house next to Bentley Priory at Stanmore, hitherto occupied by the RA side of the Command. The shoulder flash of AA Command was a fully drawn bow and arrow pointing upwards in black on a red ground. I was interested to find that this new Mess had a terracotta plaque, high up in the eaves of this mansion, engraved with just such a bow and arrow. I supposed that it had inspired the shoulder flash as an appropriate symbol.

By now, I had two other worries on my mind. One was that Phyl had told me that she was now pregnant with our first child, which was due around the first week in May. She had, of course, been slung out of the QAs on this account and was living with her family in Folkestone. Although we had decided not to start a family until the war was over, we hadn't expected things to be quite as quick as this. The English Electric Co had offered me my job back and at a salary much less than I was getting as a Major on the Staff and we had to consider that as yet we had nowhere of our own in which to live.

Another worry was that I had picked up some bug on the sole of my foot in Italy and was now suffering from a bad case of verrucas. These were very painful and the HQ's MO had nothing to offer me except the superfluous advice to wear clean socks every day. He sent me periodically to the nearest Army Medical Centre for treatment, where they sought to dig out the infected parts. This greatly restricted my movement and made me less inclined to suffer gladly the fools with whom I was dealing.

Eventually, because all the Army Med Centres locally were being closed down and I was having to travel to somewhere in East London by train, which took up most of my day and rendered me little use to the HQ, it was decided to send me for civilian surgical treatment to the Mount Vernon Hospital somewhere south of Watford. Here, I was put under a general anaesthetic and the offending warts were burnt out. This finally eliminated the problem, but I didn't return to the HQ until some time in February.

Shortly afterwards, I received my Release Notification, informing me that the Secretary of State for War thanked me for my service and was graciously allowing me to retain the Honorary rank of Major. It was accompanied by a booklet that had tear-out pages entitling me to a complete set of civilian clothing and the notification that, after the completion of my 108 days Release Leave, I was being put on one of the Reserves with effect from 11 July 1946. I was to report to the Release Centre at Otley in the West Riding of Yorkshire on 25 March 1946, for the necessary release formalities to be completed.

So, my military career crept quietly to an end. I said goodbye to my erstwhile friends at HQ AA Command, leaving them to unravel the personnel problems remaining, entrained for Otley and turned up at the Centre.

Here, I joined the queue of other officers to hand in my trusty .38 revolver (never fired in anger) and was passed on into a sort of civilian gents' outfitting department store, where teams of elderly, but efficient and well trained, counter salesmen fitted me out with a suit, an overcoat, a shirt and tie and a pair of shoes. I was able to choose what I wanted and the "sales staff" were on hand to ensure that my selected items properly fitted me and that I was satisfied with them. It was all very businesslike and I was provided with a cardboard carton into which my new belongings were neatly and expertly packed.

In all, it took me about an hour to leave the Army and I caught the shuttle coach running to the railway station still in my Service Dress uniform, with polished buttons, Major's crowns on my shoulders and all, incongruously carrying the bulky cardboard carton that marked me out as one of the new civilians.

I heaved a deep but somewhat nostalgic sigh of relief. No 123237 Honorary Major, War Substantive Captain Montgomery, D, was returning to civil life six years after he had left it.